GUERRILLEROS
AND NEIGHBOURS
IN ARMS

The Cañada Blanch / Sussex Academic Studies on Contemporary Spain

General Editor: Professor Paul Preston, London School of Economics

A list of all published titles in the series is available on the Press website. More recently published works are presented below.

Peter Anderson, *Friend or Foe?: Occupation, Collaboration and Selective Violence in the Spanish Civil War.*

Margaret Joan Anstee, *JB – An Unlikely Spanish Don: The Life and Times of Professor John Brande Trend.*

Richard Barker, *Skeletons in the Closet, Skeletons in the Ground: Repression, Victimization and Humiliation in a Small Andalusian Town – The Human Consequences of the Spanish Civil War.*

Germà Bel, *Infrastructure and the Political Economy of Nation Building in Spain, 1720–2010.*

Germà Bel, *Disdain, Distrust, and Dissolution: The Surge of Support for Independence in Catalonia.*

Carl-Henrik Bjerström, *Josep Renau and the Politics of Culture in Republican Spain, 1931–1939: Re-imagining the Nation.*

Kathryn Crameri, *'Goodbye, Spain?': The Question of Independence for Catalonia.*

Mark Derby, *Petals and Bullets: Dorothy Morris – A New Zealand Nurse in the Spanish Civil War.*

Francisco Espinosa-Maestre, *Shoot the Messenger?: Spanish Democracy and the Crimes of Francoism – From the Pact of Silence to the Trial of Baltasar Garzón.*

María Jesús González, *Raymond Carr: The Curiosity of the Fox.*

Helen Graham, *The War and its Shadow: Spain's Civil War in Europe's Long Twentieth Century.*

Angela Jackson, *'For us it was Heaven': The Passion, Grief and Fortitude of Patience Darton – From the Spanish Civil War to Mao's China.*

Gabriel Jackson, *Juan Negrín: Physiologist, Socialist, and Spanish Republican War Leader.*

Xavier Moreno Juliá, *The Blue Division: Spanish Blood in Russia, 1941–1945.*

David Lethbridge, *Norman Bethune in Spain: Commitment, Crisis, and Conspiracy.*

Antonio Miguez Macho, *The Genocidal Genealogy of Francoism: Violence, Memory and Impunity*

Carles Manera, *The Great Recession: A Subversive View.*

Nicholas Manganas, *Las dos Españas: Terror and Crisis in Contemporary Spain.*

Jorge Marco, *Guerrilleros and Neighbours in Arms: Identities and Cultures of Antifascist Resistance in Spain.*

Martin Minchom, *Spain's Martyred Cities: From the Battle of Madrid to Picasso's* Guernica.

Olivia Muñoz-Rojas, *Ashes and Granite: Destruction and Reconstruction in the Spanish Civil War and Its Aftermath.*

Linda Palfreeman, *Spain Bleeds: The Development of Battlefield Blood Transfusion during the Civil War.*

Isabelle Rohr, *The Spanish Right and the Jews, 1898–1945: Antisemitism and Opportunism.*

Gareth Stockey, *Gibraltar: "A Dagger in the Spine of Spain?"*

Maria Thomas, *The Faith and the Fury: Popular Anticlerical Violence and Iconoclasm in Spain, 1931–1936.*

Dacia Viejo-Rose, *Reconstructing Spain: Cultural Heritage and Memory after Civil War.*

GUERRILLEROS AND NEIGHBOURS IN ARMS

Identities and Cultures of Anti-fascist Resistance in Spain

JORGE MARCO

Cañada Blanch Centre
for Contemporary
Spanish Studies

sussex
ACADEMIC
PRESS

Brighton • Portland • Toronto

The right of Jorge Marco to be identified as Author of this work has been asserted in accordance with the Copyright, Designs and Patents Act 1988.

2 4 6 8 10 9 7 5 3

Original publication in Spanish under the title *Guerrilleros y vecinos en armas: Identidades y culturas de la resistencia antifranquista* (2012). Publisher: Comares.

First English publication in hardcover 2016, reprinted in paperback 2017, by
SUSSEX ACADEMIC PRESS
PO Box 139, Eastbourne BN24 9BP

Distributed in North America by
SUSSEX ACADEMIC PRESS
ISBS Publisher Services
920 NE 58th Ave #300, Portland, OR 97213, USA

Published in collaboration with the Cañada Blanch Centre for Contemporary Spanish Studies, London.

British Library Cataloguing in Publication Data
A CIP catalogue record for this book is available from the British Library.

Library of Congress Cataloging-in-Publication Data
Names: Marco, Jorge, author.
Title: Guerrilleros and neighbours in arms : identities and cultures of anti-fascist resistance in Spain / Jorge Marco.
Other titles: Guerrilleros y vecinos en armas. English
Description: Chicago : Sussex Academic Press, 2016. | Includes bibliographical references and index.
Identifiers: LCCN 2015041030| ISBN 9781845197520 (hbk : alk. paper) | ISBN 978-1-84519-868-8 (pbk : alk. paper) | ISBN 9781782842934 (mobi) | ISBN 9781782842941 (pdf)
Subjects: LCSH: Andalusia (Spain)—Politics and government—20th century. | Guerrillas—Spain—Andalusia—History—20th century. | Government, Resistance to—Spain—Andalusia—History—20th century.
Classification: LCC DP302.A53 M3813 2016 | DDC 946.081/3468—dc23
LC record available at http://lccn.loc.gov/2015041030

Typeset & designed by Sussex Academic Press, Brighton & Eastbourne.
Printed by TJ International, Padstow, Cornwall.

Contents

The Cañada Blanch Centre for Contemporary Spanish Studies

In the 1960s, the most important initiative in the cultural and academic relations between Spain and the United Kingdom was launched by a Valencian fruit importer in London. The creation by Vicente Cañada Blanch of the Anglo-Spanish Cultural Foundation has subsequently benefited large numbers of Spanish and British scholars at various levels. Thanks to the generosity of Vicente Cañada Blanch, thousands of Spanish schoolchildren have been educated at the secondary school in West London that bears his name. At the same time, many British and Spanish university students have benefited from the exchange scholarships which fostered cultural and scientific exchanges between the two countries. Some of the most important historical, artistic and literary work on Spanish topics to be produced in Great Britain was initially made possible by Cañada Blanch scholarships.

Vicente Cañada Blanch was, by inclination, a conservative. When his Foundation was created, the Franco regime was still in the plenitude of its power. Nevertheless, the keynote of the Foundation's activities was always a complete open-mindedness on political issues. This was reflected in the diversity of research projects supported by the Foundation, many of which, in Francoist Spain, would have been regarded as subversive. When the Dictator died, Don Vicente was in his seventy-fifth year. In the two decades following the death of the Dictator, although apparently indestructible, Don Vicente was obliged to husband his energies. Increasingly, the work of the Foundation was carried forward by Miguel Dols whose tireless and imaginative work in London was matched in Spain by that of José María Coll Comín. They were united in the Foundation's spirit of open-minded commitment to fostering research of high quality in pursuit of better Anglo-Spanish cultural relations. Throughout the 1990s, thanks to them, the role of the Foundation grew considerably.

In 1994, in collaboration with the London School of Economics, the Foundation established the Príncipe de Asturias Chair of Contemporary Spanish History and the Cañada Blanch Centre for Contemporary Spanish Studies. It is the particular task of the Cañada Blanch Centre for Contemporary Spanish Studies to promote the understanding of twentieth-century Spain through research and teaching of contemporary Spanish history, politics, economy, sociology and culture. The Centre possesses a valuable library and archival centre for specialists in contemporary Spain. This work is carried on through the publications of the doctoral and post-doctoral researchers at the Centre itself and through the many seminars and lectures held at the London School of Economics. While the seminars are the province of the researchers, the lecture cycles have been the forum in which Spanish politicians have been able to address audiences in the United Kingdom.

Since 1998, the Cañada Blanch Centre has published a substantial number of books in collaboration with several different publishers on the subject of contemporary Spanish history and politics. An extremely fruitful partnership with Sussex Academic Press began in 2004. Full details and descriptions of the published works can be found on the Press website.

One of the themes followed by the series has been the consolidation of the Franco dictatorship. This was examined in 2011 in terms of the cultural reconstruction of the country in two complementary works by Dacia Viejo-Rose, *Reconstructing Spain: Cultural Heritage and Memory after Civil War* and Olivia Muñoz-Rojas, *Ashes and Granite: Destruction and Reconstruction in the Spanish Civil War and its Aftermath*. In subsequent years, works on the brutal repression and its contemporary resonances were published by Richard Barker, S*keletons in the Closet, Skeletons in the Ground: Repression, Victimization and Humiliation in a Small Andalusian Town* (2012), Francisco Espinosa Maestre, *Shoot the Messenger?: Spanish Democracy and the Crimes of Francoism. From the Pact of Silence to the Trial of Baltasar Garzón* (2013) and most recently Antonio Míguez Macho, *The Genocidal Genealogy of Francoism. Violence, Memory and Impunity* (2015). The present volume examines the military challenge to the regime from those who refused to accept defeat. *Guerrilleros and Neighbours in Arms* by Jorge Marco was hailed on its publication in Spain in 2012 for its innovative approach. It is notable for placing the Spanish struggle in a wider context of European anti-fascism but above all for its subtle analysis of the role of kinship, neighbourhood and friendship groups in the mobilization and organization of guerrilla groups.

Series Editor's Preface

Despite the succession of lavish victory parades organised in the spring and early summer of 1939 in Spain's major cities and despite the boastful declarations of the new dictator, the Civil War was not over. Until the end of the 1940s, Franco's armed forces were obliged to undertake military operations against *guerrilla* groups that carried out vain, albeit heroic, attempts to reverse the result of the war. In a sporadic way the Civil War, or violent resistance against the establishment of the Francoist State, continued until the withdrawal of the last *guerrilla* units in the early 1950s. Despite the existence of a considerable literature in Spain, including large numbers of memoirs by individual fighters, very little has been published in English which is one of several reasons to welcome this highly original study by Jorge Marco.

In the 1940s, in so far as there was any opposition to the Franco regime, other than the purely passive, it was of a military nature. The most dynamic and representative cadres of the Spanish left had been decimated during three years of bloodshed. Half a million survivors fled into exile where those who did not have the luck to reach Latin America were swept up by the whirlwind of European war. Those who were left behind faced a savage repression. The anti-Francoist forces not only faced state terror, they were also hindered by internal divisions. Within this gloomy overview there were two groups of anti-Francoists who, for different albeit related reasons, managed to avoid the worst consequences of internecine hostilities and concentrate on a single primordial task, the struggle against the dictatorship. These two groups would be the nuclei of the anti-Francoist *guerrilla* forces. The first, from 1939 to 1944, were the so-called *huídos*, Republicans separated from their units during the Civil War who opted to take to the hills rather than surrender. The second, from 1944 to 1951, were the Spanish *maquis* who played a crucial role in the French resistance and, with the gradual collapse of the Germans, were able to turn their gaze to Spain. Dr Marco's study, the best kind of history from below, provides vivid portraits of a representative group of men who fought in the Civil War, then in the French resistance and finally, and often fatally, in Spain once more.

The great majority of the defeated faced, at worst, prison or the firing-squad; at best, life as second-class citizens unable to find work without certificates of political reliability and good conduct issued by parish priests and local Falangist chiefs. A few had the chance to go on fighting. After initially avoiding surrender by fleeing to the hills, the **huídos** were convinced that, to avoid death or prison, they had to fight on. Within a few months of the end of the war, there was a significant number of *guerrilleros* in rural, and especially mountainous, areas. There it was easier to hide, to avoid the patrols of the Civil Guard and even to find the wherewithal to live, either with the help of sympathetic peasants or by hunting and collecting wild fruit. The principal activity of the *huídos* was defensive, their initial objective simply survival. The repression, hunger and, above all, the intense weariness left by the titanic struggles of the previous three years ensured that there would be no popular uprising in support of the *huídos*, who were condemned to a hard and solitary existence.

Nonetheless, on occasions they were able to emerge from their defensive positions. Attacks were carried out against Civil Guard barracks, local Falangist offices, and Francoist town halls. They constituted a constant irritant for the regime. In so far as the controlled press mentioned their activities, it was to denounce them as acts of banditry and looting. However, in some rural areas the activities of the *guerrilleros* had the effect of raising the morale of the defeated population until, that is, the savage reprisals taken by the authorities took their toll of popular support. In the autumn of 1944, there came about an important change. Many Spanish **maquis**, after having played a crucial role in the French resistance, responded to signs of German collapse by moving towards the frontier with Spain.

For various reasons, the PCE (*Partido Comunista de España, the Communist Party of Spain*) enjoyed a certain pre-eminence within the *guerrilla* The individual rank-and-file *guerrilleros* were Socialists, anarchists, Communists or simply anti-Francoists. However, the anarchist and Socialist movements in exile were irreparably divided. In consequence, the senior Communist cadres in the South of France were readily able to fill the vacuum and simply assumed the leadership of the Spanish *maquis*. One of the most perceptive elements of Jorge Marco's study is his analysis of the crucial, and at times contradictory, role of the PCE in the construction of the anti-Francoist opposition. The Communists took the initiative in constructing a national *guerrilla* organisation on the basis of the vague structures created by the *huídos*. The spontaneous groups of Asturias and Galicia had already united as the so-called *Federación de Guerrilleros de Galicia y León*. This structure was adopted by the Communists. They created on paper a nation-wide network of divisions and detachments which often had no basis in fact. Where there were authentic units, they were under the command of a Communist general staff. The invention of the so-called *Ejército Guerrillero* (Guerrilla

Army) was not just a symptom of Communist triumphalism but also a propaganda device to give the impression of greater strength and so perplex the Francoist authorities and raise the morale of the *guerrilleros* themselves and also of their sympathisers who, at enormous risk, gave them food and medicines.

In the autumn of 1944, the existing groups in the interior requested help from the exiled PCE leadership in France. The venture was organised virtually as a conventional military operation with little by way of security. Its preparation was an open secret, with recruiting broadcasts by Radio Toulouse and Radio Pirenaica from Moscow. Before leaving for the south of France, some *guerrillero* units were the object of public tributes and large send-offs by the people of the French towns and cities where they had participated in the resistance. The PCE ordered its organisations in the interior of Spain to prepare for an immediate popular insurrection but the regime was fully prepared.

Beginning on 9 October 1944, approximately 12,000 men of the invading army began to enter Spanish territory, principally through the Pyrennean Val d'Arán. Snow-covered for most of the year and sparsely populated, it was an area of shepherds and wood-cutters, a place barely appropriate as the *foco* of a popular uprising. Despite the ostentatious military structure set up by the Communist leaders of the *maquis*, the invasion was largely improvised. It flouted the obvious fact that a conventional military incursion played into the hands of Franco's huge land forces. Nonetheless, the invaders chalked up their successes, some units advancing over one hundred kilometres into the interior. In some individual actions, they roundly defeated units of the Spanish Army and held large numbers of prisoners for short periods. In the last resort, however, the 40,000 Moroccan troops under the command of experienced Francoist generals, Yagüe, García Valiño, Monasterio and Moscardó, were too much for the relatively small army of *guerrilleros*. Hopes of triggering off an uprising were always remote given the intense demoralisation on the Spanish Left, which had still not recovered from the trauma of defeat, was ground down by the daily repression and only distantly and vaguely aware of what was happening in the North. The regime's iron control of the press ensured that the invasion took place in a deafening silence.

In the last resort, the numerical superiority of Franco's forces won the day. In most encounters the *guerrilleros* of the invading force were outnumbered by at least four to one and finally forced to retreat. Thereafter, the Partido Comunista de España rapidly switched to an entirely different *guerrilla* tactic. It was now decided that a more realistic tactic was the gradual infiltration of small groups of *guerrilleros* across the French frontier after which they would link up with the existing groups of *huídos*. However, as Dr Marco demonstrates, the *huídos* sometimes rejected attempts at unification and maintained their independence. Nevertheless, arriving with food and arms, hardened PCE militants trained in the French resistance or even in the Ukrainian *guerrilla* were able to organise relatively efficacious *guerrilla* units. However, the idea that the *guerrilla* would be the catalyst of a popular struggle sufficiently broad-based to intensify international hostility against the Franco regime was a vain hope given the ever stronger anti-Communism of the Anglo-Saxon powers.

Civil Guard barracks were attacked, trains were blown up and electrical power lines were brought down. The reaction of the peasantry appeared, at first, to be passively sympathetic, especially when the **guerrilleros** undertook specific actions by request, such as the burning of municipal archives to impede the collection of taxes. Jorge Marco provides a rich social history of the guerrilla, demonstrating the importance of local community and family, friendship and neighbourhood relationships. The Spanish *guerrilleros* saw themselves as the vanguard of a future invading army and, therefore, did not devote much effort to sinking roots among the local peasantry. In any case, after three years of civil war and five more of State terror, the majority of the population had enough to cope with merely surviving the prevailing famine without in addition taking part in the great uprising which was the objective of the *guerrilla*. In the long term, the *guerrilla* was doomed to failure.

Nevertheless, for a few years, from 1945 to 1948, the *guerrilla* was a considerable irritant to the regime. Part of the Communist tactic was to inflate the importance of the *guerrilla* by inventing a national structure of *ejércitos guerrilleros* for each region of the country. The forces deployed in the anti-*guerrilla* struggle, primarily the Civil Guard but also regular units of the Army, of the Spanish Foreign Legion and of the Spanish native police, the *Regulares Indígenas*, were under the impression that they were fighting tens of thousands of *guerrilleros*. It is difficult, given the exaggerations of both sides, to calculate the exact numbers of the men and women who participated in the *guerrilla* but it is likely that it was around 7,000.

Given the difficulty of establishing *focos* or liberated zones, the peasantry began slowly to reject the *maquis*. When, as occasionally happened, the *guerrilleros* were able to capture a village and fly the Republican flag from the town hall, they invariably had to withdraw when Civil Guard reinforcements arrived. At that point, violent reprisals would be taken against villagers accused of giving succour to the *guerrilleros*. Between 1947 and 1949, the regime pursued a scorched earth policy with entire villages put to the torch. The process of peasant rejection of the *guerrilla* was accelerated by another tactic used by the Civil Guard under General Manuel Pizarro Cenjor. It consisted of the creation of special units of agents-provocateurs, known as *contra-partidas* (counter-guerrilla bands) which looked, talked and behaved like real *guerrilleros* but were really *agents-provocateurs*. They would imitate the routine of the authentic guerrilleros, enter a village and, by asking for food and shelter, encourage sympathisers to come forward. Once support networks had been revealed, they would be dismantled with brutality. At other times these fake guerrilleros would simply rampage through villages, raping and plundering. The combined effect of these special operations gradually made it impossible for the real *guerrilleros* to return to villages where they had once been welcome. Once they could no longer count on peasant sympathy, which was the case by the late 1940s, they were obliged to steal simply to survive. That gave substance to the regime claim that they were never more than bandits. Both suspected *guerrilleros* and mere sympathizers were frequently arrested and without trial murdered by the application of the so-called *'ley de fugas'* (prisoners shot in the back 'while trying to escape').

In fact, it had become obvious by 1948 that the much-awaited uprising was not going to take place. With the French frontier subjected to military vigilance, it became ever harder to get supplies of food, weapons and ammunition. There was no organized evacuation nor even a formal order to withdraw. A long forced march began in 1950 in response to deteriorating conditions within Spain. The last units did not leave Spain until well into the 1950s. They had been, as Jorge Marco demonstrates, both the first and the last of the anti-fascist resistance movements in Europe. It is his considerable achievement to place their struggle marginalized in the European resistance narrative.

Acknowledgements

This book has been written and rewritten over the years in Madrid, Granada, Almería, London, Gandia, Preston Candover, Saint Hilary, Nottingham, Exeter and Bath. In each of these places, and in many others through which I have passed, I have been helped by many people in very different ways.

I am greatly indebted to Gabriela Águila, Gregorio Alonso, Luciano Alonso, Peter Anderson, Miguel Ángel de Arco Blanco, José María Azuaga, Óscar Bascuñán, Ana Cabana, Julián Casanova, Chris Ealham, Candela Fuentes Navarro, Álvaro García, Carlos Gil Andrés, Gutmaro Gómez Bravo, Eduardo González Calleja, Magdalena González Martín, Helen Graham, Claudio Hernández, Stathis N. Kalyvas, Éric Lair, José Luis Ledesma, José María López Sánchez, Ana Martínez Rus, Jesús Martínez, Antonio Niño, Luis Enrique Otero Carvajal, Daniel Oviedo Silva, Rubén Pallol, Alejandro Pérez Olivares, Livia D. Rocha Magalhães, Óscar Rodríguez Barreira, Eusebio Rodríguez Padilla, Fernanda Romeu Alfaro, Francisco Sánchez Pérez, Secundino Serrano, Alison Sinclair, Andrés Sorel, Sandra Souto Kustrín, Gareth Stockey, Ramiro Trullen Floria, Jaime Valim Mansam, Ángel Viñas, Charlotte Vorms and Mercedes Yusta Rodrigo. Their suggestions and conversations have helped to improve this book substantially.

I would like to express my infinite gratitude to Enrique Belda , Rafael ' Soda ' Galan, Germán García, Ana Martinez Ruz, Mari Pepa, Carlos 'Patron' and Alfonso Prado Artiach, who have had to endure my obsessions for many years, and who have offered their love and friendship in return.

A very special thank you to the Quero family, especially to Dolores, Eduardo and Maria, for their help, love and generosity. It is an honour to be part of your family.

I would also like to express my immense gratitude and remembrance to Julio Arostegui, who was my PhD supervisor and died unexpectedly in January 2013. I could not have had a better teacher and I miss him very much.

I owe great thanks to Paul Preston for the generous support he has shown me over the years, especially for welcoming me to the Cañada Blanch Centre for Contemporary Spanish Studies at LSE, and for his huge support with the publication of this book. I must also say a special thank you to Carl-Henrik Bjerstrom who, as well as being a friend and a great historian, translated this book into English. His work has been masterful and his comments and questions have forced me to reflect upon and clarify my ideas and thoughts. I am also grateful to Martin Darling and Robert Abrahams, who offered extremely useful help with the final review of the text. Likewise, I thank Sussex Academic Press for their work and trust in this book.

I must express a huge thank you to my family on both sides of the sea. To Ewa, Gareth and Geraint Thomas, for having made me feel welcome for many years in southern England and Wales. Thank you for the delicious meals, the beautiful Polish-Welsh Christmases and the vocabulary that I have learned (or that I pretend to have learned) in the cryptic conversations about the mining valleys of South Wales and Doctor Who.

My eternal gratitude to my parents, Jose Luis and Conchi, who have worked tirelessly to provide for our family. I know you're proud of me, but no more than proud than I am of you. Many thanks also to my wonderful brother Roberto, whose commitment to the people who most need his help continues to inspire me.

Finally, I want to dedicate a huge thank you to Maria for being brilliant in general and for helping me so generously in this new and sometimes bewildering life which we are embarking upon in a new country with new jobs. Thank you for questioning me and for making me think and reflect on a thousand and one ideas. Thank for 'esa dicha creciente que consiste en extender los brazos, en tocar los límites del mundo como orillas remotas de donde nunca se retiran las aguas'.

List of Abbreviations

ACCPCE	Archivo del Comité Central del Partido Comunista de España.
AGA	Archivo General de la Administración.
AGG	Agrupación Guerrillera de Granada.
AGLA	Agrupación Guerrillera de Levante-Aragón.
AGM	Agrupación Guerrillera de Málaga.
AGE	Agrupación de Guerrilleros Españoles.
AHN	Archivo Histórico Nacional.
AMI	Archivo del Ministerio del Interior.
ANFD	Alianza Nacional de Fuerzas Democráticos.
ATMTS	Archivo del Tribunal Militar Territorial Segundo.
ATTMA	Archivo del Tribunal Togado Militar nº 23, de Almería.
CEHGC	Centro de Estudios Históricos de la Guardia Civil.
CNT	Confederación Nacional de Trabajadores.
EGA	Ejército Guerrillero de Andalucía.
FAI	Federación Anarquista Ibérica.
FAL	Fundación Anselmo Lorenzo.

FES-
  AHCCOO
	Fundación Estudios Sindicales. Archivo Histórico
	  Comisiones Obreras.

FFF	Fundación Francisco Franco.
FIJL	Federación Ibérica de Juventudes Libertarias.
FJS	Federación de Juventudes Socialistas.
FNTT	Federación Nacional de Trabajadores de la Tierra.
FPI	Fundación Pablo Iglesias.
JEL	Junta Española de Liberación.
JJLL	Juventudes Libertarias.
JJSS	Juventudes Socialistas.
JSU	Juventudes Socialistas Unificadas.
JSUN	Junta Suprema de Unión Nacional.
PCE	Partido Comunista de España.
PSOE	Partido Socialista Obrero Español.
REI	Radio España Independiente.
TNA: PRO	The National Archives: Public Records Office.
UGT	Unión General de Trabajadores.

UJCE   Unión de Juventudes Comunistas de España.
UN   Unión Nacional.

Introduction

The bell sounded at the *Gran Cinema*. It was twenty to eleven at night and the fight was due to start in five minutes. Fans arriving late thronged around the entrance to snap up the remaining tickets. The doorman inspected the tickets and showed the spectators to their seats. That summer night the *Gran Cinema* was hosting one of its last boxing matches. A few months later the building would be demolished. In its place emerged one of the most emblematic facades of modernist Madrid: that of the San Carlos Theatre.

Inside the cinema everything was ready. The ring was in the middle of the room and surrounded by dozens of folding chairs occupied by friends, fans, boxers, and the curious. The audience consisted mostly of men. Although a variety of social backgrounds were represented, most of the men were workers, many of whom were arguing passionately. Despite its aristocratic origin, boxing had gelled in Madrid's working-class neighbourhoods. The flat roofs with clothes hanging on washing lines and the workshops with grease-stained floors had been converted into improvised gyms where young men practiced the jab, cross, hook and uppercut with electrifying enthusiasm. In the main hall, white shirts and workers' hats outnumbered double-breasted suits and felt hats. According to elitist voices in the press, boxing was a 'savage' form of entertainment, but, nonetheless, some gentlemen (*señoritos*) were attracted to this contact sport.

The calendar showed it to be July 17th. However, this July 17th did not fall on a Friday, nor was the year 1936, when an attempted coup d'état triggered the start of the Spanish Civil War. This July 17th fell on a Wednesday and the year was 1927. The crowd eagerly awaited the start of the match while discussing the latest announcement from the Treasury: Juan March, well-known businessman, banker and smuggler, had lost his monopoly on tobacco in the Moroccan colonies.

Ramón Vía, a callow youth of sixteen, born in the Puente de Vallecas district of Madrid, waited impatiently for his baptism to commence. The son of a Madrilenian cutler and a seamstress, he had been born into a poor and austere home with seven siblings. He did not drink, nor did he like to dance. He did not frequent cafés. From an early age, he had helped his mother to mend and iron socks. At eleven he left school and at thirteen was already working "shifts like a full-grown man". He liked sport and, in his spare time, built beds from iron and wood.[1] In five minutes, however, he would have a life-changing opportunity. In five minutes the third annual amateur boxing championship for the region of Castile would begin. The winners of each bout would represent Castile in the national championships that would take place a few days later in Barcelona. Vía was determined to sieze the opportunity by beating his adversary: Julián del Amo. Their fight marked the beginning of the event. Vía, being only 1.65 metres tall and weighing about 48 kilos, competed in the flyweight category. The bell rang one last time and Vía jumped into the ring with his leather gloves and his knee-high socks as his friends cheered on hearing his name announced. He was the pride of Vallecas and, win or lose, he had managed to transcend the city's barriers in order to represent his working-class neighbourhood in the bourgeois centre of the capital.[2]

In fact, Ramon Vía's boxing career was extremely short. After his defeat in the *Gran Cinema* he fought for the second and last time on June 16th, 1928, in the *Ideal Polistilo*, a skating arena next to the gardens of El Retiro, which opened its doors for boxing events on summer nights. That night all eyes were on the clash between Emilio Martínez, champion of Castile and until recently challenger for the national crown, and the "tough Basque blocker and great puncher" Echegaray. In the second match of the night, Vía faced Sánchez Calvo.[3] It was his last fight. The young boxer from Vallecas married his girlfriend and decided to hang up his gloves for good. From that moment Vía turned to battles outside the ring. Like thousands of young Madrilenians, on 14 April 1931 he celebrated the proclamation of the Republic in the capital. For the young cutler from Vallecas, who had previously harboured dreams of becoming a boxer, the change of regime led to a political awakening.

At the beginning of 1932, Ramón Vía joined the cutlers section of the workers' association El Baluarte, part of the socialist union UGT, and soon became one of the organisation's spokespersons. The young man may not have impressed with his movements in the ring but he had character, capacity for leadership, and talent as a speaker. An avid reader, he spent his nights by a small gas lamp devouring books and pamphlets found in the socialist workers' meeting house, the Casa del Pueblo.

His first confrontation with the authorities came in October 1934. Ramón Vía participated actively in the revolutionary strike of that month and, for the first time in his life, was arrested and imprisoned. Found guilty of military rebellion, he spent months separated from his family while he serveded his sentence. On July 17th 1936 a group of army generals launched the coup d'état which would mark the start of the Spanish Civil War. It was a new July 17th, nine years after his first fight in the *Gran Cinema*, when Ramón Vía returned to the city centre. However this time, he was not wearing leather gloves and shorts. Armed with his bare fists, he once more travelled into the city to defend the future of the working class.

Ten years later, in the spring of 1946, the newspaper *Ataque*, the propaganda outlet of the High Command of the Spanish Guerrilla Army, initiated a national and international campaign in support of one of the "heroes of the Resistance". The "exemplary fighter" referred to was none other than Ramón Vía, the callow youth from Vallecas who had gone from being a nineteen-year old amateur boxer to, successively, a revolutionary union leader, a major in the Republican Popular Army during the Spanish Civil War, a communist leader in the Camp Morant concentration camp in Algeria, a member of the French resistance in Marseille, a collaborator with the British and North American intelligence services in Vichy, an instructor of guerrilla fighters in Oran (Algeria) and, finally, a leader of a guerrilla unit in Spain. On November 15th 1945, he was arrested by the police and six months afterwards, on May 1st 1946, together with twenty-five other inmates of the Provincial Prison of Malaga, he participated in one of the most spectacular prison escapes of that period. Three weeks later his hide-out was discovered. The Civil Guard surrounded the house, and, after an intense shoot-out, he fell, his body riddled with bullets.[4]

This brief biography of Ramón Vía shows the close links between the Spanish Civil War, the anti-Francoist resistance and other antifascist resistance movements in Europe. The anti-Francoist guerrilla was a movement which fought against Franco's dictatorship between 1939 and 1952. For fourteen years, thousands of guerrilla fighters, operating in all the mountainous areas of Spain, confronted one of the most brutal dictatorships in Europe. Its activities commenced before the Second World War and extended into the Cold War period, making it both the first and the last of the antifascist resistance movements in Europe. In spite of this, it has been marginalized in the European resistance narrative.

Although Franco sent 47,000 Spanish soldiers to Germany to fight in the Wehrmacht against the Soviet Union, Spain did not officially enter the Second World War, which still provides the principal chronological framework of the European resistance movements against fascism. Moreover, the battle of the anti-Francoist guerrilla in this period was not fought against foreign occupying forces, but against the indigenous form of fascism that had triumphed in Spain as a result of the civil war. As a result, the anti-Francoist guerrilla fell outside the model of antifascist resistance established by French historiography, which has dominated this field for decades.[5]

In 1945, while people in most parts of Europe celebrated the victory against fascism, Franco unleashed a wave of violence to consolidate his dictatorship in Spain. In this situation, the anti-Francoist guerrilla did not demobilise but continued to fight. The protraction of its activities beyond the end of the Second World War transposed the anti-Francoist guerrilla to a new context: that of the crystallising Cold War. This further complicated its position in the traditional model of antifascist resistance in Europe.[6] Ultimately, the small size of the anti-Francoist guerrilla and the marginal importance of the 'Spanish problem' in the international agenda of the post-war period condemned the Spanish experience to oblivion.

This book aims to correct this deficiency. To do so, it is necessary to break with old interpretations of antifascist resistance movements based on occupation and a restrictive chronology tied to the Second World War. Studies of European resistance movements must incorporate all experiences emerging on the continent, including their specific qualities, without constructing an ideal model. It is also essential that such studies refer to antifascist cultures, which emerged in inter-war Europe and in the 1930s in particular. There is one event which meets all these criteria and cannot be ignored: the Spanish Civil War.

Millions of young Spanish antifascists and about 36,000 foreign volunteers, the majority Europeans, from fifty-four countries participated in what was known as the first battle against fascism in Europe. However, the Spanish Civil War was not only important because of its transcendental impact on the collective imaginary of international antifascism.[7] It also provided thousands of young Europeans with vital combat experience, which was fundamental to the subsequent development of antifascist resistance in their respective countries.[8] Moreover, when the Spanish Civil War ended, thousands of Spanish exiles joined the resistance in Europe, especially in France, where they participated in significant events such as the Liberation of Paris. This history of constant transferrals and interchanges must not be obscured by national resistance narratives of a parochial and myth-making kind.[9]

The narrative of antifascist resistance in Europe has not only excluded important experiences like that of Spain but has also painted an excessively monolithic picture, focusing all too often on exclusively ideological and political perspectives. New histories of antifascist resistance should combine microhistory, anthropology, and cultural history in order to construct new narratives that highlight the plurality and heterogeneity of this transnational phenomenon. This is the perspective adopted in this book, a perspective which the author hopes will prove useful for a broader understanding of antifascist resistance movements in Europe.

Two models: Neighbours in arms and modern guerrilla

International studies of guerrilla movements have often oscillated between partisan romanticism, on the one hand, and uncritical confirmation of counterinsurgency perspectives, on the other, producing accounts which tend to be either mythologizing or criminalising.[10] To a great extent, these characteristics can also be found in the Spanish historiography on the anti-Francoist guerrilla. Both discourses have created distorted and homogenised images of the anti-Francoist guerrilla which persist today.[11] The resistance myth, in particular, has generated a stereotype of the guerrilla fighter as a politicised peasant with an extensive activist background and a strong ideological imprint. The Agrupaciones guerrilleras, created by the Spanish Communist Party (Partido Comunista de España, hereafter PCE), have been upheld as the most common and widespread organisational model in Spain. Other groups and guerrilla fighters not conforming to such stereotypes have been declared anomalies. Historians have typically explained such "exceptional cases" by pointing to evolution over time and ideological differences between communists, socialists and anarchists.

The former argument claims that the conditions of the first period (1939–1942) only allowed dispersed and isolated forms of resistance to develop. The new international context from 1943 onwards and the arrival from abroad of guerrilla units tied to the PCE meant that a few "men who tended towards banditry" were converted into "guerrilla fighters who acted in accordance with certain ideas".[12] To a large degree, this analysis simply reproduces the discourses of the PCE at the time.[13]

The latter argument is based on the ideological profiles of the guerrilla fighters. The conflict between socialists, anarchists and communists was intense, and integration into the new Agrupaciones guerrilleras, organised by the communists from 1944 onwards, depended entirely on whether or not the guerrilla fighters were affiliated to the PCE. Socialists and anarchists, in particular, distrusted any communist proposal and therefore preferred to form their own guerrilla organisations or maintain their status as independent groups.

The intention of this research is to propose an alternative model of interpretation. Without wishing to downplay the influence of chronological factors or ideological conflicts this study is intended to show that the analytical ranges of both perspectives are limited and insufficient. This approach stems from a recognition of the fact that there were distinct types of "resistance", and that these were configured in accordance with the diverse experiences, motivations, political cultures, traditions of collective action and collective imaginaries of the guerrilla fighters.[14]

The anti-Francoist guerrilla emerged in a rural environment and the majority of its members were peasants. Within this context, the plurality of responses was much greater than hitherto suggested by historians. In order that these hidden elements emerge clearly, two new categories have been devised: *neighbours in arms* and *modern guerrilla*.

At the end of the Spanish Civil War a small number of people fled to the mountains. Thus, the first armed groups were formed around local communities and comprised mostly neighbours and family friends. Their activities initially centred on pure survival, but they gradually developed a broader set of activities with a clear political character. Nonetheless, their operational area and political impact was still confined to the local community. The *neighbours in arms* model constituted the most widespread form of resistance in Spain until 1944. Henceforth, exiled political organisations, and especially the PCE, tried to incorporate these autonomous groups into "real guerrilla units" which adopted the new methods of the *modern guerrilla*. Occasionally these small armed groups consented to their absorption into the Agrupaciones guerrilleras, as these units were called, but at other times they rejected any attempts at unification and defended their independence. This rivalry was more extensive than historians have recognised, and its emergence, as well as its anthropological, rather than ideological, roots, form the two central vectors of this study.

Although the construction of two clearly differentiated models may produce inflexible and unnuanced explanatory images this largely depends on how they are used. Hermeneutic tools are means to an end rather than an end in themselves. None of the armed groups analysed in this book fit perfectly into one or other model. The categories *neighbours in arms* and *modern guerrilla* have not been created to classify armed groups but to illuminate areas that still remain obscure. These categories have permitted analysis of independent groups without recourse to discourses of anomia, which facilitates an understanding of their proper character and meaning. They have also functioned as analytical instruments to penetrate the most sophisticated guerrilla structures and to deconstruct certain stereotypes and recurrent myths appearing in the historiography. Figuratively speaking, these categories must therefore serve as a conceptual scaffolding which allows close observation of issues that would otherwise have been discernible only from a distance. Once the issues in question have been analysed, the scaffolding must be dismantled so that the nuances appear once again in their complex entirety.

Neighbours in Arms and Modern Guerrilla

	Neighbours in Arms	Modern Guerrilla
Organisational tendency	Independent	Unifying
Internal Structure	Horizontal	Vertical and hierarchical
Area and action level	Local	Supralocal (regional/national/international)
Strategy	Survival, traditional guerrilla war	Insurgency War, modern guerrilla
Social Composition	Peasant	Command level: workers and white collar Grassroots level: peasant
Origin of guerrilla fighters	Native	Command level: external and native Grassroots level: native
Collective Experience	Low or medium	Command level: high Grassroots level: low or medium
Internal Cohesion	Primary groups (kinship, neighbourhood and friendship)	Affinity groups (political) and primary groups
Size	Smaller than 40 members	Larger than 40 members
Discipline	Dissolute	Strict and regulated
Propaganda	None, except for propaganda of the deed	Newspaper, radio, international campaigns, occupations of villages, etc.
Repertoire	Traditional	Modern and Traditional

In some respects these concepts suffer from great imprecision, which complicates their use in different geographical and chronological settings. In order to make the concepts *neighbours in arms* and *modern guerrilla* useful in other contexts, from the antifascist resistance movements in Europe to the guerrillas in Asia, Africa, and Latin America, twelve analytical variables have been identified. These can be broadened, modified, or complemented as required in other research projects. The variables chosen concern three fundamental aspects: the characteristics of guerrilla actions, the experience of guerrilla members and the structure and organisation of groups.

The reader will notice how no reference is made to the ideological orientation of the groups or the guerrilla fighters. There is a simple reason for this: ideology can not be considered a defining variable. Spanish groups belonging to the categories *neighbours in arms* and *modern guerrilla* included among their members a mixture of socialists, anarchists, communists, republicans and members without previous party affiliation. The only exception, as will be seen later, is confined to the command structures of the Agrupaciones guerrilleras, where a communist dominance was evident. This new approach permits analysis of the nature of guerrilla action and the social and political roots of the armed struggle, which largely transcended ideological frameworks.

Existing studies of armed resistance in Spain have focused on the large Agrupaciones guerrilleras organised by the PCE from 1944, paying little attention to the multitude of small armed groups operating across Spanish territory at the same time. There are two fundamental reasons for this: (1) the Agrupaciones guerrilleras achieved the greatest degree of hegemony and prominence of all armed organisations, and (2) it is relatively easy to find documentation relating to these groups in the archives. However, this tendency has in fact generated a distorted image of the anti-Francoist guerrilla, claiminging a degree of unity and convergence that had little to do with reality.

This study compares the 64 armed groups that have been identified and localised in eastern Andalusia, of which only three were Agrupaciones guerrilleras (Appendix: Table 1). That as many as 64 groups actually existed in Andalusia demonstrates in itself the anti-Francoist guerrilla's high degree of fragmentation.

On analysing the twelve variables described above, 48 groups exhibited characteristics approximating to those of *neighbours in arms*, while only 15 approximated, to various degrees, to the model of *modern guerrilla*. Thus, only a quarter of the armed groups in eastern Andalusia possessed the characteristics typically used to describe the armed anti-Francoist resistance. However, the majority of the 15 groups described as *modern guerrilla* could in fact be seen as *neighbours in arms* when many of their individual features are considered. Nevertheless, they have been placed within the category of *modern guerrilla* due to their national ambitions and their positive response to integration within the Agupaciones guerrilleras.

It should be noted that this initial classification only gives a general idea of typical characteristics. In time, groups which originally exhibited characteristics associated with *neighbours in arms* ended up transforming themselves, integrating or being absorbed into groups showing characteristics associated with the *modern guerrilla*. Moreover, members of resistance movements did not always stay in the same groups; rather, there were constant exchanges of guerrilla fighters. Sometimes these exchanges took place between armed groups of similar characteristics, but they could also occur between *neighbours in arms* and *modern guerrilla* groups or vice versa. All these elements must be kept in mind when analysing a phenomenon that was not only plural but also very dynamic.

However, if a graphic of the resistance movement is prepared on the basis of its members, the distribution of *neighbours in arms* and *modern guerrilla* groups looks different. Research in eastern Andalusia has identified 1,038 guerrilla fighters, representing approximately 95% of all guerrilla fighters active in the region. Using this data as a starting point, the guerrilla fighters incorporated into at least one of the 15 *modern guerrilla* groups represented a total of 65%, while about 50% were part of a group of *armed neighbours*. Thus, up to 15% of the guerrilla fighters active in eastern Andalusia participated in both forms of resistance (Appendix: Graph 1).

This simple classificatory sketch is only intended to show the enormous complexity, plurality, and heterogeneity of the anti-Francoist guerrilla. As stated previously, the intention here is not to establish a classification of groups, but to use both models and the twelve analytical variables as tools with which to recognise and explain the diversity of the guerrilla movement in Spain.

The best strategy for such a task is to study the guerrilla movement in a region like eastern Andalusia, which is large enough to contain a broad diversity of armed groups yet also small enough to allow for micro-historical analyses. Eastern Andalusia was home to approximately a thousand guerrilla fighters, approximately one eighth of the total number of guerrilla fighters in Spain. The guerrillas in Andalusia were also the most active in the whole country with the greatest number of combat incidents, robberies, kidnappings, and deaths of government forces being registered in this region, with Andalusia also having one of the highest rates of sabotage and murder of civilians. The Agrupación Guerrillera de Granada (also called, at different times, the Sixth Battalion (Sexto Batallón) and the Agrupación Guerrillera de Málaga) was, together with the Agrupación Guerrillera de Levante-Aragón, the most important communist organisation in the whole of Spain. These factors make Andalusia a perfect place to study the anti-Francoist guerrilla movement.

The PCE and the modern guerrilla

The characteristics of the modern guerrilla are not tied to any particular ideology but are simply a set of tools and structures that can be adopted by groups of diverse types. In the case of Spain, however, it was the PCE who made the greatest effort to transform the anti-Francoist resistance according to this model. That is not to say that the *modern guerrilla* was a model available exclusively to armed groups linked to the PCE, nor that all armed communist groups adhered to it. Nonetheless, the PCE was undoubtedly the organisation that worked most intensely to implement the *modern guerrilla* model in Spain, and for this reason the PCE receives special attention here.

The PCE became the main point of reference within the anti-Francoist guerrilla in the middle of the 1940s, although its presence in the guerrilla movement had been scant, even insignificant, in the previous years. In the aftermath of the Spanish Civil War, most of the PCE leadership had gone into exile and thousands of party activists found themselves behind bars. This situation was similar to that of other organisations forming part of the anti-Francoist opposition. What made the PCE a special case was the signing of the Non-Aggression Pact between Germany and the Soviet Union, which, between 1939 and 1941, tied the party's hands in its fight against Franco. After the collapse of the pact in June 1941, the PCE tried to recover the initiative but its negligible influence inside Spain complicated its plans. From 1941, the PCE continuously insisted on the need to transform the armed resistance in Spain. The anti-Francoist guerrilla was a font of heroism and generosity but needed to be reorganized and reconceived:

> Guerrilla war must not be a collection of isolated and somewhat desperate struggles. The guerrilla fighter must be an armed anti-Francoist combatant whose operations are in tune with political necessity (. . .). It is imperative to improve the armaments of the guerrillas and provide them with munitions. We must perfect the fighting and combat techniques in accordance with military principles. We believe that the working class and its vanguard should consider the actions of the guerrilla fighters a superior form of the struggle.[15]

The armed anti-Francoist resistance had to be transformed into "a true guerrilla army", insisted the PCE. Between 1941 and 1943 such slogans had no effect at all inside Spain. The first PCE intervention of any magnitude was "Operation Reconquest of Spain", launched in the autumn of 1944. The timing was largely due to external factors, especially the new turn in the course of the Second World War and its psychological effects. If the military initiative had resided with the Axis until 1943, from then onwards a series of Allied victories began to raise the hopes of the opposition in Spain. A defeat of fascism in Europe would bring about the defeat of Franco's dictatorship. In this context, the idea of triggering a popular uprising through a guerrilla invasion from France began to be discussed by the leaders of exiled political organisations, particularly the PCE. Such an operation would be facilitated by the fact that the French resistance movement contained thousands of Spanish combatants and that the PCE had insisted that these exiles must not be dispersed, but, rather, organised in a few Spanish units. In April 1942, Jesús Monzón, leader of the PCE in France, founded the XIV Cuerpo de Guerrilleros Españoles, which he renamed, in the middle of 1944, Agrupación de Guerrilleros Españoles (AGE). Following the liberation of Paris, the AGE consisted of 8,000 or 9,000 guerrilla fighters who relocated to the south of France in order to cross the border and set up a base on Spanish territory.[16]

"Operation Reconquest of Spain" involved a guerrilla invasion from across the French border through the Valle de Arán and other strategic points in the Pyrenees. The operation had three fundamental objectives: to bring about a national uprising, to establish a zone controlled by the insurgents, where a provisional government could be installed and to link the Spanish conflict to the European conflict, so that the destiny of the Franco dictatorship would be tied to that of other fascist dictatorships in Europe. The operation failed to achieve any of these goals but the consequences within the PCE and the guerrilla movement would nonetheless prove crucial.

The failure of "Operation Reconquest of Spain" was used by the PCE leadership to initiate an internal purge, described in Chapters 2 and 3. It was from this moment that the Central Committee led by Dolores Ibárruri managed to recover control of the PCE in France and Spain. A critical role in this process was played by Santiago Carrillo, a young political leader who became the right hand of Dolores Ibárruri and the central reference point of Spanish communism in subsequent decades.[17]

When he took charge of the PCE in France, Santiago Carrillo assumed the leadership of the communist guerrilla in Spain and was to be the chief author of the guerrilla transformations which subsequently took place. Carrillo devised a plan to reform the anti-Francoist guerrilla and transform *neighbours in arms* into "a true guerrilla Army".[18] The plan had four fundamental objectives: to regain the PCE's control in the Spanish interior, to improve the tools of the armed struggle, to turn the PCE into the main force of the anti-Francoist opposition and to overthrow Franco's dictatorship. The last goal was never achieved although the other three objectives were effectively accomplished.

The transformation of the anti-Francoist guerrilla was not a simple task.

The PCE had to develop a very precise plan. First, it selected its most experienced activists in the armed struggle to go to Spain and act as instructors and leaders. These activists had extensive combat experience from the Spanish Civil War and the Second World War, when they were integrated into the French resistance. The PCE also established a guerrilla school in the south of France, where hundreds of activists learned the techniques and tactics of the *modern guerrilla*. Highly active from 1944, it had to close in 1950 as a result of the banning of the PCE in France. The guerrilla school operated secretly behind the façade of a timber yard where the guerrilla fighters worked in the morning and received political and military instruction in the afternoon.[19] These training centres allowed the PCE to form hundreds of activists which, once prepared, were sent to Spain. The process was similar to that of the Greek guerrilla, which had its guerrilla schools in neighbouring countries such as Albania, Bulgaria, or Yugoslavia.[20]

There are few surviving documents relating to the instructors at the guerrilla school, although examination of the syllabus leaves little doubt as to their high degree of competence. In most cases they must have been communist party officials who had held a military post during the Spanish Civil War and the French Resistance. However, they also included some former Spanish students and teachers at the Soviet Military Academy in Frunze (capital of Kyrgyzstan). At least one contingent of these NKVD-trained teachers arrived in France in 1945 from Yugoslavia, where they had been employed as military instructors.[21]

The few documents available do not permit study of the evolution of the syllabus at the guerrilla school in Toulouse. However, they certainly reveal two important facts: (1) the great familiarity of the school's instructors with the material taught, which contained specific sections on strategy, tactics, organisation, propaganda, arms, social support, etc. and (2) the instructors' interest in traditional forms of irregular warfare as well as the new approach of the *modern guerrilla*.[22] In the surviving programme from 1946 there is an explicit reference to the "history of guerrilla movements". In this section, the students not only learned about the strategies used by the Second World War resistance in "Russia, Czechoslovakia, Poland, France, Yugoslavia, and Greece", but also considered "guerrilla movements in the present: Palestine, Indonesia, Vietnam, Greece, and Spain".[23] As a report by the PCE Central Committee stated, it was necessary to study the emergence of guerrillas in "different countries, make comparisons, and draw on previous experiences in order to apply these in Spain".[24]

The transformative plan of the PCE required the new activists trained in guerrilla schools to take command of armed groups in order to enforce the necessary changes as soon as they arrived in Spain. New leaders returning from exile had to create new kinds of groups, called Agrupaciones guerrilleras, in every region. These would serve as organisational bases incorporating the multitude of autonomous groups which acted independently. The Agrupaciones guerrilleras were conceived of as political-military organisations under the control of the PCE.[25] Together, the regional Agrupaciones formed the National Guerrilla Army.

Despite the complexity of the unification process, between 1944 and 1946, the new leadership managed to implement its model in several regions of Spain.

Name	Territory
1st Agrupación	Cáceres, Toledo, Ávila, southeast of Madrid and north of Badajoz and Ciudad Real.
2nd Agrupación	Ciudad Real, Córdoba, Jaén, Toledo, Cáceres and Badajoz.
3rd Agrupación	Córdoba, south of Badajoz and Ciudad Real.
4th Agrupación	Galicia and León.
5th Agrupación	East of Ciudad Real, south of Cuenca and west of Albacete.
6th Agrupación	Cádiz and western Málaga.
Agrupación Guerrillera de Málaga / Agrupación Guerrillera de Granada	Granada, eastern Málaga and zones adjacent to Almería and Jaén.
Agrupación Guerrillera de Levante-Aragón	Teruel, Valencia, Castellón, Cuenca and neighbouring zones.

The Agrupaciones guerrilleras were clear examples of the new *modern guerrilla*, where politics took precedence over military tactics, propaganda and psychological warfare became central, and political infrastructure was seen as a decisive factor.[26] The transformation of the guerrilla movement following this model had wide-ranging consequences. Between 1939 and 1944 the PCE's first clandestine organisations at regional and local level did not maintain relationships with armed groups in the mountains. Any contact would endanger the structure of the clandestine organisation, claimed the leadership inside Spain, although the new guerrilla units sent by Carrillo disagreed and criticizeded these leaders for their attitude. The situation changed radically from 1945. From that point onwards, clandestine organisations were not only obliged to maintain close relationships with the Agrupaciones guerrilleras, but also to serve as their basic support network, their main source of information and their reserve of future recruits. The guerrilla and the clandestine organisations became so closely interwoven that the latter decided to refer to themselves, at local level, as "guerrilla fighters of the plains". From then on, the direction and orientation of the Agrupaciones guerrilleras depended on the political leadership within the clandestine organisations, which was superior to the military commander leading the guerrilla in the mountains.

Internal communication patterns between local and regional committees also developed over time. Initially, coordination was mainly achieved through a chain structure, which aimed to organise the grassroots through direct contact established without any system. One person simply created ties with another who, in turn, was tied to another, thus forming a chain. This organisational method made it easy for Franco's dictatorship to break up the clandestine organisations, which led to the development, from 1943, of a new modality: *troikas*. A *troika* was a unit of three people. Every member of a *troika* had contact with someone who formed part of another *troika*, and so on. The structure was vertical and pyramidal, which, theoretically, made it more resistant to repression. However, police activity continued to have a devastating impact. From 1945 onwards there was a new order from the exterior: they were to disband the *troikas* and form cells in the workplace. Different cells were integrated into a 'ratio' and several 'ratios' formed a sector. The sectors, in turn, answered directly to the Local, Regional, and National Committees. This model was also vertical and pyramidal, but sought to anchor the operation in the workplace rather than in personal relationships, as was the case with previous models.[27]

The PCE aspired to transform the armed struggle in Spain by adopting the techniques and methods of the *modern guerrilla*, but, despite their efforts, the success of the change was limited. They faced rejection from a great number of autonomous groups which preferred to maintain their traditional forms of action, organisation, and independence. Meanwhile, the internal rivalry within the PCE in Spain hindered the implementation of new directives, a task which was further complicated by the intense repression of the Franco dictatorship. A combination of obstacles thus limited the transformative project envisioned by the PCE.

The model established in 1945 remained stable until 1948, when resistance reached an important turning point. From 1947 the repressive politics of the dictatorship had ceased to be directed exclusively at guerrilla fighters and also began to target local committees and support networks. The Agrupaciones guerrilleras immediately began to suffer the consequences. By this time, the anti-Francoist resistance was also completely isolated internationally, forcing it to resort to theft or the black market to supply itself with weapons. Faced with this precarious situation, the PCE's Central Committee decided to seek help from "comrade Tito".

A number of factors explain why the PCE turned to Yugoslavia for help. The Spanish cause was well supported in the recently created Socialist Federal Republic of Yugoslavia. Among the approximately 1,700 International Brigaders of Yugoslav origin who fought in the Spanish Civil War, about 250 managed to return to their country, where they played a vital part in the first phases of resistance against the occupying German forces. Popularly known as *Španci* (the Spanish in Serbo-Croat), they acquired great political and social prestige. No less than thirty of them reached the end of the Second World War as generals, while another fifty-nine were awarded the title "Heroes of the People".[28]

The Spanish Civil War thus permeated the collective imaginary of the new Yugoslav socialist republic. Belgrade had also become the place of residence of certain distinguished PCE members, some of whom worked as advisors to the Yugoslav Chief of Staff. Moreover, the Tito government gave logistical support to the Greek communist guerrilla in this period. Equally importantly, in September 1947, Moscow had launched a successor to the Communist International, named Kominform, which had its formal seat in Belgrade.

According to Carrillo's testimony, Marshall Tito's response was largely indifferent. The Yugoslav air force did not have sufficient range to drop arms on the east coast of Spain and then return to the Adriatic. Tito also asked the Spanish delegation if they had discussed their plans with Moscow, a question which made the Spanish leaders uneasy. Years later he explained to Carrillo that he thought the proposal was a trap, devised by Stalin in order to enable the Soviet leader to accuse the Yugoslav leadership of disobeying his orders. In reality, the Spanish communist delegation was not yet aware of the crisis brewing between Belgrade and Moscow.[29]

The tension between the Soviet Union and Yugoslavia came to a head at the second meeting of the Kominform, when Tito's Republic was expelled for not following Soviet directives.[30] Stalin, conscious of the gravity of the schism created, ensured that the other communist parties maintained their discipline. In this context the Spanish delegation's visit to Belgrade a few months previously suddenly became a problem. In order to clarify the position of the miniscule PCE, Stalin called a meeting at the Kremlin in October 1948. This was attended by a Spanish delegation consisting of the General Secretary of the PCE, Dolores Ibárruri, Santiago Carrillo and Francisco Antón. The PCE delegation spoke for a few hours with Stalin, the Foreign Minister, Molotov, the Soviet official Voroshiloc, and one of Stalin's most faithful allies, Mijail Suslov.

The Spanish delegation began by insisting on its absolute loyalty to the Soviet Union and to Stalin, after which it engaged in harsh self-criticism which included a sudden rejection of *titoism*.[31] Once the issue was resolved, those present proceeded to discuss the strategy that the PCE should adopt against Franco's dictatorship in Spain. The basic idea expressed by Stalin was that they must not forget the traditional Leninist approach of working and infiltrating the unions. Did this mean that Stalin advised against a continuation of the armed struggle? The testimonies of the protagonists are not clear in this regard. It seems that Stalin did not explicitly reject armed action, but rather stressed the idea of developing the clandestine struggle within the official unions of the dictatorship as a preferable course of action.[32]

After the meeting, the PCE modified its stance regarding the guerrilla movement, which came to be known as the "change of tactics". The Agrupaciones guerrilleras were not to have an offensive character, but rather should be converted into political instructors and organisers of the peasantry:

> The greatest resource of this guerrilla movement is not, despite its high value, its inexhaustible spring of heroism and combat willingness, but its political wealth, its growing understanding of the role it has to play in the political and revolutionary education of the masses (. . .). The guerrilla fighters of our fatherland have realised that their role is not only to attack the Civil Guard and the Falangists, the assassins of the people. They know, and this knowledge is gradually being turned into practice with increasing intensity, that they are something more valuable: they are and must be propagandists, political instructors, organisers of the people and the peasantry. Every guerrilla fighter, and above all every guerrilla leader, must be a political leader and an organiser of the peasantry.[33]

The change of tactics was hampered by two fundamental problems. Firstly, new directives did not reach all Agrupaciones guerrilleras, who were increasingly isolated owing to the regime's persistent harassment. Secondly, the conversion of guerrilla fighters into political instructors may have seemed viable from the comfort of an office in Paris or Moscow, but was far removed from the reality of guerrilla life in the Spanish mountains. In a context marked by the constant aggression of the army, the Civil Guard and the counterinsurgency groups, the change in direction was practically impossible.[34]

Faced with the mounting contradictions between the orders of the PCE leadership in exile and the brutal reality of life in the mountains, the guerrilla movement in Spain faced a slow death. By 1950 there were only two surviving units, the Agrupación Guerrillera de Levante-Aragón and the

Agrupación Guerrillera de Granada, whose vitality had begun to decline rapidly. Two years later, in 1952, the PCE decided to abandon the path of armed struggle. The demobilisation of the guerrilla was chaotic and the PCE did little to help the process. They organised only one evacuation operation for the last guerrilla fighters of the Levante-Aragón area, while the rest were left to their fate.[35] Dozens of guerrilla fighters died in their desperate attempts to reach the frontier, very few managing to reach exile.

With the exception of a few individual figures who remained in hiding or made incursions into Spain to carry out sabotage or other forms of action,[36] the guerrilla movement in Spain disappeared after the PCE called for demobilisation in 1952. Four years later the leaders of the party launched a manifesto entitled "For national reconciliation, for a democratic and peaceful solution to the Spanish problem"[37] where it definitively renounced the armed struggle as a means to overthrow the Franco dictatorship. There was not a single reference to the anti-Francoist guerrilla in the document. The times were changing and old heroes became troubling shadows of the past.

PART ONE

Guerrilla Identities

Chapter 1

From Peasants to Soldiers, from Soldiers to Guerrilla Fighters
Youth, masculinity and camaraderie

It is this [battle] which has hammered, chiselled, and strengthened us and made us what we are. This war (. . .) shaped us in combat, to the point where we will continue to be combatants.

(*La Guerre comme expérience intérieure*, Ernst Jünger)

The first signs of spring had just appeared when, in 1944, the streets of Paris awoke to the sight of a ubiquitous red poster. In the upper part were the portraits of ten members of the FTP-MOI (Francs-tireurs et Partisans – Main d' œuvre immigrée) and the questioning headline: "The Liberators?". In the lower part were photos of derailed trains, a weapons arsenal and a pair of bullet-riddled corpses. Beneath these images, the Nazi propaganda poster exclaimed "Liberation by an army of crime!" In this way the occupying troops sought to link the urban guerrilla with crime and terrorism. However the red poster ended up becoming a symbol of the resistance.[1]

In addition to its iconic message, the poster provided a synthesis of some of the most common features of resistance members in France: their often international origin, their youth, and their predominantly male gender. Subsequent research has confirmed this image by presenting a portrait of the typical partisan as a young man of about thirty years of age.[2]

The profile of the anti-Francoist guerrilla fighter in Spain shares two features with the French *maquisard*: their youth and their gender. However, if the two profiles are compared in socio-economic terms, important differences can be observed: while the French resistance evinced great socio-professional heterogeneity, the anti-Francoist guerrilla consisted mostly of peasants. Youth, masculinity, and rural life, understood in the context of previous experiences and, particularly, the experience of the war, are the main reference points of this chapter. It follows an accumulation of

life lessons that first turned young men from a rural background into republican soldiers, and, years later, anti-Francoist guerrilla fighters.

A peasant guerrilla

The urban guerrilla played a marginal role in the anti-Francoist resistance.
Its activities were concentrated in Madrid, Malaga, Granada, and, above all,
in Barcelona and its industrial belt. Of the approximately eight thousand
guerrilla fighters that were active in Spain, only about a hundred operated
in the "concrete jungle", as the anarchist theorist Abraham Guillén defined
the urban nuclei where the armed struggle took place.[3] The rural predominance of the anti-Francoist guerrilla was such that the contemporary
vocabulary itself directly reflected this fact. The population referred to the
guerrilla fighters as "those among the hills" or "those in the mountains".
The identification of guerrilla fighters with a geographical reference is in
fact a very wide-spread practice. In Colombia or Mexico they were know by
the same name, in Greece they were known as "those from above", while
the Korean and Malaysian guerrillas were variously called "the people in the
mountains", "from the hill" or "in the jungle".[4]

In the case of eastern Andalusia, 90% of the guerrilla fighters were
linked to the primary sector: 80% to the agricultural sector and 10% in
activities related to livestock or mountain resources. Urban workers represented only 5%, while the percentage of members belonging to the liberal
professions was negligible (Appendix: Graph 2). The numbers may vary in
other Spanish regions, especially in the north, where the guerrilla included
more miners, but they correspond nonetheless to a general pattern, showing
the profoundly rural character of the guerrilla in Spain.

This profile indicates commonalities and differences with other resistance movements in Europe. In the French case there were important
differences between *departments*, but, in general terms, French resistance
groups displayed enormous socio-professional diversity and the peasantry
tended to represent only 10% of the membership.[5] However, in the south
of France and in Greece the peasantry formed the greatest part of the resistance movement, showing a clear rural profile from the beginning.[6]

Within the peasantry, the Spanish historiography has traditionally
stressed the importance of the *jornaleros* (landless day labourers) in the anti-
Francoist guerrilla. This assertion has no empirical foundation; it is based
on old Marxist paradigms in which day labourers were ascribed the characteristics of a rural proletariat possessing a high degree of class
consciousness.[7]

The reality in Andalusia was very different. The weight of the anti-Francoist guerrilla was above all and repeatedly carried by the so-called "men of the fields", that is, small farmers and leaseholders of humble origin but with some small property or resource to exploit. Together they constituted 68% of the resistance membership, in contrast to day labourers who constituted 12% (Appendix: Graph 2). The socio-economic profile of the guerrilla in Spain varied in relation to territory,[8] and to draw a general map it would be necessary to conduct detailed studies in each guerrilla area.

The huge presence of small-holders in the anti-Francoist guerrilla in eastern Andalusia was related to two fundamental factors: (1) the fact that there were a large numbers of small-holders in the areas where conditions permitted resistance to develop, and, (2) the fact that the small-holding peasantry constituted a sector which mobilised in the 1930s in support of the Second Republic, joined the Republican Popular Army during the war, and were consequently targeted by the Francoist repression in the post-war period.

Andalusia has been represented historically as a territory characterised by the dominant presence of *latifundios* (large estates) and *jornaleros*. In recent decades, however, researchers have unearthed a more complex reality. Western Andalusia corresponds to this traditional view, but, in eastern Andalusia, there was a different distribution of land, which gave great demographic weight to small-holders.[9] These were also more numerous in mountainous areas, which they shared with the majority of the Andalusian guerrilla fighters.

But the prominent role of the small-holder in the Andalusian guerrilla does not only undermine old Marxist clichés with regards to the *jornalero*, but also adds nuance to the theory of the rural middle classes as supporters of counterrevolutionary and fascist ideologies in Europe.[10] Whether historians should ascribe to an entire socio-economic group a particular political inclination or attitude towards the dictatorship is debatable,[11] and more so if the most humble sectors of the peasantry are taken into consideration; sectors situated on the borderline between propertied and the property-less, between poverty and survival. Small-holders were often a source of social support for Francoism,[12] but they were also the backbone of the resistance against the dictatorship.

Ties between small-holders and progressive political forces can be found throughout the Republican period. During the first Republican biennium (1931–1933), the politics of the Spanish Socialist Party (Partido Socialista Obrero Español, hereafter PSOE) and the socialist union UGT (Unión General de Trabajadores) and its agrarian federation, the FNTT (Federación Nacional de Trabajadores de la Tierra), defended the interests of small-holders, leaseholders, and sharecroppers. It is true that between 1934 and 1936, socialist rhetoric adopted many postulates associated with the *jornaleros*, which led to a loss of influence among middling sectors of the peasantry,[13] but the rupture was far from complete.[14] It must be remembered that the political positioning of individuals is not exclusively articulated in functionalist terms, as if it were a strategy devised simply on the basis of economic interests. Rather, it must be seen as a product of various social and cultural components, including family traditions, personal loyalties and disagreements, and so on.[15] Moreover, after the revolutionary spring of 1936, the PSOE articulated once more – despite the FNTT's enormous resistance[16] – various concessions to small-holders; "The agrarian politics of the Socialist Party must be: to respect small property and to consider a small-holder anyone who possesses an amount of land that he can work using his own means".[17]

The exponential growth of the PCE, the Spanish Communist Party, during the war played a vital role in this development. Communist campaigns against agrarian collectivisations and in favour of small-holders, reinforced by communist leaders in charge of the Ministry of Agriculture, allowed the PCE to attract thousands of small-holding peasants to its ranks.[18] "For Republican order! Respect the property of small-holding peasants!", stated the posters of the Ministry of Public Instruction, also led by a team of prominent PCE leaders.

Finally, it must be remembered that throughout the three-year-long war, many small-holders joined the ranks of the Republican Popular Army, either voluntarily, or, from 1937, through conscription. Regardless of their original political positions, at the end of the war they returned to their villages, and as a result of their having been Republican soldiers, they suffered the repression of the dictatorship. Their small properties were often confiscated by the authorities and given to supporters of the victorious *movimiento*.

All these factors begin to explain why, despite its prominence among sectors supporting Francoism, some members of the small-holding peasantry mobilised as guerrilla fighters in the resistance.

Youth and gender

Like other resistance movements in Europe, the anti-Francoist guerrilla in Spain was composed mainly of young men. Only two investigations have compiled statistical facts regarding the age of guerrilla members in Spain: one focusing on the area of Levante and another on the provinces of Málaga and Granada.[19] The results of their statistical investigations highlight the prominence of youth in the resistance.

The present work on eastern Andalusia only reinforces this picture. The results (Appendix: Graph 3) confirm that the resistance was mostly formed by youths and men aged between 14 and 29 (52%) and men in the first phase of maturity, that is, aged between 30 and 39 (36%), who represented 88% of the total number of guerrilla fighters. The percentage of those under 18 years old was very low since all armed groups – *neighbours in arms* as well as the *modern guerrilla* – demanded that fighters reach military age before joining the resistance. Only in extreme cases of repression did they allow, as an exception, a minor to join the guerrilla. At the other end of the spectrum, those older than 40 years constituted only 12% of the total.

In terms of gender, the results are more emphatic still. The anti-Francoist guerrilla was a masculine and patriarchal sphere where women were completely marginalised. As will be discuses later, the work of women was related to other, peripheral areas of the armed struggle. Of the 1,038 guerrilla fighters identified in eastern Andalusia, only three were women, and, in Spain as a whole, the number must have been somewhere between thirty and forty.[20] Young males were clearly the engine of the antifascist resistance in Europe, but what factors might explain their dominance in the anti-Francoist guerrilla? What were the factors that made young men the main protagonists in the anti-Francoist resistance?

Youth is a social construct that changes throughout history. Its characteristics vary in relation to other contemporary factors: class, gender, environment (rural or urban) etc. Universalising models have insistently indicated that a key factor facilitating the mobilisation of youth is young people's independence and lack of responsibilities. In reality, such theories problematically take a specific western conception from the second half of the twentieth century to be a permanent condition of youth.[21] As Alberto Melucci suggests, questions revolving around young men's mobilisation can only be answered through empirical studies that provide information on the particular characteristics of youth in every context.[22]

In 1940s rural Spain, the family was a vital production unit in which young men played a fundamental role.[23] At the same time, marriage and fatherhood came at an early age. The marital status of guerrilla fighters in the armed anti-Francoist resistance was evenly balanced between married and single men, which makes it clear that issues of independence and pre-existing responsibilities were not a relevant factor in their mobilisation.

What perspective should be adopted then? In the case of the anti-Francoist guerrilla, the focus must fall within a socio-cultural framework which is sensitive to two crucial influences: the long-term history of young men's mobilisation, and the experience of war. Both clearly influenced the development of the resistance.

The process of economic, political, and social modernisation in Europe from the end of the nineteenth century favoured the growth of civil society, and, with this development, there emerged a new political subject of great importance: young men. The first indications of the mobilisation of young men appeared at the beginning of the twentieth century, but it was during the First World War and the inter-war period that they became historical agents of major significance. Political groups, conscious of the importance of youth, initiated targeted recruitment campaigns and youth organisations quickly multiplied within the new political movements of the time: fascism, socialism, and communism.[24]

The same phenomenon could be observed in Spain, albeit with a certain delay. The first youth organisations linked to political parties or unions emerged in the first decades of the twentieth century but did not become significant political agents until the Second Republic. From that moment, these organisations started to gain autonomy, their own identity and an ability to formulate proposals and demands related specifically to youth.

On the left, the national students' federation (Federación Universitaria Escolar, FUE), the Federation of Socialist Youth (Federación de Juventudes Socialistas, FJS), the Iberian Federation of Libertarian Youth (Federación Ibérica de Juventudes Libertarias, FIJL) and the Communist Youth Union of Spain (Unión de Juventudes Comunistas de España, UJCE) embodied the rise and strength of youth mobilisation. The same process could be observed among the Spanish right and the regional nationalisms, as seen in important groups like the youth organisation of the conservative party, Acción Popular (Juventud de Acción Popular, JAP), the conservative students' union (Sindicato Español Universitario, SEU), the Traditionalist Youth (Juventudes Tradicionalistas), the Basque Youth (Juventudes Vascas) or the Youth of the Catalan State (Juventut d'Estat Català). Youth organisations played a crucial role in the Second Republic, which was marked by a profound process of radicalisation, especially from 1934. From then on the new political movements took on the role of the vanguard and became the leading innovators of new forms of collective action.[25]

Having offered this general sketch of political youth organisations' evolution, it is also necessary to introduce some nuances to the picture. While it is true that youth organisations saw an increase in membership during the Second Republic their practical impact on youth activities was still limited. According to Sandra Souto, the FJS boasted about 20,000 members by April 1934, while the UJCE claimed to have 11,000 on their books in June 1933 – a figure which was no doubt exaggerated.[26] In fact, the vertiginous growth of youth organisations only really took off during the war.[27]

A second issue that needs to be clarified is the masculine predominance within the youth organisations. Research into the mobilisation of young women in Spain is still scarce, but some tendencies can already be observed. In general terms, it is clear that the first initiatives appeared at the beginning of the twentieth century, although their social impact was limited and restricted to a minority. As in the case of men, it was the Spanish Civil War that generated an important increase in the mobilisation of women, although this case also exhibited some particular characteristics.[28]

War experience

The coup d'état on July 18th 1936 prompted a political change which, for the first time, led to widespread mobilisation of women, yet failed to break old gender roles and ideals. The greatest rupture occurred in the first weeks after the military insurrection, as the Republican zone was experiencing a fully-fledged revolution. The old social order seemed to collapse and during the summer of 1936 a small number of young women fought in the antifascist militias together with their male comrades. The initiative came from women who sought to eliminate old behavioural patterns, engaging in front-line battle in the same conditions as the men, but, ultimately, the situation was transitory. Within a short time, the *milicianas* were forced to lay down their arms and women's organisations themselves disseminated the slogan that came to define women's role during the remainder of the war: "Men to the battle front, women to the home front".[29]

The reasons for this went deep, but during the First World War, the soldier became a stereotype for a new masculinity, an ideal in which beauty, bravery, or camaraderie displaced previous models. They were warrior men in action; they lived, killed, and died bonded by trench solidarity and blood. The new masculine ideal provided the foundation for the 'new man' propagated by fascist movements in Europe. But the cultural archetype was not exclusive to fascism; it permeated all social and ideological strata. The new masculine stereotype surrounding the working classes, for example, left a deep mark on socialist and other left-wing discourses at the time.[30]

Studies of the dissemination of a new masculine model in Spain are recent and in the majority of cases they refer to conservative movements.[31] Even so, early investigations show the stereotype of a new masculinity having an impact on the left too, reinforcing values like virility, strength and sacrifice. Some of the clearest examples can be seen in the Asturias revolution of 1934, in the new culture of paramilitary organisations that emerged from youth movements, and, above all, during the Spanish Civil War.[32]

Representations of men in Republican propaganda clearly indicate a strengthening of the new masculine ideal. They depict naked and muscular torsos: men, warriors; aggressive and brave. Pilots were called "Iron men", and sailors distinguished themselves through their courage. "Strong men: to the Front!" exclaimed one of the posters by the PSU. "More Men! More Arms! More Munitions!" said another by the UGT. "To attack is to win. Everyone attack as one man!." On the battle fronts, in the trenches, Republican soldiers shared this masculine ideal, which relegated women to the home front. During the period of the resistance, this same model remained in place, with its clearly defined ascriptions of gender roles.

The Spanish Civil War caused the greatest mobilisation drive and the greatest political recruitment levels in Spanish history, the explosive mobilisation process having one major protagonist: young males. "All youth united for Spain", said a poster of the JSU showing a clenched fist and an iron chain with the initials of various youth organisations (JSU, JJLL, and JIR). As Helen Graham has made clear, the massive enlistment did not come from "people in arms" as a whole or even the organised labour movement; rather it came "overwhelmingly from the young (in this case male), unskilled and *previously unmobilised* sectors".[33]

However, it is also important to remember the large proportion of peasants in the new Republican Popular Army. A PCE report written in July 1937 highlighted the strong presence of the peasantry among their ranks. The report analysed 69 brigades, composed of 183,015 soldiers in total. Of these, 92,410 were peasants, 64,929 urban workers and 23,650 were described as "others".[34] In other words, the Popular Army was made up of young men who were for the most part peasants and who, in a majority of cases, had no previous experience of collective political action. This was the dominant profile of those mobilised in the Republican zone.

There were two forms of recruitment during the war: voluntary enlistment and conscription. The coup d'état led to the disintegration of the Army, which created space for the spontaneous formation of popular militias on the Republican home front. However, the activity of the militias only lasted for a few months.[35] With the creation of the Fifth Regiment, the PCE launched the first initiative aiming to transform the militias into a regular Army. Subsequently, the government of Largo Caballero took steps in the same direction. Popular militias and regular units which had remained loyal to the Republic were integrated into the newly created Mixed Brigades, which served as the backbone of the new Republican

Popular Army.[36] Even so, the government did not feel secure enough at this stage to implement unpopular measures like conscription by the traditional mechanism of drafts. Instead, it relied on a "general mobilisation" of a voluntary kind.

The situation changed after the fall of Málaga in February 1937. The loss of one of the Republican strongholds in the south triggered a campaign driven on various political fronts to immediately introduce military conscription. The PCE, once again, was one of the greatest advocates. The first governmental institution to introduce conscription was the Catalan Generalitat, which at the time had certain autonomous powers relating to defence. Five days later the Republican government announced its decision to recruit new combatants. From that moment, until the end of the war, conscription was achieved by calling up drafts.[37] The militias managed to mobilise around 120,000 volunteers, while the conscription system from March 1937 mobilised around 1,700,000 recruits.[38]

Historians have stressed the importance of political affiliation in the formation of the militias and the Mixed Brigades. In the militias the relation between politics and recruitment was relatively close, since the popular militias were first formed by political parties and unions and since loyalty and internal cohesion was thus based on ideological affinity. In this sense, it is possible to talk about socialist or anarchist militias, for example. In the case of the Mixed Brigades, the situation is more complex. Although many of the Mixed Brigades were created from previous militia groups, it is possible to observe a greater ideological diversity in these units. A report on the political affiliation of the soldiers of twenty-three Mixed Brigades in July 1937 describes units composed of socialist, communist, anarchist, and republican party members, as well as soldiers without any known party membership. On the other hand, there were also Mixed Brigades which exhibited a much greater degree of political homogeneity, as was the case of the Fifth Regiment, where the communists dominated from the beginning.[39]

The focus on political identities has at times led historians to underplay the vital importance of primary groups (family, neighbours and friends) in the formation of the militias and Brigades. It should be remembered that the majority of militia fighters and soldiers mobilised during the war lacked any previous experience relating to collective action and did not belong to any political organisation. The importance of primary groups in the Army and the tradition in European societies of recruiting on the basis of neighbourhood have been explored in a long-standing historiography. Conscription to armies such as those of Britain, Germany and France, and later to specific units, was carried out in accordance with primary groups, especially those formed on the basis of neighbourhood bonds. The creation of army units on the basis of primary groups helped to secure strong internal cohesion as they were composed of soldiers with strong personal bonds which reinforced sentiments of solidarity, union, and loyalty.[40]

The popular militias in the Spanish Civil War, especially in the rural sphere, were organised in every municipality on account of kinship, neighbourhood and friendship. Social mobilisation *from below* relied on the structures and internal social networks of the local community. A similar process occurred in the mobilisation of social support for the coup.[41] The same phenomenon can also be observed in the Mixed Brigades, despite their being products of forced recruitment *from above*. New recruits actively sought a way to join units with soldiers from their own region and, as far as possible, ensure that their unit would be stationed as close as possible to their place of origin.[42] That said, military units changed throughout the conflict. Increasing militarisation of the Popular Army and the necessities of war often broke these initial bonds, thus enforcing geographical mobility and the integration of recruits from different regions.

The theory of primary groups has had a great impact on studies of the German army during the Second World War. Some researchers even came to suggest that German soldiers had been mobilised and maintained their internal cohesion through primary groups, without any need for ideology.[43] In contrast, writers like Omer Bartov disagree with such limited and one-sided positions. In his study on Wehrmacht units on the Eastern Front, he observed that throughout the war, as the numbers of casualties grew, the original core of primary groups was broken up with the introduction of new replacements. Thus camaraderie and the "devotion to the cause" gained increasing importance. The theory of primary groups cannot negate, in other words, the importance of ideological affinities, just as political ties cannot hide the influence of primary groups. As Bartov suggests, both mechanisms of mobilisation and internal cohesion were compatible and complementary.[44]

This is the model that should be applied to the mobilisation and formation of the militias and Mixed Brigades in the Spanish Civil War, where primary groups and ideological affinities operated simultaneously. Let us consider the ideological dimension. The new Popular Army was created as an army with marked political character. Thousands of young soldiers enrolled in the youth organisations of different parties and syndicates, thus participating in the largest mobilisation process in Spanish history. The Unified Socialist Youth (Juventudes Socialistas Unificadas, JSU), a product of the Federation of Socialist Youth (FJS) and the Communist Youth Union of Spain (UJCE), had more than 300,000 members by January 1937, while the Iberian Federation of Libertarian Youth (FIJL) counted between 130,000 and 150,000 members by May of that year. Both organisations supplied recruits to the new Popular Army which the government built to defend the Republic on the battlefield.[45] The key to this undertaking was the mobilisation of an important number of young men who until now had remained on the margin of the political conflict in Spain.

I have shown in a previous book how the *war experience* produced a profound transformation in the collective conscience and mentality of thousands of young men, who, until that moment, had remained aloof from social issues. The trenches became a school where they learned to read and write while receiving military training and ideological schooling.[46] The Ministry of Public Instruction and Fine Arts published textbooks which linked the teaching of core subjects to political conflicts in Spain. The trenches, as well as the home front, were covered in flyers, posters and wall-newspapers while young recruits attended public lectures, talks and assemblies.[47] The new political commissariat became a part of the Popular Army and took responsibility for the political education of the soldiers.

The new Republican army ceased to be a conventional army in order to become a "Popular Army" (not to be confused with a revolutionary army) and "Antifascist Armed Forces", as the Government called it in spring 1937.[48] Moreover, political organisations like the PCE created schools specifically to educate army units; each provided hundreds of new recruits with some form of training or instruction. The profoundly ideological character of the Army and the war left a mark on a generation of young antifascists who had learned to defend their rights and their ideas with arms. Thus, the war became a genuinely transformative experience for thousands of young individuals, an experience from which young combatants emerged with personalities and identities that bore little resemblance to those they had exhibited before their recruitment.

The experience of war and the strong generational sentiment were vital in the development of the armed anti-Francoist resistance. Young men had undergone a powerful socialisation process in which sentiments, taught lessons and life experiences converged.[49] George L. Mosse was one of the first writers to underscore how war experiences can be an important mobilising factor between ex-combatants and later generations. The experience of war is multifaceted, and, just as it prompted feelings of sadness and disgust, it was also remembered by many veterans as the happiest years of their lives.[50]

Camaraderie, belonging and internal solidarity within a unit living under the constant threat of death were some of the most widespread feelings among ex-combatants.[51] Testimonies repeatedly recall this connection and the strange sensation of emptiness and defencelessness that made itself felt as the war ended, when the Popular Army was disbanded and its soldiers had to return home or go into exile. Carlos Jiménez Margalejo, one of those young republican soldiers, wrote a novel about the war with an illustrative title: *Those of us who were eighteen*.[52] Sometime afterwards, in a memoir which dealt with the end of the conflict and the experience of exile, he delivered an extraordinary description of that feeling:

> All my life I had been profoundly individualist, hating everything that would tie me to others. Now I was so terribly lost that when I was separated from the little group for a few instances, I desired nothing more than to return to it and rest my back against a friend, to feel his life and her solidarity. We must have behaved like children wanting their mothers. We needed animal contact to feel safe. We went towards an undetermined end, but we did so in a group, united with one another through shared misfortune.[53]

The war experience had such emotional impact among the young Republican soldiers that it came to underpin a sense of generational identity. Many protagonists have spoken of that shared sense, of that feeling of collective belonging. Santiago Carrillo, one of those youths, spoke of the *war generation*: "those who were about twenty years old in 1936".[54] The concept of historical generations is complex and has at times been associated with others such as age group and cohort, which originated in sociology and demography.[55] In this sense, the generation or the cohort can be considered "the aggregate of individuals who experience the same events within the same time interval."[56] Young Spanish antifascist soldiers felt that they shared such experiences, just as the youths of the French Resistance did, according to the work of Olivier Wieviorka.[57]

Ex-combatants and resistance

Vicente Castillo, lieutenant in the 147th Mixed Brigade and, years later, member of the Provincial Committee of the CNT in Granada, succinctly described the feelings that accompanied the demobilisation of the Popular Army and the return home: "Our trust did not extend beyond the many we had known since the beginning and our guns".[58] This was the context in which the resistance emerged. Before a wave of repression, some youths decided that there were only two possible responses: camaraderie and arms.

The return to civilian life at the end of the war was traumatic for

Republican soldiers for two reasons. Until now historians have highlighted how their status as defeated made them targets of the repression, but the war also had other effects that were felt among ex-combatants. Young soldiers marching to the front went through important changes in terms of mentality, culture, and even their place within a social structure. When they returned home they were different "men". The adaptation of these young soldiers to a world that had changed radically was complex.[59] It is only when their status as defeated and repressed is added to this picture that it is possible to get some sense of the enormous challenges and pressures they had to face in the post-war period.

The testaments of ex-soldiers recall the experience of war and life in the trenches as a particularly difficult moment in their lives, plagued by death, by losses and fears, but many also view the experience through a different lens, describing that period as a time of hopes, desires, and happiness. They were young, soldiers, and, for the first time, they felt like individuals and collective subjects, protagonists not only of their own lives but also of something bigger and more exciting: history. Many of them had left their local community for the first time and began to experience life as young adults.

The end of the war put an end to all expectations and brought in their stead exclusion and repression. The new status as defeated was not easy to accept for ex-soldiers who a few months earlier had had a rifle in their hands. They went from enjoying the power of arms and the prestige of the soldier to total defencelessness, humiliation, prison and even death. Three years before, had a war not come in between, their response might have been different, but the experience of the war had transformed them. To take up arms once more and flee to the mountains in order to fight the dictatorship may have been a difficult choice, but the rupture was not that radical when they had lived in a war environment during the previous three years. The following section will show how and where the traces of war can be observed in the anti-Francoist resistance.

The first step is to analyse the age groups of members of the anti-Francoist guerrilla in order to establish a link with their war experience. The resistance was for most part made up of young men born between 1911 and 1920, that is, those who were between 16 and 25 years old when the war started and between 19 and 28 years old when it ended. A second contingent of guerrilla fighters was formed by the age groups coming immediately before and after this one: those born between 1906 and 1910, on the one hand, and those born between 1921 and 1925, on the other; that is, those who were 26–30 and 11–15 years of age when the war started and 29–33 and 14–18 when it ended (Appendix: Graphs 3 and 4).

The close relationship between the experience of war and the resistance can be observed when analysing drafts mobilised in the war period. During the three war years the Republican government called up twenty-eight replacement drafts. Ultimately all men between the ages of 18 and 45 were subject to conscription to the Republican Popular Army.[60]

Even so, the drafts were not equally important, nor did they fight at the same time. For this reason I have divided the replacements into two blocs: those I call the primary drafts (born between 1906–1920), formed of young recruits between 18 and 30 years old, who formed the core of the Popular Army; and the secondary draft (born between 1893–1905), composed of older men (from 35 to 45 years old) who were mobilised according to the necessities of war, though typically for secondary roles.

If a link is established between the drafts mobilised by the Republic during the war and the age groups of members of the anti-Francoist resistance it can be shown that in eastern Andalusia the majority of guerrilla fighters had formed part of the central nucleus, the primary drafts, of the Popular Army. A total of 58% of guerrilla fighters belonged to the primary drafts (born between 1906 and 1920) during the Spanish Civil War, while only 13% were mobilised in the secondary drafts (born between 1893 and 1905). That is, the young men that formed the core of the Popular Army during the war was also the group that later formed the majority in the resistance. Another interesting aspect is the high number of guerrilla fighters, constituting as much as 29% of the total, who did not fight in the war as a result of their young age, that is, guerrilla fighters who had no prior combat experience at all (Appendix: Graphs 4 and 5). In the following pages I shall now analyse each of these cases.

The experience of war and the feeling of camaraderie in particular favoured the organisation of groups with members taken from old Popular Army units. The importance of primary groups in the creation of the militias and the Mixed Brigades meant, moreover, that in many cases, various cohesive factors operated simultaneously: kinship, local identity, friendship, and camaraderie. The importance of primary groups in the creation of the guerrillas will be dealt in a later chapter, and so the focus here will be on the impact of camaraderie. Establishing what Popular Army unit guerrilla fighters had belonged to during the war is not always easy, but, even so, I have been able to make the links in a few cases.

The first comrade to join "El Yatero" in the mountains was Jesús Salcedo from Murcia. Both men had formed part of the same Mixed Brigade in the Popular Army. At the end of the war Jesús Salcedo was detained and sent to Caravaca Prison. After surviving an execution by firing squad, from which he escaped under the cover of darkness, he began a long journey on foot from the province of Murcia to Quéntar (Granada), where he was reunited with his wife (who he had met during the war). The first news he received on arrival was that his old comrade from the Brigade, "El Yatero", also a native of Quéntar, had taken to the mountains. At the end of the war "El Yatero" had been driven to a concentration camp where he had repeatedly seen how Francoist army trucks, accompanied by members of the Falange, rounded up dozens of prisoners to be shot at daybreak. Rather than wait for death amongst the mud and the barracks, "El Yatero" decided it would be better to risk his life escaping from the concentration camp and heading for the mountains, where he could at least confront the "fascists" face to face and defend himself, if only with a simple hunting rifle. Upon learning the fate of his friend, Jesús Salcedo left for the mountains that same night, and, together with "El Yatero," formed the first armed resistance group in the province of Granada .[61]

A similar sentiment, forged by camaraderie in times of war, can be observed in other cases. Various members of the "hermanos Clares" group belonged to the organised militia in the village of Güejar Sierra and once the new Popular Army was formed, they joined the 78th Mixed Brigade. All of them were reunited in the mountains at the end of the war or after several years in prison.[62] For them, however, the war had not ended and they decided that the best way to continue the struggle was to join up with their old comrades. Similar circumstances applied to several neighbours from Loja, who had joined the 79th Mixed Brigade during the war and years later reconvened with their old neighbours and comrades in the Agupación Guerrillera de Granada.[63] It was common for ex-soldiers who left prison to look for their old comrades in the mountains and continue the fight, as can also be seen in the group called "Culito de Salar".[64] Camaraderie, together with loyalties deriving from local identities, kinship, and friendship, was one of the key elements shaping the formation of guerrillas in the post-war period.

The repression was particularly ferocious when directed against those who had fought with the Popular Army. Young men had been mobilised to a greater extent than anyone else during the war and consequently were one of the groups to suffer the most from the repression. It is understandable, then, why those who had fought in the war accounted for a majority of the guerrilla fighters (71%). However, how do we explain the 29% of guerrilla fighters who had no previous combat experience?

The majority of these guerrilla fighters, who were children during the war period, joined the resistance after having collaborated in some way with the guerrilla. Once they were 'branded', that is, discovered by the authorities, they had little choice but to flee to the mountains in order not to be arrested. As will be shown later, kinship bonds between guerrilla fighters without previous combat experience and those with war experience were very common. This is key to any understanding of why many of these young men became part of the guerrillas. However, there may also have been a certain feeling of frustration among those age groups who had observed the conflict from the home front and who were prevented from joining the fighting by the end of the war.[65] Furthermore, the guerrilla fighter was a heroic and attractive figure among certain sections of the population – particularly at local level and within the family sphere. This was a further factor influencing young men, who may have developed a desire to emulate the guerrilla fighter's example.

All of these factors played a part, but the antifascist guerrilla, and espe-cially the Agrupaciones guerrilleras led by the PCE, also actively disseminated ideas in order to recruit new guerrilla fighters. The young played a particularly prominent role in this process.[66] I will address this question in greater detail in another chapter, but it should be highlighted here that calls to "anti-Francoist youth" – appealing directly to a genera-tional identity – were common in the propaganda. It was no coincidence that from 1945 the head of the PCE-led guerrilla movement was Santiago Carrillo, General Secretary of the Unified Socialist Youth (JSU). The guer-rilla units sent from abroad to reinforce the resistance in Spain also belonged, for the most part, to the JSU. The guerrilla fighters saw them-selves as young antifascists. Giving expression to this identity, the Agrupación Guerrillera de Granada sent a message welcoming the creation in 1945 of the World Federation of Democratic Youth, conceived as a forum for antifascist youth in particular, with "excitement and joy".[67]

Generational identities also had an impact on ideological debates. The PCE, a marginal party during the pre-war Republic, became the most important political organisation in the course of the war – a transformation in which the International Brigades and the JSU played a significant part. The International Brigades, mobilised by the Comintern, offered a true reflection of international antifascist youth. The JSU, in their turn, repre-sented Spanish socialist and communist youth, although the organisation had in reality been absorbed by the communists.

During the Spanish Civil War, the Soviet Union and the PCE became models of political and cultural modernity and thus held a great attraction for young Spaniards. At that time a clear generational divide emerged between a politics associated with modernity and the future, linked to communists and the PCE, on the one hand, and the old and outdated, asso-ciated with the socialists and the PSOE, on the other. This generational rupture, which exhibited both cultural and ideological aspects, could still be observed when the PCE tried to unify different independent guerrilla groups years later. Socialist activists, more reluctant to engage in guerrilla action, were referred to as "old socialists" and "old politicians" by the new generation of young communists, more favourably disposed towards the armed struggle.[68]

Gender roles in the guerrilla

The experience of war reinforced Spanish combatants' ideal of masculinity, which explains the low number of women joining the anti-Francoist resistance as guerrilla fighters. Antonia Triviño, the niece of an Andalusian guerrilla fighter, recalled how her grandfather repeatedly said that "there was hope here because the men were tough".[69] Guerrilla fighters were "manly" and "strong".[70]

This image of guerrilla fighters' masculinity was commonplace at the time, but its implications were two-fold: it created a guerrilla identity, while at the same time reinforcing a distinction between those who went to the mountains ("the manly ones") and those who preferred to stay in their homes, despite their precarious positions as defeated. Salomé Perez, daughter of José Pérez Moles, remembers how her father had to endure severe pressure in his village after being freed from prison. Nobody gave him work; he had to report to the headquarters of the Civil Guard three times a day and the humiliation was constant. But, in addition to this, the fact that he remained in the village meant that his masculinity was questioned, and not only by the community of the defeated to which he belonged; a neighbour in the village, a distinguished Falangist, repeatedly insinuated that "you are not a man unless you go to the sierra".[71] At the beginning of 1947 José Pérez Moles finally went to the mountains to join the guerrillas.[72]

Gender divisions in the Spanish resistance movement were deeper than in the French case. While it is true that the masculine ideal was operative in mobilisation campaigns launched both from exile in Britain and from the interior, historians have highlighted how there were differences compared to the period of the First World War. Women did join the army and the clandestine French resistance, although in small numbers. The figure of the *partisanas* was not very widespread, but they acquired an important role in the cities through the urban guerrilla organisation (FTP). In the rural sphere, by contrast, where gender roles were more pronounced, the integration of women in the guerrilla was practically non-existent.[73]

The gender division of labour established in the Republican zone during the Spanish Civil War was largely maintained in the anti-Francoist guer-

rilla. The rhetoric of political organisations and the Agrupaciones guerrilleras with regards to women was reminiscent of the last conversation
between Dora and Annenkov, two members of a nihilist cell portrayed by
Albert Camus in his work *Les justes* (*The Just Assassins*). "Then do something
for me", Dora begs her companion. "Give me the bomb. [. . .] Yes, give
me the bomb . . . next time. I want to throw it. I want to be the first to
throw." To which Annenkov responded without thinking: "You know
quite well it's against our rules for women to be in the firing line".[74]

In their statutes, the Agrupaciones guerrilleras explicitly prohibited
women from staying in the mountains. Exceptions could only be made in
cases of danger.[75] Old stereotypes of femininity were still dominant in the
political cultures of the left, stereotypes that were far removed from the
masculine attributes of the guerrilla fighter. The taboo of sexuality, associated with old feminine myths of perversion, vice, and depravation, also
carried significant weight in this issue. The presence of women in the mountains might awaken the sexual appetites of the guerrilla fighters and
generate internal conflicts that would in turn undermine the discipline that
communist leaders tried to impose. Santiago Carrillo himself claimed that
women, despite their scarcity in the Spanish resistance movement, were to
blame for the decadence of the anti-Francoist guerrilla in its last phase. That
was when "corrupting elements appeared: women, drink, and the squan-
dering of money" stated one of his reports.[76]

PCE directives were always clear with regards to the role that women
should play in the armed struggle: "Help our heroic guerrilla fighters!"
demanded Dolores Ibárruri in the International Women's Day celebration
on March 8th 1946.[77] A woman's place was on the home front, performing
supportive tasks. Their silent work as go-betweens, providing logistical
solutions as well as information, allowed the anti-Francoist guerrilla to
survive for more than a decade.

The majority of these women began to help the guerrilla for strictly
personal reasons. A father, brother, or husband had escaped to the mountains and she tried to protect them. However, what began as a family
commitment often ended up as a strong political commitment to anti-
Francoism. The role of women as go-betweens for the guerrilla, together
with the help given to imprisoned family members, became the two greatest
politicising experiences of Spanish women during the 1940s, a journey
which took them, as Fernanda Romeu Alfaro has pointed out, "from the
walls of the cemetery to the guerrillas".[78]

Chapter 2

Carrillo's Men
PCE and the anti-Francoist guerrilla

Being communist involves more than just belonging to a party; it requires faith. There was a great sense of romanticism among us. Communism had a religious component.

(Santiago Carrillo, *El País Semanal*, December 11th 2011)

Exile and reconstruction (1939–1943)

The Spanish Civil War ended with an internal civil war on the Republican home front. The coup against Republican Prime Minister Juan Negrín, led by Colonel Seguismundo Casado and supported by a majority of socialists and anarchists, provoked an armed confrontation with PCE activists, loyal to the Republican leader until the last moment. At the same time, internal divisions within the socialist family, which had begun to form in the 1920s, now produced irreconcilable conflicts which hastened the disappearance of the primary reference point for the labour movement in Spain. The powerful anarchist movement experienced a similarly fragmented post-war situation, in which large organisations crumbled into a multiplicity of new committees and tendencies. The open wounds sustained by the Spanish left during the war took decades to heal. Intense hatreds, insults, and suspicions were exchanged over the years, which did not facilitate cooperation and collaboration in the resistance.

The PCE was the organisation that most clearly defined the political strategy of the anti-Francoist opposition, although initial steps in this direction were far from easy. The Second World War broke out only five months after the end of the war in Spain, and the Non-Aggression Pact signed by Nazi Germany and the Soviet Union left communist leaders and activists in a difficult situation. This volte-face by the PCE – operating under the command of the Comintern – provoked internal dissent, desertion of members and expulsion of the sectors most critical of the party. Yet the bulk of the membership remained faithful to Stalin's directives. Faith in the "supreme leader of the international revolution" was practically unassailable among the communist rank and file. Reason and common sense rejected the idea of any kind of pact with Nazi Germany, but the first task of any card-carrying communist was to defend the "only socialist country on the face of the earth" and obey the directives of its "supreme guide". The German–Soviet pact left the PCE even more isolated than it had been at the time of the Casado coup. The pact intensified the conflicts with the rest of the opposition, who could not understand how they could accept Stalin's new strategy, a strategy which made them allies of European fascism.[1]

On July 22nd 1941, Nazi Germany invaded the Soviet Union, *de facto* breaking the non-aggression agreement signed in 1939. One month later, the Mexican delegation of the PCE – finally liberated from the constraints imposed by Moscow – launched their proposal for a National Union. The objective was to unite all anti-Francoist political forces, including the "civilised right", to fight the Franco dictatorship under the leadership of the PCE. But the manifesto was more lenient towards sectors of the moderate right than to organisations on the left, who were fiercely criticised and mocked.[2] The tone of the proposal did not break the PCE's isolation, and the idea of a National Union would not have any practical relevance until two years later, when Jesús Monzón presided over the establishment of the Supreme Council of National Union (Junta Suprema de Unión Nacional, hereafter JSUN) from inside Spain.

Jesús Monzón became a central figure from 1942 as a result of the dispersion of the PCE leadership in the early post-war years. At the end of 1939, the Comintern ordered that the national leadership of all communist parties take the precautionary measure to leave Western Europe. All members of the Central Committee of the PCE consequently left France to take up residence in Mexico or the Soviet Union.[3] This decision created a power vacuum in party structures in the south of France, where the greatest number of exiled Spanish communists lived.

In this precarious situation, the PCE in France began to be directed by Jesús Monzón, a medium-ranking party official who had not formed part of the national party leadership. General Secretary in the miniscule Provincial Committee of Navarra during the Second Republic, he had occupied the post of civil governor in Alicante and Cuenca. Together with the last leaders of the PCE, Jesús Monzón managed to leave Spain in the spring of 1939 for Oran, although he was transferred to France shortly thereafter. From France he organised the evacuation of thousands of Spanish refugees to Latin America and the Soviet Union, and then took charge of the organisation of the fragmented PCE, which suffered from a lack of orientation in the absence of the national leadership. He was helped in this task by a small number of relatively prominent officials who had not left France, such as Carmen de Pedro, who was the former typist of the Central Committee, Gabriel León Trilla and Manuel Azcárate.

The PCE delegation led by Jesús Monzón in France grew in step with the French Resistance and gradually acquired real strength. The large number of Spanish communist activists in the country, the incorporation of a significant proportion of these in the *maquis*, and their proximity to Spain, made it the most powerful organisation in the exiled anti-Francoist opposition.

During 1942 and 1943, Monzón not only strengthened the PCE in France but also sent various delegates to Spain. The absence of communist leaders within the country after the war had generated a power vacuum which was filled from the beginning of 1941 by Heriberto Quiñones, an old Comintern agent of central European origin.[4] Tensions between Quiñones and the Central Committee in exile rapidly worsened and soon became so acute that the PCE's Mexican delegation sent two party activists to assassinate him at the end of 1941. It was only his detention by the Francoist police on 31 December that saved him from being killed by his own comrades.[5] The activists sent from France by Monzón from 1942 were ordered to eradicate any trace of *quiñonismo* and restore the complete control of the party.[6]

The politics pursued by Monzón in France and within Spain followed the directives disseminated by the Central Committee of the PCE. While it is true that Monzón enjoyed a large measure of autonomy this was largely a result of the circumstances. Clandestine existence under the Vichy regime in France made communications with the party leadership in Mexico and Moscow extremely difficult. This autonomy, together with Monzón's strategic position as he took control of the party in France and Spain, soon provoked a new crisis within the PCE.

With the permission of the Central Committee, Jesús Monzón made contact with members of the Spanish right, including some military figures, in an attempt to create a broad oppositional front against Franco's dictatorship. Between 1942 and 1944 he also developed a plan to expand the guerrilla war in Spain, although this was never became reality. In the spring of 1943, exactly two months after the dissolution of the Comintern, he decided to cross the border and settle in Spain. Monzón was convinced that European fascism faced an imminent defeat, which made it imperative to initiate preparations for an armed insurrection in Spain.

In September 1943, acting in conjunction with Allied advances on the battlefield and emulating the politics of Charles de Gaulle and Jean

Moulin,[7] Monzón issued a call for the creation of the Supreme Council of National Union (JSUN), an organisation that aimed once more to unite all anti-Francoist opposition groups, including Catholics and Monarchists. Individual expressions of support aside, his call did not resonate among other political forces; rather it had the opposite effect. Socialists and republicans in exile interpreted JSUN as a new stratagem of the PCE and responded by launching their own organisation, the Spanish Liberation Committee (Junta Española de Liberación, JEL) in November 1943.[8]

The struggle for control of the PCE

Santiago Carrillo and the official histories of the PCE claim that the conflict between the Central Committee and Jesús Monzón predated "Operation Reconquest of Spain". Carrillo disguised the dispute as an ideological and tactical battle, when in fact it was a struggle for the control of the party in France and Spain. According to the party's official account, Monzón advocated a guerrilla invasion, while the Central Committee proposed a gradual infiltration of guerrilla fighters in Spain. In fact, by 1944, the PCE as a whole was convinced of the inevitable success of "Operation Reconquest of Spain". The retreat of fascism and the rise of the resistance in Europe brought a wave of enthusiasm which touched everyone from the communist rank and file to the national leadership. "Spain's hour has come" they proclaimed to all who would listen.[9]

Both the French delegation's creation of the JSUN and the insurrectional call issued by Monzón were applauded by the PCE's Central Committee.[10] Dolores Ibárruri delivered exhortations from Moscow in support of a "guerrilla movement, the vanguard in the struggle for the Reconquest of Spain".[11] In October 1944, Enrique Lister, a distinguished member of the Central Committee, had an interview with Comintern leader Georgi Dimitrov, who set out Stalin's view on the "Spanish problem". They had to organise a unitary government in exile presided by Doctor Juan Negrín, backed inside Spain by guerrilla action.[12] The presence of a healthy number of Spanish combatants – between 8,000 and 9,000 – at the French border, ready to extend armed action from France into Spain generated an atmosphere of frenzy and exaltation among the PCE leadership.[13]

At this moment, Santiago Carrillo was a young PCE leader serving as General Secretary of the JSU. At the end of the war, he had broken publicly with his socialist past in a letter to his father, and in the first disputes over the control of the PCE in exile, he had shown his firm loyalty to the woman who ended up being his General Secretary, Dolores Ibárruri "Pasionaria". But from the end of 1944, Carrillo went from being a distinguished party official to being "Pasionaria's" right hand man. From then on he was the one charged with the task of ruling the PCE in France and Spain with an iron fist.

The failure of "Operation Reconquest of Spain" provided him with his opportunity. Years later, Enrique Lister accused Carrillo of taking advantage of his position as the only member of the Central Committee present in France in order to create his own personal platform from which he could rise to the highest post in the party.[14] Lister was not wrong, but it is also important to remember that Carrillo's promotion stemmed from a personal decision of the General Secretary of the PCE, Dolores Ibárruri.

Santiago Carrillo was in Mexico when "Operation Reconquest of Spain" was planned in the south of France. By June 1944 he was given the mission to go to North Africa in order to reorganise the party and place it under the orders of the Central Committee. After a complicated journey through Portugal, he arrived in Tangier in August. One of his first measures was to replace some figures in the local leadership, keeping and adding leaders who were loyal to Ibárruri. From then on, distinguished members like Ricardo Beneyto, Ramón Vía or Félix Cardador were gradually transformed into Carrillo's men. They first took over the leadership of the PCE in North Africa but later also became the most important figures in the anti-Francoist guerrilla in Andalusia. Carrillo stayed in North Africa throughout August and September 1944, training with a guerrilla group headed by another young communist leader, Ramón Vía. The aim was to form a number of guerrilla units that would disembark in the south of Spain at the same time as the guerrilla invasion was being launched across the Pyrenees.[15]

The Chief of Staff of the Group of Spanish Guerrillas (Agrupación de Guerrilleros Españoles, AGE) had planned "Operation Reconquest of Spain" under the military leadership of Generals Vicente López Tovar and Luis Fernández. The manoeuvre consisted of a number of guerrilla incursions along the Pyrenees mountain range. The first groups, aiming to disorientate the Francoist army, entered Spain in September, while the larger-scale manoeuvre began with the entry of two guerrilla brigades on the 3rd and 7th November. The operations continued for days, reaching their peak on 17 November, when around 4,000 Spanish guerrilla fighters crossed the border. But the news arriving from the interior was disheartening. The propaganda apparatus of the PCE had announced the invasion months before, which meant that the Francoist army knew about the operation and had sent a military contingent to the front. The guerrilla units were unable to advance and their casualties began to mount.[16] It was at this moment that Santiago Carrillo, who was on the point of disembarking in Spain together with a guerrilla group from North Africa, received a telegram from Dolores Ibárruri in Moscow. He was to travel to the south of France immediately and halt the operation on the orders of his Secretary General. The official version of the PCE states that Carrillo met with Luis Fernández and López Tovar shortly afterwards, convincing them to order a retreat.[17] However, López Tovar and other witnesses suggest that the decision was taken before Carrillo arrived in France.[18]

Whether or not it was actually Carrillo's order that halted "Operation Reconquest of Spain" is the least important aspect of this subject, even though historians have paid special attention to it.[19] The most significant issue is that the failure of the operation allowed Carrillo to take control of the PCE in France and establish the first bases in Spain. To achieve this he started a smear campaign against Monzón and his collaborators, accusing them of being traitors and provocateurs. Internal purges were always a key characteristic of communist parties,[20] and the PCE now initiated, although on a smaller scale than seen in other European sister parties, a similar process, revolving around the phantoms of *quiñonismo* and *monzonismo*.[21]

In December 1944, Dolores Ibárruri received the first report on the situation of the PCE in France and Spain. The report suggested that Carrillo was taking "appropriate measures" to end *monzonist* provocation, which held enormous influence in the French as well as in the Spanish delegation.[22] The "appropriate measures" consisted of an internal purge. At times this meant removing members from the leadership or excluding them from the party; at other times, it meant forcing someone to undergo a formal process of "self-criticism", which was a very common practice during these years. In the most extreme cases, the purge was carried out with the help of pistols and assassinations, which eliminated the leaders considered most "dangerous" as a result of recurring accusations of "treachery".[23]

France was liberated in the middle of this bid to regain control of the French delegation, and various members of the Central Committee began to prepare a move to Toulouse. It was necessary for the highest leaders of the party to be as close as possible to Spain in order to direct the PCE's politics in the interior. By spring 1945 various members of the PCE's Central Committee had managed to travel to France. Modesto and Lister arrived in February, after a meeting with Marshall Tito in Belgrade. Dolores Ibárruri and Ignacio Gallego arrived in May, after sitting through an interview with Stalin and having completed a long journey from Moscow to Toulouse via Teheran, Bagdad and Cairo.[24] They were joined shortly afterwards by Francisco Antón and Fernando Claudín.[25]

The power accumulated by Carrillo during the first months in France generated resentment among some members of the Central Committee, but Dolores Ibárruri supported his position. Carrillo, despite his youth, assumed definitive command of the PCE inside Spain and of the activities of the anti-Francoist guerrilla. Since 1943, the PCE had been sending distinguished party members from France into Spain, where they were instructed to infiltrate and replace the national leadership. Carrillo continued this strategy by sending men he trusted, both from the ranks of the leadership and the guerrillas. The objectives were to regain control of the party, reorganise the committees and create the first Agrupaciones guerrilleras on the basis of local armed groups. This was a slow and troubled process, as the case of Andalusia shows.

Carrillo's men in Andalusia

Before October 1944, the PCE could count on the support of a few autonomous armed groups in eastern Andalusia (Manolo "El Rubio" and "Rubio de Brecia" above all), but the party lacked its own guerrilla structure. In addition, the PCE's provincial and regional committees were weak and isolated. The party boasted its most significant presence in Malaga and Granada, but even here its influence was largely symbolic. The first Provincial Committee in Málaga was constituted behind the façade of an advertising company in 1940 but its activities were reduced to helping imprisoned members and their families. Disbanded in 1941, a new attempt to reconstruct the group was made in 1942, but with little success. In 1943, the network of committees in the province was dissolved once again after the detention of thirteen people. The following year a new Provincial Committee was set up by Manuel Campo Roldán. Its internal structure was still very vulnerable but for the first time it managed to establish contact with the Andalusian Regional Committee.[26]

The signs of PCE weakness were even more marked in the province of Granada. At the beginning of 1940 four activists tried to reconstruct the Provincial Committee but by November had all been arrested. There was a second attempt by three communist activists in 1942 but with same end result. In November of that year another three militants did manage to organise a small Provincial Committee and to establish contact with its counterpart in Málaga and the Andalusian Regional Committee. However, this was again dismantled in March 1944 after the police detained five of its members.[27]

The interprovincial coordination between different committees and the constitution of a Regional Committee in Andalusia were also marked by weakness. The first attempt came in 1942 but was undermined shortly afterwards by over twenty arrests. In 1943, a new Regional Committee led by Castro Campos and Francisco Blanco managed to contact the Central Committee, which led to the first visits by national leaders from Madrid. However, the initial push was cut short by the arrest of most its members in 1944. There was a new attempt the following year but the leadership was detected by the authorities only a few months afterwards.[28]

Between 1945 and 1947, after this period of weakness and scarce activity, the PCE saw a period of growth in Andalusia with the expansion of local and provincial committees as well as a strengthening of the Regional Committee. At the same time, the coordination and communication between different cells was more fluid and the foundations for the Agrupaciones guerrilleras were laid. The success of this mission owed much to party units sent from exile. Their work transformed the weak and atom-ized structures into more solid and coordinated organisations.

It now became clear that Santiago Carrillo's politics prioritised the task of consolidating the guerrilla front. The first teams that he sent to the region consisted of the political and military leaders of the Agrupaciones guer-rilleras, although some figures were initially assigned other tasks.

A distinguishing characteristic of the new leaders was their youth. Carrillo placed his trust in the young men of his own generation: the gener-ation shaped by the Spanish Civil War. The new leaders were between 25 and 35 years old when they returned to Spain and combined youth and expe-rience. All these men had experienced three long years of fighting in Spain and at least another four years of confinement, clandestinity, and resistance in exile. They were young communists whose lives had been shaped by the blows of combat, defeat and unfulfilled expectations. They were men of faith with unshakeable principles and irrepressible passion, men who gave their lives for a country and an idea. These characteristics turned them into the principal bastion of the anti-Francoist struggle in Spain, but at times it also reinforced the most sectarian positions.

The men who from 1945 formed the new leadership of the PCE in Spain and the communist guerrilla in Andalusia were thirteen in number. Of the thirteen, eleven were sent from exile, and ten of these were sent directly by Santiago Carrillo. Only Ramiro Fuentes Ochoa and Francisco Rodríguez Sevilla (political and military leaders of the primitive AGG) were recruited by the PCE in Spain. Alfredo Cabello Gómez-Acebo was the only one who did not come from exile under the orders of Carrillo, since he returned to Spain in February 1944, when Carrillo was still in Latin America (see Appendix: Table 2). Six of the twelve leaders sent from exile came from Algeria. Carrillo's stay in North Africa between August and October 1944 had produced a close relationship and mutual trust between him and the Algerian Committee, which was reorganised by Carrillo himself when he arrived. Three of the new members of the Committee (Félix Cardador, Ricardo Beneyto and Ramón Vía) would return to Spain under Carrillo's direction. Similarly, ten of the twelve leaders spent some part of their exile in France. Three of these participated actively in the French Resistance (Ramón Vía, "Roberto" and José Merédiz) while nine were students or teachers at the Guerrilla School in Toulouse before entering Spain ("Roberto", José Merédiz, Ricardo Beneyto, Félix Cardador, José Mallo, Luis Campos, Nicolás García, Julián Pérez and Manuel López).

The timing of the order to enter Spain did not necessarily correspond to the actual arrival of these leaders in Andalusia, as some were still carrying out previously assigned missions in other regions. Since the combined trajectories of these leaders form a complex picture, two tables have been included in the Appendix (Appendix: Tables 2 and 3) where the rank of the principal communist guerrilla leaders and their arrival in Andalusia can be observed more clearly.

Alfredo Cabello: From diplomat to guerrilla fighter

The first to arrive in Spain was the distinguished communist leader Alfredo Cabello Gómez-Acebo, although his first mission, in May 1944, had nothing to do with the reorganisation planned by Santiago Carrillo. Son of a distinguished family from Zamora, he joined the Federación Universitaria de Estudiantes (FUE) and the Juventudes Socialistas (JJSS). Together with Santiago Carrillo he was a key figure in the creation of the Juventudes Socialistas Unificadas (JSU) between 1935 and 1937, distinguishing himself for his conversational and diplomatic gifts. These strengths, together with his ability to speak several languages, led to him being responsible for JSU's international work during the civil war, a role which took him to Prague, Stockholm, London, Paris, and Geneva. A member of the leading committee of the JSU, he managed to flee to France after the war and from there to Latin America. In January 1944, after a few years in Argentina and Chile, the PCE leadership in Argentina ordered him to return to Spain to reinforce the National Union policy together with the new leader of the interior, Jesús Monzón. The steamer *Monte Ambaco* docked at Bilbao in February 1944 , where he disembarked with a new identity. After five years in exile, Cabello commenced his clandestine activity in Spain.[29]

The first mission assigned to him by Jesús Monzón was the reorganisation of the regional committee in Andalusia, recently dismantled by the
police, who had arrested over 200 activists. He arrived in Seville in May
1944 and remained there until August, when Monzón asked him to return
to Madrid to undertake a new mission, better suited to his abilities. When
he arrived in the capital in September, Alfredo Cabello was included in the
leading circle of the Junta Suprema de Unión Nacional (JSUN). He would
be responsible for establishing contact with the CNT, the PSOE and republican groups in order to incorporate them into the communist organisation.
Between September 1944 and February 1945 he held talks with various
anarchists from the Alianza Nacional de Fuerzas Democráticas (ANFD).
However, his efforts produced no positive results and the distance between
the communists and other anti-Francoist opposition forces remained.[30]

Carrillo and Cabello had had a close relationship for many years. Both
had, as mentioned, exerted a driving influence in the unification of the
Spanish socialist and communist youth organisations and had held leadership posts in the organisation created as a result, the JSU. Carrillo himself
acknowledged that Cabello had been supportive when, at the end of the civil
war, he wrote a letter denouncing his father, the socialist Wenceslao
Carrillo.[31] But that friendship was not enough to protect Cabello from the
internal purges of the PCE. Cabello's collaboration with Jesús Monzón in
the first clandestine stage (from February to December 1944) cast a shadow
of suspicion over him and created constant problems with the Central
Committee. At first, the new leaders sent by Carrillo confided in Cabello
to some degree but mistrust towards him then gradually increased.

One of the first reports sent by Carrillo's men stated that "[Cabello] has
continued making serious contributions, which is why we now use him in
the work of the UN. Apart from being important, he combines in this
regard magnificent qualities. In our judgement, he has overcome all his
difficulties and is producing good work."[32]

Agustín Zoroa, Carrillo's right-hand man in Spain, ordered Cabello to
maintain his contacts with Catholic and Monarchist sectors who were critical, albeit timidly and secretly, of Franco's dictatorship. Following this
order, between February and April 1945, Cabello organised consultations
with Manuel Giménez Fernández, member of the Sindicatos Católicos
Agrarios; with Cardinal Segura, Archbishop of Seville; and with a repre-
sentatives of the Prince of Orleans and Juan de Borbón. According to
Cabello's reports, the JSUN could count on the collaboration of three lieutenant colonels and fourteen generals who "disagree" with Franco, but
support from Catholic and Monarchist sectors would only be forthcoming
if the PCE accepted the restoration of the Monarchy and ceased all guerrilla

activities. Ultimately, none of these exchanges ended in an agreement. From April 1945, Cabello had to hide from both a wave of police arrests and from new purges carried out within the PCE.[33] More specifically, between April and September, Cabello was temporarily separated from the PCE. His earlier collaboration with Monzón made him liable to charges of "treason" and "provocation". At that time, various old colleagues of Monzón were persecuted, sentenced and even killed on the orders of the party leadership. His life as an activist, like that of many other grass-roots communists, was being scrutinized by a leadership consumed by paranoia and sectarianism.

The reports that the Central Committee received on Cabello were contradictory. Some, like that prepared by Agustín Zoroa, valued Cabello's work and claimed that even though he had worked with Monzón, he now displayed complete loyalty towards the PCE leadership.[34] However, Pilar Soler, Monzón's lover, prepared a report – or, more accurately, was forced to sign a report full of accusations against Cabello. As Monzón was arrested by police in Barcelona, Pilar had managed to escape the net and cross the border to France. Santiago Carrillo, Fernando Claudín and Ramón Ormazábal subjected her to an intense interrogation, and, since they did not agree with the report she produced, wrote an alternative version which revealed all the treasonous activity that Monzón and his accomplices had allegedly carried out.[35] Pilar was forced to sign the report, which contained very negative references to Cabello. He was accused of living a relaxed clandestine life and being unconcerned with precautions and security measures. He was also said to have extravagant manners and an inappropriate relationship with the daughter of the Chilean ambassador in Madrid.[36]

The final conclusions of the investigation stated that Alfredo Cabello had belonged to the *monzónist* wing and led a life unsuited to clandestinity. The punishment was the most common one within the PCE at this time: he was sent to the guerrillas in the mountains where work was particularly hard. Once this was decided, Agustín Zoroa sent a letter to the new guerrilla leader in Malaga, Ramón Vía, to inform him of Cabello's new posting. Ramón Vía showed up in Madrid at the beginning of September 1945, and, on September 7th, after a conversation with Cabello, the two young men took a train towards Málaga.[37]

Ramón Vía: A young Bolshevik from Vallecas

Ramón Vía was attracted to the rigour, discipline and original discourse of the PCE from the start of the war. However, he remained in Vallecas, working as a cutler, until May 1937. The offensive launched by Italian troops at Guadalajara forced the Republican government to call up the draft of 1931, and Ramón Vía was immediately incorporated into the 35th Brigade of the IV Corps of the Popular Army. Based in Hita (Guadalajara), Vía joined the PCE and was made head of the Ramón Mercader Batallion. He was transferred to the Madrid front shortly afterwards, where he was embedded in the 73rd Mixed Brigade. In 1938 he fought on the Aragón front, where he reached the rank of commandant, although his troops had to retreat until they reached the Levant.[38]

At the end of the war, Ramón Vía managed to embark on the Stanbrook, the last boat that left the port of Alicante for the Algerian coast. His wife and children were left behind, trapped in a hostile land. They would never see each other again. Ramón Vía went into exile and immediately began his new life as a stateless revolutionary.

The Stanbrook came within sight of Oran two days after the commencement of its voyage, but, as it approached the coast, it was detained by the French authorities. For weeks the refugees on the boat had to remain on the deck, exposed to the extreme temperature shifts between the African day and the night. The men, women, and children onboard, many of them dying and left without any medical care in extremely unsanitary conditions, barely survived the hunger, the lice, and the fevers. The French authorities did not know what to do with the wave of refugees arriving from Spain, and, while they were coming to a decision, Senegalese colonial soldiers guarded the boat. One month later came the official order for evacuation. Relief and joy spread among the refugees. As another survivor of the Stanbrook wrote in his memoirs, they still had no idea what the future would bring.[39]

The French authorities sent the Republican ex-soldiers to various concentration camps in the Algerian desert. Ramón Vía was first interned in the Rabi-Blanch camp but a few weeks later was transferred to Camp Morant in Boghari, located approximately 300 km. from Algiers. At that time Vía was only 28 years old, but, despite his youth, had acquired extensive experience as an activist . His rank as commandant in the Popular Army and his leadership skills earned him his colleagues' respect. In July 1939 he was nominated to take responsibility for the PCE in the concentration camp. During this period, there were around 2,500 Spanish refugees, Polish brigaders and Yugoslavs in the camp. At first, they slept on the desert sand, but, little by little, built barracks to provide shelter for between 30 and 45 people. Temperatures could reach as high as 50°C during the day.[40]

Between July 1939 and December 1940, Ramón Via organised the PCE in the extreme conditions of the concentration camp. Defeat, exile and separation from loved ones, together with the inexplicable circumstance of being detained by the French authorities, had deepened the sadness and despair felt by the refugees. To combat these feelings, Vía devised various activities to distract the refugees, and, at the same time, boost the political morale of the activists. The barracks began to be used as educational spaces. Those who were illiterate could learn how to read and write and there were also classes in French and History. Ramón himself built a workshop to make small sculptures. On July 14th 1940, the day of the storming of Bastille, the camp relaxed with a Hispano-French festival during which the refugees and the French soldiers participated in a football match and a few races. Ramón Vía, reliving his youth, organised a couple of boxing matches too.[41]

However, besides the demoralisation of the refugees, Vía had other problems to solve. The German–Soviet pact generated bewilderment among communist activists and complicated relations with socialist and anarchist refugees. Ramón Vía prepared a report explaining to his communist comrades the reasons behind the pact while also seeking to ease the conflict with other political organisations. Vía himself fully maintained his loyalty to the PCE and Comintern; as an internal Central Committee report stated, "He was a Bolshevik".[42]

Towards the end of 1940, following an order from the PCE, he escaped from the concentration camp. A few days later he was arrested and sent to a Workers' Battalion in the desert. The camps were being militarized and Spanish refugees were subjected to forced labour in the construction of a trans-Saharan railway. He remained in this situation for the following six months. In June 1941 he managed a successful escape and the PCE, now that the German–Soviet Pact was definitely broken, ordered him to France. He travelled in secret from the port of Oran to Marseille, where he immediately began to collaborate with the French resistance.[43]

His stay on the continent lasted until November 1942. The Vichy police were snapping at his heels and the court in Marseille pursued him for his contacts with the British and North American secret services, all of which prompted his return to Oran. The PCE leadership put him in charge of propaganda in North Africa and from then on he worked in a clandestine print shop. He also planned various concentration camp break-outs and organised resistance groups on Algerian soil. The courts of Oran and Algiers sentenced him to death in absentia for participating "in a plot to capture the city".[44]

The arrival of Allied troops in North Africa in November 1943 caused a radical change in the region, allowing the PCE to emerge from clandestinity. At this time the PCE committee in North Africa gave him the task of organising a group of activists who were to train as guerrilla fighters.[45] Ramon Vía, who had maintained contact with the North American secret services in France, developed closer relations with the US Army and even received military instruction, arms, munitions and radio transmitters.[46]

This collaboration continued from the end of 1943 to August 1944. Santiago Carrillo cut all contact between the PCE and the US Army when he arrived in Oran. The PCE in Mexico had already sent an order to this effect but communication difficulties had hindered its reception.[47] Carrillo included Ramón Vía in the new Regional Committee of the PCE, although Vía was increasingly focused on his guerrilla training. On 3 September 1944, after the liberation of Paris, he ordered the streets of Oran to be filled with posters which proclaimed in large letters: "AFTER PARIS, MADRID!"[48] Vía could not forget the city where he was born, grew up and fought his first fights.

The guerrilla expedition from the Algerian coast to the south of Spain, launched in parallel to the "Operation Reconquest of Spain" in the Pyrenees, was already organised when Santiago Carrillo received the order to go to the south of France. Despite the eventual failure of the Pyrenean invasion, the Algerian operation was not aborted. Ramón Ormazabal remained in Oran to organise the landing with Ramón Vía. The original plan was to send an expedition of ten guerrilla fighters every two months from North Africa,[49] but the PCE only managed to transfer three groups between 1944 and 1946.[50] A few internal PCE reports suggest that the number of guerrilla fighters sent from Africa may have reached fifty, although the three expeditions led by Vía, Meruelo and Robles actually amounted to a total of only thirty fighters.[51]

The first expedition comprised ten guerrilla fighters. The 33-year-old Ramón Vía was the leader of the group. His mission was first to organise an Agrupación guerrillera in the province of Málaga, and, once this had been achieved, extend operations across the rest of Andalusia. All expedition members were communists, faithful to the official PCE line. They had received military training and were specialised in various tasks. Vía was accompanied by his right-hand man, Ildefonso Ruiz Armenta (Head of Chief of Staff in the future Agrupación and artillery expert), Joaquín Centurión (mountain guide), Isidoro Moreira (in charge of radio transmissions and armaments expert), Pedro (forger), and the guerrilla fighters Antonio Pascual (artillery), Manuel Lozano (artillery and aviation), Eugenio Navarro, Manuel Joya and Francisco Ruiz Aguayo.[52]

At the end of October 1944, the group disembarked from a motorboat on a beach at Almuñecar, in the province of Granada , with a radio transmitter, arms, munitions and uniforms from the US Army, modified with Republican insignia and armbands. The weaponry was scarce but of good quality (four machine guns, six pistols, one Colt, and five grenades).[53] On the other hand, the weaponry of the local guerrilla was very rudimentary, consisting mostly of hunting rifles and pistols. However, despite its quality, the material carried by the guerrillas sent from North Africa had one disadvantage: the impossibility of finding munitions and parts for such modern armaments in Spain.[54] In any case, this was not the only problem which Vía had to face when arriving in Andalusia.

Encouraged by Allied victories and the achievements of the resistance, exiles in France lived in a triumphalist atmosphere which allowed them to construct a false image of developments in Spain.[55] The alleged readiness of 'the people' to rebel was only a chimera and Vía's group found a society anxious for change yet fearful and distressed. The repression of recent years had made its mark not only on the mood of the population but also on that of the activists and leaders of the PCE. The peasants were uncomfortable and suspicious when meeting strangers working in the mountains, and the arrival of the new guerrilla created problems within the party.

The relationship between Vía and the PCE committees he met in Andalusia, all of which were faithful to Jesús Monzón, was extremely troubled, the tension stemming from two distinct discrepancies leading to the same outcome: the different experiences and expectations of activists inside and outside Spain, combined with the purges carried out in the PCE. The Provincial Committee of Málaga, led by Manuel Campo Roldán, was in a weak position and had suffered various setbacks over the years. Little by little he had managed to rebuild party structure and renew contact with the Regional Committee. But Manuel was loyal to the old leadership of Jesús Monzón, and, from the start, refused to submit to the authority of Carrillo's men. For months the Provincial Committee defended this position by evading all initiatives taken by Vía and his men to establish contact.

The first attempt came a fortnight after the landing of October 1944. Ramón Vía sent one of his men, Francisco Ruiz Aguayo, to Málaga and shortly afterwards was informed of the Provincial Committee's first refusal to establish any kind of contact. In December, Vía himself came down from the mountains and spent a month in the provincial capital. However, even his presence could not change the attitudes of the members of the Provincial Committee. Vía returned to the mountains to continue his work with the construction of the Agrupación guerrillera while keeping Aguayo in the capital with the aim of solving the conflict. In February 1945, Vía returned to the city for three days and met with Aguayo. The response was still the same: the Committee rejected any contact with the guerrilla and refused to reveal their links with the Regional Committee.[56]

Faced with this problem, Vía decided to go to Madrid and seek help from Agustín Zoroa, the highest PCE authority inside Spain. Vía remained in

Madrid during the month of February while Zoroa tried to initiate some contact with the Regional Committee. All attempts failed. Both the Provincial Committee in Málaga and the Regional Committee of Andalusia openly defied the authority of Carrillo's men. On April 6th 1945 Vía returned to Málaga and tried once more to establish contact with the Provincial Committee, only to encounter the same resistance as before.[57] Internal disputes within the PCE, similarly to conflicts between different sectors of the anti-Francoist opposition, took up an excessive proportion of leaders' and activists' attention, which detracted from the most important common goal: to overthrow Franco's dictatorship.

The situation changed slowly from May onwards. The Provincial Committee abandoned its evasive tactics and agreed to hold conversations with Vía although it continued to produce excuses for not collaborating. The tension must have been palpable during the first meeting, when the positions of those present were irreconcilable. Manuel Campo warned Vía of the dangers of the armed struggle: it exposed the organisation to danger and could easily descend into criminality. In fact, Manuel Campo's arguments were only a pretext: from 1945 he had maintained contact with various local armed groups and made arrangements with the Regional Committee and the Provincial Committee of Granada relating to guerrilla activity.[58] Ramón Vía, on the other hand, accused him of passivity and cowardice. He demanded that the Provincial Committee facilitate contact with autonomous guerrilla groups and provide him with two activists who could form part of a committee of go-betweens. In the following meeting, they discussed the "Open Letter from the Delegation of the C.C. of the Interior", a document prepared by Santiago Carrillo criticising the *monzonista* tendency.[59]

The Provincial Committee eventually provided two activists for a guerrilla committee but continued to put obstacles and hindrances in the way of Vía's work. In Zoroa's words: "The P. organisation, or rather its leadership, which is composed of idiots, is against the development and activity of a guerrilla".[60] Ramón Vía used direct threats in his last meeting with Manuel Campo. Either the Committee accepted the orders of the PCE leadership or it would be expelled. Although it has not been possible to find any document containing Manuel Campo's reply, eight days later he, together with the rest of the Provincial Committee leadership bar one, were arrested. The police operation led to over one hundred arrests and successfully dismantled the PCE network in Málaga.[61]

The dismemberment of the Provincial Committee one week after the threat by Ramón Vía raised suspicions. The tactic of filtering information to the police in order to resolve internal conflicts was not alien to clandestine organisations, although there is no direct proof that such methods were used in this case. Either way, whether by chance or design, the fall of the Provisional Committee was celebrated by Vía, who was now free to implement official policy and reorganise the party in accordance with the requirements of the armed struggle. As he stated in a report:

> The blow [that is, the fall of the Provincial Committee] helped us to eliminate the passivity encrusted at the top of the Party. During the repression there were moments of true panic which allowed us to know better those who remained. I made an effort to help the grass-roots, the guys who had no title but were firm, who have seen plenty of people trying to break them. They were told that they had one foot inside and one foot outside of the Party. Ultimately, despite imperfections and defects, the goal was to prevent the sinking of the Party, and it can be assured that this has been achieved.[62]

After the fall of the Provinicial Committee, Ramón Víá left the mountains to take charge of the reconstruction of the PCE in Málaga. First, he travelled to Madrid to seek help from the National Committee. He needed experienced men who could engage in political tasks in addition to guerrilla work. Agustín Zoroa offered him two men, promising him that he would send reinforcements the following month. The first was Alfredo Cabello, who had just been punished by the party and obliged to work with the guerrilla due to his improper conduct. The identity of the second is not known. On September 7th 1945 the three returned to Málaga and at the end of October two new reinforcements arrived: Ramiro Fuentes Ochoa and Luis Campos Osaba.[63]

Vía's task was to organise a new structure in Málaga, where the urban guerrilla and the party would be perfectly interlinked. He wanted to employ the young men of the old Provincial Committee who had not been arrested and had proved their courage and loyalty. Their age and short activist history, free of direct confrontations with the law, allowed them to go unnoticed by the authorities. To this end, Ramón Vía interviewed Francisco Martín Ramírez, a 25-year-old communist who, by chance, had fought as a legionnaire in the Francoist army during the war. Given his status as a 'Francoist' in the eyes of the authorities, Vía thought him the person best suited to lead the urban guerrilla in Málaga. The new organisation called itself the "Musketeers of the Plains", in order to distinguish themselves from the mountain guerrillas, their brief being to aid the guerrilla, disseminate propaganda, and, when necessary, orchestrate some form of expropriation in the city.[64] In reality, the "Musketeers of the Plains" was the only project that Ramón Vía managed to implement after his visit to Madrid.

In the last report prepared by Vía, dated October 1945, the guerrilla leader suggested that he had already given some control of the party to the new recruits, who had established contact with 125 activists in the capital and a few more in the province.[65] Vía had also delegated some responsibilities to the men sent by the National Committee. Alfredo Cabello's mission was to contact local guerrilla groups and unite them in an Agrupación while Fuentes Ochoa and Campos Osaba began the job of reconstructing the Provincial Committee.[66] "My opinion is that continuing without delay will give the Party the weight it should have. Our friends here are very enthusiastic".[67]

However, on November 15th 1945, Ramón Vía was arrested. At that moment only two months had passed since the arrival of Alfredo Cabello in Málaga. In the case of Fuentes Ochoa and Campos Osaba the situation was even worse, as they had only spent two weeks in the city. Without knowing any activists, the recently arrived leaders had to take charge of the local organisation and the "Musketeers of the Plains" as well as the non-existent Provincial Committee and the Agrupación guerrillera that Vía was creating in the mountains.

Faced with the arrest of Ramón Vía, the first decision made by the new leaders concerned the guerrilla. Alfredo Cabello organised an assembly in the mountains to unite the armed groups which he had approached in the previous two months and called for a vote on who should be the new Head of Chief of Staff in the recently created Agrupación Guerrillera de Málaga. The assembly, disorientated by the arrest of Vía, decided to choose the person who seemed to be his right-hand man in the mountains: Alfredo Cabello.[68] At that point all kinds of alarm bells must have rung in the National Committee led by Agustín Zoroa. An activist who was among the best trained in guerrilla warfare had been arrested and his replacement was a party member only recently criticised by the leadership and who was now paying for his sins in the mountains. Cabello completely lacked military training and had moreover accepted the post without consulting the National Committee. Ramón Vía's guerrilla project, the only one of real significance in Andalusia, was in danger of collapsing totally.

Agustín Zoroa decided to intervene on two fronts. Simultaneously with the fall of Vía in Málaga, the rebellious and undisciplined Regional Committee of Andalusia (which had been loyal to Monzón) had also been dismembered in Seville. Zoroa's strategy was to create a new, reliable Regional Committee in Seville and link this to the local leadership in Malaga. To do this he had to send a party activists specialised in the armed struggle. Thus, in January 1946, the three most important leaders of the Andalusian PCE in the post-war period arrived: Rafael Armada Rus, Ricardo Beneyto and José Muñoz Lozano, also known as "Roberto".

"Roberto": The reluctant leader

The future military leader of the Agrupaciones Guerrilleras de Málaga and Granada, José Muñoz Lozano, had grown up, like Ramón Vía, in the neighbourhood of Vallecas. He was born in Ciudad Real in 1914, but his family moved to Madrid when he was still a child. Four years younger than Vía, it is possible that the two crossed paths in the street, even though their life trajectories were different. At a very young age, he had started working as a bellboy in Hotel Ritz, one of the most luxurious hotels in the city. The youngster, who must have been bright, received good tips from the wealthy guests who frequented the hotel and occasionally earned extra money helping gentlemen who used the casino. However, his father, worried about the company surrounding him, made him quit the hotel, managing to find him a job as an attendant in a famous Madrid perfume shop: Perfumerías Gal.[69]

In 1932, when José Muñoz turned 18, he decided to seek more independence and leave his working-class neighbourhood. Using his modest savings, he rented a small flat in a residential area in the northern part of Madrid. His new home was only two streets from his workplace, but the move also seemed to represent a clear attempt to climb the social ladder.[70]

The young José Muñoz Lozano did not initially show any interest in politics, other than his casual support for the new Republic. His life continued along these lines until the start of the Spanish Civil War. In 1936 José was doing his military service in Zamora but the coup d'état was announced when he was on leave in Madrid. What should he do in this situation? Following the advice of friends, he went to the UGT offices in Puente de Vallecas to sign up, but his application was rejected. He subsequently reported to the headquarters of the CNT, where the response was the same. Despite the endorsements of his friends, none of the organisations would take on a young man who until that moment had seemed concerned only with himself. Faced with these two set-backs, José Muñoz decided to visit the Círculo Socialista de Pacífico and there, where nobody knew him, he was finally accepted.[71]

During the war, José Muñoz's military career progressed swiftly. After his enlistment in the Círculo Socialista he became a sergeant in the 8th Battalion and was sent to the Guadarrama mountains. The battalion was disbanded twenty days later and his unit was incorporated into the 2nd Steel Company, where he was promoted to brigadier. Before the end of the war, he was transferred to the 5th Regiment, the Popular Army unit where the PCE achieved the greatest hegemony and in whichall the officers were members of the PCE. After spending a month in the unit, José Muñoz decided to tear up his Círculo Socialista card and join the JSU and the PCE. His decision was probably influenced by peer pressure and even a degree of opportunism, but what may have begun as a tactic ended up as a real commitment.

After joining the PCE he continued to advance rapidly. First, he was promoted to captain and in May 1938, while serving in the 46th Brigade of "El Campesino", he reached the rank of commandant. The young bellboy at the Hotel Ritz would never have dreamt of a military career of such distinction. Although his career was very different from that of Ramón Vía, both young men from Vallecas ultimately shared a similar fate. In February 1939, after retreating from the attacking Francoist Army, his unit crossed the French border, laid down their arms and demobilised.

José Muñoz was immediately sent to the concentration camp at Saint Cyprien, in the south of France, where the PCE appointed him head of the officials' barracks. However, in February 1940 he was transferred to the camp at Argelès-sur-Mer where he formed part of the PCE leadership until June 1941 when he accepted a German offer to work at a submarine base in Lorient on the coast of Brittany.[72] The PCE advised its members not to collaborate with the Germans but many, fed up with inactivity and hunger, took these voluntary jobs in order to leave the camp and improve their situation.[73] José Muñoz, true to his rebellious and individualistic spirit, decided not to comply with the policy established by the PCE. In the following years, the coast of Brittany, with its submarine base and fortifications , became an attractive destination for many exiled Spaniards and a place where the PCE began to extend its influence.[74]

José Muñoz stayed at the submarine base in Lorient until February 1944, when, just before the Allied armies' landing in Normandy, the old commandant of the 5th Regiment joined the French resistance. It seems that a colleague recommended he do this in order to regain the trust of the PCE leadership and, as seen on other occasions, José Muñoz had a talent for seizing an opportunity.[75]

The military experience that José Muñoz had acquired during the Spanish Civil War was now an advantage. Those in charge of the resistance in Indre et Loire in central France ordered him to take command of the guerrilla movement in the area, leaving him in control of four *departments*. He remained in this position for six months, until a German bullet hit him in the knee. At the beginning of September, after a quick and perhaps insufficient recovery lasting only twenty days, he returned to the front with a Division which united all the guerrilla groups in the region.[76] Shortly thereafter he organised five new Brigades composed of some 1,700 troops. His was subsequently incorporated into the Chief of Staff of the 204th Brigade and the military leadership of an FFI Battalion.[77]

José Muñoz's impressive military record in the Spanish Civil War and the French Resistance was not overlooked by the new PCE leadership. By the end of 1944 the guerrilla school at Toulouse was training hundreds of exiles to return to Spain as guerrilla fighters. One of the branches of the school, the centre at Argenton-sur-Creuse, asked for his help as instructor. He performed this task for several months. However, José Muñoz's military profile made him an ideal candidate to work on the reconstruction of the PCE within Spain. Santiago Carrillo arranged a meeting with Muñoz and asked him to form his own group and start the preparations to establish an operational base in Spain.

José Muñoz was reluctant to accept the offer. The wound sustained to his knee during the 1944 campaign had left him lame, which meant he would be of little use in the mountains. Carrillo responded with a simple promise: his work would focus exclusively on political and military matters, completely unrelated to guerrilla activities.[78] To oppose the wishes of Carrillo was anything but easy at that time, and in May 1945, José Muñoz crossed the French border and entered Spain with two other PCE members. Although he found it hard to believe, it had been six years since he had last set foot in Spain. Now, with all the experience of his thirty years and several war wounds, he returned to Spain as a seasoned guerrilla fighter.

José Muñoz crossed the French border with a *nom de guerre*: "Roberto". His first mission was to construct a Republican Army of the North.[79] The guerrilla had established a strong presence in Santander and the goal was to organise a similar Agrupación in the Basque Country with the help of the guerrilla groups which arrived from France. The first problems emerged in August and September when a series of police raids dismantled the Regional Committee and forced the few survivors (Ramiro Fuentes Ochoa and Campo Osaba) to flee to Madrid.[80]

The precarious situation suffered by the guerrilla and the PCE, united by financial necessity, led "Roberto" to plan a bank robbery. Two go-betweens from Bilbao and one guerrilla fighter from Santander took part, together with "Roberto", making off with a haul of 20,000 pesetas.[81] The weeks passed and the Republican Army of the North failed to take root in the Basque Country. The last blow came in November, when "Roberto" met with José Merédiz Víctores "Tarbes", head of a guerrilla group which had arrived from France in mid-April 1945. While the meeting was taking place in Bilbao, the four guerrilla fighters in the group were arrested in Guernica. "Roberto" then ordered "Tarbes" to go to Madrid, where he would receive instructions regarding a new posting. "Roberto" himself took an alternative route and reported to the National Committee in Madrid. The guerrilla project in the Basque Country had failed.[82]

"Roberto's" trip to Madrid coincided with the successive falls of the Regional Committee of Andalusia and the Provincial Committee of Málaga. Agustín Zoroa was certain that this expert guerrilla, war-time commandant in the Popular Army, Head of Chief of Staff in the French Resistance and teacher at the guerrilla school at Toulouse, was the ideal person to direct Cabello. Yet the new mission assigned to "Roberto" was, in fact, much more ambitious that this, aiming to unite, organize and direct all guerrilla groups in Andalusia. The task was complicated, not least because "Roberto" refused to go up to the mountains. As he had said to Carrillo, his knee injury would not allow it. The National Committee accepted this restriction and thus "Roberto" became the highest military authority of the communist guerrilla in Andalusia.[83]

Armada and Beneyto: Leaders in the shadows

"Roberto" arrived in Málaga in January 1946. Despite the city's normally pleasant climate, that winter was harsh in the provincial capital. Around the same time, two new members of Carrillo's team, Rafael Armada Rus and Ricardo Beneyto Sapena, took up residence in Seville and reconstituted the new Regional Committee of Andalusia. Rafael Armada Rus was a young activist from Córdoba whose war trajectory was the same as that of hundreds of soldiers. Conscripted when the military rising was first proclaimed, he remained in the Francoist zone until January 1937, when he deserted and crossed over to the Republican zone. He was incorporated into the Popular Army and went into exile in France after the fall of Catalonia. With help from the Spanish Refugee Evacuation Service (Servicio de Evacuación de Refugiados Españoles, SERE) he then moved to Mexico.

In October 1944, the PCE delegation in Mexico proposed that he return to Spain on a mission to strengthen the party and the struggle against Franco's dictatorship. On April 30th 1945, after a long journey through Chile and Argentina, he disembarked with a false passport in the port of Bilbao. During his first months in Spain he played an auxiliary role: Agustín Zoroa used him to organise the JSU in a couple of Madrid neigh-bourhoods. However, his big moment came in January 1946. Zoroa had observed with interest the discipline and training of the young communist, who was 31 years old at the time. The fact that he was from Córdoba would also help him to lead the PCE in Andalusia and consequently, in January, he was ordered to take the post as General Secretary of the new Regional Committee to be organised in Seville.[84]

Accompanying Rafael was Ricardo Beneyto, an old acquaintance of Carrillo's. Born in a village in Albacete but a Madrid resident since childhood , he had joined the PCE in 1935, having first belonged to UGT and JJSS. According to internal PCE reports, he came from a "petit-bourgeois" background and was one of the founders of the Sindicato de Dependientes de Comercio in Madrid. In October 1934, he took part in the general strike in the capital. He was 24 years old at the time. After joining the PCE, he also became a member of the JSU the following year. During the Spanish Civil War he held different positions in a variety of units: Head of the Defence Militias of Madrid, Commissar of several armoured train and tank battalions, and then Political Commissar in several brigades in the Agrupación Centro-Sur de Extremadura. The Casado coup caught him unawares in the Levant together with various members of the Central Committee. On March 28th 1939, before the imminent defeat of the Republic, he left Spain together with a large group of party leaders (Uribe, Claudín, Checa y Zarapain) heading for Oran.[85] He left his hopes, his dreams and his defeated fatherland behind, as well as his wife and two children. The latter had to abandon their comfortable middle-class lives and adjust to life in the narrow confines of a small flat in post-war Madrid.[86]

While the PCE organised the evacuation of the most important party leaders to North Africa, the rank and file remained in hostile territory. Beneyto was interned in Camp Morand, where he met Ramón Vía. Both activists, born in 1910, were 29 years old at that time. The two became part of the PCE leadership in the concentration camp, until, at the start of 1940, the Party leadership in Spain ordered Beneyto to escape. In February, taking advantage of an excursion with the Disciplinary Company of Miritja, he managed to break away without being caught.

The clandestine life of Beneyto, who spent most of his energies helping fugitive communists in Algeria, lasted little more than a year. In mid-1941, he and other members of the recently created North African Committee were arrested by the Vichy police. Brought before a military tribunal, he was sentenced to forced labour in the gaol at Lambesse, where he survived abuse and slavery until November 1943, when US troops occupied the territory. The liberation of Algiers brought freedom to all Spanish refugees in labour detachments and prisons. Beneyto was reunited with Vía the same month and both began to work on the reconstruction of the PCE in Algeria.

When Santiago Carrillo arrived in Oran in August 1944 in order to purge the PCE committee in North Africa, both Beneyto and Vía retained his trust.[87]

In mid-1945, Carrillo asked Beneyto to leave Algiers and relocate to the French border in the Pyrenees. He thought that Beneyto could be very useful in Spain but would require specific training at the guerrilla school in Toulouse to fulfil his potential. In December 1945, after a brief period of training, he crossed the border with a false passport and went from Barcelona to Madrid. Agustín Zoroa briefed him on his task within a couple of days. He was to base himself in Seville and rebuild the new Regional Committee of Andalusia with Rafael Armada Rus. He would be responsible for areas relating to the armed struggle, taking the role of Political Chief of the Guerrillas of Andalusia. Under his command was "Roberto", the Military Chief of the resistance.[88]

The last person to arrive in the region was José Merédiz Victores, alias "Tarbes", the youngest of the Andalusian leaders sent by Carrillo. Merédiz was born in 1919 in Oviedo and although he had little political training, he stood out as a result of his experience and understanding of guerrilla tactics. After the Spanish Civil War, in which he was a soldier, he was interned in a concentration camp in France and then joined the French resistance shortly afterwards. When Paris was occupied, the PCE sent him to the guerrilla school in Pau, where he received specialist training in sabotage. Eight months later, in April 1945, he entered Spain as the leader of a guerrilla group. His unit, composed of another four fighters, was intended to strengthen the armed struggle in the Basque Country. However, everyone apart from Merédiz was arrested at the end of 1945. Following the instructions of "Roberto", "Tarbes" went to Madrid, where he contacted the National Committee, who soon informed him of his new mission: to work under the orders of Ricardo Beneyto and "Roberto".[89]

Six young men aged between twenty-five and thirty-five, born in different regions of Spain and following very different trajectories, assumed responsibility for the organisation of the armed anti-Francoist resistance in Andalusia. They were all communists, and, apart from Alfredo Cabello, had all been sent by Carrillo. They were his trusted team. Cabello, the young student activist during the Republic; Vía, the boy from Vallecas who dreamt of being a boxer; "Roberto", the sweet-talking lad from Perfumería Gal; Armanda Rus, the intrepid Cordovan; Beneyto, the businessman from Chamartín; and "Tarbes", the impatient teen. All their dreams and youthful desires had been crushed by the coup d'état in 1936. Their lives had been trapped in the hardships of war, defeat, exile, concentration camps and resistance; nine years of suffering and struggle which had aged their faces and eyes. But these physically aged men were not yet old. They still felt an ever-present hope, an unstoppable desire for change which drove them to reject the security of a future in exile and place themselves once more in the line of fire. They were men of faith and action who, without any reward, returned to Spain to continue the antifascist battle that had begun in 1936.

The Central Committee of the PCE, which had been dispersed since the end of the war, recovered total control of the party in Spain at the beginning of 1946. The autonomous direction of Quiñones, first, and the influence of Jesús Monzón from 1943 prolonged the internal disputes amongst the PCE's leadership in Spain. The failure of "Operation Reconquest of Spain" provided an excuse to condemn the strategy of Monzón and allowed Santiago Carrillo to take charge of the French delegation. From then on, Carrillo sought to break the power of Monzón in Spain and to that effect sent dozens of leadership teams and guerrilla fighters. This process, marked by intense conflict, lasted from October 1944 until the start of 1946.

The period when political opportunities were most favourable for change in Spain coincided with the moment when unity of action among anti-Francoist forces proved impossible and when the PCE was fighting a bitter internal war over the control of the party. Internal divisions within the PCE undermined any possibility of success in its project to extend the guerrilla war in Spain. By January 1946 all local, provincial, and regional committees formed under Monzón had disappeared as a result of repression and persecution by the new leaders arriving from exile. The units sent by Carrillo restructured the PCE in the interior and poured all their energies into the armed struggle. However, by the time the guerrilla project began to take shape, it was already too late.

Chapter 3

The Long Journey Towards Unification
Resolution and resistance

We must spark a guerrilla war in the whole of Spain.

(Dolores Ibárruri, 27th September 1944)

After the end of the Spanish Civil War dozens of people abandoned their homes and entrenched themselves in the mountains. Those first men were simply fleeing the reprisals, the detentions and the assassinations that were taking place in their villages. At that point they were not thinking about any kind of guerrilla project. With time, the number of escapees in the mountains grew and they began to organise themselves in small armed groups. News of "the men of the sierra", packaged in heroic and epic format, were enthusiastically received by republican communities in exile.

The PCE interpreted the emergence of these autonomous guerrillas as a clear indication of an insurrectional atmosphere permeating Spain. The reality was very different, but such was the understanding that prevailed among communist leaders at the time. Short and medium-term strategies were formed on the basis of a simple diagnosis: there was a desire to over-throw the dictatorship in Spain but no agent to lead the battle. The local guerrillas emerging after the Spanish Civil War were laudable examples of heroism and sacrifice, but in reality they were also ineffective. The PCE had to accept its responsibility and take charge of the armed struggle in other to overcome the serious problems with disorganisation, political confusion and passivity in the anti-Francoist guerrilla.[1]

Both the French delegation directed by Monzón and the later leadership operating under the orders of Carrillo tried to eradicate the problems of the anti-Francoist guerrilla by developing an ambitious partisan project, first sketched out in early 1943. The first condition was that the resistance accept the leadership of the PCE, "the patriotic vanguard against criminal

Francoist tyranny".[2] The second condition was that the different autonomous armed groups had to renounce their independence and unite in new Agrupaciones guerrilleras: a new kind of guerrilla organisation with a military structure subject to the political guidance of the PCE.

The model proposed by the PCE collided head on with the complex reality of the resistance in Spain. Three factors – at times isolated and at other times combined – contributed to the opposition of many local guerrillas to the directives of the PCE: (1) the long period during which they had acted autonomously made them very reluctant to cede their independence, (2) the ideological conflicts with socialists and anarchists and 3) the very nature and experience of groups of *armed neighbours*.

In this chapter I will focus on the constant attempts made by the PCE in Andalusia to coordinate local guerrillas. Between 1943 and 1947, the PCE sought continuously to unify the autonomous groups into one movement, yet we may distinguish between two different stages. In the first period, coinciding with the leadership of Jesús Monzón (1943–1944), the PCE cautiously approached local groups in order to negotiate their adherence to the Junta Suprema de Unión Nacional (JSNU), an organisation without its own guerrilla structure. Between 1944 and 1947, by contrast, the PCE led by Santiago Carrillo focused on the creation of the Agrupaciones guerrilleras. The new communist guerrilla leaders tried to incorporate local groups within the Agrupaciones, increasing the pressure in the unifying process. This was often forcefully rejected and sometimes persuasion techniques morphed into intimidation and aggression, which produced significant confrontations.

La Junta Suprema de Unión Nacional and the autonomous guerrillas (1943–1944)

The guerrillas emerging in the post-war period had a marked sense of independence, but it was nonetheless common that they maintained relations with other groups in their area and occasionally engaged in collaborative action. The collaboration depended to a great extent on the experience of the members, their attitude towards local and national action and their personal connections. In Granada province the "Yatero", "Sevilla", "Clares" and the "hermanos Quero" groups operated independently within their area, although at times they joined forces in operations on a larger scale. Every group had a strong attachment to their local community, but between members of the four groups – all natives of the neighbouring villages – there were also strong links of kinship and friendship, which facilitated coordinated action in the region. The idea was to cooperate every now and then, to come together for a specific action and then return to each group's territory. This was the case in May 1941, for example, when they assaulted a venue belonging to the Falange in Purullena; on 1 December that same year, when they attacked a cable car station in Sierra Nevada; or on 20 August 1942, when they kidnapped a General of the Francoist army.[3]

The relationship between local guerrillas and political organisations was very complex and depended to a great extent on the sensibilities of the members of each group, on the strength of each of the organisations and, above all, on their attitudes towards independence and the mechanisms of internal solidarity among the guerrilla fighters. The "Yatero", "Sevilla", "Clares" and the "hermanos Quero" groups were ideologically very heterogeneous. The majority of their members came from socialist backgrounds, but there were also anarchists, communists and guerrilla fighters without any defined political identity. The fundamental cohesive bonds within these groups were of friendship, kinship, and neighbourhood loyalty, not ideology. Political organisations' respect (or lack of respect) for this kind of solidarity, based on primary groups, had a profound impact on their relations with local guerrillas.

In 1943 the Provincial Committee of the CNT in Granada managed to rebuild a structure in the capital and to establish contact with the guerrillas in the area. The intention of the CNT, and later the ANFD, was never to unify the guerrillas but to collaborate and help resistance groups by providing infrastructure, escape networks and arms. In fact, the work of the CNT and the ANFD in matters relating to the armed struggle were subordinated to the decisions made by the guerrillas: it was the guerrilla groups that made decisions while the CNT and ANFD offered support. This situation may have arisen as a result of the weakness of both organisations. In any case, the guerrilla groups did not feel that their independence was being threatened when establishing contact and relations with the CNT or the ANFD. The situation would be very different with regards to the PCE, although here too some differences can be observed relating to the weakness or strength of the PCE in specific periods.

In the province of Granada the PCE had tried various times to reconstruct a Provincial Committee, but it was only at the end of 1943 that the party had managed to create a system of some stability. The Committee only lasted for four months, which made it impossible to establish any kind of relation with the guerrillas. Even so, during its short life it is possible to observe some features which characterise the first period. The leader of the Provincial Committee, Emilio Marino, managed to contact the Regional Committee and had various meetings with Manuel Castro Campos, its

General Secretary. In one of these, held in December 1943, Manuel Castro suggested that he immediately form some relationship with local guerrilla groups. The orders transmitted from the French delegation stressed the necessity to extend the National Union and to this end it was important that the autonomous guerrillas joined the new organisation. Emilio Marino, who disregarded the order, resolutely opposed this idea: to liaise with the guerrillas would be reckless "since they were closely supervised [by the authorities] and would entail a grave danger", but above all because contact with the guerrillas would be make little sense since "in fact these were not composed of idealists but fugitive bandits".[4] This perception within the PCE of the groups of *armed neighbours* as criminals came to the fore on various occasions and naturally caused significant conflict.

The most immediate consequence of the politics of the Provincial Committee was the non-existent influence of the PCE over the local guerrilla groups in the province and the greater presence of the CNT. The local guerrilla groups led by "Yatero", "Clares" or the "hermanos Quero" in 1943 maintained close contacts with the CNT in Granada and above all with the delegate in charge of guerrilla relations, José Bueno Liñán. In October 1944, the leader of the "hermanos Quero" represented all independent groups in Granada at an ANFD meeting in Madrid, aiming to establish some form of coordination among the guerrillas and inform them of a possible delivery of arms from abroad.[5] Since the arms did not arrive, various members of the "Yatero", "Clares" and the "hermanos Quero" groups met in December 1944 at a farmhouse on the outskirts of Güejar Sierra. The ambition was to prepare an attack on an army barracks or work with a military official who could supply them with contraband arms. The operation took place in Granada on 6 January 1945 but ended in failure.[6] In any case, what is important is to underline how these groups, despite their strong local and independent identities, did not reject coordinated action on a municipal level, though such action was always carried out with the greatest respect for each group's independence.

In the province of Almeria the situation was similar, although certain elements were different. If the groups clearly displayed the characteristics of *neighbours in arms*, it also seemed that ideological issues played a more important role here. In fact, armed resistance in Almeria was only a marginal phenomenon, comprised of approximately fifty guerrilla fighters throughout the post-war years. In spite of this anarchists and communists were engaged in a constant dispute over the political leadership of the movement.

The Provincial Committee of the PCE in Almeria was not reluctant to contact the guerrillas. On the contrary, it wanted to redirect the resistance towards the National Union from the end of 1943. In September 1944, they managed to construct a cross-ideological federation of armed groups in the province, although the structure was very precarious. The decision whether to join the platform led by the anarchists and the socialists (ANFD) or that led by the communists (JSUN) produced serious internal conflict. The foundational document did not include any explicit commitment to either organisation. The mistrust grew to such proportions that it became necessary to establish a code of mutual respect stating that no member was allowed "to engage in politics or proselytism of any kind that may offend or distance the organisation's components".[7]

The agreement between anarchists and communists in the province of Almeria is important for its exceptional character, although specific circumstances also produced similar agreements in other parts of Spain.[8] However in reality this was a hollow commitment. Internal disputes continued during subsequent months, and the federation never acted like a united and organised group. Ideological tensions between communists and anarchists increased while further friction was created by the tendency of certain groups to act independently.

This can be seen in the case of Manuel Pérez Berenguer, alias "Mota", leader of a small group of only five members. A miner affiliated with the UGT during the Republic, Manuel Pérez had joined the rifle corps at the start of the Spanish Civil War and been stationed on various fronts as a Republican soldier. At the end of the war, after having spent some time in hiding, he decided to flee to the mountains. At the beginning of 1944 he came to work together with the group led by Juan Nieto Martínez, also known as "Cuco", who was the highest ranking leader in the province together with Sebastián Romero Magaña, though ultimately "Mota" preferred to work independently. In September 1944, after the federation had been created, the Provincial Committee of the PCE sent a letter "to comrade Manuel Pérez Berenguer", criticizing his attitude and reminding him that he had to respect the discipline and the command structure of the new organisation. Only through the federation would he cease to be a "vulgar deserter and a bandit" and become a guerrilla fighter. "The Party demands this", the letter from the Provincial Committee concluded. Manuel Pérez Berenguer did not accept the ultimatum and continued on his independent path until January 1945, when he was arrested. In his testimony before the military judge he suggested that despite the efforts of the PCE, the majority of the guerrilla fighters "are not disposed to adhere to any discipline but prefer to follow their own will".[9]

The PCE received its greatest support in this period in the province of Malaga, but this did not mean that the independent guerrillas joined the

National Union project *en masse*. The difference stemmed from the fact that two local guerrillas, those led by "Manolo el Rubio" and "Rubio de Brecia", showed from the first moment a strong interest in politics and the national dimension of the armed struggle, thus transcending in some aspects the model of *neighbours in arms*. They contacted the Provincial Committee of the PCE at the start of 1944 and began a process of unification, albeit with few results. Other local groups had no interest in uniting. Given that both the PCE and the two groups lacked at this time the coercive capacities needed to impose their will on the other groups, the process failed and both remained limited to their small fields of action. Primarily, this was because neither of the two groups came numerically to exceed forty combatants. Even so, both cases show that there were local guerrilla groups with a supralocal outlook and ambitions to enhance the scale of the resistance.

These kinds of processes are often seen in the first stages of the creation of guerrilla movements and historians have consequently tried to distinguish between this kind of group and those who correspond more to the model of *neighbours in arms*. Both typologies share common features, but there are also important differences, above all in qualitative terms. Microhistorical and anthropological perspectives can help us to discover the features which make these differences apparent.

Agrupaciones and independent guerrillas (1944–1947)

The arrival of Carrillo's men changed the panorama of the resistance in Spain, but the process was slow, much slower than historians have suggested. In the case of Andalusia, the changes began haltingly from the end of 1944 and were not complete until 1947. It took over two years to complete Carrillo's mission.

The figure of Ramón Vía has often been studied from a heroic perspective, shaped by his arrest, his escape from prison and subsequent death in battle. Ramón Vía became one of the martyrs of the guerrilla movement in Spain, celebrated alongside Cristino García Granda or Juan Vitini, but there has been little analysis of his effort in the mountains.[10] From now on I will focus on his work in the guerrilla groups and the enormous difficulties they had to overcome when organising a small centre of guerrilla activity in the province of Malaga.

As outlined in the previous chapter, in October 1944 Ramón Vía landed in the south of Spain together with nine guerrilla fighters arriving from North Africa. His initial mission was to establish contact with the independent groups in the province of Malaga, construct an Agrupación guer-rillera and once secure in the area, extend operations to adjacent territories. He soon realised that the project was more complicated than he had imagined. The first problem derived from the PCE itself. Only days after his arrival, the Provincial Committee demonstrated their refusal to collaborate with the new units sent by Carrillo. In fact, between October 1944 and July 1945 Ramón Vía completely lacked a supportive structure while also being barred from making any contact with local guerrilla groups. Those most inclined towards unification, the groups led by "Rubio de Brecia" and "Manolo el Rubio" – both based in the west of Malaga province – remained faithful to the *monzonist* Provincial Committee. In this situation, Ramón Vía, completely isolated in hostile territory, sought to make first contact with the independent guerrilla groups in the east of the Malaga province.

The PCE in exile had created an unrealistic image of the guerrillas in Spain, bestowing them with an insurrectional power which rapidly vanished before the eyes of Vía. In one of his first reports, Vía pointed to the "passivity" and the "confusion" prevailing among the guerrilla groups in the area.[11] The first local group he contacted was led by Antonio Sánchez, alias "Tejero". Among his members was Antonio Urbano "El Duende", who was the uncle of Joaquín Centurión, the mountain guide who Ramón Vía had brought from North Africa. This family link allowed Vía to approach the group, but he soon realised that "Tejero's" men diverged greatly from his idea of what a guerrilla movement should be.

"Tejero" was born in the village of Nerja in 1917.[12] A member of the UGT during the Republic, he enlisted in the Popular Army in the Spanish Civil War and remained a Republican soldier throughout the length of the conflict. He decided not to surrender to the authorities once the war was over and commenced his life in the mountains. During the first years he lived in the area around Nerja, helped by his friends and families. His life at that time had little to do with the idealised image of a guerrilla fighter. "Tejero" had a hunting rifle to defend himself in case he was discovered by the Civil Guard but dedicated his daily life to a small vegetable plot and attempts to make charcoal which he then sold to his friends.

His situation remained unchanged until January 1944, when two neigh-bours from Nerja, Antonio Urbano "El Duende", an old republican carabineer, and Miguel Arrabal "Montañés", and old socialist activist, also fled to the mountains. The two had to flee after the authorities discovered an arsenal of arms sent by the PCE from North Africa to help future guer-rillas. Both had been responsible for hiding the arms, but when these were found by the Civil Guard, they felt afraid and left to join "Tejero". The three were soon joined by a friend from neighbouring Almuñécar, Francisco

Cecilia, who escaped from the Provincial Prison of Huesca at the start of 1944. Ramón Vía asked Joaquín Centurión to help him contact his uncle's group, but Vía could not believe what he saw when he met the four guerrilla fighters. All were armed with hunting rifles but had never engaged in any form of armed action. The four men spent their time making charcoal in the mountains, which they then sold on the black market in the village. With the money received for the coal they would buy essential goods to survive in the mountains.

Ramón Vía gathered the four neighbours and told them that from that moment they were incorporated into the Sixth Battalion (the first name of what would become the Agrupación Guerrillera de Málaga). Thus "Tejero" became a leader of a communist guerrilla movement in Malaga but the tensions between Vía and the group were constant. The group led by "Tejero" showed clear signs of indiscipline and a desire to maintain their independence. They also resented deeply having to leave the area of which they were all natives. Ramón Vía warned "Tejero" that he had to change his attitude on various occasions, until the crisis came to a head in 1945. At that time several members of "Tejero's" unit left the group to join the unit led by Vía.[13] Finally, towards the end of 1945, Vía temporarily demoted "Tejero" and threatened that he could permanently lose the leadership of his unit. When the trial period was over the whole unit would be forcibly incorporated into the recently created Agrupación Guerrillera de Málaga (AGM) and those who were guilty of indiscipline or tried to act independently would be punished.[14]

A few members of the original group displayed complete loyalty to the new guerrilla, but in other cases dissidence remained latent for years to come. In 1948, when the Agrupación was led by "Roberto", two of the original members of the local group – "Tejero" himself and his friend "Majoleto" were executed by the guerrilla after being accused of indiscipline and dissidence.[15] A deeper analysis of this kind of internal violence within the guerrilla movement in Spain can be found in Chapter 5. Here I will return to the experiences of Ramón Vía during his first months in Spain.

In February 1945, Ramón Vía travelled first to Malaga and then to Madrid with the intention to solve the problem with the Provincial Committee. When he went to the capital, Vía had fourteen guerrilla fighters in his group, but upon his return at the beginning of April, not only had this number not risen, but it had actually been reduced to eleven. The departures resulted from two confrontations with the Civil Guard. Vía wrote in a report that he found the group in complete disarray and that morale was very low. Most of the men were thinking of deserting and felt that each one should simply go "where they thought best".[16] It should be noted that after four months in the mountains, Ramón Vía's group did not manage to stir any interest among the peasantry in the area or the local guerrillas, which continued to act independently and, in fact, had a much greater operational force than the guerrilla leader recently arrived from North Africa. Initial expectations had vanished in a head on collision with actual reality: the PCE was divided in Spain, the autonomous guerrillas preferred to maintain their "passive" and "local" approach to the struggle. Furthermore, there was no insurrectional atmosphere and the peasantry was reluctant to collaborate with foreign guerrilla fighters who they did not know. All these factors constituted significant obstacles to the expansion of the guerrilla model advocated by the PCE.

Despite these problems, Ramón Vía did not give up. It is not known what arguments he used to convince his eleven guerrilla to remain with him. It is probable that his talk referred to discipline, the particular strength of the PCE and, above all, to the favourable international context. The impending Allied victory would change the situation completely. "Everything was discussed", Vía stated in his report, "and arranged so as to allow further work."[17]

The group did not disband, although the circumstances continued to be unfavourable. The men were in a lamentable condition not only politically, but also materially. Mountain marches had worn out the footwear of the fighters and everyone walked almost barefoot. In response to this situation, on 23 April 1945, Vía organised an expedition to the village of Fornes, where there was shopkeeper selling traditional canvas shoes (*alpargatas*).[18] Some reports suggest that the guerrilla chose this shop because they had been informed that the owners had become rich on the expense of the village. Ramón Vía and José Gutiérrez "El Gato", a young man who had just joined and was one of the most distinguished guerrilla fighters in the Agrupación, entered the shop with the proclaimed intention of buying twelve or thirteen pairs of shoes. According to Vía's testimony, "he wanted us to pay for the shoes, but Gutiérrez, a very violent man, refused." When the guerrilla fighters left the shop, the young shop attendant began shooting at them, hitting both of Via's feet. "El Gato" responded immediately, attacking the aggressor. Two years later a unit from the Agrupación killed the shop attendant in retaliation for what happened that night.[19]

The wounds Vía sustained were not serious and "without complications, and they healed rapidly".[20] However, the following month the group received another blow: one of the guerrilla fighters arriving with the North African expedition was wounded and arrested by the Civil Guard. Ten days later there was another confrontation.[21] As a result of these setbacks, the group was effectively forced into a corner, and threatened with extinction. It was in this situation that Vía issued his threatening ultimatum to the Provincial Committee led by Manuel Campo Roldán: either they obey the orders given by the National Committee or they would be expelled from the party. Eight days later the whole Provincial Committee save the organisation's secretary was arrested, and the guerrilla group led by Vía, having almost disappeared, began slowly but surely to increase their influence in the area.[22]

In France, Carrillo wrote a report for Dolores Ibárruri on the state of the resistance in Spain. The excessive optimism which permeated PCE strategy at the time is evident from this account:

> The most active and best organised guerrilla forces – constituting the core, as it were, of the whole movement in which they operate – are the Agrupaciones guerrilleras, which are organised and led by the Party. With their example, it may be said that these Agrupaciones began to break the tendency of passivity and degeneration seen in some of the groups moving around the mountains. The Agrupaciones do not by any means comprise all guerrilla fighters known to exist in the areas where they operate, but there is no doubt that they are a starting point for any attempt to unify all current guerrillas and extend and broaden this movement.[23]

At the beginning of August 1945, after the fall of the Provincial Committee, Vía moved to Malaga and abandoned life in the mountains for good. From that moment he directed the guerrilla group from the city, leaving the group in the hands of Manuel Jurado Martín, a young communist who from 1942 had organised the PCE in various villages in the province. Manuel had been one of the few local PCE activists who had been inclined to collaborate with after Vía's arrival in Malaga. When the Provincial Committee was arrested, Manuel managed to escape the raid and flee to the mountains, where Vía put him in charge of the guerrilla.

At the end of August 1945, Vía returned to Madrid and informed Zoroa about the situation. The party and the guerrillas were decimated, but the arrest of the Provincial Committee had removed all obstacles and it was now possible to begin to a more constructive phase. What he needed were loyal activists with both political and military training. In September, Vía returned to Malaga with Alfredo Cabello and Zoroa's promise to send new units from Madrid. Even so, Zoroa criticised him for still not having been able organise a Guerrilla Army, almost a year after his landing in Andalusia. He was to gather the leaders of independent groups as soon as possible and properly establish, through a constituent congress, an Agrupación de Guerrilleros de Málaga.[24]

The task to contact all independent guerrilla groups and call the constituent congress fell to Alfredo Cabello, while Vía organised the "Musketeers of the Plains" in the capital.[25] Cabello's mission was complicated, but some work had already been done. The first organisational plan divided the Agrupación into a Chief of Staff composed of three members and five guerrilla groups stationed across the mountains around the province of Malaga.[26] The units had been selected by Vía. They included his original group and the four independent groups which he first contacted: 1) the group led by "Tejero", which was now completely integrated in the Agrupación, 2) the group led by "Rubio de Brecia", which had been the first to be approached, 3) Vía's original group, now led by Manuel Jurado, 4) the group led by Fernando Arias García, "Costeño" and 5) the group led by "Manolo Rubio".[27] The total number of guerrilla fighters amounted to thirty-five.[28]

Of the four local groups selected by Vía, two were problematic. The group led by "Tejero" had been completely incorporated in the new Agrupación, though not without resistance. The situation was worse with respect to "Costeño's" group, whose members were unwilling to support unification. When taking on the task of integrating all guerrilla groups in the area, Alfredo Cabello decided that his first mountain visit should go to the splinter party. Cabello made contact with the group at the beginning of September 1945 and remained in their company for two weeks. His report leaves no room for doubt regarding the open conflict between the PCE and the groups of *armed neighbours*. Alfredo Cabello described how he participated together with the "Costeño" group in a kidnapping on 18th of September. When the moment came to split the ransom, he was amazed by what he saw. The usual practice among groups of *armed neighbours* was to divide the loot equally between their members. If the group had any contact with a political organisation, the organisation received the same sum, as if it were another part of the collective, or a donation. This was how "Costeño" divided the money from the kidnapping. The total sum obtained was 150,000 pesetas; 144,000 was shared out between the guerrilla fighters and the remaining 6,000 pesetas was given to Cabello to finance the PCE.[29]

The Agrupaciones guerrilleras abolished this practice as soon as they had created their own structures, as it was considered an indication of "banditry". All the money raised through kidnappings or robberies was kept by the Agrupación while the guerrilla fighters were paid a monthly salary of 500 pesetas. The practice of splitting the money equally caused the greatest conflicts between the groups of *armed neighbours*, who tried to maintain it, and the new guerrilla leaders of the PCE, who tried to eradicate it.

Ramón Vía did not know "Costeño" personally but the reports that he received made him "see that there was something odd" about this group. Although "Costeño" did not know it, the visit by Alfredo Cabello was his last chance. Vía warned Cabello "to be very careful with this man". In a subsequent report Vía stated that "it did not take long to prove that they were dealing with a *provocateur* who was dangerous as a result of his abilities and audacity".[30] In this case, Vía and Cabello concluded that "Costeño" and his lieutenant were leading the local armed group towards banditry and that their presence impeded a peaceful integration of the group into the Agrupación. The only solution was the physical elimination of both men. The operation had to be carried out with discretion, as the PCE could not be seen to be involved in the matter. The intervention of an outside force would not be well received by the guerrilla members, and their deaths should therefore look like the result of an internal dispute. Thus Alfredo Cabello delegated the assassination to one of the members of the group, Emilio Fernández, who had a history of personal feuds with "Costeño".[31] Ramón Vía sent a detailed report to Zoroa under the heading "fight against provocation", where he offered his version of events:

Sometimes his political position was close to the flag with the hammer and sickle, sometimes close to that of the FAI. He behaved terribly towards his group members, who hated and feared him. His military objectives were to steal indiscriminately wherever he could. His morals were those of a vulgar bandit, as he made a mother of his own sister, had three wives and bought land with the money that he stole. The civil guard knew that he spent months in his parents' house yet his family was never disturbed; the house was not even registered. All this was known by the peasants and patriots, who hated him to death. When the group were going to split the money taken most recently, he drew his gun and took 40,000 pesetas. This gave rise to a violent argument which turned bad and considering his attitude and all the precedents, the decision was taken to get rid of him and his lap dog (the only one who followed him). The operation went well, but the lap dog escaped after having been shoot at twice. This caused great alarm, as everyone knew what this element was capable of doing. The situation was particularly serious considering that, between the civil guard, moors and *regulares*, there are currently about 8,000 men [stationed in the area], because this figure, the leader, had previously refused to leave the area, despite the orders received. Thanks be given to a patriot who could stop "the dog". Had it not been for him the situation could have led to a real catastrophe.

A great deal of this is due to the fact that our friends do not adhere to the rules of a conspiracy, nor did they choose a special group of activists to be used in these cases. Even the family members of the one who has been purged know what has happened, as do the go-betweens and a whole bunch of people who should have been kept in the dark, which has made it necessary to break with a number of go-betweens, resources and support which are not easily replaced.[32]

The creation of the Agrupación Guerrillera de Málaga

After the elimination of "Costeño", Alfredo Cabello travelled across the mountains in order to make contact with other groups expected to participate in the constituent congress.[33] A few days later, on 28 September, the PCE published a flyer and issue 18 of the newspaper *Por la República*, where the sections "Propaganda Commission" and "Organising body" of the Federación Guerrillera de Granada-Almería-Málaga-Jaén appeared for the first time.[34] The constituent congress was scheduled for October, but the problems with "Costeño" and an encounter between Cabello and the Civil Guard delayed the meeting. A new meeting was planned in the last week of November 1945, but a new incident, this time of enormous consequence, changed the situation once again. Vía, the first guerrilla leader sent by the PCE to Andalusia, was arrested on 15th of November after being denounced by a colleague who had recently deserted.[35]

The arrest of Vía changed the plans developed by the PCE's National Committee with regards to Andalusia. The news arriving in Madrid from Malaga was increasingly alarming. Cabello had not postponed the Agrupación's constituent congress, which was held, in the absence of Vía, in December 1945. In view of Ramón Vía's arrest, the attending guerrilla groups had agreed to grant the political leadership of the newly founded Agrupación Guerrillera de Málaga to Cabello, a man who had been criticised by the leadership of the party. From the perspective of the National Committee, nothing could be more dangerous: the command of the first Agrupación guerrillera created in Andalusia after a year's hard work was left to a suspicious *monzonista* who was redeeming his past. The first decision taken by Zoroa to halt any internal division was to send to Malaga province a guerrilla expert: "Roberto". His mission was to supervise Cabello and take charge of the military leadership of the future Guerrilla Army in Andalusia. At the same time, Zoroa insisted on a creating a new Regional Committee in Seville and a political leadership of the guerrilla in Andalusia as a whole under the command of Ricardo Beneyto, as it was necessary to maintain firmness and discipline within the party.

The overriding priority of the new Regional Committee was the development of the guerrilla struggle. Thus it was necessary to unite and organise dozens of autonomous groups who at the end of 1945 were still operating independently in Andalusia. In western Malaga province Alfredo Cabello continued his work under the watchful eye of "Roberto", but other centres of resistance (the province of eastern Malaga-Cádiz, Granada, Jaén and Almeria) remained territories without any PCE influence.

In December 1945, Santiago Carrillo ordered that a second expedition of guerrilla fighters, led by Emeterio Meruelo, previously a lieutenant coronel in the Spanish Army, be sent from North Africa. The expedition landed in Almeria. From Almeria they could unite different groups and connect with Malaga, but also this expedition was boycotted by local leaders. The Provincial Committee of Almeria shunned all contact with the guerrillas, and eventually the group led by Meruelo, lost in the mountains without any support network, was eliminated by the Civil Guard in a clash which caused four deaths, five arrests, and one deserter.[36]

Confronted with such problems, Ricardo Beneyto and "Roberto" focused the efforts on the Province of Granada, where there was a higher number of independent guerrilla fighters. "Roberto" was not allowed to leave the Province of Malaga, as he had to monitor every step taken by Cabello, and therefore asked Agustín Zoroa to send José Merédiz Víctores "Tarbes" to help. He had arrived in Madrid after his hasty escape from the Basque Country and had been ordered to take charge of the urban guerrilla in Madrid, but considering the needs of the group in Malaga, Zoroa sent him as a reinforcement.[37]

"Tarbes" arrived in Malaga in February 1946 and had his first interview with "Roberto". His task was to make first contact with local guerrilla groups in Granada and facilitate the process of unification. Ramón Vía had briefly established contact with the Provincial Committee of Granada in April 1945 but the go-between had gone missing.[38] While "Tarbes" began his work in the Province of Granada, another guerrilla expedition arrived from North Africa. In view of the failure of the Meruelo group in Almeria, Carrillo decided to organise a new landing in Malaga in order to strengthen the work of "Roberto" and Beneyto. A group led by Enrique Robles and José Chicano disembarked on the Malaga coast in February 1946. A few days later, after contacting Cabello and "Roberto", José Chicano assumed the command of one of the units in the recently created Agrupación Guerrillera de Málaga (hereafter AGM).[39]

Alfredo Cabello left the mountains and began to direct the AGM from the city of Malaga. Every fifteen days he received reports from the four units comprising the AGM by May 1946. Earlier efforts now appeared to bear fruit and the AGM began to operate as an Agrupación guerrillera, increasingly removed from the usual practices of the groups of *armed neighbours*.

Yet there were still issues with the integration of some groups. The old unit led by "Tejero" was still problematic. Moreover, Joaquín Centurión, member of Vía's expedition and nephew of one of the original members of the group, proclaimed "admiration" for and attachment to this group, whose practices were still linked to the old model of *armed neighbours*. "Political guidance" had not produced any results in this group and Cabello feared a betrayal from Joaquín, who was also annoyed with the Chief of Staff for not having offered him the command of a unit. The problem was critical since the "Tejero" group, which included various socialists, began to flirt with the idea of joining the ANFD and create their own independent group. In May 1946, Cabello finally decided to intervene directly to show that the Chief of Staff was not going to tolerate any indiscipline. It were no longer a simple group of *armed neighbours*, but formed part of a Guerrilla Army where one had to respect the chain of command. Cabello's orders were concrete: "Tejero" was demoted again, as he had been in Vía's time, but he was now removed from the leadership of the unit definitely and replaced by José Cecilia, one of the independent fighters who, despite being a member of the group from its inception, showed greater "consciousness" and "loyalty" to the PCE. At the same time, the group remained under the command of the 2nd Company, led from that moment on by José Chicano, one of the guerrilla fighters arriving with the third expedition sent to Andalusia from North Africa.[40]

But at this time, Alfredo Cabello also had a more important issue to deal with in the city of Malaga. On 1st of May 1946, Ramón Vía took part in a spectacular escape from Malaga's Provincial Prison together with twenty-five prisoners. Although it has occasionally been suggested that the PCE organised the break-out, Vía himself admitted that both the planning and the preparation were carried out by a number of anarchist prisoners.[41] The situation was complicated and there was an air of suspicion. On the one hand Vía distrusted the new PCE leadership in Malaga and the guerrilla Chief of Staff, as demonstrated in the letter he sent to the National Committee. Fearful of any kind of leak, revenge or careerism, Vía decided not to communicate his escape plan to anyone: "and so even comrades forming part of the Party leadership have been surprised by my getaway."

Vía's plan was to retake the command of the AGM and develop "a vast plan for an immediate struggle", but the National Committee's silence forced him to abandon the project and instead to take refuge in a house where he awaited new orders.

The anxiety in Madrid must have been substantial. Ramón Vía had been one of their most loyal and combative activists, but to confer on him the leadership of the party and the AGM after six months in prison would have been imprudent. No one wanted to think that he could be an informer but security protocols had to be respected. Vía's letter, responding to another sent by the National Committee, show perfectly the mixed feelings of the young communist leader. On the one hand he was disappointed by the party's caution in not restoring him as the leader of guerrillas, and he did not refrain from referring to the ingratitude and betrayal of some leading activists, although he never revealed their identity. On the other hand he showed discipline and his deep loyalty to the PCE. He was willing to take whatever post the leadership considered appropriate. However the only thing the National Committee wanted to do at that moment was to remove him from his refuge in order to avert further danger.

Cabello y "Roberto" were given the responsibility to orchestrate his escape as soon as possible, but a string of mistakes caused the fall of the party in Malaga. Alfredo Cabello was arrested on 21 May 1946, and four days later the police discovered Ramón Vía's hide out. The death of Vía following a shoot-out affected the activists deeply. The concurrence of events made the National Committee suspect that Cabello had revealed the location of Vía's hideout, though in reality he did not collaborate with the police. The report filed by his interrogators proves that Cabello did not inform on any of his colleagues.[42]

However, the PCE began to highlight his *monzonist* past as well as his "bourgeois" and "disordered" life, ostracising him completely. However, these were not times in which it was possible to be calm. A witch-hunt was organised against the young leader who since 1944 had risked his life for the liberation of Spain and for his loyalty to the PCE. He was repudiated by all his comrades in prison until his execution on 6 April 1948. Marginalised on the block and in the cells, he was always seen walking alone without anyone calling his name. Insults and public ridicule was all he got from his fellow sufferers. He, however, maintained his composure, defended his innocence, and remained faithful to the PCE until the day he died.[43]

In as little as four days the two highest guerrilla leaders in Malaga had been eliminated. "Roberto" was immediately summoned by the Regional Committee in Seville; he was asked to provide an explanation for recent events. After a long conversation, Rafael Armada and Beneyto accused him of negligence. The reasons for this are not clear, but all indications point in the same direction. In March 1946, a group of the "Musketeers of the Plains" robbed one of the offices belonging to the insurance company "El Ocaso" with catastrophic results. Up to eighty party activists in Malaga were arrested after the police caught one of the robbers. "Roberto", the master mind of the robbery managed to escape Malaga and hide in Almeria until the danger had passed. Not only had his decision brought a great blow to the party, but it also led to his absence from Malaga at a time when he was sorely needed.[44]

Everything suggests that the Regional Committee of Andalusia accused "Roberto" of negligence for these reasons. After an initial conversation in Seville, "Roberto" and Rafael Armada went to Madrid for a meeting with Agustín Zoroa; their case had to be settled directly by the National Committee. Declared guilty, the punishment for "Roberto" was that most commonly meted out to PCE leaders at the time: he had to return to the mountains to "redeem" himself in the eyes of the party. "Roberto" alluded to his knee problems and the promise made by Carrillo, who had given him his word that he would only work in cities, but the decision was made. Nothing could be done against the judgement passed by the National Committee. From that moment onwards, he continued being the military chief of the guerrillas in Andalusia, but now he would base his operations in the mountains.[45]

The first PCE expedition to Andalusia, led by Ramón Vía, took place in November 1944. At that time the Allied forces, with the collaboration of the resistance, had liberated France. The defeat of the Axis was imminent, but the future of Spain was still undecided. Political divisions among exiled organisations hampered a solution to the "Spanish problem". The victorious western democracies, led by United Kingdom, were not particularly interested in intervening in Spain, and the plurality of discrepant voices in exile did little to change their position. Spanish Republican organisations wasted time and energy in their struggle for hegemony while the perfect political opportunity slipped through their fingers.

Two years later, completely excluded from international fora, they continued their fight against Franco's dictatorship on their own. During those two years the PCE had proved incapable of founding a coherent guerrilla movement in Spain. The conflict between communist, socialists and anarchists, as well as internal struggles for the control of the PCE, had consumed most of the energies of its leaders and grassroots activists. Neither had they understood the nature of the resistance in Spain. In eastern Andalusia, by 1946, there was only one small Agrupación guerrillera, operating within the limits of the Malaga province. The attempts made by Vía,

Cabello, "Roberto" and Beneyto to unite the local guerrillas had not borne fruit. The situation changed in mid-1947, but by then the opportunity for political change in Spain was gone.

The origins of the Agrupación Guerrillera de Granada

"Roberto's" new phase in the mountains continued along familiar lines. The unification process in the eastern zone of Malaga had made progress but in Granada, where the largest number of independent guerrillas was to be found, the situation was still unresolved. This area had more guerrilla fighters than any other in Andalusia, yet the PCE had not managed to incorporate a single one within its structures. "Tarbes" had been making arrangements since February 1946, but with few results. He had maintained contact with the local guerrillas led by "El Yatero", "El Sevilla", "Hermanos Clares" and "Hermanos Quero", but none of them were interested in unification. Only the group led by "Polopero", operating in the Sierra Nevada, seemed willing to join the Agrupación, but the party lost contact with this group at the end of 1946. Even so, "Tarbes" began to produce the first internal documents of a fictitious Agrupación Guerrillera de Granada, in which he occupied the role as "Head of the Agrupación".[46]

The tendency of "Tarbes" to make decisions without adhering to the directives of the Regional Committee annoyed Beneyto, who decided to substitute him immediately. In September 1946, he sent Ramiro Fuentes Ochoa to take his place. Fuentes Ochoa was a young communist activist who had begun to work secretly for the PCE after being released from prison. As was the case with Cabello, he had to complete a trial period and express self-criticism for his collaboration with Monzón in 1944. At the end of 1946 he was rehabilitated and Beneyto offered him the political leadership of the guerrilla in Granada.[47] His mission was to manage all the contacts with local guerrillas first established by "Tarbes" and unify all groups in an *Agrupación Guerrillera*.

The task given to Fuentes Ochoa was not easy. First of all he had to overcome the grudges of "Tarbes", who initially refused to recognise his authority. Eventually he gave Fuentes Ochoa the contacts, but further obstacles remained. The only local guerrilla group showing a clear interest in unification, the group led by "Polopero", continued to show no signs of life. The group led by "El Sevilla" accepted the terms of the new Agrupación but this was the smallest group in Granada, consisting of only four members. The "Hermanos Clares" group were reluctant and expressed doubts, while the rest of the groups rejected any kind of unification outright. Faced with this situation, Fuentes Ochoa only managed to persuade a few guerrilla fighters to collaborate on an individual basis. Even so, he put together a provisional Chief of Staff for the still non-existent Agrupación, consisting of three commanders: Ramiro Fuentes Ochoa himself, Francisco Rodríguez "El Sevilla" and Antonio Castillo Escalona.[48]

In October 1946, "Roberto" went up the sierra to assume command of the Agrupación Guerrillera de Málaga, but his aim was still to extend the Agrupación towards the eastern zone of Andalusia. To speed up the process, Ricardo Beneyto and Rafael Armada Rus moved from Seville to Granada. Although Fuentes Ochoa had not made any great progress in the unification of local groups – as only the "Hermanos Clares" group accepted, in part, a close collaboration – in December they finalised the preparations for the official constitution of the most active Agrupación guerrillera in the whole of Spain. On 24th of December 1946, the most senior PCE leaders in Andalusia – Ricardo Beneyto, Rafael Armada Rus, Ramiro Fuentes Ochoa and "Roberto" – met in Granada. The justification for the dinner was to declare "Roberto" military chief of the new Agrupación Guerrillera de Granada (AGG), a product of the fusion of the Agrupación Guerrillera de Málaga and the small guerrilla nucleus organised by "Tarbes" and Ochoa in Granada.[49]

The following phase was centred on the task of incorporating the guerrillas operating in Almeria. To this end, Beneyto ordered "Tarbes" to contact the guerrilla groups in that area, but the mission ran into complications.[50] The local guerrilla leaders, "Nieto" and "Magaña", had tried to contact the guerrilla groups in Granada, but with no results. An agreement ending hostilities on the national level between communists, socialist, and anarchists had been sealed in the spring of 1946, as the JSUN (an exclusively communist organisation) had been dissolved and the PCE incorporated into the Alianza Nacional de Fuerzas Democráticas (ANFD). The new context facilitated, if only momentarily, the signing of an accord between the different guerrilla groups in Almeria and the formation of a Agrupación with twenty guerrilla fighters and four units.[51]

Ricardo Beneyto considered it vital to contact his leaders as soon as possible in order to realise their integration into the recently created AGG. The dream of one coordinated guerrilla group in Andalusia seemed to be coming true. On 12th of January 1947, "Tarbes" went to the village of Gérgal to establish contact with two go-betweens of the Chief of Staff of the Agrupación in Almeria, but the authorities arrested him that same day. Among confiscated material the Civil Guard found notes with the heading "Notes on the creation of a technical manual for the fabrication of explosives and sabotages." Realising that they had captured someone important, they communicated Granada and transferred the detainee immediately.[52]

The arrest of "Tarbes" and his collaboration with the Civil Guard had a catastrophic impact on the PCE and the communist guerrillas in Andalusia. The first consequence was the arrest of Ramiro Fuentes Ochoa on 17th of January 1947, only five days after the capture of "Tarbes" in Gérgal and three weeks after the appointment of "Roberto" as the head of the new AGG. Three days later the General Secretary of the Regional Committee of Andalusia, Rafael Armada Rus, was arrested in Granada, together with another of the militants sent by Carrillo from France, Nicolás García Béjar. A number of go-betweens in the village of Monachil were also detected and two of them were subjected to the "Ley de Fugas" – a historic form of extra-judicial murder by which prisoners were shot while supposedly trying to escape. All suspicions pointed in the same direction: "Tarbes" had become an informer.[53]

During the two following months, between February and March 1947, "Tarbes" and the Civil Guard lieutenant Manuel Prieto López travelled the provinces of Madrid, Seville, Malaga, and Córdoba in search of Ricardo Beneyto, the political chief of the communist guerrillas in Andalusia, but all investigations were fruitless.[54] In view of this failure, "Tarbes" suggested he operate as informer after re-establishing contact with Beneyto and "Roberto" in the mountains. When they were found, he would alert the Civil Guard so that they could make the arrest. The authorities accepted his proposal and "Tarbes" reappeared in the mountains in April 1947. A few days later, "El Sevilla" became aware of his presence in the area. He was detained by two guerrilla fighters and interrogated by "Sevilla" himself. "Tarbes" defended himself by saying that he had escaped by jumping off a truck as he was being transferred from the Civil Guard barracks, but "El Sevilla" did not believe him. The young guerrilla fighter knew he had been caught out and, facing certain execution, decided to flee the guerrilla base where he was held. "Tarbes" managed to escape but shortly afterwards was detained once again by "El Sevilla". This time he was executed on the spot.[55]

Informers were one of the greatest problems of the guerrilla movement. They affected both the *modern guerrilla* groups and groups of *armed neighbours*, although the *modern guerrilla* groups were more vulnerable to their activities. Links based on kinship and friendship, often underpinning groups of *armed neighbours*, reduced to a great extent the danger of betrayal, although this danger was never completely eradicated.[56] By contrast, the *modern guerrilla*, based fundamentally on ideological solidarity and cama-raderie, constantly suffered its attrition. Throughout the years, the police forces of the dictatorship had also improved their counterinsurgency techniques, eventually perfecting their means of infiltration of political and guerrilla organisations.[57] The greatest calamity suffered by the *modern guerrilla* was the conversion of various high-ranking leaders into informers. In the case of Andalusia, no fewer than three of its six leaders ("Tarbes", "El Sevilla" and "Roberto") ended up collaborating with the police and thereby delivering a number of mortal blows to the guerrilla movement.

By May 1947, when these events took place, the unification between the AGM and the AGG had still not become reality, despite the agreement of December 1946. "Roberto" was organising various units of the AGM in Malaga and did not turn up in Granada until September.[58] After the arrests of "Tarbes" and Fuentes Ochoa, "El Sevilla" became the head of the AGG by default, although only a dozen of guerrilla fighters had accepted the plan for unification. The rest of the local groups continued to reject completely the integration with the AGG and preferred instead to maintain their independence.

When "Roberto" arrived in Granada in September 1947, a conflict broke out with "El Sevilla" and the small group of guerrilla fighters who had accepted unification. They had supposedly accepted the authority of "Roberto", but in reality they continued to operate as *neighbours in arms*, without showing any interest in changing their practices. The AGG organised by "Tarbes" and Ramiro Fuentes Ochoa, subsequently led by "El Sevilla", had only really assumed a "federal" form which facilitated the kind of cooperation seen among groups of *armed neighbours*. Upon his arrival in Granada, "Roberto" ended the arrangement allowing each group to act independently in its territory. At the same time, he imposed military discipline and abolished the practice of splitting money obtained through kidnappings and robberies. From that moment each guerrilla fighter would earn a monthly salary of 500 pesetas. The consequences of these measures adopted by "Roberto" were immediate. "El Sevilla", for example, decided to leave the Agrupación and the armed struggle. Taking refuge in a cave in the outskirts of his municipality, he remained hidden until 1951, when he voluntarily gave himself up to the local authorities. He worked as a police informer for various years. The group led by Rafael "Clares", the only local guerrilla which had accepted some degree of integration, decided to reject any ideas of unification and maintain their independence once they saw the measures adopted by "Roberto".[59] Only the group led by "Polopero", with which Roberto finally managed to make contact in April 1948, ended up joining the AGG and accepting PCE dominance.[60] After the fall of Ramón Vía, Agustín Zoroa wrote a report to Santiago Carrillo addressing the failure of the PCE to unite the autonomous guerrillas:

There are at least three to four thousand guerrilla fighters in the mountains in our country. However, we have not been able to establish relations, to effectively control and to integrate in our Agrupaciones more than five hundred of them. The general picture suggests that insofar as we fail to reach them, the immense majority of guerrillas have succumbed to passivity, and there are extensive tendencies of banditry, especially in Andalusia.[61]

The results of the unification process led by the PCE in eastern Andalusia are illustrative. Of the forty-three autonomous groups operating between 1944 and 1947, twenty-one rejected outright any proposals for integration, thirteen accepted such proposals reluctantly or under threat. Only eight were openly in favour (Appendix: Table 4).

From mid-1947, the situation changed radically, but the transformation of the guerrilla movement in the region resulted neither from the strength nor the conviction of the PCE. Most of the independent groups disappeared as a consequence of repression ("Capacho", "Mota", "Quero", "Galindo", "Matías", "Peste", "Cencerro", "Jubiles", etc.) or decided to abandon the armed struggle and flee abroad as foreign intervention became increasingly unlikely ("Yatero", "Baza" and "Ollafría").

From 1948, in contrast to the fragmentation of earlier periods, there were only eight active guerrilla groups in eastern Andalusia, three of which were led by the PCE: 1) AGG – the most potent one – in the provinces of Malaga and Granada, 2) the miniscule Agrupación Fermín Galán, formed of the old groups led by Bernabé López Calle (anarchist) and "Manolo el Rubio" (communist), in the provinces of western Malaga and Cádiz and 3) the depleted 2nd Agrupación led by "El Gafas", operating between Córdoba, Ciudad Real, and northern Jaén. Four of the five remaining groups had survived the repression and unification processes, showing characteristics typical of groups of *armed neighbours*: the groups led by "El Matías" and the "Clares" in Granada, and the groups led by "Cencerro" and "Sixto Marchena" in Jaén.

From that moment, the new and much more concentrated distribution of resistance in Andalusia prompted most people who "headed for the mountain" to join the Agrupaciones guerrilleras. The enhanced coercive capacities of the Agrupaciones also hindered the emergence of new groups of *armed neighbours*, which were rapidly incorporated by the PCE. The only exception was the group led by "Laño", a small communist guerrilla group in Malaga which formed in 1948 and maintained its independence until 1949, when its last survivors joined the AGG, though not without conflicts and discord.

The last great confrontation between groups of *armed neighbours* and Agrupaciones guerrilleras took place, as the next chapter will show, in January 1949, when the AGG attacked the Civil Guard barracks in Güejar Sierra. Outraged by the invasion of *their* territory, the group led by the "Clares" responded by offering themselves *en bloc* to the Civil Guard and its counterinsurgency unit.[62] The AGG had violated one of the fundamental norms of the *neighbours in arms*: respect for the local community and territory.

Chapter 4

"A Strange Guerrilla Group"
Identities and local community

My sympathies were always with those who I considered anti-Francoists. My leftist friends in the village and I formed a block against the neighbours of the village of Cortiguera, a traditional rival, who were mostly Falangists. Thus we created strongly polarised identities around a traditional rivalry between communities and superimposed on this a political enmity, even though neither party understood much about politics.

(*Guerrillero contra Franco*, Francisco Martínez López)

The testimony of Francisco Martínez alias "Quico", an anti-Francoist guerrilla fighter in León, shows the dynamics of two identities at work in local communities: one identity of a local character and another of political character. The primary focus of this chapter is the penetration, superimposition, and coexistence of both these identities in the rural sphere. The analysis is not reduced to a simple definition of identity frameworks but rather considers the dynamics which shaped these, that is, the processes of construction, repression, fragmentation and transformation to which they were submitted.

The formation of these identity frameworks in the post-war period must be analysed from a long-term perspective. Collective identities in both rural and urban spheres underwent great change at the end of the nineteenth century and in the first decades of the twentieth and the processes of mobilisation during the Second Republic and the Spanish Civil War drastically redefined collective identities once more. To understand the dynamics of identity during the Spanish post-war period and in the anti-Francoist guerrilla especially, it is necessary to study these preceding transformations.

Identity-forming factors operating in the context of armed struggle on local levels included political affinities, power strategies, individual and collective survival strategies and "primordial loyalties" that were of enormous importance to the peasantry. In the post-war years, relations of patronage, kinship, friendship and traditional neighbourliness in the countryside were subjected to immense pressures and adjustments. These are analysed in detail in this chapter.

Hybrid identities

The author who has sketched the development of Spanish peasant and neighbourhood identities with greatest precision is Jesús Izquierdo. Originally, the Spanish word for peasant – *campesino* – only served to distinguish between those who were "always in the countryside (*en el campo*)" and those who inhabited the pre-modern urban world. Throughout the centuries, the word *campesino* retained this meaning, until a semantic shift gradually occurred in the second half of the nineteenth century. The original attributes of "life in the countryside" were replaced by two fundamental elements: work in the fields and its relation to property. Thus a new meaning of the word *campesino* emerged in urban centres, first in progressive liberal thought and later in the discourses of parties and unions of the left.[1]

The turning point came between 1918 and 1920. Those three years, generally known as the "Bolshevik triennium", were marked by intense agrarian conflict.[2] It is possible that agrarian mobilisation processes had reactive origins, but the experience of these processes were also likely to have a transformative impact on participants' sense of identity. On some level, the new "class" attributes of the word *campesino* had "entered the consciousness of the participants in the conflict". For the first time, these participants could now appropriate the initially alien concept.[3]

The term *campesino* acquired its greatest importance within the modern political culture seen during the period of the Second Republic, when it became an identity framework aiding the mobilisation of the rural population. Political parties and unions were aware of its mobilising power, which prompted them to adopt strategies actively reinforcing peasant identities. Moreover, this process was also subject to political competition, influencing the term's meaning. Certain groups, like the communists, established a direct link between the peasantry and class, thus suggesting an analogy with the urban proletariat. Republicans and socialists, by contrast, considered the peasantry to include both smallholders and leaseholders, who were the base of their new Agrarian Reform project. Social Catholicism, for its part, sought to define the peasantry through a discourse stressing traditional values, excluding all potential references to "class conflict".[4]

The Spanish Civil War prompted the greatest mobilisation process in the history of Spain and the peasantry played a prominent role in popular militias and Popular Army units. The effects of rapidly increasing political awareness could be felt on both home and military fronts and a key element in this change was the strengthening of the peasantry's political identity. "Peasant youth! The JSU knows your heroism and your contribution to the fight against fascism" said one Republican poster.

There is no doubt that the new, politically loaded peasant identity became a central reference point in agrarian societies in the first decades of the twentieth century, but studies of this identity must not exclude other more enduring community frameworks and, in particular, those linked to neighbourhood relations. Jesús Izquierdo highlights that "by 1936, the centuries-old neighbourhood loyalties that had united members of rural communities despite their socioeconomic differences were facing unprecedented competition from partisan identities finding expression in old words charged with new meaning".[5]

The relation between old neighbourhood identities and new peasant identities must be analysed from the perspective of competition and conflict, but this illuminates only one aspect of the issue. Individuals tend not to abandon one identity simply to assume a new one. Assimilation is not, in other words, the only mechanism allowing us to understand identity conflicts. In some cases it is possible to observe transparent or "pure" identities, but for the majority of people the adoption process is partial or shared, which means that in most cases identities are hybrid.[6]

In large sectors of rural society the new peasant identity was adopted without old neighbourhood identities being renounced. Both identities came into frequent conflict and the dominance of one over the other varied according to various factors. This was the context, within local communities, in which the anti-Francoist guerrilla emerged and developed.

Cultural anthropology has shown more interest than other disciplines in the territorial and social frameworks of identity. In these studies it is possible to observe various levels of identity: local, regional, national.[7] Family, street, and village are the three levels of local identity. From these three basic units a common sense of belonging is constructed, reinforced by shared symbols and rituals. Furthermore, different kinds of festivities (*mozos*, *quintos*, *casados*, *gremios*, etc.), local symbols either religious or secular in character (*patrón*, *virgen*, *fuente*, etc.) or inter-local conflicts reinforce the construction of a local identity.[8] These processes recur in all municipalities, but identification and intra-communal bonds are stronger in small to medium-sized communities, where the interaction between neighbours is more frequent, and in mountain villages, where inhabitants live in a greater degree of isolation. As Carlos Gil Andrés has suggested:

> The village, as a basic social unit, generate a sense of identity and belonging to a community, relationships rooted in work and the neighbourhood, solidarity and emotional bonds which allow people to recognise their common interests and act together in what they believe to be their defence.[9]

This sense of belonging to a local community did not exclude the possibility of internal conflict. In fact, research on local communities has identified two areas of conflict: one relating to matters internal to the community and one relating to community action vis-à-vis the exterior.[10] Social conflicts within rural communities were constant throughout the nineteenth century and the beginning of the twentieth. The important if limited changes in the agrarian economic system after the crisis at the turn of the century, the centralisation process and increase of state control, and the appearance of new ideologies all transformed and deepened the internal rift within rural communities. Throughout the decades, amidst the clamour of collective action, the breach between those who controlled the means of power and those in subordinate positions became ever wider. This process soon led to the emergence of collective identities more antagonistic in character.

From the beginning of the twentieth century the polarisation of society was becoming increasingly sharp, but beyond certain common elements, the identities of the distinct camps were hardly homogenous. One of the first authors to analyse social conflicts during the Second Republic and the Civil War from the perspective of collective identities was Rafael Cruz, but his work reduces the political conflict to one between two identities: the *popular* and the *Catholic*. He thereby forgets other important collective identities relating to class, nationality, neighbourhood, etc. and he neglects, above all, their hybrid character.[11]

Historians have also been tempted to explain the conflict with reference to a dichotomy between power-holders and subordinates, but as Javier Ugarte claims, the conflicting identities had deep roots and cannot be understood exclusively in terms of class or ideological divisions. Community relations were articulated through a complex network of personal connections and primordial loyalties. These connections and loyalties, which could stem from "concrete interests and quarrels, sometimes within the family, friendship, patronage, etc.", constituted the central nuclei of every bloc.[12] What needs to be addressed therefore is the relation between local identities and collective identities shaping the conflict.[13]

Social science has addressed one of the most complex issues in society: the nature of hybrid identities. In this field, analysis tends to explore two dimensions: the social struggle between collective identities, on the one hand, and the internal conflicts that take place within each individual, on the other. Individuals comprise various identities (relating to their individual subjectivity, family, community, nation, ethnicity, religion, gender, age...) which interact in a constant process of negotiation, conflict, and transferal. As a result of this multiplicity, individuals often face situations in which different loyalties collide and leave little room for a simple resolution.[14]

The complexity of the matter can be observed at moments when social conflicts find expression in political violence. This was the case during the Second Republic, yet the social implosion of peasant communities during the Spanish Civil War and the first years of the dictatorship caused particularly harrowing damage to the social fabric in rural areas. José Luis Ledesma has analysed how "internal divisions and struggles" coexisted with "community solidarity" on the Republican home front before external intervention. Where the military rebellion did not succeed, it unleashed a social revolution. In many of these municipalities, rural inhabitants occupied farms and collectivised land, but they also detained and even assassinated a significant number of neighbours. However, the particular dynamics of such events were not homogenous.

Studies have shown that detentions of neighbours could have two motives: to hand over the person to the enemy or to protect the person from attacks by the militia. There is a military paradox relating to deaths of neighbours: on some occasions the assassination is carried out by the neighbours themselves, on other occasions it is carried out by militia men from other villages with the help of locals acting independently, but there are also cases where the victims are protected by the community. In these cases, the local committee, which tended to be the most important political authority in the wake of the social revolution, would deny the existence of any rightists in the village and the visiting militiamen would leave without committing any crime. Thus local solidarity could intervene to stop external aggression, even in moments of extreme social conflict. In other cases, by contrast, internal conflict and political identities would override community unity.[15]

Studies of the war-time rebel zone and the post-war period point to the same patterns of action. At times the violence was meted out from within the municipality and at other times it was local authorities who protected the local community from external violence (from the militias or army). The general atmosphere in the post-war period was asphyxiating. Local authorities and neighbours devoted to the Francoist *movimiento* subjected the defeated to processes of social control, exclusion and constant humiliation. Their collaboration with the military courts, with the Civil Guard, with the

Falange, or their direct participation in the repression through denunciations or the formation of paramilitary groups was constant. But such
activities did not completely eliminate certain forms of internal solidarity,
as seen in written statements clearing neighbours of political suspicion.[16]

These mechanisms were also at play in the resistance. It is clear that
villages experienced great internal polarisation in the post-war period, that
the line between victors and vanquished was clearly drawn, and that this
caused a rift in local communities. Yet local norms and loyalties were also
maintained, which meant that both mechanisms operated simultaneously.
If the repression and social exclusion engineered by Franco's dictatorship
often relied on the initiative and collaboration of neighbours, the victims
of robberies, kidnappings and even assassinations carried out by the guerrillas, too, had in many cases been singled out by another member of the
local community.

My ambition here is not to suggest an equivalence of responsibilities,
which would be impossible when comparing state repression and the guerrilla, but to highlight the importance of local dynamics. It was common
that the guerrillas questioned the motives of neighbours forming part of
local committees or those performing supporting roles. At the other end of
the scale, it also happened that independent guerrilla fighters intervened to
prevent an action against a neighbour of their village. In Frigiliana,
according to David Baird's account, the guerrillas "wanted to kill all the
rich, but [a local guerrilla fighter] got in the way and none of the rich were
touched".[17] The rupture and/or conservation of community loyalties regulated to a great extent violent guerrilla action on local levels, which is in
itself a common phenomenon in these kinds of armed conflict.[18]

Once the complex mesh of relations formed between different identities within local communities has been elucidated, it is possible to analyse
its relevance in the anti-Francoist guerrilla movement and its impact on
the nature of the resistance. The political and national focus of efforts to
recognise and commemorate the guerrillas in Spain and elsewhere has not
facilitated this kind of analysis, but its approach is essential to any
attempt to understand and explain the complexity of a phenomenon like
the resistance.[19]

Primary groups and resistance

Many of the armed groups formed at the end of the war had a common
origin: neighbourhood loyalties, kinship, friendship and the camaraderie
emerging in Popular Army units during the conflict. The last variable was

analysed in chapter 1, so I will now focus on what is known as primary groups: neighbourhood groups, kinship groups, and friendships. Primary groups can be considered the most fundamental form of social relations, a group in which an individual participates in immediate, direct and personal ways. Individuals then join other, secondary, groups like school, the army, and political parties, etc. The basis for guerrilla mobilisation was established through primary groups, just as guerrillas' characteristics, conduct and modes of action were determined by the loyalties and values defining these groups. A study of informal networks is therefore crucial to an understanding of the internal dynamics within local communities and, above all, the processes by which the groups of guerrilla was formed.[20]

Most groups forming part of the armed anti-Francoist resistance movement included members who were related in some way. Fathers, brothers, sons, nephews, cousins, and sons-in-law: these kinds of family links were common among guerrilla fighters in one group. The mechanisms of socialisation, recruitment, and the specific dynamics of repression, which attacked the immediate family of the guerrilla fighter, reinforced this situation. However, it is necessary to distinguish between groups where kinship bonds co-existed with neighbourhood links and/or political affinity and groups in which family relations were key to internal cohesion, that is, situations where a family, a lineage, a clan became the cement of a guerrilla group. This second kind was rare, but a few examples can be found in Andalusia.

It is not easy to identify kinship relations between guerrilla members. Direct relations (father, son, brother, etc.) can be inferred through surnames, but such evidence is not sufficient. Indirect relations (son-in-law, nephew, godfather, etc.) are even harder to identify, which means that in both cases it has been necessary to refer to documents and oral testimonies. Following this premise, I have identified six groups primarily operating on the basis of kinship bonds: "Obispo", "Juan Apaños", "Costilla", "Chaparos", the "hermanos Matías" and the "hermanos Quero".

Groups exhibiting these characteristics were relatively small in size: none of them had more than twenty members. Group leadership always fell to a member of the family and activities were restricted to the local community and surrounding villages. None of the groups agreed, when the time came, to join the Agrupaciones guerrilleras, preferring instead to maintain their independence.

The predominant kind of family relation in these groups was that between brothers: Obispo (2), Juan Apaños (2), Chaparros (3), Matías (3) Quero (4); and cousins: Obispo (3), Costilla (2), Chaparros (5), Quero (6).[21] Three of the six groups were named after a surname or a family nickname:

the "hermanos Chaparro", the "hermanos Matías", and the "hermanos Quero". This was not common, but neither were these the only examples. The identification of a guerrilla group with a family name can also be found, for example, in the "hermanos Clares" and the "hermanos Galindo", but the internal cohesion of these groups was primarily based on neighbourhood loyalties.

All groups which based their internal cohesion on kinship fit the model of *neighbours in arms*, but not all groups of *armed neighbours* were formed around kinship. In fact, neighbourhood loyalties were the most common base for internal cohesion. A detailed study of every single group would be repetitive, so I will analyse only a few cases as concrete examples.

Three guerrilla groups operated in the northern side of the Sierra Nevada, the area closest to the provincial capital Granada: the "hermanos Quero", the "hermanos Clares" y "Yatero". The three groups, which collaborated closely, were formed between 1939 and 1942. Many of the guerrilla fighters knew each other from before the war and there was a fluid interchange of members between the groups. The first, the "hermanos Quero", established internal cohesion on the basis of kinship, even though it also came to include ten members who were unrelated to the family but linked to the group through friendship and local loyalties. Still, the core of the group was formed around kinship.[22]

The group led by "El Yatero" was formed in 1939 by two escapees: Juan Francisco Medina "El Yatero" and Jesús Salcedo. The first was a native of Quéntar and the second joined the neighbourhood through marriage. In this case, it is also important to remember the influence of soldierly camaraderie, as both had belonged to the same brigade during the war period. In any case, the "El Yatero" group was being formed by locals of the area, but specifically by inhabitants of Quéntar, where the group originated. Throughout its existence (1939–1947), it incorporated 37 guerrilla fighters, and I have been able to identify the place of residence of 34 of these: Quéntar (14), Cogollos Vega (4), Purullena (3), El Fargue (2), Cenes de la Vega (2), La Peza (2), Granada (2), Málaga (1), Monachil (1) y Zújar (1). Only two guerrilla fighters originally came from communities outside the geographical area and their incorporation related to a change of residence, in the first case, and personal relationships, in the second. The group set up a base in the mountains around Quéntar and its activities were restricted to the villages in which the guerrilla fighters had lived. The communist leadership organising the Agrupación Guerrillera de Granada tried to incorporate them, but the group maintained its independence, with the exception of four of its members, who ultimately abandoned the group to join the AGG.[23]

The "hermanos Clares" group was formed in mid-1941 by five escapees, all of them local to Güejar Sierra. The leader of the group, Rafael Castillo Clares, and his brother Félix, who replaced him after his death, were born in the village of Ocaña (Almería) but had moved to Güejar Sierra as small children. As in the previous case, the group's original members were all from the same municipality, though later additions also came from neighbouring villages. Throughout its existence (1941–1949), the group incorporated 29 guerrilla fighters, and I have identified the place of residence of 28 of these: Güejar Sierra (11), Dílar (3), Quéntar (3), La Peza (3), Almería (3), Agrón (2), Murtas (1), and Monachil (1). In the case of the "hermanos Clares", there were six guerrilla fighters who came from villages located far from the area in which the guerrilla operated. This was a result of the fact that the group "joined" the first incarnation of the Agrupación Guerrillera de Granada (1946–1947) for approximately a year and a half. In fact, during that time the group maintained its independence, although it was formally a part of the fictitious AGG. In mid-1947, when the AGG managed to establish a real presence in the area and sought to incorporate the "hermanos Clares" in practice as well as theory, the group resisted and decided to retain their independence. This development will be analysed in greater detail later on. In any case, the operational characteristics of the group were the same as those seen in the group led by "El Yatero". Based around Güejar Sierra, it did not extend its activities beyond the area delineated by the communities of its own guerrilla fighters.[24]

The examples given were not exceptions but rather the norm when considering independent armed groups in Andalusia. They were formed by neighbours in a particular village, who then included new members from adjacent communities. Kinship, friendship, and camaraderie reinforced the internal cohesion of these groups, whose operative area was restricted to that surrounding their own local communities. In most cases this limitation was not a result of the "poverty of the struggle" seen in the first period but rather the fact that group action was shaped by experience, local identities and members' conception of collective action.

The unwillingness of a large number of independent groups to join the Agrupaciones guerrilleras led by the PCE can now be understood from the perspective of this "clash of mentalities" rather than the classic model emphasising ideological struggle. A key question in the conflict between *neighbours in arms* and the *modern guerrilla* was whether the armed struggle should be organised on a local or national level, or, that is to say, whether it should take the form of a traditional guerrilla war or a modern guerrilla war.

In a classic 1928 study of insurrection, Ho Chi Minh established the traditional Marxist interpretation of rural partisan movements when offering the following reflections:

> Historical experience of guerrilla warfare in various countries shows that initially it is characterized by small engagements of only local significance. This is the result of the weakness and limited numbers of the guerrilla units, and the low level of awareness among the peasants of their goals – due to their lack of experience, and to the absence of any adequate influence of the proletarian party in the countryside. The fundamental aim of the guerrilla detachments in this period is to defend the peasants of the area in question (. . .). Subsequently, as the revolutionary upsurge increases in the countryside (. . .) guerrilla detachments no longer limit themselves to operating in their home area. They venture out from their own villages or districts, gradually transform themselves into flying columns of varying strength, join up with detachments from the neighbouring areas and become emboldened to undertake larger-scale operations.[25]

Ho-Chi-Minh's interpretation of the motives which prompted the peasantry to adopt such local forms of armed insurrections was adopted by other Marxist authors like Eric Hobsbawm.[26] This theory, based on an evolutionary model of collective action (primitive v. modern) and the vanguard role of the urban proletariat, has its limitations.[27] However the circulation of these ideas show the importance that Marxist analyses attributed to the scale of the conflict and consequently how the PCE viewed local resistance groups in Spain.

A good example indicating the problems that the *modern guerrilla* faced can found in the case of six inhabitants of a small village in the province of Malaga who decided to flee to the mountains in May 1944.[28] The escape was prompted by two Falangists' harassment of the six men, who had been distinguished military figures during the Second Republic and formed part of the local Revolutionary Committee during the war. Facing the threat of arrest, the six villagers decided to steal a few hunting rifles from a forest ranger and seek refuge in the mountains. But their plan was to remain within the areas belonging to the municipality. From there they would attack local authorities and when the time came, they would liberate their village. This was the outlook of groups of *armed neighbours*, an outlook which harmonised perfectly with a traditional localism characterising peasant mobilisations during the nineteenth century and remaining predominant in agrarian conflicts during the Second Republic.[29]

The conflict between the six guerrilla fighters and the *modern guerrilla* came a few days later, when three guerrilla fighters sent by "Rubio de Brecia" "warned them that they could not remain a separate group and had to unite with others in the sierra". The six local men, though fearful of outsiders, decided to follow them and arrange a meeting with "El Rubio". The guerrilla leader warned them that he would not tolerate any kind of "banditry" and that they had "to enlist in the guerrilla organisation of the National Union, in which he was the provincial leader of Malaga". The six agreed to join the group, although the situation did not last for very long.

After a few days in the camp the six men requested a new meeting with "El Rubio". In the meeting they asked "if they could return to their own territory, that is, their municipality, where their local knowledge made life easier, which ["El Rubio"] allowed, but not without warning them that they were still part of the organisation that he led and that he would call on them when needed". Here the importance that *neighbours in arms* attached to locality is evident, but as I will show below, the *modern guerrilla* groups developed various means to counter this tendency.

With the permission from "El Rubio", the six guerrilla fighters returned to the area around their village and camped for some time at the foot of the mountains. They orchestrated a kidnapping of one of the Falangists who had threatened them and robbed a local farmhouse. But the news reached "El Rubio", who summoned them again to demand that they cease all such activities, which were the hallmark of bandits rather than guerrillas. As a result of coercion, the six men joined the group led by "El Rubio" but on new conditions. The group leader decided to implement a measure which would later be generalised within the *modern guerrilla*. To prevent a localised understanding on the battle, leaders removed guerrilla fighters from their municipality and placed individual members of local groups in different units. Relatives and neighbours were not allowed to join the same group, in order to facilitate the emergence of other kinds of bonds (based on political agreement and camaraderie). The idea was to abolish the "primitive" mindset of the peasantry and transform those *neighbours in arms* into modern guerrilla fighters.

However, the measure was not very successful. Three of the six refused to join the group and immediately gave themselves up to the authorities in the village. They would rather abandon the struggle and risk their lives than lose their autonomy and fight under the leadership of a guerrilla fighter from the "outside". The other three accepted the authority of "El Rubio" and joined the group, though this did not last long. The three men were placed in different units, but their discontent grew. "El Rubio", said one of the men, "wanted impose a military discipline which was far too severe and which we did not agree with". After an argument, "El Rubio" "threatened them by saying that there had to be unity and discipline, and if this was not the case he would impose it by force and eliminate those tried to stop him". Faced with this situation, the three deserted and reported to the Civil Guard barracks in their municipality. It had only been two months since they had been forcibly incorporated into the group. This kind of conflict between local identity and political identity, between integration and independence, between localism and action on a national scale, were not marginal but a regular occurrence.

The "manual of political-military direction in the Guerrilla Army of Andalusia", compiled by Ricardo Beneyto in 1946 and distributed to all AGM and AGG units, presented this as one of the most serious problems facing a transforming guerrilla movement:

> LOCALISM. This is an evil that gradually immobilizes and hinders unit movement and the appropriate outlook of our men. It is imperative that all comrades understand that the fight against the Falangist assassins has a *National* character (. . .). We must therefore resist the tendency of some comrades to fight only in one specific place.
>
> We know that this tendency is shaped by sentimental or family-related feelings but if we really want an efficient Army it is necessary to free men from all such pre-conceptions, which impede its development and the efficacy of the struggle.
>
> Attachment to a specific territory almost always generates passivity and non-aggression pacts with the enemy, as has already been the case in some sectors, or tolerance towards some individuals who are declared Falangists. It prevents the Chief of Staff to deploy its men where they can produce the greatest results, and thereby make their work as fruitful as possible (. . .).
>
> Politically strong comrades must contribute to this task of eliminating localism from political chiefs and unit leaders.[30]

Breaking local links: *Cuadrillas* and nicknames

Cuadrillas, which are very common in Spain, are a kind of informal collective organisation based on two primary groups: neighbourhood groups and groups of friends. One community can contain various *cuadrillas*, which share a set of common characteristics: all members belong to the local community and their incorporation depends on age (with minor variation) and gender. All members of the *cuadrilla* are considered equal in principle and tend to develop among them a strong sense of solidary and reciprocity.[31] From this perspective, *cuadrillas* allow us to observe the complexity of communities' internal dynamics, especially as expressed in intra-local conflicts. In cases where the *cuadrilla* is divided as a result of conflict, internal loyalties may facilitate the creation of consensus, and in a situation marked by political violence, the *cuadrilla* can minimize the risk run by each one of its members. If this does not happen, there is a risk that the *cuadrilla* breaks up and ceases to function as such. Alternatively, the *cuadrilla* may maintain a strong consensus in the face of conflict, which often reinforces identities and can even convert the group into a platform for more formal organisation and an agent of recruitment.

In the case of the armed anti-Francoist resistance, the *cuadrillas* played a crucial role. Many of the local organisations which supported the resistance originated in the *cuadrillas* formed by youths within the community. That said, there are important differences between the groups which I have defined as *neighbours in arms* and *modern guerrilla*. Many groups of *armed neighbours* emerged from local *cuadrillas* and, more importantly, their internal organisation and loyalty operated on the same basis. By contrast, the *modern guerrilla*, which insisted on breaking any "localist" mentality, occasionally attacked these internal loyalties by isolating them or encouraging internal desertions. The following example will show how this dynamic worked.

The AGG support base in the village of Almuñécar revolved around the local PCE organisation, composed to a great extent of a neighbourhood *cuadrilla*. In 1947, the dictatorship changed its strategy in the fight against the guerrillas and decided to focus on eliminating its social support. The Civil Guard and the Army increased their presence and pressure in the village. In this context, at the beginning of October two local youths were accused of burning the shack and mill of a prominent Falangist.[32] Fear spread among the locals and rumours began to circulate, stating that "everyone who had previously belonged to the socialist parties (. . .) and all who had been in the red zone [i.e. in the Republican zone during the civil war] were going to be arrested and imprisoned."[33]

In this situation, one of the guerrilla leaders in the area, "Felipe", called a meeting with various locals from the village in the early hours of 14 October 1947. The meeting was attended by fifteen neighbours, who after some discussion decided to join the AGG. The "clash of mentalities" and the *modern guerrilla*'s incomprehension regarding the local solidarities followed only a few hours later. The fifteen men were taken to the base camp where the Chief of Staff was waiting for them. Aiming to avoid local groups, "Roberto", leader of the AGG, separated the men and assigned them to different units. As mentioned above, this was common practice. The consequences following from this decision banishes all doubt regarding the conflict between local solidarity and identity and the *modern guerrilla* project proposed by the AGG. No less than ten of the fifteen men who enlisted in the Agrupación that night deserted within the first days or months, and another was executed (*ajusticiado*) by the Chief of Staff. Only four remained loyal to the new group.

The fifteen youths who joined the AGG as a *cuadrilla* had found themselves separated from their friends and neighbours, and the unifying link which had facilitated their recruitment was thereby broken at the very moment of incorporation. Only four accepted the situation, putting political identities and loyalties before local ones. The strategy of desertion was widespread among local groups as means to solve the conflict. But even desertion frequently showed characteristics that point to guerrilla fighters' local attachments. Most commonly deserters waited until they met other units in which they could reunite with a friend or relative, together with whom they would then flee.

Another important issue was the place of surrender to the authorities. Deserting guerrilla fighters walked dozens of kilometres and took the risk of being captured by their own ex-colleagues, the Civil Guard or counterinsurgency parties in order to report to the Civil Guard barracks of their own municipality. In the minds of the deserters, it was clear that they returned to *their* community, and therefore also a web of loyalties which may in a given moment mitigate repression or punishment. For this reason deserters always sought out a mediator before giving themselves up, an important local person with whom they had remained friendly: a priest, a civil guard, or a Falangist, etc.

The same conflict can be observed in the rites of passage and initiation employed by the Agrupaciones guerrilleras. Integration into an Agrupación guerrillera was not a simple formality. Guerrilla candidates had to go through a short trial period, after which he was made a full member. This event was celebrated in a ceremony attended by various units and the Chief of Staff. In this moment the new recruit took the guerrilla oath and was given his *nom de guerre* by the Agrupación.[34] Enrique Urbano, of the guerrilla fighters in the AGG, stated clearly that

> We didn't want nicknames in the guerrilla (. . .). Have I said that we were not allowed to keep *village nicknames* in the guerrilla? It was "Roberto" who prohibited this, and for very good reasons, since "Porrete", for example, who was this? Who were we referring to, when there were three of them in the guerrilla?[35]

In a rural environment, nicknames were a means to identify individuals within a community. On the one hand, it helped to form social networks within municipalities, delineating kinship links within villages while also indicating the limits of the community vis-à-vis the outside worlds. Nicknames could refer to an individual or a lineage, that is, they were given either to an individual or to a family. But nicknames were not simply a substitute for surnames, but placed "the power of naming in the hands of the local community, the *cuadrilla*, or the neighbourhood".[36] The nickname, then, operated on two levels: that of individual identity and that of collective identity as articulated within a community.

"Village nicknames" were handed out by the community and meant that everyone in that community could place its members in a larger web of locally significant associations. Guerrilla fighters from the "outside" had no access to this knowledge since there were not part of the local community. It is clear that the *modern guerrilla* tried to establish close relations with these communities, but they adopted strategies which effectively sought to transform locals into guerrilla fighters without considering the nature of relationships in the countryside, and this diminished their potential. The response of the *modern guerrilla* in this situation was not to create links with the community but to remove one of its members and integrate him in a new network of group relations. The result was a high number of desertions and reduced number of recruits.

There were three fundamental reasons why the Agrupaciones guerrilleras were so determined to abolish "village nicknames". Firstly, as a security measure: if someone kept the name by which he had always been known, it was easier to identify him. A change of nickname, by contrast, caused difficulties and confusion for the dictatorship's police and armed forces.

Secondly, communist morals and army discipline could hardly approve of inappropriate nicknames with a comical ring, often making more or less veiled reference to nudity or unflattering attributes (e.g. "Cagalete", "Cornudo", "Braguetas", "Alegría", "Zambo", "Chiflita", "Patamoro", "Piripi", "Culito", "Matanzas", "Gachas de Mosto", "Matagallos", "Pelandreras", "Orejón", "Mantecas", "Matutero", "Matasiete", "El Meneos", or "Pollastrón"). All these were local nicknames which had to be replaced by common and simple names when a fighter wanted to join a *modern guerrilla*, names like "Rafael", "Francisco", "Julio", "Teodoro", "Bienvenido", "Arturo", etc. The repertoire was limited, and when there were not enough names to go around, a nom de guerre would be repeated with an added number: Oscar-2", "Gallardo-2", "Mariano-2", or "Nico-3". On special occasions new recruits would be given the name of a "guerrilla martyr", like Cristino (after Cristino García Granda) or Ramón (after Ramón Vía).

Thirdly, the oath and the christening were seen as an initiation rite into the guerrilla. The Agrupación was the new family of the recruit, who should therefore cut all ties with the old community. From that moment he was no longer "Matutero", "Alegría" or "Braguetas" but "Ricardo", "Manuel" or "Fernando". The nom de guerre signified the recruit's integration into the group, but it also gave him a new identity.

The prohibition of village nicknames in the *modern guerrilla* had a clear goal: to weaken old identities and local loyalties in order to create new identities and political loyalties. From that moment recruits ceased to be *neighbours in arms* and became *guerrilla fighters*. As mentioned earlier, there was strong sense of neighbourliness in local communities. At the same time, from the beginning of the twentieth century, new identities (relating to class, politics, etc.) also came to shape relationships in rural communities. But the latter did not replace the former. Both were present and the dominance of one or the other depended on the situation. A large number of modern guerrilla fighters accepted their new identity and integrated themselves without conflict, but a significant part of them did not. About 35% of guerrilla fighters in eastern Andalusia did not join a *modern guerrilla*. Moreover, as I will show in greater detail below, the desertion rates in the *modern guerrilla* was very high. These groups lost up to 32% of their guerrilla fighters as a result of desertion while the corresponding figure for groups of *armed neighbours* was only 10%.

The *armed neighbours* always retained the "village nicknames" and the local identities of their members. These would at times refer to families: los "Villenas", los "Chavicos", los "Pelaos"; at other times to kinship: "El Hijo del Machacado", "El Chato de la Pilar", "El de la Luque", "El Hijo del Cojo Ponce"; to profession: "Espartero", "Recobero", "El de las cabras", "Paco el Lechero"; or to physical characteristics: "El Tuerto", "El Cojo", "El Nariz", "El Porras", "Carasucia", "Boca Fea", "Carahermosa". In any case, most common were individual nicknames like "El Raspa", "Espantanubes", "Chamarra", "Boñiga", "Chanflute", "El Gibao", "Salsipuedes", "Patalete", "Cuarterón", "Cogollero", "Perejil", "Chorras", "Collares", "Culomojao", "Cencerro", "Chirri", "Ladilla", "Papas Fritas", "Bicarbonato", "Pezuño", "Olla Fría", "Cantaor", "Marranica", "Chorra", "Potaje", "Chorrohumo", "Pollito", "El Rata", "Puñalá", "Berraco", "El Bicho".

A native of village was a full-fledged member of the community from birth. Those who were not born in the village and had immigrated acquired the status as locals after being residents for various years. Even so, the community often used nicknames to indicate the difference and point to immigrants' place of origin. Pitt-Rivers has observed how neighbours who originally came from elsewhere were known as "el Gaditano" [the man from

Cádiz], "el Andaluz" [the Andalusian], or, as in his case, "el Inglés" [the Englishman].[37] This social differentiation can also be observed in the case of the guerrilla fighters. Firstly, members of local communities distinguished clearly between those guerrilla fighters who were natives – not only of the area but of their specific municipality, and those who were from the outside. Ángel Sánchez García, a peasant from Frigiliana – recalled in an interview how, on one morning in 1947, he ran into a group of guerrilla fighters from the mountains:

> I recognized Vicente, one of the Artabús brothers – that's the nickname they had – and one called Lomas, who came from the hamlet Acebuchal. The others were strangers. There was one from Torrox who was carrying a Russian machinegun, and the others had pistols.[38]

As the quote makes evident, two of the guerrilla fighters were considered to be local: one from the same municipality, Frigiliana, and another from El Acebuchal, a small hamlet in the mountains. The word *stranger* is applied to the rest of the fighters, including the man from Torrox, a village located about fourteen kilometres away. When guerrilla fighters came from more distant lands, the peasants stressed the difference even more. Ramón Vía, the first guerrilla leader to arrive from exile, had various *nom de guerre* but was known in the villages in the area as "El madrileño" as a result of his strong Castilian accent.[39] Locals made frequent reference to some guerrilla fighters' accents in statements made to the Civil Guard: "he had an accent that's not from around here", "he had a Castilian accent" and so on.[40] Ramón Vía came to the province of Malaga in a small boat from the city of Oran together with another ten guerrilla fighters, so when people spoke about them in the villages it was common to refer to the group as those who "came from Oran". But nicknames were used to mark differences even within the guerrillas. Occasionally these referred to other geographical locations, either because it was a fighters' place of origin or because he had lived there for many years: "El madrileño", "El bilbaíno", "El chileno", "El catalán", etc. It was also common to distinguish between villages in the local area: "Manuel de Alcázar", "El de Albodón", "Los Antequeranos", "Emilio el de Bayarque", "Rafaelillo de Lanjarón", "Culito de Salar", "Polopero", "Serafín de Cástaras", "Lozano de Lanjarón", "Rafaelillo de Calahorra", "El Viejo de la Peza", "Pepe el de Piñar", "Rafael el Malagueño", "Ramón el del Cenes", etc.

Identities in conflict

The clash of mentalities between *neighbours in arms*, attached to local environments, and the *modern guerrilla* was constant and even led to armed confrontations. In the preceding chapter I addressed the conflicts triggered by the unification processes initiated by the Agrupaciones guerrilleras. Now I will focus on the most serious cases, which clearly show how the conflict revolved around issues of space and territory, among other factors.

Above I outlined the origin and local character of the "hermanos Clares" group. Although they operated with complete independence, they were formally incorporated into the precarious Agrupación Guerrillera de Granada for approximately one year and a half (1946–1947). In 1947, when the AGG sought to incorporate them in practice as well as theory, "hermanos Clares" refused and continued to maintain their autonomy. The Agrupación never managed to establish a strong presence in the area. Locals preferred to join guerrillas from the area ("Yatero", "Clares", "Quero") rather than the Agrupación guerrillera. The guerrillas of *armed neighbours* became, despite their small size, organisations of serious competition and, in the view of the PCE, impediments to the transformation of the resistance.

Even so, the "hermanos Clares" and the AGG maintained a verbal agreement between 1947 and 1948. Units from the Agrupación could cross the mountains of Güejar Sierra but not carry out operations in the villages of that area. To the "hermanos Clares", this was *their* territory. The situation changed in January 1949. By then the AGG had over two hundred armed men in the mountains and decided to put an end to the veto imposed on them by a group of *armed neighbours* which at that moment consisted of no more than five guerrilla fighters.

On January 6th 1949, taking advantage of the Magi festivities (*Reyes Magos*), a messenger told the "hermanos Clares" group that the AGG planned various sabotages and an attack on the Civil Guard barracks four days later. They could join the operation or, if they preferred, hide. The five guerrilla fighters were surprised and upset by the news. These groups were very territorial and the "hermanos Clares" could not believe that the AGG were going to operate on *their* territory. The five guerrilla fighters had a meeting and decided, after eight long years of struggle, to give themselves up to the Civil Guard, to inform the authorities of the AGG's intentions and defend the village against an "alien party". According to a transcription of one of the guerrilla fighters' testimony, subsequently given before a court martial:

They got together to share ideas after a meeting had produced complete disagreement with an *alien* party which had arrived in the outskirts of the village of Quéntar. They decided to tell the Authorities of the Civil Guard Command what had happened, giving themselves up as a group and preparing to localise the *alien party* a few days later, in collaboration with the forces of public order . . . [41]

Such events prove the importance of territory and local identity to these guerrilla fighters. That was *their* field of action, an area belonging to *their* community and only they had the right to raid it. If someone from the outside tried to attack, they defended the community. This did not always happen, but in this case it is clear how local identities prevailed over political identities.

The five local guerrilla fighters pointed to the place where the AGG intended to commence the attack on the barracks and organised an ambush together with a number of Civil Guards, killing two guerrilla fighters and one go-between. The *Agrupación* had not respected the rules of the local guerrilla and this, though it may seem extreme and incomprehensible, was the response. From that moment, the fate of the five ex-guerrilla fighters would take different turns. They worked actively in a counterinsurgency brigade for several months, fighting the AGG on their own territory, but in October 1949, when all AGG units in the area had been eliminated, the consensus between the five men broke.

Félix "Clares" and "Espantanubes" opined that once the problem with the AGG had been resolved, they should return to mountains and resume the armed struggle. "Ponce", "Chorra" and "Cotorra", by contrast, thought that such a decision would be suicidal. Moreover, the Civil Guard had promised them that they would be rewarded for collaborating. Félix "Clares" y "Espantanubes" stuck to their decision nonetheless and deserted the counterinsurgency unit at the end of October 1949. Their new phase in the mountains did not last a week, however. Their three previous colleagues knew all their usual routes and hide-outs and on November 2nd 1949, they caught "Clares" and "Espantanubes" near Tocón de Quéntar. After nine years of fighting, of shared loss and misfortune, they suddenly stood face to face on opposing sides of the battlefields. They knew that the armed struggle against Franco's dictatorship had long lost any real meaning but each still had to choose the outcome of that defeat: death or the bitter taste of treason.

The bodies of Félix "Clares" y "Espantanubes" were sent to the municipal cemetery while "Ponce", "Chorra" and "Cotorra" continued to work with the counterinsurgency. In May 1950, once the problem of guerrilla activity in the area had been solved definitely, they were discharged and sent to prison. Their contributions to the death of twenty guerrilla fighters and one go-between gave them strongly reduced sentences. "Chorra" and "Cotorra" were freed at the beginning of 1951 after their case was dismissed. "Ponce" was sentenced to eight years and one day in prison but was released on probation in February 1953.[42]

It would be easy to judge, from the vantage point of today, those men who first gave their lives to fight a dictatorship and then took the lives of others just to save their own. Their actions cannot be justified, but in this context it is instructive also to recall the words written by Bertolt Brecht in his 1938 poem *To Those Born Later*:

> You who will emerge from the flood
> In which we have gone under,
> Remember,
> When you speak of our failings,
> The dark time too
> Which you have escaped.[43]

All men are responsible for their actions, but we should never ignore the context in which events took place. It is precisely in this regard that the totalitarianisms of the twentieth century show their cruellest and most modern tendency: to pressure men and women, desperate and fearful for their lives, to denounce, betray or even kill their own friends, relatives, and colleagues.

PART TWO

Anatomy of Resistance

Chapter 5

"I Swear on My Honour as a Guerrilla Fighter"
Discipline, recruitment and desertions

I swear, on my honour as a patriotic guerrilla fighter, to make every effort and sacrifice demanded by the struggle to reconquer Spain, my fatherland, independent and free (. . .). I swear to maintain discipline and faithfully carry out the orders of my superiors in the Guerrilla Army, the armed branch of the National Union.[1]

(Guerrilla oath in Spain, 1944. *National Union*)

The Agrupaciones guerrilleras adopted military symbols and rituals. Both resources were used to reinforce the political identity of the resistance externally as well as internally. The population could not be allowed to mistake the new guerrillas for criminals but neither were they to be confused with *neighbours in arms*. The Agrupaciones had to project a new image, the image of a true guerrilla army. Similarly, the guerrilla fighters who joined the Agrupaciones had to be conscious of their *new* position. They were no mere *neighbours in arms* but rather *real guerrilla fighters* who formed part of a national liberation movement.

   This chapter will focus on four fundamental aspects. Firstly, it aims to describe the structure of the Agrupaciones guerrilleras, which operated on military organisational principles. One of the immediate consequences of this transformation was the application of a strict disciplinary code within the *modern guerrilla*. The military structure and discipline of the *modern guerrilla* produced important differences compared with the *neighbours in arms*, organised as local groups with more relaxed codes of conduct. But, crucially, the new model of a *modern guerrilla* also insisted on new ways to dismiss guerrilla fighters from the rank and file. One of the most dramatic examples was the physical elimination (*ajustamiento*) of guerrilla members by the Agrupaciones guerrilleras themselves. However, as the following analysis will show, this was not the only practice to demonstrate important differences between *neighbours in arms* and the *modern guerrilla*.

Symbols and rituals

The "Pledge of Allegiance" was one of the new rituals adopted by the Agrupaciones guerrilleras. All guerrilla fighters joining an Agrupación had to go through a *rite of passage* similar to that found in conventional armies. The Chief of Staff and the different units comprising the AGG typically had regular meetings at their base camp every six months. On these occasions units commonly introduced new recruit, who had to take the oath before the Chief of Staff.

The most widespread formulation was the one found in the epigraph of this chapter, introduced by Jesús Monzón in 1944, when he created the JSUN, and later adopted, with some modifications, by the Agrupaciones guerrilleras. Once the oath had been taken, the ceremony continued and the new recruit was given his nom de guerre and guerrilla uniform. Manuel Gómez, a guerrilla fighter in the AGG, recalled how he was given "a uniform consisting of one pair of corduroy trousers, one khaki-coloured shirt, one t-shirt, one white shirt, one brown winter coat and a beret".[2] Material conditions did not allow all guerrilla fighters to have a complete uniform, but they had to wear something which would distinguish them from other groups in the mountains and identify them with the Agrupación. They usually wore an armband with the colours of the Republican flag and the initials E.N.G. (Ejército Nacional Guerrillero, National Guerrilla Army) while officers wore a red emblem stating their rank in the Guerrilla Army.[3]

The adoption of military rituals and symbols in the Agrupaciones guerrilleras was not a matter of mere formality. The PCE was the only political organisation with a clearly defined project regarding the guerrilla movement; hence the internal analysis regarding the state of the armed struggle in Spain between 1939 and 1943 and the proposal to transform the resistance from 1944. The project carried out by the PCE was very similar to the process of militarising the popular militias during the Spanish Civil War. Resistance would only be successful, the party repeated incessantly, if its forces adhered to the principles of a Single Command, Unity and Discipline.[4] Such rhetoric clearly resembled that used by communist leaders during the war: in 1937 it was the Mixed Brigades that were to transform "the people in arms" into a genuine Popular Army; now the Agrupaciones guerrilleras would transform *neighbours in arms* into a genuine National Guerrilla Army.

The new organisational model devised for the resistance was rejected by a significant number of local guerrillas, just as the Mixed Brigades had been viewed with suspicion by many popular militias. The fundamental differences between the two processes were the coercive capacity of the transforming agent and the resources of mobilisation. The militarisation of the popular militias was undertaken by the state, a weak state at first, but one which gradually regained its control over the levers of power. On the other hand, the militarisation of the resistance was impelled only by the PCE, a PCE which did not have access to state resources and even lacked a liberated area from which to work.

The PCE's transformative project faced the external resistance of dozens of groups of *armed neighbours*. However, this should not be our sole analytical concern. Organisational methods and tough military discipline produced conflict within the Agrupaciones too, which led to a high number of desertions and phenomena such as the *ajusticiamientos* (executions carried out as punishment for disciplinary offences). The historiography has foregrounded the mobilisation of dozens of people in the new guerrilla army but has paid scant attention to later processes of demobilisation or the various ways in which guerrilla fighters were excluded from the resistance movement. The fact that the militarisation process simultaneously accelerated the two antagonistic processes of recruitment *and* desertion is key to understanding the impact and limited growth of the resistance in Spain.

The creation of a guerrilla army

The PCE sought to create a National Guerrilla Army in Spain. Wherever a nucleus of armed resistance was found, PCE leaders tried to organise and unify local groups, subsume them under a single command and impose strict discipline. These mottos guided the creation of Agrupaciones in a number of places in Spain. To a greater or lesser extent, they all adopted a military structure, although the reorganisation was undertaken with varying degrees of success.

In eastern Andalusia, there were, as mentioned, at least sixty-four guerrilla groups, of which forty-seven corresponded largely to the *neighbours in arms* model. This becomes evident when analysing their organisational structures, which were based on primary groups. Friendship, kinship and neighbourhood loyalties tended to be the dominant factors producing internal cohesion, which had characteristics similar to that of *cuadrillas*. The groups were structured horizontally, with few, if any, hierarchical levels of command. Leadership was based on charisma and decisions were made on the basis of consensus achieved in assembly meetings or on the instructions of the leader. After 1945, when the first Agrupaciones were created, some of these groups joined the new guerrilla structures directed by the PCE, although the majority retained their independence and autonomy. What was the situation for local groups which fit the category of *modern guerrilla*? Did they all adopt a military structure? Did they all join the new Agrupaciones guerrilleras?

Before 1945 there were nine local groups which corresponded to the *modern guerrilla* model in eastern Andalusia. Their internal organisation differed little, in fact, from that of groups of *armed neighbours*: a majority was formed on the basis of family and neighbourhood relations, they tended to have a horizontal structure and the leadership role was largely based on charisma. The fundamental difference was that these characteristics were not rooted in the nature of the group (as was the case with *neighbours in arms*) but rather in the conditions of the armed struggle in the first period. Their ambition was always to transcend the geographical limitations of their work and build national connections which would allow them to fight the dictatorship effectively. For this reason their response to the Agrupaciones guerrilleras and the leaders returning to Spain from exile was very different to that of typical groups of *armed neighbours*.

In regions where geographical factors made it possible to maintain direct contact with the Agrupaciones, local *modern guerrilla* groups ("Rubio de Brecia", "Cuarterón", "Collares" and López Quero) joined the new guerrilla organisations without difficulty. In regions where they were more isolated, local *modern guerrilla* groups tried to create their own Agrupaciones guerrilleras. In the province of Cádiz and in western Malaga, the group led by "Manolo el Rubio" first formed the Agrupación Stalingrado and later, together with Bernabé López Calle, the Agrupación Fermín Galán. In the province of Almeria similar efforts were made to create an Agrupación de Guerrilleros de Almería, although the rifts between anarchists and communists complicated the process. Finally in eastern Malaga the groups led by "Rubio de Brecia", "Casero" and "Cuarterón" also tried, unsuccessfully, to establish a new guerrilla organisation.

None of the Agrupaciones which emerged on the initiative of local *modern guerrilla* groups but failed to secure the collaboration and direct help of communist leaders returning from exile (Agrupación Stalingrado, Agrupación Fermín Galán and Agrupación de Guerrilleros de Almería) managed to transform their organisation in any significant way. Despite the new nomenclature, their structure remained largely unchanged, and so they cannot really be counted as a new kind of guerrilla organisation.

In eastern Andalusia there were three Agrupaciones guerrilleras organised by communist units returning from exile: the AGM (eastern Málaga), the 2nd Agrupación (Jaén and Ciudad Real) and the AGG (eastern Málaga and Granada). All these formed part of the National Guerrilla Army and successfully adopted a military structure and discipline, very different from the rest of the *modern guerrilla* and, of course, the *neighbours in arms*. But the consolidation of a guerrilla army with an effective military structure was a slow and incremental process, beset with enormous difficulties. The development can be illustrated with reference to changes taking place in the AGM and AGG. As outlined in Chapter 3, the AGM began the militarisation process showing a number of weaknesses, while the AGG, under the direction of "Roberto", became the culmination of the guerrilla project in Andalusia.

The AGM (known in the first period as the 6th Battalion) was created in November 1944, after the landing of ten guerrilla fighters led by Ramon Vía. Despite initial difficulties, by the spring of 1946 the Agrupación had a Chief of Staff and four units in the mountains, as well as the "Musketeers of the Plains" in the provincial capital.[5] However, the arrest of the AGM's military leaders – Ramón Vía in November 1945 and Alfredo Cabello in May 1946 – caused the "Musketeers of the Plains" to disband and put a brake on the growth of the Agrupación as a whole.[6]

The transformation of the AGM arrived with the new leadership of "Roberto", once he was relocated to the mountains. At the end of 1945, the Regional Committee of Andalusia appointed him as military chief of the Andalusian Guerrilla Army (Ejército Guerrillero de Andalucía, EGA), a fictitious structure which in fact only included the units enlisted in the primitive AGM (6th Battalion). As described in Chapter 3, his mission was to liaise with local guerrilla groups in the provinces of Málaga, Granada and Almería, a mission which had little success. During this period, he worked from Málaga and Seville. In October 1946, however, the national leadership and the Regional Committee obliged him to lead the embryonic guerrilla army – that is, the AGM – from the mountains. One of his first decisions was to realise the dream of Ramón Vía by extending the units' operations to the province of Granada. For this reason, at the beginning of 1947, the Agrupación changed its name to Agrupación Guerrillera de Granada-Málaga or, simply, Agrupación Guerrillera de Granada (AGG).[7]

The AGG adopted a proper military structure and organisation from 1947. The Agrupación was then composed of a Chief of Staff, assembled by the guerrilla's military chief, General "Roberto", and by four guerrilla fighters in charge of logistics, internal discipline, intelligence, and agitation and propaganda. A unit composed of ten men, known as the Liaison Group, was responsible for the protection and personal safety of the Chief of Staff. The AGG started with two battalions: the 6th, which operated as far as the eastern parts of Málaga province, and the 7th, operating in western parts of Granada province. In May 1948, the 8th battalion was created, when the local group led by "Polopero" managed to re-establish contact with the AGG. The new addition limited its operations to the southern slopes of the Sierra Nevada and the Granada coastline (Appendix: Table 5).[8]

The leadership of the battalions was delegated to a group of senior staff, led by a commander and a lieutenant (Appendix: Table 6). Every battalion was divided into companies and these, in turn, were divided into units. The 6th and 7th battalion each had two companies, which were composed of two units (Appendix: Table 7). Every unit contained ten guerrilla fighters, although the actual numbers varied according to the numbers of guerrilla fighters in the mountains. The leadership of the unit fell to a lieutenant or captain while a sergeant performed the role of an assisting officer. The rest of the unit was composed of the troops, that is, by the guerrilla rank and file.[9] The appendix includes an organigram of the AGG at its strongest moment, that is, between 1948 and 1950, when the organisation had incorporated over 200 guerrilla fighters to its ranks.

A study of the military structure of the Agrupaciones guerrilleras and their chain of command permits analysis of the strategy employed by the PCE to implement their model of resistance. One of the issues highlighted above revolves around the important difference between locals and outsiders in any given geographical context. Guerrilla fighters from other regions were rarely present in groups of *armed neighbours* and local *modern guerrilla* groups while the Agrupaciones included the majority of guerrilla fighters who were not local to the area where they were based. The relatively extensive military and political training of these "outsiders", in combination with their often greater loyalty to the PCE, meant that they tended to occupy most leadership positions in the Agrupaciones, while indigenous guerrilla fighters were found in mid- and low-ranking positions and, above all, the rank and file. The appendix contains three tables (5, 6 and 7) showing data relating to guerrilla fighters with officer's status within the AGM and the AGG, ordered according to rank: 1) organisational leaders, 2) Chief of Staff and senior leadership and 3) unit leaders. The data includes the post and/or highest officer rank of each guerrilla fighter, the dates when he occupied this post, the Agrupación to which he belonged and whether or not he was indigenous to the area where he was stationed.

The stark division between the top leadership, which was mostly non-local, and lower levels of command, mostly occupied by local guerrilla members, clearly demonstrates the PCE's desire to control all aspects of the guerrilla movement from above. However, it also indicates an awareness in the party that the Agrupaciones guerrilleras could not be effectively deployed without the presence of the most political of local guerrilla fighters in their officer ranks. It was necessary to achieve a certain balance between centrally appointed guerrilla leaders, in whom the PCE placed their greatest trust, and indigenous guerrilla members, even though this ambition could not be allowed to override one of the basic ambitions of the Agrupaciones: to eradicate the *localist* tendency underpinning the passivity of indigenous guerrilla fighters.

As mentioned previously, one of the means most commonly used to excise *localism* was to break up local groups and place their members in different units. The aim was to break the solidarity of primary groups and instead reinforce internal cohesion through soldierly *camaraderie* and political affinities. The ability to separate friends and neighbours rested largely on the coercive capacity of each group. In fact, the local modern guerrilla tried to implement this strategy but without success. However, the Agrupaciones guerrilleras, with their internal disciplinary codes and courts, were in a better position to enforce this division of local groups immediately.

The AGG provides an exceptional example of this procedure. With the aim of eradicating *localism*, "Roberto" continually altered the composition and operational area of his units. Approximately every six months, the Chief of Staff gathered all units of the three battalions in one of their camps.[10] The Chief of Staff then handed out new instructions, evaluated the progress of every unit and reorganised the groups. There were at least five general AGG meetings of this kind between 1947 and 1949.[11] In addition, the senior leadership of every battalion also changed unit compositions regularly.

This strategy was ultimately counter-productive for the Agrupaciones and caused a series of unforeseen problems. One of the fundamental characteristics of irregular warfare derives from the mobility of guerrilla groups, that is, their ability to stage surprise attacks and disappear once they have been carried out. The success of this tactic hinges on two conditions: a geographical space which, as a result of its particular characteristics, cannot be easily controlled, on the one hand, and detailed knowledge of the terrain, on the other. Groups of *armed neighbours* and local *modern guerrillas* could always make use of such advantages. Their members tended to act only within their own municipalities. The Agrupaciones also had a very high number of locally recruited guerrilla fighters, but the policy was to separate them from their place of origin in order to avoid *localism* and passivity. How, then, did they resolve the problem of mobility and knowledge of terrain?

The fundamental resource used by the Agrupaciones was that of the *prácticos*: local guerrilla fighters who were used as guides in the mountains. Each unit, formed by approximately ten men, was required to include one person who knew the designated area of action. In fact, the figure of the *práctico* dates back to the first landing on the Andalusian coast: the three expeditions, made by a contingent of mostly non-Andalusian guerrilla fighters, included a *práctico* among their members.[12] Their work was crucial, not only for the success of operations but also the very survival of the group. The problem was that the determination to remove indigenous guerrilla fighters from their place of origin reached such extremes that it occasionally diminished the competence of the *prácticos* and thereby also the ability and efficacy of the Agrupaciones. A farm hand who had been kidnapped by an AGG unit offered a revealing description in this regard to the Civil Guard: "there was one who was called the *práctico* and not even he knew the terrain very well because the man who declared himself captain scolded him for choosing bad routes and made it clear that they did not know their way around those mountains".[13]

Such situations may not have occurred frequently, but neither were they exceptional. Alfredo Cabello despaired in one of his last reports. He had gone to the mountains to visit one of the AGM units but no one knew the territory. The fate of the group depended entirely on the *prácticos* but these, too, seemed unfamiliar with the area. For two weeks they were lost, aimlessly wandering the mountains. They struggled to find food and shelter and even had an unexpected encounter with the Civil Guard. The *prácticos*, Alfredo Cabello concluded, "are always looking for excuses (. . .) they talk a lot, promise a lot, but ultimately they fail to deliver".[14]

Another important consequence of the determination to break up primary groups could be seen in the high number of desertions in the Agrupaciones guerrilleras. "Roberto", as the supreme commander of the AGG, introduced various measures to minimise desertions among his ranks. The first, implemented at the beginning of 1947, was a training period preceding the "Pledge of Allegiance". For six weeks, young recruits received military and, above all, political training, designed to reinforce internal cohesion through a "raising of political awareness" which would disrupt the peasantry's "localist" tendencies. Once the young recruit had completed the training period, he graduated and became an authentic guerrilla fighter.[15]

However, the initiative met with little success. Consequently, seeing that the "raising of political awareness" produced meagre results and that locals continued to desert frequently, "Roberto" considered it necessary to adopt further methods to halt this trend. When the Chief of Staff or the unit leader had doubts regarding a candidate, the conventional *rite of passage* – the "Pledge of Allegiance" – was turned into a real test of commitment. In order to prove his fidelity and loyalty to the guerrilla, the young recruit had to eliminate an enemy selected by the Agrupación. The chosen victim tended to belong to the local community, be it a Falangist, a "traitor", or a Civil Guard, although there were also cases of aggression against military figures. Considering its seriousness, this violent version of the "Pledge of Allegiance" had three aims: 1) to break the bonds of local solidarity which generated passivity; 2) to stem the flow of desertions (few guerrilla fighters who were guilty of homicide gave themselves up to the authorities) and 3) to avoid infiltration by informers.

The violent "Pledge of Allegiance" was an exception to the conventional model, but it is still necessary to analyse some examples of this practice in order to understand both its procedures and the strategies devised by candidates who had to adhere to it. Antonio Arellano sought to join the AGG at the beginning of 1947, but the Chief of Staff was suspicious of his motives: during the Spanish Civil War he had voluntarily enlisted in the Falangist militias and then fought with Franco's army for the remainder of the conflict.[16] "Roberto" summoned the aspiring guerrilla fighter for an interview. After this meeting, he requested a report from "Paco Jurite", an AGG member hailing from the same village as Antonio. "Paco Jurite" confirmed that Antonio had been a volunteer with the Falangist militias, but insisted that he was a "good guy" and that he could be trusted. "Roberto" was not persuaded by the report, especially since he feared the influence of dangerous "community loyalties". If Antonio wanted to join the AGG he had to prove his loyalty, and to do this he had to eliminate someone from his own village. The potential recruit spent eleven days at the AGG base camp. At the end of January he escaped and surrendered to the Civil Guard. This aspiring guerrilla fighter was not an informer, but the death of a neighbour seemed to him to be an excessive price to pay to join the resistance.

Around the same time, José Álvarez, too, sought to enlist in the AGG. José had an extensive history as an activist. In February 1945, he was arrested for being implicated in a "communist plot" and from February 1946, at which point he had been released, he acted as a go-between for the guerrilla. Despite his background, the Chief of Staff stated that he could only join the AGG if he killed a neighbour from his village, Felix Castán. Felix Castán had operated as a go-between for a number of years, but had recently been caught by the Civil Guard. After being subjected to torture, he had revealed some of the guerrilla's hiding places and this information had later caused the death of two AGG fighters. Felix Castán had become a traitor and the AGG were determined to execute him. On February 27th 1947, José Álvarez returned to his village, waited by the entrance to a bar, and when Felix Castán had finished playing a game of cards, he kidnapped him and took him to the mountains. That same night, José Álvarez killed

Felix Castán in front of a group of guerrilla fighters, and from that moment he was a member of the AGG, taking "Pascual" as his nom de guerre. [17]

In August 1950, four residents of Salar (Granada) decided to join the AGG. Their loyalty was beyond doubt: the four men had acted as go-betweens for years and had various relatives in the guerrilla, but the number of desertions was so high in this period that the aspiring members were given a practical test nonetheless. An AGG unit took them to the house of a Falangist farmhand in Salar, Emilio Trescastro, whom they were instructed to kill. The four men then lynched their neighbour and from that moment formed part of the AGG. [18]

However, young candidates would occasionally refuse to complete this rite of passage or else invent ways to trick the guerrilla. In July 1950, another three young men from the village of Salar applied to join the guerrilla. [19] Two of them were cousins and were related to Francisco Ruiz, a lieutenant in the AGG, while the third one had a brother in the guerrilla. The leader of the local AGG unit was informed of the their intention, but, in the face of constant desertions, decided to adhere to the procedure advocated by "Roberto". If they wanted to join the AGG the three men had to prove their loyalty by killing a Falangist field ranger from their own village. To facilitate this act, the guerrilla lent them a pistol and a hunting rifle. The three aspiring guerrilla fighters kidnapped the ranger and took him to an isolated spot in the mountains. They wanted to join the guerrilla but no one was ready to kill their neighbour. To avoid the choice between rejection and murder, they decided instead to trick the guerrilla unit leader. They fired twice into the air and told the ranger to run. That same night they met the leader of the local AGG unit and told him that the ranger had managed to escape just as they were about to execute him. The leader accepted their excuses and allowed the three youths to join the AGG despite their failure.

Three months later, on November 11th 1950, one of the three young men from Salar deserted from the guerrilla, surrendered to the Civil Guard, and began to work with a counterinsurgency group. Another of the three was arrested three weeks later, after which he too joined the counterinsurgency. Four days later, on February 10th, the third member of the group deserted. Such losses were very common in the Agrupaciones guerrilleras, despite the strict disciplinary measures imposed. Indeed, not only did the disciplinary measures fail to halt the flow of desertions; they sometimes increased it.

Discipline in the guerrilla army

A guerrilla army had to be disciplined. Without discipline, the resistance would never achieve victory, according to the oft-repeated slogans of the PCE and the Agrupaciones guerrilleras.[20] The emphasis on discipline was undoubtedly the main reason why they acquired a hegemonic position in the anti-Francoist resistance. A strictly disciplined environment was common to all units and could be observed at the most senior levels of the guerrilla hierarchy. A number of leaders in Andalusia were given posts in the guerrilla as a punishment imposed by the national leadership and all attended to their duties without protest. Alfredo Cabello, accused of being a *monzonista*, was sent to the mountains to redeem his sins. "Roberto", accused of negligence after the death of Ramón Vía and the arrest of Cabello, was ordered to lead the guerrilla from the mountains as a result. Vía himself was disappointed by the fact that he did not recover the leadership of the AGM after his prison escape but nonetheless accepted the National Committee's directives.[21] No one could question the chain of command or the slogans of the party; all resistance members had to execute the orders of their superiors with the outmost discipline. "He who begins to question the party is no longer a communist" stated one of the fundamental principles guiding communist activists at the time.[22]

All Agrupaciones had an internal Code of Discipline which regulated guerrilla fighters' conduct. The first code was formulated by the JSUN, whose model served as a basis for later versions. The Agrupaciones guerrilleras also had Disciplinary Councils dealing with oversights and minor breaches; more serious cases were handled by the Chief of Staff, the highest juridical authority in the sierra. Guerrilla fighters had to obey "without retort or amends" and show their leaders absolute respect. Such disciplinary measures were applied when the Agrupaciones guerrilleras acquired coherent military structures and a powerful coercive capacity. In Andalusia, the AGM and the 2ⁿᵈ Agrupación made significant progress in this respect, but the highest degree of internal discipline was achieved in the AGG. The regulations of the Agrupaciones not only demanded obedience and respect for superiors but also regulated various aspects of daily life, including sexual relations and alcohol consumption, two habits which were widespread in the anti-Francoist guerrilla before the arrival of the PCE and central to a significant number of conflicts. Once again there are parallels with the Spanish Civil War. During the war, the military leadership anxiously observed the high consumption of alcohol among soldiers and problems derived from a "disorderly" sex life. Venereal diseases claimed a significant number of casualties while excessive alcohol consumption diminished the fighting capacity of the units. The Popular Army tried to combat such behaviour, which had become more entrenched as the discipline of popular militias was not very strict, through various propaganda campaigns and disciplinary measures. The corresponding development in the anti-Francoist guerrilla was quite similar.

Groups of *armed neighbours* and some local *modern guerrillas* had a fairly lax concept of discipline. There was no kind of regulation in relation to alcohol, which meant that it was commonly consumed. Some guerrilla fighters occasionally returned to their villages to participate in local festivities. But the greatest danger arose in connection with parties organised in isolated farmhouses, in brothels, or even in bars located in working-class slums – parties which involved, on occasion, severe drunkenness and could be easily detected by the authorities.[23] Several guerrilla fighters, such as "Hojarasquilla" and the members of the group led by Velázquez Murillo, were arrested or killed as a result of such events.[24] *Armed neighbours* also returned with some frequency to their homes in order to visit their families, and on more than one occasion their wives and girlfriends fell pregnant – to the surprise of the authorities. They also paid regular visits to various "lovers". Guerrilla fighters cultivated a heroic image as strong, masculine, armed men living outside the law, a powerfully seductive image at the time. The most extraordinary case in Andalusia was that of Rafael Castillo Clares. A man of widespread fame as a late-night reveller and a womaniser, he had at least four lovers in the mountains, two of whom even joined the guerrilla in order to follow him wherever he went.[25]

These kinds of behaviour, which were very common among *armed neighbours* and the local *modern guerrilla*, exposed guerrilla members to increased risks and pushed relatives and social support networks into the spotlight of the authorities. This was the fundamental reason why the Agrupaciones guerrilleras tried to eradicate such behaviour. One of the first measures adopted by the AGG was the limitation of alcohol consumption among the men: "It is strictly forbidden to drink excessive amounts of wine or spirits; alcohol is permitted as long as we can perform our tasks normally and as long as we do not give the enemy the slightest chance of taking advantage of our insobriety", said one of the articles in the AGG regulations.[26] The regulations also forbade women from visiting the mountains and guerrilla fighters from visiting their homes while any kind of contact with a brothel was prohibited. A breach of this disciplinary code led immediately to a court martial before the Chief of Staff.

The strict discipline of the Agrupaciones guerrilleras had one clear effect: an increase in the number of desertions. Old members of groups of *armed neighbours*, used to more flexible routines, decided to leave the Agrupaciones guerrilleras. The example of Rafael "Clares" is illustrative. One of the first conflicts to arise after this group had joined the initial structure of the AGG related to the presence of women in the mountains. The Chief of Staff refused to allow Rafael "Clares" and his colleagues in the mountains to live with their lovers, but the group ignored the constant warnings. Their insubordinate attitude then prompted the Chief of Staff to take the drastic decision to assassinate both Rafael "Clares" and his partner at the time, Carmen "La Canela". The ultimate responsibility for this act rested with "El Sevilla", the Head of Chief of Staff, although testimonies differ with regard to the identity of the actual killer. Some sources suggest this was "El Sevilla" himself while others claim it was one of his subordinates. In any case, Rafael "Clares", although badly wounded, survived the assassination attempt. Carmen was less fortunate. The death of Carmen and the attempt on Rafael's life caused the "Clares" group's definititive break with the AGG and the beginning of hostile relations between the two guerrilla organisations.[27]

The case of Francisco López "Polopero" shows how these conflicts not only arose with members from groups of *armed neighbours* but also members from local *modern guerrilla* groups. "Polopero" was sixteen when the Spanish Civil War started. Born in Rubite and a resident of Polopos (Granada), he enlisted in the Popular Army in 1938 and reached the rank of lieutenant. At the end of the war, he was arrested, sent to a concentration camp and prosecuted. After being found not guilty, he was sent to a Workers' Battalion to do his military service. He returned to Polopos after leaving the military in 1945 and began to work as a carpenter, but in mid-1946 he made contact with the Provincial Committee in Granada. Shortly after, the leaders of the AGG, "Tarbes" and Ramiro Fuentes Ochoa, asked him to organise the PCE in various villages in the province. At the beginning of 1947, after the arrest of both leaders, "Polopero" decided to flee to the mountains and assemble a small guerrilla group. Between January 1947 and May 1948, when he established contact with "Roberto" and joined the AGG, his group operated independently in the area of the Alpujarras.[28]

"Polopero" became a member of the Chief of Staff, commandant of the AGG and leader of the 8th Battalion. However, his relationship with the guerrilla leadership was always tense. Despite being "one of the most intelligent communists to join the guerrilla",[29] according to the lieutenant coronel of the Civil Guard, Eulogio Limia Pérez, he was given a disciplinary sentence by the Chief of Staff in July 1948. Problems with discipline and a disastrous encounter with the Civil Guard prompted his demotion to captain and the loss of command of the 8th Battalion.[30] Three years later, a new conflict arose between "Polopero" and the Chief of Staff. As Miguel Salado, another member of the AGG, explained: "Relationships with women were not allowed [in the mountains], but Paco had been in the Granada Agrupación [Agrupación de Granada] where no one paid any attention to that. When the Chief of Staff was out of reach, Paco tended to look for women. This gave rise to arguments".[31]

The final straw was an incident involving the daughter of one of the guerrilla's go-betweens. "Polopero's" unit had come to Órgiva (Granada) and while they waited for the go-between to bring some supplies, Paco ["Polopero"] slapped the young girl's bottom. One of the guerrilla fighters, "Jiménez", saw the incident and reported it to the lieutenant. Guerrilla fighters had to treat women, as well as the go-betweens, with the utmost respect. Soon afterwards, the senior leadership of the 8th Battalion met and agreed on the need for disciplinary measures to be taken. The problem was that the 8th Battalion had momentarily lost contact with the Chief of Staff, the only organisational body authorised to call a court martial. Thus, it was decided to postpone the trial until contact could be re-established. Nonetheless, one immediate disciplinary measure was taken and the offender was demoted from the rank of captain to the rank of assistant lieutenant. Francisco López "Polopero" had been a member of the Chief of Staff himself and knew how far punishments could go. With this in mind, he deserted in November 1951 and gave himself up to the authorities, with whom he then collaborated as part of a counterinsurgency unit.[32]

The Agrupaciones guerrilleras insisted that all resistance members accept their individual responsibility in maintaining internal discipline. The Agrupación took precedence over individuals and the survival of the group depended on the diligence and discipline of each guerrilla fighter. From this perspective, it is possible to understand why "Jiménez" followed unit protocol and reported the offence committed by "Polopero". In this regard it should also be noted that, even though the Agrupaciones adopted a military structure, the PCE sought not to create a conventional army but rather a "class" army, as its internal documents show. The chain of command was necessary to guarantee efficacy, but, ultimately, everyone was equal, comrades with the same rights and duties: "It is crucial to understand that our discipline is not a militarist or a despotic one, as in any other Army of castes. It is discipline based on reason and consciousness, imposed by oneself (. . .) the leaders we obey are our comrades".[33]

On the basis of this premise, the Agrupaciones guerrilleras institutionalised a procedure aimed at spreading unit discipline *from below*: the individual and collective practice of self-criticism, which was widespread in communist parties at the time. The most abundant documentation related to this concerns the Agrupación Guerrillera de Levante-Aragón: a result of its close contact with the PCE leadership in exile. However, the same process could be observed in all Agrupaciones guerrilleras.[34] The units had regular meetings in which each member publicly criticised his own personal conduct and that of the group.[35] The Chief of Staff also requested private reports of the same kind. These procedures helped to maintain strict internal discipline but also served as a means to denounce colleagues for personal reasons or to initiate political or ideological purges. Several guerrilla fighters were court martialled, sentenced and executed after being accused of "treason", "demoralisation" or "provocation" in these meetings. It is not an exaggeration to say that fear and panic eventually came to dominate the atmosphere of some units, generating mistrust and suspicion among its members. As the AGG commandant Antonio Jurado Martín stated, the terror became so pervasive that no one dared to oppose an execution. Whoever did so "would have been thrown into the grave", regardless of rank.[36] The logic of violence ended up infiltrating the Agrupaciones and to disrupt its increasingly uncontrollable dynamic entailed a great risk.

The Agrupaciones' Code of Discipline applied the death penalty in the most serious cases, those involving "high treason". Such serious offences included flight before the enemy; mission failures which put the survival of the unit in danger; surrender to the enemy or attempts to persuade a unit to surrender collectively; attempts to foment disunity or undermine morale; and desertion or appropriation of money or other capital goods.[37]

The documents which refer to *ajusticiamientos* (executions) in the resistance are confusing and contradictory. In fact, they deal with one of the most widespread taboos in the anti-Francoist guerrilla, which means that testimonies in this regard enter an obscure and little known area. Nevertheless, in the provinces of Málaga and Granada, this study identifies twenty-four *ajusticiamientos*, to which another three executions might be added, although the information in these cases is less reliable (Appendix: Table 8).

Francoist literature made use of the dominant stereotypes of the period to explain the *ajusticiamientos*: bloodthirsty communist leaders with an obsession for internal purges. Other parts of the historiography have paid scant attention to the problem. The author of the present study believes that internal executions became part of guerrilla practice when four fundamental factors combined: (1) weak internal cohesion, (2) a strong political culture favouring internal purges, (3) powerful group capacity for coercion, and 4) exposure to high levels of external repression.

Internal *ajusticiamientos* were only carried out by Agrupaciones guerrilleras. Groups of *neighbours in arms*, revolving around primary group relations, achieved a high level of internal cohesion and any kind of discord consequently tended to be addressed by other means. The local *modern guer-rilla* may have experienced certain problems of cohesion when trying to integrate other residents of the area but their coercive capacity was also limited. By comparison, the Agrupaciones guerrilleras suffered the greatest problems with internal cohesion. The deliberate break up of primary groups, the rigid disciplinary regime, and the ideological conflict greatly weakened internal unity. The guerrilla fighters sent from abroad by the PCE leadership were also shaped by a political culture placing great value on the internal purge. What separated different Agrupaciones such as the AGM and the AGG was the coercive capacity. Instructions and internal reports relating to the AGM demonstrate that measures such as the *ajusticiamientos* were part of its disciplinary programme, but, as a result of its embryonic state, it was not always able to implement them. On the other hand, the AGG, having over two hundred fighters in the mountains and the struc-ture of an army, acquired the strength needed to implement measures of this kind. Thus, the AGG executed twenty-three guerrilla members while the corresponding figure for the AGM was only one. The dates are also revealing: twenty-two of the twenty-four executions took place between 1948 and 1951, when state repression against the guerrilla reached its peak. Intensified pressure from the authorities no doubt prompted stricter disci-pline in the guerrilla, which, in turn, led to increased use of radical measures to maintain it.

Establishing the real motives for an *ajusticiamiento* is always a complex task. The declarations of surviving guerrilla fighters to the Civil Guard or researchers become more diffuse when this subject is approached. The responses vary and indicate different and even contradictory feelings: guilt, remorse, justification, unwillingness to accept responsibility, or pride in having fulfilled one's duty. Moreover, the *ajusticiamiento* tended not to be due to a single motive; rather it occurred for of a diverse set of reasons. When the motives for seventeen executions are given in Table 8 in the Appendix, only the most important reasons repeated in documents and testimonies are listed.

Executions resulting from internal dissidence were occasionally related to the conflict between *armed neighbours* and the Agrupaciones guerrilleras. The assassinations of "Costeño" and "Tejero",[38] like the attempted assassi-nation of Rafael "Clares", were measures taken to discipline the most fractious leaders of groups of *armed neighbours* and set an example to other guerrilla fighters. However, there were also cases where executions had strong ideological overtones. The assassinations of Francisco López and Francisco Nieto, for example, seem to be related to their socialist member-ship and their criticisms of the Chief of Staff.[39] In the case of Ramón

Castilla, a distinguished member of the PCE, there are some indications that his criticism of the guerrilla leadership was the cause of his death, although it is more likely that it was due to an act of banditry.[40]

The eradication of banditry in the resistance movement and Spanish society as a whole was one of the principal objectives of the Agrupaciones guerrilleras. The resistance movement had a profoundly political character and actions involving crime could cause confusion and damage the prestige of the guerrilla. For this reason, guerrilla leaders would resort to executions to set examples and abolish such practices for good. The death of Alfonso Navarro was a consequence of a robbery of 5,000 pesetas which his unit committed so that he could send the loot to his family.[41] The offence of Ramón Castilla and Francisco García, executed in 1949, was even more serious: after deserting they carried out a kidnapping claiming to still be part of the AGG.[42]

Desertions also played havoc with the anti-Francoist guerrilla. The main problem was not so much the loss of personnel as the information which deserters may give to government forces and their subsequent participation in counterinsurgency units. For this reason, the death penalty was introduced as a means of reducing the number of desertions. Even so, it has only been possible to identify four instances where this penalty was actually applied. Missions aiming to localise and execute an old guerrilla member were dangerous and could only be carried out in exceptional cases.[43]

Further motives for applying the death penalty were, once again, related to matters of discipline. Article 9 of the Guerrilla Code of Discipline prescribed the death penalty for attempts to demoralise a unit, offences which led to the execution of Francisco Centurión and Antonio Corpas "Braulio". The former had suffered from depression after the death of his brother, who was also a guerrilla fighter, while the latter wanted to return home to look after his new-born daughter.[44] Victoriano Sánchez "Braulio", a surviving member of the AGG, admitted in an interview years later that "we killed 'Braulio' for an act of minor stupidity".[45]

Similar disciplinary breaches applied in other known cases. "Tarbes" was executed by the AGG after being arrested by the Civil Guard and recruited as an informer. Enrique Moreno was accused of the same crime, although the real circumstances of his "treason" are not known.[46] A somewhat different case was that of Antonio Platero, who was executed for having a relationship with a woman in his village, even though all contact with women was prohibited in the AGG.[47]

The most common method used when executing both internal and external enemies was hanging. This process had a powerful symbolic charge, but it must also be remembered that the guerrillas struggled to procure sufficient quantities of arms and munitions and therefore preferred to save their provisions for confrontations with the authorities.

The disciplinary regime of Agrupaciones guerrilleras had a complex and contradictory impact on the development of the resistance. It certainly strengthened the anti-Francoist guerrilla but it also generated significant conflicts and internal ruptures. This chapter concludes with an analysis of guerrilla members' time in the mountains and discusses different ways of leaving the resistance, matters closely related to those of discipline.

Duration of individual participation in the resistance

Existing studies have unwittingly projected a distorted image of the armed anti-Francoist resistance. The stereotype is that of a young peasant who fought Franco's dictatorship for a decade. The key role played by young men and the peasantry is highlighted in the first chapter, but, to what extent did guerrilla fighters remain in the resistance for long periods?

Forty-five percent of resistance members in Andalusia stayed in the mountains for less than one year and only ten percent remained for longer than five years. The remaining forty-five percent stayed between one and five years. There was a clear difference between long-standing guerrilla members, who can be said to have constituted the hard core of the resistance, and those whose participation was more ephemeral.

The stereotypical young peasant who fought the dictatorship for over a decade represented, in fact, only a small minority. Of the forty-five percent of guerrilla fighters who lasted less than a year in the mountains, twenty-six percent only stayed for a few hours, days, or weeks; twenty-nine percent lasted no longer than five months, while the remaining forty-five percent stayed for less than twelve months. Resistance members' average length of stay in the mountains was eighteen months. The low average length of stay, combined with the large number of guerrilla fighters whose presence was only ephemeral, helps to explain the fragility and weakness of the resistance in Spain (Appendix: Graphs 6 and 7).

But what were the factors causing these low levels of continuity in the mountains? Many young men fled to the mountains with an idealised image of the resistance. Once there, on seeing the difficult conditions of the armed struggle – the constant nocturnal marches, the lack of food, the cold, the fighting, etc. – many decided to return to their homes. Although this was undoubtedly one of the most common reasons, it was not the only one. To answer the previous question, it is necessary to consider different kinds of discharge from the guerrilla and to make further distinctions between the *modern guerrilla* and *neighbours in arms*.

Statistical analysis (Appendix: Graphs 8 and 9) clearly shows that military repression caused almost half of the losses suffered by the resistance, as 47% of guerrilla fighters died in combat, both in groups of *armed neighbours* and in the *modern guerrilla*. It mightinitially have been assumed that the larger size and stricter military structure of the Agrupaciones guerrilleras would have led to fewer losses in combat compared to the *neighbours in arms*, but this was not the case. However, the expected difference can be observed in the number of arrests. Stricter discipline and respect for security measures in the *modern guerrilla* allowed these formations to reduce the proportion of guerrilla fighters arrested to 11% while groups of *armed neighbours*, who adopted a more lax discipline, lost 29% of their members as a result of arrests.

A significant difference can also be observed in relation to desertion and voluntary surrender to the authorities. Among *neighbours in arms*, the number of guerrilla fighters choosing these options represented a mere 10%, while the corresponding figure for the *modern guerrilla* was as high as 32%. As mentioned earlier, *neighbours in arms* operated with a more solid form of internal cohesion based on primary group loyalties, compared with the *modern guerrilla*, who based its internal cohesion on political affinities. In addition, the measures taken against *localism*, especially the separation of primary group members and the imposition of strict discipline, profoundly weakened the internal cohesion of the Agrupaciones guerrilleras. It should also be remembered that the AGG, the group with the largest number of guerrilla fighters in Andalusia, suffered a great loss of members as a direct consequence of the repression from 1947 onwards. A significant portion of this group lacked any kind of prior combat experience, as it included a generation who had not fought in the Spanish Civil War. As Santiago Carrillo recognised, this fact meant that new guerrilla fighters were "weak" and hesitant: "They began to lose morale and desert. Some hid while others fell into the hands of the enemy, and once under arrest they revealed all they knew, which led to further arrests among the peasantry. This led to a general mistrust of guerrilla fighters and increased their isolation".[48]

The number of losses suffered as a result of suicide was small although there were some cases in Andalusia. Up to fifteen people took their own lives when trapped by government forces. Most of these belonged to groups of *armed neighbours*. The fact that the number is as high as fifteen is largely a product of suicides committed by members of the "hermanos Quero" group. Popular rumour had it that the "hermanos Quero" had sworn to take their own lives rather than give themselves up to the authorities. Although it is difficult to ascertain whether this was actually the case, almost half of the group opted for this course of action, which raised the group's mythical status even higher among working-class constituencies in Granada.[49]

Finally, it is necessary to highlight the difference between *neighbours in arms* and the *modern guerrilla* with regards to exile. Given the effort and resources that the PCE invested in the development and transformation of the guerrilla movement, in addition to its national and international infra-structure, it might be expected that the number going into exile would be much higher in the case of the Agrupaciones guerrilleras. In fact, the reality was very different, as only 3% of *modern guerrilla* members were exiled, compared to 8% of the *neighbours in arms*. The PCE showed no interest in evacuating the guerrilla once the armed struggle was declared to be over and dozens of guerrilla fighters were left to their fate in Spain. The only large-scale evacuation organised by the PCE was that of the last twenty-seven survivors of the Agrupación de Guerrilleros de Levante-Aragón, who fled Spain at the end of 1951 and the beginning of 1952.[50] There is only one other such case in Spain: the evacuation of thirty Asturian socialist guer-rilla fighters in 1948.[51] These are two exceptional cases in the context of the Agrupaciones guerrilleras. With regard to Andalusia, the PCE activist Armando Castillo stated in an interview that the party had planned an evac-uation of the members of the AGG, but there is no other testament or document mentioning any such project.[52]

Resistance members going into exile from Andalusia used their own resources or the evacuation structures of other political organisations. The CNT was the most active agent evacuating guerrilla fighters from the region. The Provincial Committees of Granada, Seville, and Cádiz estab-lished various routes which allowed resistance fighters to flee to North Africa or to cross the border in the Pyrenees.[53] Of the 1,038 guerrilla fighters identified in this study, no more than fifty managed to reach exile. The last six members of the completely decimated AGG had to walk almost 1,000 kilometres from the mountains of Granada to the Pyrenees. Receiving no help from the PCE, they reached the French border on October 14th 1952, one hundred days after first setting out from their Andalusian base. Once liberated by the French police, the PCE gathered the exiled guer-rilla fighters and subjected them to an internal interrogation. Each guerrilla fighter prepared a report and the six were subsequently dispersed in France and other countries in Eastern Europe.[54]

Between 1944 and 1947 the PCE transformed the guerrilla movement in Spain. The slogans of Unity, Single Command and Discipline heavily influ-enced the structure and operations of guerrilla units and became the basis for change in the resistance movement. In response to the fragmentation of the first period, the PCE managed to centralise most of the guerrilla movement. There were fifty-six different groups operating in eastern Andalusia before 1945, but the situation changed radically after the unification process. By 1947 the number of active groups had been reduced to eleven. Many had been integrated into the Agrupaciones, while others had disappeared as a result of repression or exhaustion. Although the resistance appeared to be coming to an end the military structure and internal discipline of the new Agrupaciones allowed the guerrilla movement to maintain its vitality until the early 1950s.

The militarisation process in the resistance was complex, slow and troubled. A great number of *neighbours in arms* proved hesitant or were opposed to the idea of unification, an attitude which limited the operational capacity of the resistance. At the same time, the internal cohesion of the new Agrupaciones guerrilleras suffered from evident weaknesses. The new military structure, the separation of primary group members from each other and their place of residence, and the adoption of a strict internal discipline all exacerbated such problems. Immediate consequences included the application of extreme punitive measures like the *ajusticiamientos* and, above all, the demobilisation of a large number of guerrilla fighters through desertions. The militarisation process thus had two opposite and contradictory effects: it contributed to the mobilisation of dozens of new guerrilla fighters while simultaneously causing increased demobilisation. The participation of as many as half of the total number of guerrilla fighters in eastern Andalusia was relatively ephemeral, lasting less than a year.

In short, the Agrupaciones guerrilleras were incapable of preventing desertions, of steadily increasing the number of recruits and of maintaining a stable group of active guerrilla fighters. Consequently, despite the significant innovations introduced by communist units arriving from abroad, the Agrupaciones guerrilleras always showed signs of great weakness and restricted potential. Thus, the guerrilla movement was never able to overcome its own limitations or to pose a real threat to Franco's dictatorship.

Chapter 6

Beyond Sabotage
Combat, robbery, kidnapping and murder

The only way to save life is to expose it to struggle. Fight, desert, join the guerrilla, carry out sabotage; organise, unite, fight. Only along this path can we find guaranteed freedom from slavery and death.

(*Nuestra Bandera*, Federico Melchor, April 30th 1943)

Sabots (clogs) were a common type of footwear among workers, miners and peasants in France. As a protest against the mechanisation of work taking place during the industrial revolution in the nineteenth century, some workers would throw their clogs into the machinery in order to obstruct the gears.[1] The practice of destroying machines with this simple instrument spread and the word *sabotage* acquired a broader meaning relating to all forms of labour obstruction. Soon afterwards, the word also appeared in other European languages. Sabotage, a tactic developed and used by workers themselves, was also incorporated into the lexicon of war. The increase in irregular operations gave sabotage a new status. The Second World War, which included an important guerrilla component, ultimately consolidated the use of this kind of tactic, both traditional and modern in origin.

Sabotage has been given a prominent role in partisan literature. Derailment of trains, destruction of energy sources or the interruption of communications are celebrated as the most effective, political and conscious acts of the resistance. However, in addition to sabotage, the armed groups had a larger repertoire of guerrilla action. In the case of the anti-Francoist guerrilla, there were five common methods: direct combat, robbery, kidnapping, murder and sabotage.

Compared to European antifascist resistance movements, Spanish guerrillas demonstrated relatively low levels of activity. The explanation is simple: European resistance movements developed in the context of the

Second World War, with a large mobilisation of human and material resources, while in Spain the guerrillas emerged in a post-war context and total isolation. Even so, within Spain there were important differences between geographical zones. Andalusia is notable for being the seat of the most extensive guerrilla activity. The highest levels of robbery, direct combat, assassinations and kidnapping in Spain were recorded in the provinces of Málaga and Granada. The number of killings of civilians and acts of sabotage in these areas were also the highest in the country.

Repertoires of guerrilla action

In the first years after the war, before it exercised any influence over the guerrilla movement, the PCE repeatedly insisted that it was necessary to transform the armed struggle in Spain. The guerrilla movement had to strengthen its political character and adopt various forms of modern guerrilla action which would permit it to transcend the struggle for mere survival:

> Guerrilla war must not be a collection of somewhat desperate, isolated battles. The guerrilla fighter must be an armed, anti-Francoist combatant, who operates on the basis of political need (. . .) Guerrillas' weapons must be improved and munitions provided. Fighting and combat methods must be perfected following military rules.[2]

The project of transforming the *neighbours in arms* into a "true guerrilla army" began to take shape at the end of 1944, when the PCE sent the first guerrilla leaders from its bases in exile. Chapters 2 and 3 have shown how this process was, in reality, tremendously slow and complicated, although the perception among communist leaders brimming with optimism was very different. In mid-1945 the exiled PCE leadership claimed that its intervention in the anti-Francoist guerrilla had already prompted enormous change in the movement. At this time, Santiago Carrillo prepared an initial report in which he was jubilant about the results. If indigenous groups had originally focused on "subsistence", the new guerrilla preferred to attack Civil Guard detachments and "punish murderous Falangists".[3]

In a subsequent report the PCE created a catalogue of basic aims and methods of the Agrupaciones guerrilleras. Guerrilla fighters, incorporated into "armed detachments" had to severely castigate "murderous Falangist leaders". The guerrilla also had to become an "organisation defending the interests of rural workers" and an "organisation of armed struggle against the forces of repression". Guerrilla action should seek to "gain control over arms and munitions" and "impose heavy fines on large landowners and use the revenue raised to attend to the needs of guerrilla units". Sabotage should be directed "against the property of Falangist leaders and wealthy capitalists".[4]

The efforts made by the PCE to transform the guerrilla movement in Spain certainly had an effect, although this came later and was more limited than communist leaders suggested. The new *modern guerrilla* model broadened and "modernised" the range of guerrilla action. However, it should be noted that this broadening and "modernising" was limited by the circumstances and the particular conditions in which the Spanish armed struggle took place.

In general terms, the range of action of groups of *armed neighbours* was limited to direct combat, robberies, murder and kidnappings. The *modern guerrilla* broadened this repertoire of armed action by incorporating sabotage, distribution of food, village occupations and punishment operations. It also added non-violent phenomena such as meetings, the clandestine press, propaganda and smear campaigns, which will be analysed in the following chapter.

However, the contribution of the *modern guerrilla* did not only consist of broadening the range of guerrilla action. *Neighbours in arms* and the *modern guerrilla* shared a basic repertoire based on combat, robbery, murder and kidnappings. As the following analysis will show, the *modern guerrilla* managed to modify these kinds of armed action in both technical and cultural terms.

Sabotage

On December 14th 1946, a news report alarmed the authorities in Granada: a group of guerrilla fighters had raided a dynamite store belonging to a railway company and seized fifty-two kilos of explosives, one hundred and eighty meters of fuse and three hundred detonators. The guerrilla fighter Francisco Rodríguez "El Sevilla" had worked for the railway company and knew where its deposits were located. For this reason, Ramiro Fuentes Ochoa, political chief of the guerrilla in Granada, requested that he take command over the operation. Ramiro's objective was to acquire a significant arsenal of explosives in order to carry out sabotage in the province and to show "Roberto", Armada Rus and Beneyto the strength of the guerrilla in Granada. Despite the initial success the operation was a failure as the Civil Guard discovered the hidden arsenal a few days later in some caves near the city.[5] This anecdote illustrates the precarious nature of the work carried out by the *modern guerrilla* in Spain. Sabotage was always the principal aim of the Agrupaciones, but to achieve it in practice was complicated. Some historians have conflated the anti-Francoist guerrilla's *desire* to carry out sabotage with its real extent, thus distorting the capacity and magnitude of the resistance movement in Spain.

The PCE always considered sabotage to have great strategic value. In the guerrilla school at Toulouse future guerrilla fighters learned the art of sabotage, paying particularly close attention to energy and communication networks: railway lines, trains, lorries, buses, power stations, communication masts, etc.[6] The new leaders trained at the Toulouse school and sent from France were expected to incorporate sabotage into the guerrilla's operational repertoire. Groups of *armed neighbours* did not carry out activities of this kind, making it necessary to implement models taken from modern warfare. To this end the PCE produced a variety of instructional material outlining basic guidelines, preferred outcomes and final aims of sabotage within the context of guerrilla warfare.[7]

In Andalusia it was Ricardo Beneyto, political chief of the regional guerrillas, who, more than anyone, insisted on the need to include sabotage in the guerrillas' tactics. At the end of 1946 he ordered "Tarbes" to produce a manual about sabotage techniques which could be distributed among the units. However, in January 1947 "Tarbes" was arrested. The Civil Guard confiscated his "Notes on the creation of a technical manual for the fabrication of explosives and sabotage",[8] which therefore never reached the guerrillas. Nonetheless, the guerrilla leadership in Andalusia continued to insist on the importance of sabotage. In March 1947, the AGG jubilantly announced a "wave of attacks on railways, power stations, barracks, police stations and other acts of general sabotage." These actions would "shortly increase, until they have assumed the character of a general offensive".[9]

These were the intentions of the *modern guerrilla*, although the reality of its achievements was quite different. The conditions of the armed struggle did not permit the expansion of sabotage as a guerrilla tactic in Spain, and Andalusia was no exception. Between 1943 and 1952 guerrillas in Almería managed to carry out only four acts of sabotage. In the same period, nine acts of sabotage were carried out in Jaén, twenty-eight in Málaga and thirty-four in Granada.[10] The figures for Málaga and Granada are among the highest in Spain, exceeded only by fifty-seven in Teruel, forty-five in Asturias, and thirty-nine in A Coruña. In any case, these figures show the limited extent of sabotage in the anti-Francoist guerrilla.

The problem not only stemmed from the reduced number of such operations but also from their impact . When the acts of sabotage actually carried out by the Agrupaciones guerrilleras are examined more closely, it is rare to find attacks on communication infrastructure or power stations. Most commonly they burned down the farm house of some high-profile Falangist, as was the case in attacks carried out by "Rubio de Brecia" in 1943, by the AGG in 1948, or by various guerrilla go-betweens in 1950.[11] Moreover, the statistics regarding sabotage are distorted by the dictatorship's own paranoia. Some reported cases referred to "guerrilla sabotage" of telegraph lines and railways when the act in question was probably a simple theft of wire and copper, very common at the time.[12] To conclude, in Spain, actual acts of sabotage were of little importance in comparison with other European resistance movements. The weakness of the anti-Francoist guerrilla, together with its lack of external support and supplies, greatly hindered the realisation of this tactic's practical potential.

Combat

Armed confrontation was one of the most common forms of guerrilla action. Intentional or not, encounters with enemy forces were practically inevitable, even if the units and agents varied throughout the conflict. The Civil Guard was the primary force used by the dictatorship to pursue the guerrillas. There were also various groups collaborating with the Civil Guard: "self-defence" groups composed of local civilians and organised by the town halls (especially in the first period), paramilitary groups of Falangists and Requetés (as auxiliary forces), Army units (deployed in the area between 1944 and 1951) and special counterinsurgency groups (between 1947 and 1952).[13] But was there a difference between the *neighbours in arms* and the *modern guerrilla* when they engaged in combat?

The actions of *neighbours in arms* tended to be more reactive or defensive. The main aim was to avoid armed confrontation with government forces. Direct combat only took place when the groups were ambushed or cornered. The *modern guerrilla* always accused the groups of *armed neighbours* of "passivity". The resistance had to break out from the habitual "passivity", re-activate itself and strike against enemy forces.[14] That said, despite such harsh criticisms, the *modern guerrilla* in Spain also adopted a relatively reactive posture. The intention was always to progress to an offensive phase, but, given its weaknesses it could hardly move beyond self-defence. Even so, they did occasionally carry out offensive operations, seeking to surprise the enemy.

Among these exceptional cases, the most common form of action was an attack on a Civil Guard barracks. Such operations tended to have either one or a combination of three possible motives: 1) to avenge the death or arrest of a guerrilla member or go-between, 2) to terrorize the forces playing a central role in the repression and 3) to acquire arms for the guerrilla. They chose barracks according to their location (i.e. those which were located in isolated villages or hamlets) and the number of guards on stand-by.[15]

The anti-Francoist guerrilla rarely sought to orchestrate an ambush, normally an elementary method in irregular warfare.[16] The balance of forces was too uneven, especially when the dictatorship committed ever larger military units to fight the guerrillas. In this context, when the guerrilla operated with reduced mobility and a constant lack of arms, attacks based on an ambush were reduced to a minimum. In Andalusia, such offensive operations against security forces were carried out exclusively by the AGG. The risks were so high that only two guerrilla fighters, "Roberto" and "El Gato", dared to lead them.

Antonio Gutiérrez ,"El Gato," was one of the most active guerrilla fighters in the AGG. Involved in the resistance since the time Ramón Vía, his colleagues feared and admired him in equal measure. In 1947, he requested permission from the Chief of Staff of the AGG, where he was a unit leader, to organise an ambush against a group of soldiers who were making raids in his area. On November 10th, the operation went ahead. His unit attacked the soldiers, causing three deaths and making off with a small arsenal.[17]

Five months later "El Gato" saw military action for the last time. In the Sierra de Cázulas there was an important timber business which had been adversely affected by the presence of the guerrilla. The business owners and the local authorities asked for help from the Army. From mid-1944 an Army Company was deployed in the area and began to escort workers to and from the site. The unit led by "El Gato" planned their ambush carefully. The workers tended to walk about fifty meters in front of the soldiers, so, if the guerrilla surprised the procession at a particular point on a hill, the workers would not risk getting hurt. They commenced the attack at half past five in the afternoon. As usual, the soldiers walked in a line. Located at strategic points on both sides of the valley, the guerrilla fighters waited for the perfect moment. When the soldiers arrived at the ideal point, the voice of "El Gato", ringing out from the forest surrounding the road, interrupted the march by shouting "weapons down and hands up!" The response of the soldiers was not what was expected, however. An officer gave the order to fire, leading to a battle which lasted for half an hour. The guerrilla fighters managed to kill seven soldiers, wound another five and even seize a significant amount of weaponry. However, "El Gato", the unit leader and one of the most prominent figures in the AGG, died in the battle.[18] The most famous ambush organised by "Roberto" took place on July 27th 1949 in Sierra Tejada. A large detachment of soldiers and Civil Guards was in the area on a counterinsurgency mission when they were surprised by an AGG unit. The government forces were attacked from a position higher up the mountain and after an intense, eight-hour-long exchange of fire the guerrillas retreated. The propaganda paper for the Agrupación, *Por la República*, described the event in the usual epic and exaggerated tone. Twenty-three guerrilla fighters had confronted more than one thousand five hundred soldiers and had inflicted one hundred and fifty casualties on the enemy ranks, according to the paper. In reality, although the ambush had been an undeniable success, as the guerrilla suffered no casualties and even managed to appropriate some weaponry, the battle left only one soldier dead and four wounded.[19]

The AGG only carried out actions of this kind in the period of its greatest strength, that is, between 1947 and 1950. The Agrupación had to accept its material and human limitations. This explains why the AGG had to maintain a relatively defensive strategy, despite being the group which, more than any other, hoped to advance to an offensive phase. In fact, most battles were engineered by government forces whose actions were guided by their own counterinsurgency plans, rather than those of the guerrilla.[20]

Nevertheless, the provinces of Granada and Málaga had the highest numbers of armed confrontations in the whole of Spain. Official statistics show one hundred and fifty-one battles in Granada and one hundred and forty-nine in Málaga. The number of casualties suffered by government forces were eighty-two in Málaga and seventy-three in Granada. These figures were the highest in the country, followed at some distance by Asturias with twenty-five and A Coruña with seventeen.[21]

Robberies

Objectives

Unlike other European resistance movements, the anti-Francoist guerrilla received little economic support from abroad.[22] The PCE was the only political organisation in exile with a budgetary commitment to support the guerrilla struggle, although the allocated sums were insufficient and, in any case, given exclusively to the Agrupación Guerrillera de Levante-Aragón.[23] The consequent lack of resources obliged armed groups in Spain to finance their activities through robberies. Guerrilla groups had to cover the costs of resistance members, new weapons, provisions, clothes and travel. At the same time, they had to provide economic help for guerrilla fighters' families, given that in many cases those who had fled to the mountains were the heads of the family and/or the eldest sons, who were the principal breadwinners in the rural household. They also needed to reward collaborators in their social support network (and thereby reinforce their loyalty), and pay political organisations, local and regional committees and families of imprisoned guerrilla members. Thus, the survival of the anti-Francoist opposition depended largely on the financial resources acquired, making robberies and other revenue-raising activities a crucial part of their *modus operandi*. Once again, the guerrillas in Andalusia were the most prolific in the country, orchestrating four hundred and twenty-six robberies in Granada, three hundred and ninety-nine in Córdoba and three hundred and fifty-three in Málaga.[24]

Robberies did not have the sole objective of financing the opposition; in many cases they were a means of individual survival. The material needs of the guerrilla fighters increased in step with intensified repression and the clothes and food donated by families and collaborators were not enough. The guerrilla also bought goods at local farm houses for high prices hoping this would guarantee the cooperation of the population. However, the authorities' repressive measures made it increasingly difficult to access sorely needed provisions even in this way. This was the main reason why robberies were commonly committed to secure subsistence. Guerrillas were not only looking to steal money but also food (ham, flour, salt, oil, etc.), clothes (jackets, trousers, footwear, blankets, etc.), arms (rifles and pistols), and other valuable objects such as tobacco, watches, mirrors, and combs. But how widespread were such robberies in the anti-Francoist army?

Efficacy

The only extensive and complete documentation found by the author with regard to armed guerrilla action in Andalusia is that produced by the Civil Guard at the beginning of July 1947. The report contains information on raids, kidnappings, combat and murders involving the guerrillas in the provinces of eastern Málaga and Granada between June 1946 and June 1947.[25] Of the one hundred and forty-nine recorded incidents, almost half, seventy, were robberies not involving kidnapping (Appendix: Table 9).

A significant number of these activities were carried out to acquire basic goods like food and clothes. Such robberies constituted the majority in Granada, but were less common in Malaga. The difference was not accidental but related to the type of guerrilla operating in each area (Appendix:

Table 10). The AGG did not take control over the guerrilla in Granada until the summer of 1947. The numbers given in the table therefore show the difference between the *modern guerrilla* (which had a greater presence in eastern Málaga at the time) and the *armed neighbours* (who in that period dominated in Granada).

The Agrupaciones guerrilleras developed more solid infrastructures, which made robbery less necessary as a means to guarantee subsistence. On the other hand, groups of *armed neighbours*, faced with weak infrastructures and decimated after years of fighting, found themselves increasingly forced to resort to such measures. Moreover, *neighbours in arms* tended to carry out small but frequent robberies while the *modern guerrilla* organised larger raids on farmhouses and factories which allowed them to feed the whole Agrupación for a long period of time.[26]

The *modern guerrilla* tried to integrate and transform the *neighbours in arms*, but, when this proved impossible, their main objective was to distinguish themselves from less disciplined groups. One of the main concerns of the *modern guerrilla* was that their actions should not be confused with banditry, which is why they gave all their activities a political meaning. Robberies could give rise to misconceptions, so the Agrupaciones offered pedagogical instruction to guerrilla fighters in their ranks: "it is strictly forbidden to use the word "robbery", as these are political operations of an economic kind", stated the fifth statute of the AGG.[27] These types of operation, labelled "repossessions" or "provision services", only targeted "wealthy Falangists", the "killers of our people", as the guerrillas constantly reminded the local population in their propaganda. Years later, when the Agrupaciones guerrilleras were in decline, they too began to rely on small robberies for subsistence, applying less selective criteria to the process.

However, the differences were deeper still. The *modern guerrilla* carried out robberies with greater efficacy than the *neighbours in arms*, save in exceptional cases like that of the "hermanos Quero" group, whose activity was concentrated in the urban environment of Granada.[28] The presence of a relatively large number of wealthy victims allowed them to reap greater rewards with fewer hits. Between June 1946 and June 1947, the numerous groups of *armed neighbours* in the province of Granada had to carry out thirty-five robberies to raise 204,362 pesetas and 30 céntimos while the AGM/AGG in eastern Málaga raised 351,850 pesetas in only ten robberies (Appendix: Table 11).[29] The military structure of the Agrupaciones guerrilleras allowed them to reduce the risk and maximise the returns on each action.

Profiles of victims

Victims were selected on the basis of three fundamental criteria: location, political profile and economic profile. Location refers to the victim's home address or workplace. Guerrilla fighters did not leave the mountains or their secure zones, meaning that victims had to belong to the scattered population residing in the mountains or in the nearest and most accessible villages. With regard to economic status, most victims were farm hands and millers, that is, the rural "middle-class" living in the mountains. Those farm house residents who sympathised with the guerrilla tended to become go-betweens and helped to secure provisions for the resistance. Those who did not became subject to robberies. The guerrilla had to feed itself one way or another. However, the demands for supplies, made incessantly for more than a decade, ultimately prompted a general rejection among the rural population.

Bakers and millers, who were common targets of guerrilla action, were a case apart. Both social groups typically suffered from a bad reputation among the working classes as they were often accused of manipulating weights or hoarding during times of hardship. In a post-war context marked by hunger and the black market, attacks on bakers and millers did not have a negative effect but, rather, raised the prestige of the guerrilla among the most impoverished social sectors.[30] For example, on February 20th 1948, an AGG unit attacked a flour mill in the village of Frigiliana. A few days later, the guerrilla's propaganda paper, *Por la República*, described the event as an action against the owner of the mill, "the señores Torres, wealthy Falangists who got rich on the back of our people".[31] Being Falangists and rich, were two key factors as the resistance selected its victims.

Members of higher social strata, as will be shown later, were mostly targeted for economic gain through kidnappings. In general terms the guerrilla did not bother poor peasants or rural day labourers. If a day labourer or poor peasant was included among their victims it was mostly for ideological reasons, that is, because the victim formed part of the support network of the dictatorship. However, when the guerrillas were experiencing periods of increased insecurity and shortage, robberies became more indiscriminate.

When it came to selecting victims on the basis of political affiliation, there was no significant difference between the two kinds of guerrilla. Groups of *armed neighbours*, operating in familiar territory, knew the local population well. The *modern guerrilla* could also consult indigenous guerrilla fighters in their ranks, or local committees, when selecting their victims. The *modern guerrilla* considered robberies to be a form of punish-

ment, the imposition of a "fine" deservedly paid by Falangists, local authorities and "men of the Right" who supported the dictatorship.[32] As stated
in the Instructions of the AGG: "Operations of a political-military kind
should target people who are clearly fascist and never those among whom
we could hold a recruitment campaign".[33]

However, the trust placed in local committees also entailed certain risks.
Local committees acquired great power by singling out possible guerrilla
victims, and this capacity could in turn become an instrument to resolve
personal disputes.[34] In Spain, where there was a close relationship between
armed groups and the local community, these situations were common. In
fact, political and personal motivations were in most cases interlinked. For
example, José Ferández Villoslada organised a robbery in his own community at the beginning of 1947. The operation targeted a distinguished local
Falangist who had also been Ferández Villoslada's employer a few years
earlier.[35] Although these kinds of personal relations leave little trace in
archival documentation, researchers should not forget their potential
impact.

Sharing out the spoils

Within the context of robberies, the question of how to split the money
marked a clear point of difference between *neighbours in arms* and the *modern
guerrilla*. As mentioned in Chapter 3, *neighbours in arms* shared the loot
between everyone who had participated in the robbery. Those groups who
were linked to political organisations (PCE, CNT, or PSOE) also gave a
small sum to the organisation's local or provincial committees. Once the
money had been split equally, the guerrilla fighters put part of their share
into a common pot used for arms, clothes, food and support for families of
imprisoned or dead guerrilla members. The rest of their share was kept for
individual use.[36]

The *modern guerrilla* sought to eradicate this practice, as it was thought
to encourage banditry. The Agrupaciones guerrilleras offered all guerrilla
fighters a monthly salary of 500 pesetas, which allowed the Chief of Staff
to handle financial resources centrally. When a unit belonging to the
Agrupaciones carried out a robbery, the unit leader kept the money until
he could hand it over to the Chief of Staff and report on the actions undertaken. Every unit had to account for incomes and expenses and was
expected to periodically present an overview of its accounts to the guerrilla leadership.[37]

Sharing out food

Lastly, it is necessary to highlight the distribution of food among poorer sections of the rural population as one of the practices which the *modern guerrilla* introduced to the range of guerrilla activities. These operations made it possible to give robberies a new meaning and inject them with great propaganda potential. However, attempts to distribute stolen food were rare due to the dangers this entailed and the precarious situation of the guerrillas. At the end of March 1945 an AGG unit arrived at a farm house and forced a distinguished Falangist "to hand over a great quantity of foodstuffs and clothes which were then distributed among the most needy peasant families". That same day, another AGG unit attacked a shop owned by another Falangist and "distributed the food among the hungry population".[38] Similarly, in February 1948, the AGG raided a flour mill: "our forces opened the doors of said mill and handed out all the flour that the locals wanted to take", claimed the unit's report.[39] These kinds of actions were not undertaken by *neighbours in arms*, although the popular legend surrounding the "hermanos Quero", for example, tended to represent the group as acting in the spirit of Robin Hood, handing out money to the poor. Such representations will be analysed in the next chapter.

Kidnappings

The guerrillas in Málaga and Granada made relatively frequent use of kidnappings as a means of economic extortion and punishment. Official statistics count eighty-eight guerrilla-related kidnappings in Granada and one hundred and forty-one in Málaga, followed by seventy-two in Cádiz, fifty-four in Cáceres and thirty-seven in Ciudad Real. However, the statistics are incomplete, as they do not include kidnappings carried out between 1939 and 1943 and only refer to cases which were reported to the police. In any case, the figures clearly show that the Andalusian guerrillas were also the most active in Spain in this field.

Initially the PCE was not an advocate of kidnappings, which were very common among *neighbours in arms*. Ramón Vía despised kidnappings and robberies, which he considered practices typical of common criminals and bandits.[40] Thus, the AGM minimised the number of robberies and refrained from carrying out any kidnappings while under his command. The situation changed from 1946, when "Roberto" became the military leader of the AGM/AGG. The new guerrilla leader supported these kinds of actions, which allowed him to finance the guerrilla and the party. Eulogio

Limia Pérez, a lieutenant coronel in the Civil Guard and the man responsible for the repression of the AGG between 1949 and 1952, stated in one
of his reports: "the main tactic of the head ["Roberto"] was to obtain money
so that he did not have to rely of holdups, which generated antipathy
towards the guerrilla among the peasantry and the civilian population in
general. To this end he preferred to kidnap wealthy individuals, who were
released for increasingly large sums of money".[41] The revenue raised
through kidnappings vastly exceeded that obtained through robberies
(Appendix: Table 11). The guerrillas were aware of this and kidnappings
consequently became an important activity, despite the high risks involved.
One might assume that kidnappings, as opposed to simple robberies,
required a more sophisticated guerrilla structure. However, this was not the
case, as the most common form of kidnapping was very rapid. The guerrilla
abducted a person and sent a message through an interlocutor. The ransom
was paid in less than twenty-four hours and the abducted person freed.
There was no need for large logistical networks. The simplicity of the operation even allowed *neighbours in arms*, who had weaker structures, to carry
out such kidnappings, albeit less efficiently. The larger number of wealthy
targets available to the *modern guerrilla* enabled it to extract two thirds more
from each kidnapping, than groups of *armed neighbours*.

Differences other than in the efficacy are also evident. The *modern guerrilla* saw their own kidnappings as punishment operations while those
carried out by *neighbours in arms* were considered a form of banditry. Enrique
Urbano, a member of the AGG, made the following comparison between
the AGG and local groups of *armed neighbours* in an interview: "The kidnappings that the Guerrilla carried out were not the same as those linked to the
"Clares". We did not hit out blindly, and while our operations were
supported by the people, those of the others were seen as nasty".[42] Beyond
such individual assessments, it is important to show how participants were
fully conscious of the fact that the groups represented two different resistance models, which conditioned their action in different ways.

Kidnappings had two advantages over robberies: they generated more
money and had a less negative social impact on the community.
Consequently, the profile of kidnap victims tended to be different from that
of robbery victims. The most affluent sectors of society, or at least members
of the upper middle class, as well as the most prominent local supporters of
the dictatorship (including those in official positions) were the most
common kidnapping victims. Groups of *armed neighbours* had intimate
knowledge of local inhabitants' social and political profiles, knowledge
which was also made available to the *modern guerrilla* through indigenous
guerrilla members and local committees.

Enrique Jiménez, a member of the AGG, was interrogated by the Civil Guard after deserting from the guerrilla. When asked how they financed their operations, Enrique answered that "the money was normally raised through actions against farm owners who had become rich by exploiting the black market". This was the method most frequently used by the *modern guerrilla*. For example, in July 1949, the local committee of Salar de Loja informed an AGG unit that a village farm owner was hoarding wheat in order to sell it on the black market. A few days later, the farm owner was kidnapped and released once a ransom of 60,000 pesetas had been paid.[43]

Two years earlier, another AGG unit had attacked a livestock dealer and black marketeer. "We are the Spanish guerrilla", they told him, "and you have to hand over 30,000 duros tonight [150,000 pesetas]. If you do not, we will ask for 40,000 tomorrow morning." That same night, the guerrilla sent a note to his wife: "This is to inform you that your husband is with the guerrillas and to save his life will cost 200,000 pesetas. If this sum is not provided before the deadline you will lose your husband for ever, and then we will continue persecuting you". The family managed to gather 84,000 pesetas for the next day. The guerrilla had to decide whether to accept that sum and end the kidnapping or to persevere until the requested sum was provided, although this would increase the risks of the operation. The most common outcome was that they accepted whatever money the family had managed to collect and freed the victim, even if they did not obtain the full ransom, as occurred in this case.[44]

Nonetheless, the threat of death was occasionally followed through. On August 22nd 1947 several members of the AGG kidnapped a landlord in Frigiliana. His ransom was set at 150,000 pesetas. After two days had passed, his wife asked for an extension to the deadline but received no answer. Two days later a neighbour found the corpse with a bullet in the head.[45]

Social or economic status, or activities that were contrary to the "moral economy of the peasantry", such as hoarding or extensive black marketeering, were the main criteria considered when choosing a victim. Ideological affinities often corresponded in predictable ways to these criteria, but not always. José Arrabal was a day labourer living in poverty. His economic profile was far removed from that of the typical guerrilla kidnap victim, but his political profile (Falangist) made him a target nonetheless. Six members of the guerrilla group led by "Rubio de Brecia" kidnapped him and demanded a ransom of 100,000 pesetas, which the family had no way of paying. On this occasion, however, internal solidarity networks came to the rescue. Without alerting the authorities, various neighbours met in the home of the interlocutor and managed to raise 46,000 pesetas. The guerrilla fighters accepted the sum and let José Arrabal walk free.[46]

Kidnappings were not only carried out for economic reasons, but were also a form of punishment. It was one way of applying guerrilla law . They were also intended to eradicate certain practices (black marketeering, low salaries for field workers, etc.) and to cause disaffection among locals and to disrupt their collaboration with the authorities. The main problem with these measures were their geographical limitations. As Eulogio Limia Pérez has indicated, the isolated rural environment in which the guerrillas operated restricted the effects of their actions to the hamlets and villages where they could make a direct intervention.[47]

By comparison, both kidnappings and robberies had a more extensive impact when carried out in an urban environment. The urban guerrilla in Andalusia was very small, but nevertheless managed to devise a few operations which had a huge social impact. The kidnappings of a general in 1941 and of one of Spain's most prominent bankers in 1945, both carried out by the "hermanos Quero", and the kidnapping of another distinguished military figure by the "Clares" in 1947 caused a sensation at the time and contributed to these groups' mythical status among the more humble sectors of society.[48]

Murder

Numbers and intensity

The anti-Francoist guerrilla eliminated enemies throughout the conflict, as did all resistance movements. This section will not examine deaths in combat nor executions of guerrilla fighters by their own colleagues as these issues have been dealt with earlier. Instead, the focus here will be exclusively on the guerrilla killings of civilians and the exceptional cases where the guerrilla took the lives of police and military personnel outside a combat situation.

In the terminology adopted by the guerrilla, this kind of killing was known as an *ajusticiamiento*, as it was considered a method of implementing a sentence prescribed by guerrilla justice. Although it later became a phenomenon which guerrilla fighters tried to hide, at the time these eliminations were even celebrated in the guerrillas' own propaganda: "Every murder committed by Franco will be avenged tenfold by our guerrilla forces. All who have dirty hands from killing or betraying an anti-Francoist fighter will face the punishment they deserve".[49]

However, despite the rhetorical use of terms like *ajusticiamiento*, this practice was not very widespread in Spain. The total number of murders committed by Spanish guerrillas between 1939 and 1952 was less than 1,000. In Málaga and Granada, the provinces with the highest number of victims, there were a total of one hundred and eighty-five murders in this period.[50] The Greek guerrilla in the Argolia region committed three hundred and seventy-two murders between September 1943 and 1944, a figure which amounted to 0.82% of the population. At a national level, the Greek guerrilla executed approximately 15,000 people (0.2% of the total population) between 1941 and 1944 and 4,000 (0.05%) between 1947 and 1949.[51] In Andalusia one hundred and eighty-five victims represented 0.0007% of the total population, which shows the anti-Francoist guerrillas' moderate use of this method.

Profiles of victims

The majority of guerrilla murder victims were civilians, a common feature of these kinds of conflicts.[52] The Agrupaciones guerrilleras tended to threaten civil guards or torturers within the police, but such threats were rarely followed through.[53] In Andalusia, eighty-three government agents (civil guards, service men, armed police officers) died at the hands of the anti-Francoist guerrilla, most killed in combat.

The violence committed by the anti-Francoist guerrilla was decidedly selective, in contrast to other contemporary cases.[54] The high number of local guerrillas and the rare deployment of guerrilla units to unknown territories, together with the infrequent use of elimination as a guerrilla tactic, reduced indiscriminate violence to a minimum. However, not all victims of anti-Francoist guerrilla violence were "fascists" and "Falangists", as the propaganda and internal reports of the Agrupaciones guerrilleras tended to claim.

Occasionally the victims had a clear ideological connection with the dictatorship through holding a political post or belonging to paramilitary groups. In October 1947 the AGG kidnapped three neighbours who were prominent Falangists and members of counterinsurgency groups in the area. One of them was also Deputy Mayor of the municipality. The following morning the bodies of the three men were found. They had been arranged in a triangle around a wooden stake. The corpses showed clear signs of having been brutally beaten and hanged. A note had been left on one of them which said: "FASCISTS. This is the guerrilla response to the mass killings committed by your thugs."[55]

In Andalusia, the author has encountered some cases of political assassinations carried out by the AGG, although these are fewer in number than might be expected. Some mayors were harassed and even assaulted, but, as a rule, they were not important guerrilla targets. In July 1944, for example, the "Velázquez Murillo" group attacked the brother of the mayor of Pulianas after confusing him with his brother.[56] Two years later, in November 1946, the mayor of Lagos was retained, together with another two locals, by the AGG. The guerrilla killed one of the locals but freed the mayor, who "only" suffered a beating.[57] The only other assassination of a member of a municipal organisation seems to be that of the municipal judge in Canillas de Albaida. According to the guerrilla press he was a "prominent Falangist criminal" and, in September 1947, an AGG unit kidnapped and killed him in the mountains.[58]

The story of Francisco Ortega, mayor of Torrox (Málaga) is stranger. On February 6th 1946, he emerged unscathed from an assassination attempt organised by an AGG unit and the subsequent testimony of the guerrilla unit leader is revealing. According to the guerrilla fighter, the failed assassination attempt was in fact planned by him and the mayor. The military authorities suspected that the mayor and the guerrilla had made a pact of "non-aggression". The AGG's attempt on his life was intended to dispel any doubts about his political integrity.[59] It has not been possible to verify whether the guerrilla leader's testament before the military courts was true or simply a tactic, but his argument may support an interesting hypothesis. Despite the absence of any documents which might prove such a claim, it is likely that some local authorities reached agreements with guerrilla units operating in the area. This may explain, in part, the relatively low number of guerrilla attacks on local regime officials in Andalusia. Similar tacit agreements existed between groups of *armed neighbours* and the Civil Guard during the first post-war years.[60]

The fourth and last case where a regime official was murdered by the Andalusian guerrilla concerns a magistrate of the Provincial Court of Jaén. In September 1948, while hunting in the mountains around Loja, an AGG unit acting on a tipoff from the local committee, intercepted him. The magistrate was responsible for the imprisonment of a brother of one of the guerrilla fighters in the AGG. Once the magistrate had been identified, the guerrilla killed him in front of the other hunters.[61] This is the only known case where a member of the magistrature was killed by the guerrilla in Andalusia, which again serves as an indication of the low number of assassinations of regime officials committed by the anti-Francoist resistance.

Motivation

The principal motive for the anti-Francoist guerrillas' selective assassinations was the victim's actual or presumed status as a whistle-blower or informer. As a result, the socio-economic profile of the victims was diverse. On the one hand, the author has identified a large number of victims who were landowners thought to be working for the Civil Guard and enriching themselves by exploiting their status as Falangists. The main accusation, however, was always that of collaborating with counterinsurgency forces.[62] On the other hand, a significant number were day labourers, workers and small-holding peasants. Some were fervent defenders of the dictatorship, while others were pushed to collaborate as a result of police pressure or hunger. The "Guinea" family, who lived in extreme poverty in the Sacromonte neighbourhood of Granada, acted as police informers for years and in this capacity caused various guerrilla losses. Information was passed on to the police by the father and two sons, who were consequently killed in three separate attacks by armed groups in the city.[63]

On August 16th 1949 a note was found on the school doors in Frigiliana which said: "'El Terrible' and 'El Bendita' are next to the Cruz de Napoleón. "El Terrible" and "El Bendita" were two day labourers who frequently acted as informers for the Civil Guard. The two men were found hanging from two pine trees, one in front of another. "This is the guerrilla sentence passed on all who show or tell the authorities where our units are stationed" stated the note left by the AGG on one of the dead men's pocket.[64] Dozens of similar examples can be found in official records relating to the anti-Francoist guerrilla in Andalusia.

However, the social groups who were most defenceless against the violence committed by the guerrilla were small farm owners, leaseholders living in the mountains and shepherds. Regardless of their own ideological preferences and their possible collaboration with government forces, their position between a rock and a hard place turned them into the principal victims of a conflict where both belligerent parties fought for the control and hegemony over the territory.[65]

The situation was particularly difficult for shepherds. The profession was inherited from father to son among the most impoverished sectors of the population. Boys began to supervise their first flocks when they were eleven years old. Having developed their own culture, shepherds tended to spend most of the year isolated in the mountains. Although they were part of the local community, their position within that community was of a particular kind. In this context, shepherds had to live with the presence of both guerrillas and counterinsurgency forces for a decade and more. Co-existence was impossible and often had tragic outcomes. This study has identified up to eight shepherds among the victims of guerrilla violence in Andalusia. The accusation was always the same: collaborating with the Civil Guards who were persecuting the guerrilla.[66]

A clear example of the difficult situation in which the shepherds found themselves can be found in the story of a young shepherd who poisoned a guerrilla fighter called Francisco García. The guerrilla fighter was lost in the mountains after being separated from his unit during a confrontation with the Civil Guard. When he saw the shepherd he asked for food and some wine. The young shepherd gave him something to eat from his shoulder bag, but, before handing it over, he added a natural poison used to kill wolves. This was his own revenge for the death of his father, also a shepherd, who after being exposed to continuous pressure from the Civil Guard and the guerrilla had been executed by the AGG for being an informer.[67]

Treason could also stem from within the guerrilla organisations themselves, or their social support networks. José Alcántara, previously the socialist mayor of Guajar Alto, was eliminated, together with two local Falangists, by the AGM at the beginning of 1946 for collaborating with the Civil Guard.[68] Felíx Castán died in similar circumstances in February 1947. This day labourer was a go-between for the AGG but was discovered by the Civil Guard. Worn down by hunger, threatened with unemployment and imprisonment, Castán finally agreed to collaborate. According to AGG's propaganda press, for 4,000 pesetas, Felix Castán provided vitally important information which contributed to the death of two guerrilla fighters. His treasonous act could not be pardoned and a few days later a guerrilla unit executed him.[69] Three months later, a similar case occurred, although with greater repercussions in Granada. The "hermanos Clares" group kidnapped and killed a person who until that moment had acted as an intermediary between the CNT and local guerrilla groups. The victim had accepted an offer from the authorities of 200,000 pesetas, immunity and the possibility of fleeing abroad for informing on the last members of the "hermanos Quero" group.[70]

In many cases local dynamics added to the motives indicated here. Ideological justifications or accusations of collaboration were not incompatible with more personal conflicts between local civilians, go-betweens and guerrilla fighters. In July 1950, an AGG unit decided to kidnap a landowner in Alfarnate. One of the guerrilla members, who was from the area, Victoriano Sánchez, insisted that they also kidnap the guard of the estate, with whom he had various scores to settle as when the war ended this man had made his life in the village near impossible and was also responsible for the death of Victoriano's brother. The two kidnap victims, the landowner and his estate guard, were executed by Victoriano himself, who had volunteered to carry out the act.[71]

There are certain similarities here with the murder of a Falangist landowner from Loja in January 1951. An AGG unit kidnapped him and demanded a ransom of 600,000 pesetas. During the previous year as many as thirty villagers from Loja had been forced to flee to the mountains to escape repression, and this Falangist was largely held responsible. A few hours later his family paid a large sum of money to rescue him, but the unit did not free the prisoner. Two guerrilla fighters volunteered to execute him: Antonio Roldán and Antonio Extremera. The first accused the Falangist of being responsible for his brother's death in the river many years earlier, while the second was still bitter about the fact that the prisoner had vetoed his membership in the local livestock association during the Republican years, claiming that the few goats he owned did not constitute a sufficiently large herd.[72]

Guerrilla justice

To conclude, it should be noted that there were also important differences between the *modern guerrilla* and *neighbours in arms* regarding the elimination of enemies. The Agrupaciones guerrilleras sought to implement their own guerrilla justice by creating proper structures and having court hearings in the mountains. In these hearings, presided over by the Chief of Staff, guerrilla fighters explained the charges brought against the defendant, and once the case had been carefully considered, a verdict was delivered. The defendant could be present or sentenced in his absence. However, this model of guerrilla justice could only be followed in particular conditions. As units often had little contact with the Chief of Staff, it often fell to the unit leader to deliver and implement the sentence. "Roberto" claimed in his testimony to a Francoist court that 95% of killings committed by the AGG resulted from initiatives taken by unit leaders and that he would normally give post-hoc permissions for these when reading units' operational reports. It is possible that "Roberto" tried on this occasion to offload responsibility onto his subordinates. However, it is also true that the dispersion of AGG units in the provinces of Granada and Málaga often made meetings with the Chief of Staff impracticable.[73]

The following is one of the few documented cases of a court hearing held in the mountains by the AGG: on February 5th 1949 the unit led by "Felipe" kidnapped two residents of Alhama in Granada, Francisco Márquez Navas and his cousin, José Márquez. Both were immediately brought before "Roberto". Having gathered the Chief of Staff and over seventy guerrilla fighters, the hearing began. One of the guerrilla fighters described the nature of the charge: Francisco Márquez, a fifty-year-old peasant, informed the Civil Guard of the presence of an AGG unit. As a consequence of this tipoff the Civil Guard had been able to surprise the guerrilla unit and cause the death of "six comrades". The Chief of Staff listened to the allegations and the defendant's plea before sentencing him to death. Márquez was hanged that same night. His cousin was released. The following two notes explaining the sentence were found in the dead man's bag:.

> The execution [*ajusticiamiento*] of this individual is due to the elimination of the guerrilla fighters who arrived from exile and were captured by the henchmen paid by Franco.
>
> When the shepherd who watched over this man's flock came to his house to ask for food for our comrades, he did not hesitate in sending it, but he immediately told the repressive forces [about what had happened], which caused the death of my comrades.
>
> The Guerrilla Army does not forget such crimes nor does it forgive those responsible. The justice of the guerrilla may be delayed but eventually it reaches into every corner where criminals hide.
>
> Guerrilla Army of Andalusia. Agrupación de Granada. On the orders of the High Command.
>
> Informing spies. This is guerrilla justice for all who show or tell [the authorities] the camps or movements of our units. The same goes for all who have harmed our people. AGRUPACIÓN GUERRILLERA DE GRANADA.[74]

The *modern guerrilla* always left notes on the corpses so that the authorities would know the outcome of the court hearing and the reasons for their death.[75] The aim was obviously to eradicate any collaboration between the civilian population and the authorities and show that their actions were not to be confused with simple criminality. Groups of *armed neighbours* never held formal hearings in the mountains and explanatory notes were only occasionally left by the "Clares" and "Yatero" groups while both were operating under the influence of the AGG.[76]

Chapter 7

Voices of the Resistance
Propaganda and communication

Every act of the guerrilla army ought always to be accompanied by the propaganda necessary to explain the reasons for it. (. . .) The most effective propaganda is that which is prepared within the guerrilla zone. Priority will be given to the diffusion of ideas among natives of the zone, offering explanations of the theoretical significance of the insurrection (. . .). In this zone there will also be peasant periodicals, the general organ of all guerrilla forces, and bulletins and proclamations. There will also be the radio (. . .). Propaganda should be of a national, orienting type (. . .). is this [battle] which has hammered, chiselled, and strengthened us and made us what we are. This war (. . .) shaped us in combat, to the point where we will continue to be combatants.

(*La Guerra de guerrillas*, Ernesto *Che* Guevara)

Propaganda is typically informative and persuasive in character. The sender sends a message with the intention of influencing the "opinions or actions of other individuals or groups for predetermined ends and by psychological manipulation".[1] The use of terms like *manipulation* or *persuasion* should be understood in a sociological sense, without value connotations, as propaganda can be used to encourage everything from the extermination of a community to solidarity between peoples. It is a form of social communication which can be put to multiple ends; it intervenes in the construction of internal (we) as well as external (they) identities, and it serves as an extraordinary tool of social mobilisation, harbouring the power to threaten enemies and establish frameworks for collective action.[2]

Throughout history, propaganda has always been an indispensable resource in the management of power relations and conflicts. As a form of social communication, propaganda acquired new status in the middle of the nineteenth century and was granted even greater importance in the first decades of the twentieth. The emergence of radio, the expansion of communication channels and the growth of receptive audiences were fundamental to this process. Mass society transformed the stage of the struggle: new agents assumed a greater role and the mechanisms of social communication and control adapted to new circumstances. Access to cultural production triggered a slow but gradually expanding process of democratisation of media and the production of meaning.[3] In this context, propaganda took on a new dimension, incorporating new techniques and distribution channels and becoming "one of the most powerful instruments of the modern world".[4]

Although it was not the only factor, there is no doubt that new forms of social communication prompted important shifts in approaches to irregular warfare, which, in turn, favoured the emergence of the *modern guerrilla*. Concepts such as "psychological warfare" and "propaganda war" were adopted by guerrillas and counterinsurgency centres, who made use of new propaganda resources and techniques. However, in the case of the anti-Francoist guerrilla, there were important differences in this regard resulting from its internal heterogeneity. While the *modern guerrilla*, which was very conscious of the power of modern propaganda, made use of a wide range of resources, groups of *armed neighbours* used social communication methods that were more traditional in the countryside.

Propaganda and the modern guerrilla

The *modern guerrilla* was aware of the fact that the armed struggle not only depended on the Agrupaciones guerrilleras, but also on an extensive network of local, regional and national committees. If the guerrilla were to link all these organisations in a coherent campaign, some communication apparatus was required at each level. Thus the anti-Francoist opposition, and especially the PCE, provided the guerrilla movement with a variety of propaganda instruments.

Radio España Independiente

One of the principal propaganda channels run by the PCE was Radio España Independiente (REI), better known as *Pirenaica*. Established by Dolores Ibárruri in Moscow in July 1941, *Pirenaica* was, for forty years, one of the very few news outlets evading censorship (the others being the BBC, Radio Francia Internacional, and the press reports of the British consulates).[5] As a tool of propaganda, the REI had important advantages over other media. Firstly, it had an unrivalled power to reach a wide audience. Any longwave radio located anywhere in Spain could tune into the broadcast, which guaranteed national coverage and minimised risks, even when the message was brought to the most remote corners of the country. Secondly, the transmission of the message through a spoken medium allowed the PCE to reach a greater audience, as Spain remained a country with high levels of illiteracy. Lastly, the medium allowed the party to broadcast new slogans to the whole country at once and thereby avoid confusions and temporal dislocations.

In terms of the guerrilla struggle, the REI made important efforts to mobilise popular support for the resistance from 1943. That year, Dolores Ibárruri began broadcasting speeches in support of the guerrilla, a theme she would return to with increasing frequency during 1944, until guerrilla-related propaganda reached its peak during the Operation Reconquest of Spain in October and November. Propaganda broadcasts remained a resource in the guerrilla struggle, but, from 1947 onwards, the REI made considerably fewer direct references to the resistance. Even so, the station continued to disseminate news regarding guerrilla activities in Spain as a whole, to denounce the crimes of the dictatorship and to inform people of the names of "traitors" and "Falangists" who had been eliminated.[6]

The PCE organised three landings of guerrilla fighters in Andalusia. It was no coincidence that the three groups were equipped with radio transmitters and counted among them a specialist in radio technology.[7] The radio allowed them to intercept Civil Guard and Army communications, make contact with different guerrilla groups and receive the general directives via *Pirenaica*. Dolores Ibárruri highlighted the importance of the radio in a talk clearly aimed at groups of *armed neighbours* and broadcast on REI in December 1944:

> LISTEN, LEADERS OF GUERRILLA DETACHMENTS
> You, guerrilla fighters, have arms and you have courage. You are prepared to risk your lives at any moment. But you proceed without method. One day you cut the communications between Madrid and Valencia, the next day you derail a train in Despeñaperros, and the next you attack a group of Falangists . . . You are saved by virtue of incredible and heroic efforts. But, to some extent, you fight how people fought in the War of Independence [the Peninsular War, 1808–1814] (. . .). Force has to be supplemented with astuteness. And in the guerrilla wars of today, the radio can and must be seen as a valuable aid.[8]

Guerrilla press

The printed press was the most important and the most widespread propaganda medium in Spain. There were fewer advantages, but print media had some strengths that radio lacked. On the one hand, in comparison with radio, a message in the printed press was less widely circulated. Distribution networks tended to be local or regional, although there were newspapers, such as *Mundo Obrero*, which operated at a national level. Even so, distribution was hampered by evident difficulties which also exposed organisations to serious risks. The PCE's decision not to establish separate structures for the party and the guerrilla resulted in numerous problems, especially from 1945 onwards, and the distribution of the guerrilla press provides some of the clearest examples. Both local and regional committees in Andalusia fell after the police had followed their distribution channels, and the presses were confiscated once the party apparatus was dismantled.[9]

Moreover, the printed press could only reach a limited audience, given the high levels of illiteracy in the country. It is true that there had long existed the tradition among poorer social sectors of having news items or other texts read aloud to them. A group would gather around a reader and he or she would transmit the text vocally. A large number of the illiterate population would access written information in this way.[10] The AGM and the AGG used this method in various mountain villages. José Rodríguez, better known as "Pepe the Teacher" was hiding in the Montes de Málaga after being imprisoned for a brief period in a concentration camp. During the Republican period he had been President of the Workers' Society of the socialist union UGT in Fuengirola and was consequently afraid of further reprisals in the post-war period. As soon as he arrived in the mountains he began to give classes in selected farm houses in the area, and, from 1946, the PCE made him responsible for the distribution of clandestine press and guerrilla propaganda. As he himself admitted in his subsequent testimony to the authorities, he would gather sympathetic locals in a farm house and read aloud the propaganda received from the party and the guerrillas.[11]

The difficult conditions caused by censorship and high production costs greatly limited the publication frequency and continuity of the clandestine press. The Interior Ministry exercised strict control over legal printing equipment, ink and paper.[12] Thus, the PCE and the *modern guerrilla* were forced to create their own clandestine print shops using paper duplicators. The material was in most cases bought from foreign sources and delivered to Spain by merchant ships, the merchandise having to bypass several obstacles before reaching its destination.[13] In any case, the productive capacity of clandestine print shops was significantly diminished by the difficulty of obtaining materials and the constant arrests of committee members.

The production models adopted by the clandestine press and its limited distribution can only be understood in this context of instability. The resistance would occasionally produce properly printed material, but, in most cases, the guerrilla press operated with manually typed, or even hand-written, copies of an original text. This is a crucial fact, especially in relation to issues of distribution. Prints made with a duplicator could be distributed in their thousands, whereas texts copied on a typewriter or by hand were never produced in numbers exceeding a few dozen. This situation not only affected the scale of distribution but also increased the risks associated with subversive propaganda production. A copy of a mechanically printed text did not change hands as much as one that was manually copied as there were more copies to go around. The greater circulation of manually copied propaganda items prompted closer contact between resistance members, which increased the risk of being discovered by the authorities.[14] All these factors caused considerable discontinuity in publication patterns and significant confusion with regards to the communication and reception of party directives.

That said, the nature of the clandestine press certainly encouraged a stronger local and regional focus, compared with national media like Pirenaica. This is important, not least because the mechanisms of identification have a stronger impact, the closer people imagine themselves to be.

The clandestine press in 1940s Spain was fragmented and sporadic in character. There were publications linked to different political organisations (PCE, CNT, PSOE, etc.) which also had separate publications at regional and local levels. There also emerged specific titles relating to the guerrilla and the prisons. With regard to the guerrilla press, there were an estimated 42 different titles in Spain, the most notable of which belonged to the Agrupación Guerrillera de Levante-Aragón and the Ejército Guerrillero de Galicia.[15]

The clandestine press was very fragmented in Andalusia too. In terms of character and distribution, it was, broadly speaking, divided into two types. Firstly, it is necessary to distinguish between publications with a national outlook and those with a predominantly regional focus. Secondly, it is possible to distinguish between publications focused purely on the guerrilla struggle, on the one hand, and more general publications linked to political opposition, on the other, even where the latter included news items and slogans concerning the guerrilla (Appendix: Table 12).

The PCE was the organisation with the greatest media presence in eastern Andalusia; it published eight clandestine titles, compared to CNT's three. Although the exact print run of these publications is not known, the structural differences between the two organisations and their propaganda apparatus during the 1940s suggest that the PCE press was more widely distributed in Andalusia than its anarcho-syndicalist counterpart.[16]

Roughly what kind of print runs may the guerrilla press have had? In Galicia, the newspaper *El Guerrillero* achieved a print run of 800 copies. Newspapers like *Mundo Obrero* had, in its national version, a print run of 9,000 copies, which was possible because the publication was printed in France.[17] According to the internal reports of the PCE, the newspaper of the AGM/AGG, *Por la República*, reached a print run of 4,000 copies, although the usual characteristics of each issue (which was copied out on a typewriter) suggest that the average print run could hardly have been higher than 300 copies.[18]

In any case, the numbers show that there was a rough balance between the clandestine press at national level, which comprised five titles, and that at regional level, comprising six. However, regional publications also had different geographical coverage and focus. The six regional titles in Andalusia were *Mundo Obrero* (regional supplement), *Voz Obrera*, *Solidaridad Proletaria*, *Unidad*, *Por la República* and *Resistencia*. The first three, published by the Regional Committee of the PCE, based in Seville, were distributed in the whole of Andalusia, while the fourth was restricted to Málaga and the last two to Málaga and Granada. Of the eleven publications, four focused purely on the guerrillas: *Reconquista de España*, distributed throughout the peninsula and published by National Union (Unión Nacional) organised by Jesús Monzón; *Ataque*, also distributed nationally and published by the High Command of the Guerrilla Army; *Por la República*, ostensibly the newspaper of the Guerrilla Army of Andalusia but in reality published by AGM and later AGG; and *Resistencia*, published by the same organisation. All belonged to the PCE.

In the national clandestine press, the focus was predominantly on international and national news. In the regional press, by contrast, there were three levels of information (national, regional, and local), although regional and local affairs were prioritised. This strategy enabled the guerrilla to establish contact with rural populations through mechanisms of local identification, which could then be upgraded to regional, national, and international levels. Even so, the difficult conditions regarding distribution significantly hampered the mobilising potential of the clandestine press.

One of the greatest problems of the clandestine press was that it relied, in most cases, on the enthusiasm and voluntary sacrifice of its social base. This support was necessary but insufficient for its expansion. From its headquarters in France, the editors of *Reconquista de España* encouraged its readers inside Spain to work as journalists and distributors of the clandestine press. All they needed was pen and paper, "although typed contributions would be preferable, copied with a duplicator or a printer".[19]

The basic idea was that "every Spaniard" would be "a contributor to *Reconquista*". Similar notions were expressed by other guerrilla papers, such as *Resistencia*, which asked "all comrades and all patriots in general to send us a contribution". The AGG had an internal reporter embedded in every group: "every guerrilla or Resistance unit must include a correspondent of the Resistance".[20] Oppositional forces made every effort to distribute and thereby widen the readership of the clandestine press, but the scarcity of materials and the repressive measures adopted by the state hindered any possible expansion.

Guerrilla papers did not have regular sections like conventional newspapers, but the overall format tended to be the same in every issue. Descriptions of guerrilla operations, slogans and texts communicating basic party directives occupied the most prominent positions. The most common exhortations asked that the working classes collaborate with the anti-Francoist guerrilla in its fight against the dictatorship:

> Peasants, workers, patriots everywhere. Help unconditionally the Guerrilla Army to fight and annihilate the exploiters who enrich themselves by robbing the fruits of your labours and the executioners who torture and kill the Spanish people and ruin our fatherland.[21]

In addition to such texts, it was common to add a few articles regarding the national and international situation and a few poems, songs, or drawings by the guerrilla fighters themselves. On December 6th 1948, a contingent of more than six hundred Army soldiers and Civil Guards attacked the AGG's base camps. The military operation was a failure because, despite finding the camp, they did not capture any guerrilla fighters and suffered various casualties. A few days later, "Paquillo" published a poem in *Por la República* which mocked one of those Civil Guards, portrayed as a feeble and cowardly creature compared to the brave and courageous guerrilla fighters:

> Alaminos moans and cries
> high on the mountain;
> Alaminos begs,
> kneeling on the ground.
> Alaminos goes to hide;
> they look in every corner;
> they call; he does not reply;
> he ducks behind the rocks.
> Alaminos ends up fleeing

before reason catches up with him,
and running down the footpath
the poor man loses
even the rustic buttons
on his worn jacket.[22]

Propaganda structures

The interest shown by the *modern guerrilla* and the PCE in various propaganda techniques is evident in their organisational structures. In the 1940s, the provincial, regional and national committees of the PCE were divided into four sections: the General Secretariat, the Secretariat of Organisation and Finance, the Secretariat of Unions, and the Secretariat of Agitation, Propaganda and Military Organisation.[23] It was no coincidence that the PCE integrated responsibilities relating to agit-prop and the armed struggle in one Secretariat. In fact, both aspects of its work were closely related.

The Agrupaciones guerrilleras had their own propaganda apparatus. The directives issued by the guerrilla leadership in exile were clear: "Our units must try to establish solid structures for the dissemination of propaganda and ensure that this propaganda ends up, by all means imaginable, in the hands of all anti-Francoists, wherever they are, and that it is read by the largest number possible".[24] Ramón Vía, leader of the AGM in Málaga province, had a clear understanding of the importance of propaganda in the guerrilla struggle. As part of his underground work in Oran he was responsible for PCE's propaganda apparatus in North Africa and set up various illegal print shops.[25] One of his obsessions was the creation of a propaganda structure within the guerrilla, but the difficult conditions slowed down the project. In September 1945, he created the "Musketeers of the Plains" in the city of Málaga as an auxiliary organisation with two fundamental objectives: to engage in propaganda work and form a core of guerrilla reservists. But, as described previously , the life of the Musketeers was particularly short. In May 1946, the police arrested Alfredo Cabello, which led to another thirty arrests and the complete dismemberment of the group.[26]

The AGG, led by "Roberto", also created its own propaganda apparatus. Francisco Sánchez, better known as "Paquillo", was head of the Press and Propaganda section between 1947 and 1951, that is, for most of the AGG's existence. Within the Agrupaciones, the post as head of propaganda was reserved for guerrilla members who combined at least two special qualities. Firstly, they had to be fiercely loyal to the PCE and be well regarded by the Politburo. The PCE files on Francisco Sánchez clearly show the kind of profile needed for the job: "political conviction (. . . .) and absolute loyalty to the Party (. . .) Disciplined (. . .) Great capacity for self-sacrifice".[27]

Secondly, candidates for this post also had to be well educated, at least to a level which allowed them to manage the propaganda apparatus. Francisco Sánchez was a bricklayer by trade, although some guerrilla fighters claimed he had been a seminarian. "He was funny and knew how to say things in writing", recalled one of his colleagues in the guerrilla much later.[28]

Meetings, occupations and propaganda

From its beginnings, the *modern guerrilla* was very aware of the importance of direct propaganda in social mobilisation processes. The Andalusian guerrillas' *Manual of political-military orientation*, edited by Ricardo Beneyto, made reference to a whole repertoire of propaganda activities that were relevant to the guerrillas. Propaganda should be disseminated by:

> organising meetings and assemblies in farm houses, factories, workshops and villages, where the objectives of our struggle can be explained simply (. . .); distributing [printed] propaganda material among the population close to and within our operational zone (. . .); taking villages if, only for a few hours, in order to raise the Republican flag in as many places as possible. It is crucial that no operation, regardless of size, is carried out without political explanation (. . .) this will greatly reinforce antiFrancoist sympathy towards us and strengthen their morale in the struggle against Franco.[29]

Meetings, assemblies, leaflets, village occupations; all were valid means to explain to rural societies the reasons for the guerrilla struggle, increase support among the peasantry and mobilise the most active sectors. In Spain, it was not common for guerrillas to occupy villages. The risks were high and the results often counter-productive. On the one hand, occupations could widen the social support base, reduce local levels of collaboration with the Civil Guard (as a result of increased fear of the guerrillas) and even aid recruitment. But, on the other hand, they could also have devastating effects. After a guerrilla occupation, the Civil Guard usually increased their repression, and, in many cases, this led to the complete destruction of local support networks and collaborators. For this reason, the *modern guerrilla* only carried out a handful of occupations, after which it halted such operations as a result of their severe repercussions. Even so, there are a few examples to study.

On the night of March 1st 1946, an AGM unit occupied the small hamlet of Guajar Alto, located in the province of Granada. The unit gathered all the locals in a square and one of the guerrilla fighters took the initiative of starting a village meeting. Later, as they left, the guerrilla virtually covered the streets in leaflets, both in the temporarily occupied village and in a neighbouring community. The results were immediate. Two locals from Guajar Alto joined the Agrupación guerrillera that same night. However, the authorities also responded without delay. The day after the event, both villages were occupied by the Civil Guard and various locals were arrested, among them a socialist who had been mayor during the Republican years.[30]

In February 1948, a day labourer who worked on the estate belonging to the Marquesa de Cázulas decided to join the AGG.[31] Three weeks later a number of units occupied the estate. The guerrilla killed a few sheep and organised a great feast with the estate employees. "At the end of the dinner, the workers listened to a political talk which explained the rationale of our struggle (. . .); only thus can we be free of Francoist terror".[32]

There are various cases where the dates chosen for local propaganda activities were highly symbolic. At dawn on April 14th 1946, the anniversary of the proclamation of the Second Republic, a number of PCE members hung 25 printed flags around the streets of Granada.[33] A similar occurrence took place on April 14th 1950, when the city awoke to find hundreds of leaflets celebrating the Republic.[34] In February 1948, the Chief of Staff of the AGG ordered all its units to occupy villages in their area and to hand out propaganda in commemoration of February 16th, the day the Popular Front won the general elections in 1936.[35]

However, despite such propaganda efforts, the *modern guerrilla* occasionally found it hard to communicate with the peasantry. The guerrilla did not always adapt its language to the language of the village, which meant that its messages often appeared cryptic and indecipherable to rural audiences. "We don't understand many of the words you are using", said a Russian peasant to a Bolshevik leader during the Russian Revolution.[36] The *modern guerrilla* faced a similar situation in Spain. Constant references to leaders like Lenin, Stalin, Santiago Carrillo or Dolores Ibárruri, or debates and propaganda littered with "urban" political terminology confused and unsettled sectors of the peasantry. A member of the Agrupación Guerrillera de Levante-Aragón acknowledged, in a way, these communication problems: "Of course many peasants were not sufficiently educated to explain very clearly or even tell us what demands they wanted to put forward".[37]

This guerrilla member took peasants' minimal education to be the cause of their communication problem, when, in fact, it was a consequence of each group using different codified languages. All kinds of communication require some knowledge of a common code between sender and receiver. Yet it was not the case that the *modern guerrilla* had a general communication problem with the peasantry in Spain. An "urban" political vocabulary had slowly penetrated rural communities in the first decades of the twentieth century, and the *modern guerrilla* tried to adapt their language, although there is no doubt that complications arose. In any case, the communication issues involved not only vocabulary but also disparate cultural frameworks.

International campaigns

One area where the heads of guerrilla propaganda and the secretaries of Agitation, Propaganda and Military Operations at provincial, regional, and national levels all worked together was international campaigns to denounce the repression of the dictatorship. When successful, these initiatives gave rise to wide-ranging collaboration. Information was sent through various communication channels (internal reports, guerrilla press, etc.) from the PCE inside Spain to its exiled leadership, who distributed it to different national delegations. These then mobilised all support and resources in a campaign which was also coordinated with other international support organisations.[38]

These campaigns were developed through a wide range of activities: workshops, demonstrations, meetings, publication of articles, leaflets, and flyers, protests in front of Spanish embassies and consulates, lobbying of political parties, parliaments and governments of foreign countries in order to pressure them to condemn the dictatorship.[39] When the campaigns were successful, the results were communicated in the opposite direction, from exiled groups abroad to party leaders inside Spain. The clandestine press reported on condemnations issued abroad, which often generated enthusiasm and hope among the most politicised social sectors. "Political, cultural, and religious organisations throughout the world; eminent personalities of science and the arts and governments of democratic countries have taken interest in the life of the two celebrated Spanish Republicans", said one of the leaflets published by the Regional Committee of the Andalusian PCE in connection with the campaign against the death penalty for Santiago Álvarez and Sebastián Zapirain.[40] There was a reduced sense of isolation, which occasionally facilitated mobilisation.

However, not all attempts to mount an international campaign were successful. So how many of them did in fact have a real impact abroad? Documents pertaining to the British Foreign Office suggest that only seven campaigns achieved significant visibility on the international stage,[41] although studies of other sources may modify this conclusion somewhat (Appendix: Table 13).

The PCE was the only Spanish party maintaining an important propaganda section with the capacity to mobilise the resources and social support necessary to organise international campaigns. All seven campaigns shown to have had some impact were organised by the PCE. All of them also aimed to overturn death sentences, which suggests that the emotive reaction to such phenomena harboured great mobilising potential in an international context. Of the seven campaigns, five related to one person only. The individual focus of the campaign facilitated the manipulation of personal identification processes and made it possible to symbolically fuse the biography of a single individual with Francoist brutality and repression as a whole. The other cases related to a pair (Álvarez and Zapirain) and a group of nine people, whose distinguishing characteristic in in this context was their youth (seven of the nine detainees were 18 years old or younger at the time of their arrest).

It is also significant that fourteen of the sixteen people at the centre of these campaigns were directly related to the anti-Francoist guerrilla: one as a national leader (Agustín Zoroa), another as regional political leader (Ricardo Beneyto), three as military guerrilla leaders (Juan Vitini, Cristino García Granda and Ramón Vía), and nine as new recruits, allegedly intending to form a guerrilla cell. Only two cases related to people outside the guerrilla movement: Santiago Álvarez and Sebastián Zapirain, who were both members of the Central Committee of the PCE in Spain. The case of Agustín Zoroa falls into both categories, as he was the Political-Military head of the guerrilla under the leadership of Jesús Monzón, but then the General Secretary of the PCE in Spain after the fall of Zapirain.

The myths surrounding the guerrillas held enormous mobilising power, especially at the particular historical moment when the campaigns achieved their greatest visibility. The peak came between 1945 and 1947, that is, just as the Second World War had finished and the partisans enjoyed great prestige in many places across the continent.[42] Many Spanish Republicans had participated in the antifascist struggle as partisans and there was a widespread sense of gratitude and indebtedness towards Spanish antifascist fighters in Europe. In fact, Juan Vitini and García Granda had participated in the liberation of France and were considered national heroes.[43]

The international campaigns organised by the PCE before 1945 largely failed to resonate. War developments in Europe left little space for such initiatives. From 1948 onwards, PCE campaigns again had negligible international impact. The new logic of the Cold War and the "fight against communism" silenced all campaigns denouncing the dictatorship. This situation remained unchanged until 1962, when the European left began to formulate a new alternative discourse that allowed campaigns against Franco's dictatorship to regain their international resonance. This was the case with the communist leader Julián Grimau and two young anarchists, Granado and Delgado, the following year.[44] Thereafter, European campaigns maintained a consistent visibility until the end of the dictatorship.

Radio, press, occupations and meetings, distribution of propaganda, international campaigns: all these means were employed by the *modern guerrilla*, which was highly aware of its importance in modern wars:

> Our propaganda is the equivalent of the heavy enemy artillery that we do not yet have and is in many cases more efficacious than such artillery (. . .).
>
> Our propaganda is our voice and our ideas, which are rapidly communicated from one to another. It provides us with sympathisers, friends and collaborators. It also corrects mistakes and undermines the lies disseminated by Falangists and their lackeys. Our propaganda strengthens and encourages thousands of men and women to join the fight, men and women who are profoundly anti-Francoist but do not participate actively in the struggle because they do not know how.[45]

So, did groups of *armed neighbours* make similar use of propaganda resources?

Communication and *neighbours in arms*

An analysis of groups of *armed neighbours* shows an absence both of propaganda structures and the instruments used by the *modern guerrilla*. None of the local groups organised occupations or meetings in the villages, nor did they launch national or international campaigns. They did not have a clandestine press, nor did they publish leaflets or flyers, and they lacked the equipment to send radio broadcasts. Nonetheless, it would be a mistake to assume that *neighbours in arms* had no means of transmitting their message of opposition to the dictatorship. They had their own forms of social communication but it is necessary to adopt an anthropological approach to decipher the codes and tools employed to this end.

Rumours constitute a principal communication resource in irregular warfare, especially in that waged by *neighbours in arms* (and, to a lesser extent, the *modern guerrilla*) in Spain. As various authors have shown, rumours can be a powerful form of communication, and, as they spread through social networks, they require no material infrastructure. The creation of rumours was a common way of spreading news or ideas before the emergence of modern communication media. However, these modern inventions did not eliminate the need for oral communication, which remained particularly important in peasant societies. It combined a set of characteristics which were of significant benefit to the guerrilla: zero cost, low risk, fast, wide-ranging dissemination and difficult for the authorities to trace. The rumour, called a "weapon of the weak", was used daily by subaltern groups, be it as a means of quotidian resistance or as a means of supporting the armed resistance.[46] It proved to be a highly effective resource.

However, rumours were not the only means of communication employed by the *neighbours in arms*. These groups had a close relationship with their area of action. In most cases, guerrilla fighters operated within their local community. This resulted in the inhabitants of that community knowing perfectly well both the identity of local guerrilla fighters and the reasons for their escape to the mountains. Moreover, although groups of *armed neighbours* were conscious of the fact that the fight against the dictatorship ultimately had to be fought at national level, they acted according to local cultural codes . Hence their operational reach was limited to a small area: *their* area, which most of these groups had no interest in extending i. For many of their members, the tools of modern propaganda were alien to their own life experiences, yet the circumstances of local groups encouraged them to use another propaganda strategy, one which had a long tradition within the Spanish left: *propaganda by the deed*.

Propaganda by the deed is a concept which has generated a large body of theoretical literature. Historically it has been linked to revolutionary anarchist tactics developed by the ideologue Mihail Bakunin, although its origins can be traced to the French socialist Paul Brousse or the Neapolitan Carlo Pisacane. In any case, propaganda by the deed was advocated by new anarchist theorists like Enrico Malatesta or Carlo Cafiero, who, in the Naples Congress of 1876, defined the "insurrectional deed" as the most efficacious of all forms of propaganda. The "insurrectional deed" did not include attacks against society but rather referred to different techniques of agitation such as strikes, meetings, risings and occupations, aiming to trigger an insurrectional movement. While it is true that propaganda by the deed often tended towards terrorism the original meaning of the concept was conserved until the 1930s, at least in the Spanish case.[47]

There were a certain number of anarchists in the Andalusian groups of *armed neighbours* but these were a clear minority compared to the socialists, as were the communists. In the 1930s, socialist unionism in rural areas in eastern Andalusia had acquired much greater importance than any anarchist option, which was concentrated in the cities of Málaga and Granada. Groups of *armed neighbours* obviously engaged in armed propaganda but this was not due to any commitment to anarchist tactics. This was instead a basic form of direct informal communication which did not require any great resources to achieve its aims.

"Words might well be what man uses when he has nothing else", said Flora Davis in her book about non-verbal communication.[48] A simple gesture or posture establishes a form of social communication between the sender and receiver, capable of transmitting messages without the mediation of words. Due to its symbolic character, collective action is also a form of social communication charged with messages.[49]

The relationship between the guerrillas and the local community was complex and tended to have a paradoxical character, as various authors have indicated. Those locals who found themselves outside the law formed their own group and thereby seceded from the community. Nevertheless, in many ways they remained a part of the community, with which they shared loyalties, local co-ordinates and symbolic codes.[50]

Thus, all guerrilla operations had a clear meaning for affected locals. When they carried out a robbery, a kidnapping or a murder, the message could be deduced from the character and identity of the victim. All individuals form part of different social networks, in which they occupy a symbolic place. The smaller the group, the greater the symbolic charge attached to each individual member. When studying any form of guerrilla action, researchers tend to look at a single attack against an individual of whom very little is known. However, contemporary inhabitants who knew the symbolic coordinates of local networks would not only see the identity of the individual but also the symbolism of his or her social position. In this way guerrilla actions became attacks against *caciques* (rural political bosses), *señoritos* (affluent snobs), *falangistas* (Falangists), or *chivatos* (informers), to give but a few examples, each carrying a specific significance.[51]

This symbolism was connected to characteristics which were not necessarily present in reality, although the symbol could carry considerable force nonetheless. Sebastián Navas, a peasant living in a small village in Málaga where the guerrilla was active, recently explained: "there were no *señoritos* here. Those who had more land called themselves *señoritos*, but they weren't really rich. They were Franco supporters".[52]

These symbolic systems were often hidden to the outside observer. Few testimonies touched directly on murders committed by the guerrilla. Fear continued to be an inhibiting factor among the inhabitants of the mountains but their accounts give at least some insight into the fabric of local symbolisms. Interpersonal relations, at times conditioned by long-running conflicts, were also part of the dynamics of violence and tend to be difficult to bring to the surface. Murders and robberies were occasionally prompted by personal motives and locals were very aware of the nature of these. Should personal motives play a clear part in an attack, the prestige of the guerrilla would suffer significantly. However, the population did not interpret guerrilla activities uniformly: where some highlighted elements of personal revenge, others emphasised the social or political nature of an attack. In any case, if the guerrilla wanted to maintain a level of social support within a community, it could never transgress consensual moral codes established by that community. There was a clear distinction between "just and legitimate" violence and that seen as "unjust, unnecessary, and wanton murder".[53] These distinctions may seem odd in peaceful and democratic societies, but they are extremely important in societies marked by high levels of violence and oppression.

Guerrilla action (a robbery, a kidnapping or a murder) sent out multiple signals. Although everyone interpreted the symbolic character of the act through the victim, the conclusions reached could be very different. Those who identified with the values or the symbols represented by the victim may have felt fear and indignation while for those who identified the victim with something negative (a symbol of repression, power, etc.) the act could give rise to a profound feeling of "justice".

The power of the guerrilla myth

Groups of *armed neighbours* utilised simple and direct means of propaganda, but like the *modern guerrilla* they were also helped by other cultural resources of comparable importance. The French anthropologist Levi-Strauss indicated that "nothing comes as close to mythical thought as political ideology". Both kinds of thought are imbued with feeling, faith, and passion.[54] The relationship between myth and politics is not a result of mere coincidences but rather a mutual influence which constitutes a direct link. Political myths are powerful resources in the construction of identities and collective mobilisation, which also makes them key tools in social communication. For these reasons, political myths have played a particularly important role in the mass societies of the nineteenth and twentieth centuries.[55]

Political myths offer a window onto the beliefs, values, and feelings of a community. George Sorel, one of the most important theorists of political violence in the nineteenth century, remarked in a letter to the French historian Daniel Halévy that "A myth cannot be refuted, since it is, fundamentally, identical to the convictions of a group, being the expression of these convictions in the language of movement".[56] Sorel thus laid down the basis for some of the beliefs later informing Mussolini's propaganda. As Emilio Gentile has shown, the ideologues of Italian fascism were very conscious of the mobilizing force of political myths, as well as their potential to shape collective consciousness.[57]

This is not a secondary issue. Similar observations can be made regarding German Nazism and Soviet communism.[58] Wars and revolutions have proved particularly fertile ground for the construction of contemporary political myths and the guerrilla struggle, often invisible, yet typically given a romantic air, was a suggestive subject for these kinds of representations. The Mexican revolution would seem incomplete without the political myths surrounding guerrilla figures such as Emilio Zapata and Pancho Villa, just as the Cuban revolution and its extension in Latin America in the 1960s and 1970s is inseparable from the myths of Fidel Castro and Ernesto *Che* Guevara.[59] These people have become part of the collective imaginary. More importantly, in every process in which they participated, their myth was an operative factor facilitating mobilisation and the construction of collective identities.

Both *neighbours in arms* and the *modern guerrilla* used myths as a cultural resource aiding recruitment, mobilisation and identity construction, although each group would have different communication tools at their disposal. Groups of *armed neighbours* nourished their myths through direct action and rumours, while the *modern guerrilla* added their whole propaganda apparatus to these resources. However, when analysing political myth it is important to distinguish between those myths which circulated at the time of struggle and consequently had an impact on contemporaneous society and those which were constructed decades later. This appears to be a simple distinction but occasionally mistakes have been made when authors have transferred later mythical constructions to a period when they did not form part of a lived reality.[60] Oral testimonies are not trustworthy in this respect. Reconstructions of past events from memory can easily be distorted by associations which emerge after the event in question. Hence, written documents must be the fundamental source of material for this kind of analysis.

Political myths transcend normality. Dozens of guerrilla groups operated in Spain, but only a minority achieved a mythical status: "Bernabé" in Asturias, "Juanín" in Cantabria, "Foucellas" in Galicia, "Girón" in León and "Sabaté" in Barcelona, to mention the most representative examples.[61] In

Andalusia, the most notable cases were those involving Ramon Vía and "Roberto", within the *modern guerrilla*, and the "hermanos Quero", among the *neighbours in arms*. The following analysis will focus on the latter, which is of particular importance.

Between 1940 and 1947 at least sixty guerrilla groups operated in eastern Andalusia. Many were of a similar size to that of the "hermanos Quero", i.e. sixteen members throughout its existence, and others were actually larger. Agrupaciones guerrilleras such as the AGM and the AGG covered large tracts of territory in their operations; they possessed important propaganda tools and structures and would even engage in international campaigns. The "hermanos Quero" group did not employ such means. Their operational area was restricted to the city of Granada, where they nonetheless managed to establish one of the most powerful political myths of the era. The Spanish guerrilla were given different labels: run-aways, maquis, *fuxidos*. In some areas of eastern Andalusia guerrilla fighters simply called themselves *queros*, thus referring to the group whose name had effectively become a regional synonym for guerrilla.[62]

The myth of the "Quero" was constructed without recourse to any modern propaganda machinery, emerging solely on the basis of propaganda by the deed, word of mouth and rumours. Aided by such phenomena, spectacular actions such as a prison break, a donation to friends or family, a kidnapping of a distinguished figure (e.g. a general or a banker), a visit to the military judge or a robbery committed in broad daylight in the centre of the regional capital, gave them an air of invisibility, invincibility and generosity similar to that described by Hobsbawm in his studies on bandits.[63]

The myth became so powerful that the collective imagination attributed various operations to the"hermanos Quero" which had, in fact, been carried out by other groups, such as the kidnapping of Colonel Milans del Bosch, an action by the "Clares" group, and the killing of police inspector Julio Romero Funes, carried out by the "Velazquez Murillo" group.[64] Rumours inflated the legend and subaltern groups created and disseminated new and ever more fantastical stories, interspersed with curious anecdotes and details. For example, it was said that the "hermanos Quero" met in central Granada and had lunch in restaurants where they left a generous tip and a note which said: "The hermanos Quero have eaten here".[65] It was a way of constructing an oppositional narrative: a hidden and subversive discourse. A hero who becomes a myth is a symbol: a symbol representing the dream of freedom and justice.[66]

In his reports on the anti-Francoist guerrilla in the province of Granada, Eulogio Limia Pérez, a lieutenant colonel in the Civil Guard, made various references to the mythical character of the Quero group. In 1941, he mentioned the "popularity which it has acquired throughout the years", and the following year, he emphasized the "audacity" of the group and the ease with which its members walked the streets despite being recognised by the people. By 1943 the myth was well-established: "the group acquires great prestige (. . .) feeding the popular imagination through audacious acts by these wrongdoers, who undoubtedly serve the aims of political agitators". In 1945 he claimed that the group had "reached the zenith of its prestige (. . .). The audacity of the group cannot be denied".[67] Similar comments were made in the reports of the local Falange and the state security services (Dirección General de Seguridad, DGS), who stated that "a legend is being constructed" around the "hermanos Quero".[68]

Political myths like that surrounding the "hermanos Quero" kept a dissident identity alive. The civil population contributed to and strengthened the armed struggle through such symbolic, rather than confrontational, practices. Political myths were collective constructions shaped both by the guerrilla and by society: a symbolic cultural resource which disrupted the hegemonic discourses and imagery of the dictatorship. The Francoist authorities were very aware of this effect and utilised all resources at their disposal to combat the resistance off the field of battle as well as on it. The guerrilla would not be definitively defeated until the guerrilla myths surrounding them were also dead and buried.

Chapter 8

The Invisible Front
False guerrillas and crime

The category of resistance cannot be made to exclude its (supposedly) 'primitive' or 'lumpen' forms of manifestation. There is another problem about the political definition of resistance. (. . .) the binary division between resistance and non-resistance is an unreal one. The existence of those who seem not to rebel is a warren of minute, individual, autonomous tactics and strategies which counter and inflect the visible facts of overall domination, and whose purposes and calculations, desires and choices resist any simple division into the political and the apolitical.

(*Power/Knowledge*, Colin Gordon in Michael Foucault)

The Francoist dictatorship labelled the guerrillas "criminals", "offenders" and "bandits". The aim was to deny the guerrillas' political character and thereby delegitimize armed resistance. The Agrupaciones guerrilleras used a similar method against groups of *armed neighbours*. At best they insisted that such groups were disoriented and in need of a clearer political profile,[1] but, in many cases, *neighbours in arms* were dismissed as bandits. Miguel Salado, a member of the AGG, claimed that the *neighbours in arms* with whom he had had contact – the "hermanos Quero" and the "hermanos Clares" – "were not guerrillas; they were bandits. They did not want to carry backpacks; they wanted to live in houses. They did not leave their villages, and the money they got was all for themselves. They wanted to be independent and take orders from no one. For me it was like José María *El Tempranillo* [a famous Spanish bandit in the nineteenth century]".[2]

The models *neighbours in arms* and *modern guerrilla* are not only abstract analytical tools. Members of the armed resistance were very aware of the differences which set the two kinds of guerrilla apart. However, beyond such distinctions, there are also two co-existing and complex phenomena which are not always easy to identify and isolate through archival documentation. First, there are traditional forms of peasant crime, which, in this period, could be disguised as guerrilla action. Groups engaging in such activities cannot be considered integral parts of the armed resistance, although their history and development is still important to historians of the resistance, as this chapter will show. Secondly, there are locals who formed part of guerrilla groups but who then crossed the line into pure criminality, either alone or with other group members. Both phenomena are diffuse and difficult to identify and prompt us to reconsider once more the nature of the anti-Francoist guerrilla and the particular character of peasant resistance.

In Spain, the 1940s were marked by hunger and misery. The devastating impact of the war, the thousands of workers (labour-power and human capital) interned in prisons and concentration camps, the purges taking place in all economic sectors and the autarchic politics of the dictatorship all contributed to an economic collapse. Production remained below pre-war levels until the beginning of 1950, with disastrous social consequences.[3] Ration cards did not solve problems of malnutrition; the population continued to suffer calorie and protein deficiencies, making them more vulnerable to diseases. In these conditions of marginalization, social segregation and acute poverty, survival strategies often operated at the limits of legality and contributed to a rise in begging, prostitution, fraud and property crimes.[4]

Robberies and theft were part of the traditional repertoire of day-to-day resistance among the peasantry and became one of the most common features of the post-war conflict in rural Spain.[5] From a long-term perspective, it is clear that robberies and theft increased dramatically in the 1940s, which undermines the conventional idea that the dictatorship successfully imposed "long-await social peace" after the civil war.[6]

False guerrilla fighters

In order to present the phenomenon as clearly as possible and propose a set of analytical criteria, this section will differentiate between three types of false guerrilla fighters: (1) those who deliberately claimed the identity of guerrilla fighters in threatening letters, (2) those who carried out robberies in temporary groups, and (3) those who lived in the mountains permanently but were only involved in banditry.

Threatening letters

The assumption of a guerrilla identity was a relatively common practice in both rural areas and cities and would often find expression in a letter demanding money. The use of anonymous letters as a means of extortion had deep roots in both popular and elite culture in Europe. Consequently such cases must be understood as an adaptation of traditional practice.[7]

The anti-Francoist guerrilla regularly sent threatening letters. Together with the Agrupaciones guerrilleras, local and provisional PCE committees sent threatening missives to Civil Guard barracks to ensure a passive response to resistance activity.[8] The PCE and the guerrilla also sent letters to mayors, municipal officials and distinguished Falangists, demanding the cessation of punishments meted out to guerrilla fighters' family members or neighbours.[9] The most common letter was one demanding money which would then be used to fund the resistance. This practice was predominant among *neighbours in arms*, although the *modern guerrilla* would also occasionally resort to it.[10] The rest of this section will focus on those individuals who falsely claimed to be guerrilla fighters in order to exploit the fear that the anti-Francoist guerrilla could generate for their own benefit.

Pretending to represent a guerrilla group in a threatening letter was common in the 1940s and many of these threats were never reported. The profiles of the perpetrators vary greatly, although the majority were men between the ages of twenty and thirty-five. Most came from a rural working-class background, although the phenomenon also existed in the cities. A very large proportion of these fraudsters had been excluded from the labour market and society in general as a result of their or their relatives' political history, but there were also young followers of the dictatorship with frustrated personal ambitions. In his novel *La larga marcha*, Rafael Chirbes describes a feeling which was very widespread among young working-class men who had supported the coup d'état of July 1936: they were theoretically among the victors; their war medals and blue shirts "were meant to open all doors", but time passed and they remained imprisoned by the same poverty, staring at the same grey horizon ahead.[11]

Francisco Gómez, a young man from Albondón, provides a perfect example of the survival strategies employed by some young peasants from the 'winning' side in the war. He had continued his military service after the official end of the conflict, but, having completed his training, he returned to his village, where he quickly found himself in the same situation as before the war. He decided to move to another village in the same province, where he presented himself as a maimed war veteran. This new identity gained him certain privileges, but not enough. On April 14th 1946, he handed over a letter to a neighbour, claiming it to be from a group of guerrilla fighters. The day was not chosen arbitrarily: a date as significant as that of the proclamation of the Second Republic reinforced the political nature of the missive. In any case, the letter left no room for doubt.

It contained a short message, written in capitals: "[WE ARE] THOSE IN THE MOUNTAINS. WE WANT 3,000 [PESETAS]". However, the letter had been written by Francisco himself, not the guerrillas. Shortly afterwards, he was arrested by the Civil Guard and sentenced by court martial to four years' imprisonment.[12]

Manuel Jaime, a butcher from Málaga, provides a contrasting case. A member of the UGT in the Republican period and a soldier in the Republican army during the civil war, Jaime suffered repression and social segregation as a result of his political history, and, by 1947, he was drowning in debts. However, the fear that the guerrilla instilled among certain social sectors gave him an opportunity to amass a significant amount of money without taking any great risks. He therefore decided to send an anonymous letter to a previous employer threatening to kill him if he did not pay 15,000 pesetas:

> We have saved your life various times but we also know how to take it if you don't give us the money we need, (. . .) remember that we freed you during the red [Republican] period and we also know that you belonged to the Brothers of Charity in prison in order to console the poor wretches who they hanged, so we know everything.[13]

Both the groups of *armed neighbours* and the *modern guerrilla* made great efforts to suppress these practices, which they considered to be a kind of banditry. If the two examples above show anything, it is a personal resentment towards the dictatorship – a resentment rooted in different experiences and motives yet in both cases leading to the false adoption of a guerrilla identity as an individual survival strategy in conditions of extreme hardship.

Group robberies

In his work on the Spanish post-war period, Michael Richards suggests that a predominant concern with survival in the 1940s led to a marginalisation of social consciousness in favour of an individual consciousness, which weakened any attempts to organise collective political action. The two examples given above may reinforce this idea, but what they show is, in fact, only part of social reality. The dictatorship designed political strategies to encourage atomization and social fragmentation but its success did not fully materialise until the end of the 1940s, when the generation mobilised during the Second Republic was definitively defeated. Society then turned inwards to focus on private life and individ-ualist strategies.[14]

The constant reformation of political organisations, the continued exis-tence of the anti-Francoist guerrilla and the collaboration of thousands of peasants as go-betweens clearly demonstrate that collective consciousness was not yet extinguished. Moreover, as other authors have indicated, the low material standards of life in the post-war period prompted the devel-opment of particular forms of group solidarity responding to acute scarcity. Group robberies, a practice that was widespread in the post-war years and deeply rooted in the rural sphere, were a perfect manifestation of this specific kind of solidarity, which may at times have been diffuse but nonetheless stemmed from an evident sense of frustration, dissatisfaction and injustice.[15]

Throughout the 1940s, the Ministry of Justice was extremely worried about the rise in property crime and particularly by the very young age of most of the offenders. A sharp rise in crimes committed by underage youths had been observed since the end of the civil war. Among the fundamental factors causing this rise were the extreme poverty of the post-war years, the dynamics of social segregation, unfulfilled expectations and the generally violent climate following the military conflict.

The authorities attributed the phenomenon of "wayward youths" to the corrupting influence of two heroic male models: the figure of the guerrilla fighter and the gangster of American cinema. In 1948, the state prosecutor claimed to know of "various gangs of petty thieves who, led by a gang leader, operate in a manner influenced by cinema and certain novels". In Málaga, "where the problem of abandoned children is particularly grave, the authorities have noted crimes of astonishing audacity, like the kidnap-ping of a six-year-old child, carried out by a group of small desperados between the ages of twelve and fifteen in imitation of the *Bandidos de la Sierra*".[16] But such emulation was not solely restricted to robberies and hold-ups. As the authorities themselves recognised, "the kidnappers are no simple run-aways [i.e. guerrilla fighters], but rather miscreants who, shel-tered by the terror that the gangs have instilled in the population, (. . .) dedicate their time to carrying out [all kinds of] hits which produce signif-icant material gains".[17]

The extreme conditions of survival drove hundreds of people to commit these types of crime. One of the most common strategies was to work in gangs based on primary groups (groups based on kinship, friendship and neighbourhood links). Luis Amador was a young man who, in 1943, was doing his military service in Seville. The economic situation in the parental home was desperate and his call-up had made matters worse as it deprived the family of crucial contributions to the domestic economy. Such situations explain why dozens of recruits deserted from their military service in order to secretly return to their homes: one of the most traditional forms of day-to-day resistance found among the peasantry.[18] Luis did not desert, but, in May, while on leave, he and a group of relatives and neighbours carried out several robberies, claiming to be "reds on the run". In three days they attacked six farm houses in the vicinity of the village. They demanded money in each of the six homes, but, as they had selected their victims indiscriminately, they found themselves mostly robbing poor peasants and day labourers. The spoils accumulated after three days amounted to no more than a few kilos of food.[19]

Judicial documents contain numerous cases of robberies carried out by others in similar circumstances and who often claimed to belong to the resistance. Local authorities and the military sometimes managed to distinguish this kind of peasant crime from the robberies carried out by the anti-Francoist guerrilla. Peasant gangs often used masks and scarves as they typically lived in the neighbourhood where they committed their crimes and feared being recognised. In contrast, members of the resistance never hid their faces, not even groups of *armed neighbours*. Being aware of this difference, the authorities in Málaga managed, for example, to identify three disguised youths who claimed to be part of the guerrillas when attacking a bus in the city.[20]

Banditry

Groups formed by locals to carry out robberies and hold-ups were, alongside petty theft and black marketeering, the most common extra-legal survival strategy of the time. These groups tended to have a temporary character, as each member returned home having committed the crime. A less widespread phenomenon was banditry, that is, groups who lived in the mountains and were entirely dedicated to robbery. The dictatorship used these groups to manipulate the old myth of Spanish banditry and conflate them with the anti-Francoist guerrilla. There was no connection between the two , but the official rhetoric, constantly repeated, eventually took hold in the population to some extent. The groups dedicated solely to robberies and hold-ups were not very numerous although there were some notable cases. The antecedents and typology of this kind of group are complex: some were led by life-long criminals while others revolved around people who were marginalised due to their political history and had resorted to robberies as a means to survive.

"Sargento [Sergeant] Chamorro", for example, was a career criminal. At the start of the Spanish Civil War he was serving time in a prison in Cádiz but was freed when the town was occupied by Francoist troops. Upon leaving prison, he volunteered to join the army, where he reached the rank of sergeant. He was a member of the Falange. However, at the end of 1939 he robbed his unit's safe and deserted. For some time he drifted around the province of Lérida, where, after making himself known to the police, he compiled various "registers" of houses where people of "red" backgrounds could be found. The local authorities arrested him, but he managed to escape shortly thereafter. The police thought he had fled to France, but "Sargento Chamorro" returned to his home village in Jaén where he assembled a group composed of various relatives and neighbours. Between 1942 and 1943, this group carried out robberies, hold-ups, and kidnappings which were both violent and indiscriminate. Many of his victims were simple day labourers. He even raped and killed his own cousin, who had become pregnant by him. In December 1943, the group was disbanded after the arrest of its last members. The Civil Guard were surprised to discover that both the members of the group and many of its collaborators were colleagues from the Falange or well-known Rightists. In March 1944, the six detainees were sentenced to death and executed.[21]

The story of Felipe Cabello, on the other hand, follows a different path, a path which reveals the complex nature of peasant crime in the post-war period. Felipe was 14 years old when Francoist troops occupied his village in the summer of 1936. His elder brother was captured and killed by a Falangist squadron while he and his family, known to have socialist sympathies, managed to escape to the Republican zone. Felipe joined the JSU during the war, although his young age prevented him from fighting in the Popular Army. Once the war had ended the family returned to their village in the hope of recovering some normality, but the father was arrested and imprisoned. At this point, Felipe Cabello was 17 years old and had suddenly become the head of the family.[22]

The family situation during the following two years was extreme. His father remained incarcerated and no one would give him work on account of his family's history. At the end of September 1941, driven to desperation, Felipe went to the mountains and committed a number of robberies. From then on, he remained in the mountains and started to call himself "El Enmascarado" [the masked man] since he wore a mask to avoid being recognized. He stayed in the mountains for four months, robbing farm houses and assaulting travellers and locals passing along the paths of Alhama.

However, on January 24th 1942, "El Enmascarado" saw his adventure come to an end. That day he held up two muleteers returning from work, carrying their day's pay. One of them said, "I've got five pesetas, which is what I've earned for a day's work. Are you going to take this money?" "El Enmascarado" told him to hand over the wallet. By doing so he transgressed the moral codes of the community: to steal from the "rich" was permissible, and even celebrated, among large sectors of society, but to take from a worker, an equal, was unacceptable.[23] The two muleteers asked a few colleagues for help and found the aggressor's hideout. Armed with hunting rifles, they shot Felipe in the leg and took him to the Civil Guard barracks.

Survival strategies involving crime can be linked to a variety of profiles and motivations and stories like those of Felipe Cabello or Manuel Jaime illustrate three important points. Firstly, it is clear how politically moti-vated segregation and social marginalization pushed dozens of individuals towards crime. Secondly, family traditions or even personal political activism did not guarantee that individuals automatically opted to join the resistance. Large numbers of people with extensive political experience rejected the option of joining the anti-Francoist guerrilla and decided instead to pursue individual survival strategies including theft, robbery, hold-ups, extortion, etc. Thirdly, these practices tended to be indiscrimi-nate in character. Unlike the modus operandi of the resistance, there was no previous selection of victims. Some variation can be observed (in the case of Manuel Jaime, who sent a letter to his previous employer), but it was common for this crime to have a horizontal character, that is, the perpetra-tors often chose victims who belonged to the same socio-economic group as themselves. A similar trend can be observed regarding denunciations.[24]

Beyond the moral judgements passed by members of the Agrupaciones guerrilleras on groups of *armed neighbours*, the historian is sometimes faced with complex dilemmas when trying to interpret the meaning of specific actions carried out by local armed groups. It is often difficult to distinguish between groups of *armed neighbours* and those more closely related to tradi-tional group robberies. An analysis of motivations does not necessarily resolve the situation; indeed, it can lead to more confusion. As various authors have pointed out, there are a multitude of reasons why people may join an insurgent group and among these the political and ideological factor may be secondary. Issues relating to security, money and personal consid-erations can all serve as important incentives for an individual to participate in a guerrilla movement, as may expectations regarding conflict resolution, the behaviour of community networks and primary groups or even simple curiosity and attraction to danger.[25]

One of the least studied motivations, perhaps owing to its rational and pragmatic character, far removed from the altruism otherwise associated with the resistance, is the purely economic.[26] However, there were men who joined the resistance, even the Agrupaciones guerrilleras, principally for economic reasons. The monthly salary of 500 pesetas paid to guerrilla fighters in the Agrupaciones (as long as the economic resources of the specific Agrupación in question allowed it) constituted an extremely powerful attraction for the peasantry, whose salaries tended to oscillate between 150 and 300 pesetas in the best of cases. In the context of the hunger and misery which marked Spanish society in the 1940s, the money offered by the Agrupaciones made a significant difference.

In fact, the Agrupaciones guerrilleras used the salary as an incentive to mobilise guerrilla fighters. Enrique Jiménez recalled how a neighbour who had joined the guerrilla visited him at the farm house where he worked and gave him money, "so that the family could eat", and "promised him that he would earn 500 pesetas every month if he joined the men who wandered the mountains". Enrique, forced by necessity, accepted the offer and joined the AGG.[27] Similar situations applied to other guerrilla fighters, like the goatherd José Castillo. His family lived in extreme poverty and José became the head of the family aged 15, when his father died. As he was incapable of earning the money needed to sustain the family he joined the AGG at the end of 1950, after the Chief of Staff had made him undergo a violent initiation rite which involved attacking a soldier with an axe. When he arrived in the mountains he only had two teeth left, "as he only ate sugar cane", but was able to try meat for the first time in his life.[28]

As these examples suggest, economic reasons formed a significant part of the spectrum of incentives which prompted people to join the resistance: not all who joined the guerrillas had a clear political profile (at least not before joining). However, any attempt at categorisation which describes the guerrillas as the home of the politically aware and criminal groups as creations of those who could only conceive of individual survival is further complicated by peasants who decided to pursue individualistic strategies despite having political backgrounds. What criteria should be used, then, to distinguish between groups of *armed neighbours* and *cuadrillas* who adopted more day-to-day forms of resistance? This author believes that the stress should fall on the intentions of the group, that is, the thin line which separates pure survival from a more politically "conscious" form of action against the dictatorship, albeit at a local scale. It is also possible to observe significant differences with regard to the types of actions carried out and the selection of victims. The resistance, be it *neighbours in arms* or the *modern guerrilla*, did not *only* engage in actions which were economically motivated and applied more selective criteria when choosing their victims, typically targeting people with a particular political profile and/or higher socio-economic status. On the other hand, ordinary *cuadrillas* restricted their activities to those which produced an immediate economic gain (theft, robbery, and kidnappings) and tended be indiscriminate in their selection of targets.

Between resistance and crime

So far groups and individuals who falsely claimed a guerrilla identity or adopted survival strategies outside the resistance have been analyzed. However, some individuals followed a path which took them from day-to-day resistance to the armed opposition or, more problematically, made them oscillate between the two and thereby constantly cross the thin line between the anti-Francoist guerrilla and crime.

The first scenario scarcely poses an analytical problem. Some people decided initially to pursue individual survival strategies (principally theft), but, when discovered by the Civil Guard and at risk of being arrested, they fled to the mountains and joined the guerrilla.[29] Many of these people were already economically marginalised as a result of their political history, but this was not always the case.

Those cases involving individuals who blur the line between resistance and crime are more complicated. Previous chapters have explained how the Agrupaciones guerrilleras combatted banditry, both within and outside their own organisations:

> We must destroy the weeds of banditry and provocation. Where such temptations arise either individually or collectively, we must repress them with an iron fist, without any hesitation. Some acts of banditry committed by murderous Falangists disguised as guerrilla fighters have helped the Francoist regime to unleash smear campaigns against us, trying to reduce our work as men who fight for the fatherland and for their ideals to that of bandits and assassins (. . .).
>
> When people of this ilk are discovered, they should be given the same treatment as their Falangist masters. Not a single bandit must be allowed to infiltrate our units, nor live in our municipalities, provinces or regions.
>
> A purge of degenerates of this kind will make people confide in us (. . .). Where Falangist bandits carried out robberies or committed crimes before their elimination, we must avoid any risk of confusion by disseminating our propaganda denouncing and condemning, energetically and publicly, any such action.[30]

The Agrupaciones guerrilleras strongly condemned all forms of petty criminality and used a variety of means, including murder, to suppress it. The introduction to this chapter has shown the negative conception that Agrupaciones had of *neighbours in arms* with regards to crime. However, *neighbours in arms* also took a firm stance against such activities. The group led by "Belloto", formed of various neighbours from Loja and Alhama, was active between 1941 and 1942. On a number of occasions one of its members took advantage of his position as a guerrilla fighter to rob shepherds in the area. When "Belloto" discovered this he threatened to kill the man if he continued his criminal behaviour. The effect was immediate and no further offences were committed by the guilty guerrilla member.[31] The "hermanos Quero" responded in a similar way when they found out that one of their members had carried out various robberies and engaged in blackmail independently of the group.[32] Nonetheless, the measures adopted by the resistance to eradicate petty criminality did not prevent the fact that individual strategies continued to carry significant force among the peasantry and even within some resistance groups. The following section will analyse a concrete case related to a group which emerged in the south-east of Granada province.

Antonio López, alias "Culito de Salar", was 36 years old when he fled to the mountains in December 1941. He had bought a horse, but was crippled by debt and consequently decided to join a group of *armed neighbours* who operated in the area: that directed by "El Belloto".[33] The group had appeared at the beginning of 1941, and, by the time "Culito" joined, comprised eight men from Loja, Alhama, and Antequera. The group's career was short-lived. They were caught by the Civil Guard after carrying out a robbery in February 1942. Five died in the encounter and "Belloto" was arrested.

From that moment, "Culito de Salar" led a new group of *armed neighbours*, formed of friends and neighbours from Loja and Alhama. In April they were joined in quick succession by three new guerrilla fighters: "Roque" had escaped from a Disciplinary Battalion in Cádiz; "Casado", a go-between for the "Belloto" group who had fled to the mountains after being discovered by the Civil Guard; and "Cornudo", who had escaped from the municipal gaol just before being transferred to a provincial prison. All three, like "Culito de Salar", had been socialist activists during the Republic and had participated in the war as Republican soldiers.

The group reached full strength in November 1942 with the arrival of "Espartillo", a young deserter from the Francoist Army.[34] Between 1942 and 1947 the group led by "Culito de Salar" operated independently in the mountains of Loja and Alhama. Following the most common procedures of the *neighbours in arms*, they focused mostly on holdups and kidnappings while being supported by a social network of locals, among whom two were particularly important: "El Mariscal" and his-brother-in-law, "El de las Cuevas". However, the group did not normally live together, nor did they really act as a group. Occasionally they would unite to carry out an operation, but most of the time they lived in couples and could go long periods without having any contact at all with each other. At times they would even cease all activities in order to hide and survive solely with the help of go-betweens.

They continued in this way until February 1947 when they decided to disband. The group had suffered several arrests and only "Culito de Salar", "Cornudo" and "Espartillo" remained.[35] The international context was not conducive to further armed resistance, and, on a personal level, the relationship between "Culito de Salar" and "Cornudo" had never been good. "Cornudo" continued to lead a solitary existence in the sierras while "Culito" and "Espartillo" laid down their arms and secretly left for Barcelona. Having assumed new identities, both ex-fighters stayed in Barcelona for a year, working on construction sites.

However, things changed in May 1948. After several months of privations, toiling away as illegal construction workers, they arrived at a simple conclusion: work was hard and the pay miserable. Life in the mountains was also hard and could even cost one's life but, at least, there were some advantages. From their point of view, it would be better to go to Granada and "collect" their pay cheque from the rich. Consequently both returned to their village and its mountains. However, the new group exhibited important differences compared to the previous one. Whereas in 1942 they had formed part of a group of *armed neighbours* who fought the dictatorship, albeit with an exclusively local focus, they were now a group motivated primarily by economic concerns. Although the political element had not completely disappeared the line between the guerrilla and pure crime was becoming increasingly blurred.

"Culito" and "Espartillo" were joined by another young man from their village, "Campañito". They had met while working on a building site in March 1948 and the two friends had persuaded their new acquaintance to come with them. "Campañito" had come to Barcelona in May 1947. His father, a socialist, had been imprisoned, and, due to his family history, no one in his village would employ him. After completing his military service, he decided to seek work elsewhere and send the money to his family.[36] The idea of returning to his village and living in the mountains was attractive, as it allowed him to be close to his family while helping them economically.

In August 1948 the group incorporated further reinforcements when four neighbours from Loja joined the three returning from Barcelona. "Cordero" had been sentenced to 30 years' imprisonment for having been a Republican soldier and a socialist activist and had just been given probation. A similar situation applied to "Retorcido", a CNT activist and Republican soldier who had fought with "Culito" during the war and had also been released on probation . Both faced ostracism as a result of their political history. They were joined by two young local men, aged 20 and 21 : "Chanflute", whose father and brother had been shot after the war, and "Lino".[37] It might be expected that these additions, who had a clear political profile, would push the group towards the model of *neighbours in arms*. However, the line between politically motivated guerrilla activity and pure crime remained diffuse.

The group operated independently between May and October 1948, when the situation in the mountains was different to in "Culito's" early days as a guerrilla fighter. The AGG had patrolled the area from 1947, trying to unite all the local guerrillas and to stamp out any form of banditry. The municipalities of Loja and Alhama fell within the operational zone of an AGG unit led by "Crescencio", and, in October 1948, "Crescencio" contacted "Culito" to inform him that the AGG would not tolerate any petty crime in the area. His group had two options: to join the AGG or to disappear.

The seven members of "Culito's" group agreed to join the Agrupación, but "Crescencio" was suspicious of "Campañito", the youngster who had just arrived from Barcelona. Consequently, the unit leader demanded that "Campañito" take a violent "Pledge of Allegiance" by killing Felipe Cabello, also known as "El Enmascarado", the young man whose history was outlined earlier in this chapter. The reason was simple: after his detention Felipe Cabello had denounced several neighbours in Alhama, which had led to the arrest and imprisonment of fifteen people.[38] He had been freed from prison in February 1948, but, according to the Local Committee, had since been collaborating with the Civil Guard in their campaign against the guerrillas. Even so, "Campañito" refused to carry out the killing. In response, "Crescencio" gave the young man 100 pesetas and ordered him to leave Granada. "Campañito" did as he was told and returned to Barcelona.[39]

The other six members of the group were taken to the AGG base camp to meet the Chief of Staff. "Roberto" and his lieutenants welcomed them and they were incorporated into the AGG, who gave them their monthly salary of 500 pesetas, a uniform and food. As usual, the original group was immediately broken up and each member assigned to a different unit.

The group led by "Culito" did not stay with the Agrupación for very long. After four months of military discipline, four of its members –

"Cordero", "Retorcido", "Chanflute" and "Espartillo" – deserted with another guerrilla fighter, "El Nene", who had lived in the mountains since June 1946. The five took the opportunity to desert during a large-scale operation against a flour mill at the beginning of 1949. The operation involved several AGG units, which meant that the members of "Culito's" group were temporarily reunited and could desert together. At this point there were only two members of the original group left in the AGG: "Lino", whose nom de guerre became "Anastasio" and "Culito" himself, who took the name "Narciso".

Why did the guerrilla fighters desert? According to the testimony of "Espartillo", the problem was that "there was very strict discipline; people were frequently punished and generally treated cruelly. In addition, the entire income from hold-ups went to the unit, and they [the guerrilla fighters] received only their monthly salary of 500 pesetas, which was not always paid out".[40]

The five deserters hid in a farmhouse belonging to a go-between who remained loyal to their old group, "El Mariscal". During their first few days they planned a kidnapping in the area around Loja. The idea was to pose as members of the AGG, carry out the kidnapping, share out the money and then split up and leave Granada. The kidnapping took place in early February 1949. Having been paid a ransom of 300,000 pesetas, the deserters took 60,000 pesetas each. They remained in hiding for fifteen days, after which, four of the five ("Espartillo", "Chanflute", "Retorcido" and "Nene") left Alhama, and, after walking for a few nights, arrived at village about 100 kilometres away in the province of Jaén from where they took a train to Barcelona. The only one to stay in Alhama was "Cordero", who continued to hide out in the farmhouse belonging to "El Mariscal".

At this point, "Cordero" began to plan a new kidnapping. This time the two go-betweens for the old group led by "Culito": "El Mariscal" and his brother-in-law "El de las Cuevas", were going to participate, together with two new deserters from the AGG: Ramón Castilla and Francisco García. Both Castilla and García were being hunted by the AGG Chief of Staff and had sought refuge in "El Mariscal's" farmhouse. In late March 1949, the three deserters and the two go-betweens, pretending to be members of the AGG, kidnapped the son of a proprietor in Santa Cruz del Comercio, in the province of Granada. The ransom note they sent to the family contained clear signs of their having adopted a false identity:

> Agrupación guerrillera de Granada inform you that if between 11 and 12 you have not brought the sum of 100,000 pesetas, you will have to start looking for your son's body.

The messenger with the money must come on a horse and when he goes down the road to the cortijo he should sing "vuela vuela palomita"[fly fly little dove] and then you have to cross a bridge in front of Valenzuela up to the Gallina tower and from there to El Camisón, and he has to come on his own, if anyone is with him, the captive pays.

And if you tell the Civil Guard we'll kill the whole family and we wish you health and kindness because if all the money is brought nothing will happen but if one peseta is missing we will kill the captive. Greetings and LONG LIVE THE Democratic Republic![41]

The kidnapping ended in disaster. One of the kidnappers, "El Mariscal", who had never fled to the mountains and had continued to live a normal life in the village, worried that he might have been recognised by the victim. Fearing the risk of being denounced, he decided to kill the young man.[42] The news spread rapidly and soon reached the Chief of Staff of the AGG. The AGG would not tolerate their name being used to commit crime and murder; their orders were to eradicate any forms of banditry. Soon afterwards, the local committee in Loja learned the whereabouts of Ramón Castilla and detained him. He was handed over to the Chief of Staff, sentenced in the mountains and executed. Francisco García met the same fate; he was sentenced to death and killed by members of the AGG on an unknown date.[43]

While these events were taking place in Granada, the history of the four deserters who fled to Barcelona progressed in a similar fashion. Their first idea was to cross the French border. During February they remained in hiding until they found a guide who knew the routes across the Pyrenees. Once a deal was negotiated, the four set off towards Andorra but abandoned the trek when they reached the Cardona, where the path became too difficult. On their return to Barcelona, they met with a surprise: "El Mariscal", his brother-in-law and their wives had fled Granada after the failed abduction and had come to seek refuge. For the next fortnight the new arrivals remained in hiding in a hostel, until news came that the situation had calmed down. It seemed the Civil Guard believed that the crime had been committed by the AGG and did not suspect them. As the Chief of Staff of the AGG did not know about their participation either, the two go-betweens returned to Alhama with their wives at the beginning of March 1949.

Between March and July 1949 the four deserters embarked on a path that was clearly criminal and in some sense comparable to the development of other groups in the resistance. While still residents of Barcelona, they would travel in pairs, every two weeks, to Madrid and from there to

Alcauete (Jaén) and then on foot to Loja or Alhama. Over a few days they would carry out robberies and kidnappings, returning to Barcelona once they had amassed a substantial sum of money. In this new phase, they were accompanied by another old go-between and "Campañito", the youngster from Alhama who decided not to join the AGG when the Chief of Staff demanded that he kill an informer.[44] In April 1949, "Cordero" was arrested in a tavern in Almedinilla (Córdoba) during one of these journeys.

The group of deserters was definitively disbanded on 20th of July 1949. "Retorcido" had met a girl and, in May, the two went to her village in the province of Murcia. In mid-May he wrote a letter to "Campañito", who was still living in Barcelona, suggesting they plan a new series of hold-ups in Loja, where they could take advantage of the August celebrations in honour of the patron saint. However, the letter was intercepted by the Civil Guard, who promptly arrested "Retorcido". The following day "Campañito" was arrested together with his girlfriend on the train from Valencia to Cartagena. The three remaining members of the group: "Nene", "Chanflute" and "Espartillo", were arrested in Barcelona with their partners a few days later, as a result of the interrogation to which "Retorcido" and "Campañito" were subjected.

A court-martial sentenced "Nene", "Cordero", "El Mariscal" and "El de las Cuevas" to death. They were executed almost immediately. "Espartillo", "Retorcido", "Chanflute" and "Campañito" received thirty years in prison.

The only two members of the old group led by "Culito de Salar" who remained in the AGG met a different fate. "Lino" died in a confrontation with the Civil Guard on 4th of May 1949. "Culito" only survived a little longer. In early 1951, "Roberto" decided to offload the oldest and least combat-fit guerrilla fighters, who he considered a burden, and, to this end, created a new unit called Group L (for *lisiados*, i.e. war wounded). "Culito" was appointed unit leader. According to some testimonies, "Culito" was not pleased when he heard the news and communicated his dismay directly to "Roberto". Such segregation was below the dignity of a guerrilla leader and a communist and if he had survived without the AGG before he would be able to do so again. "Culito" gathered his ten men, and after making a speech, the group deserted in pairs, leaving each to decide freely whether to turn themselves in to the Civil Guard or remain in the mountains. "Culito de Salar" decided not to give himself up. He was 47 years old and had 14 years of combat experience. Now alone, he died in an encounter with the Civil Guard on 4th of June 1952, according to some versions. According to others, he died when a shepherd poisoned him in his sleep.[45]

The story of the group led by "Culito de Salar" shows, in richly nuanced ways, how guerrilla fighters' lives could follow very different paths. It was initially a group of *armed neighbours* who occasionally drifted dangerously close to banditry. They then dissolved, only to later reunite and join an Agrupación guerrillera. Some members remained in the resistance while others deserted and dedicated themselves solely to crime. The thin line between resistance, survival and crime was continuously and stealthily re-negotiated. The group led by "Culito de Salar" was not an exception within the multifaceted resistance movement in Andalusia, although it would be wrong to ascribe its particular experiences to all *neighbours in arms*. Ultimately, this case reveals a grey area which cannot be ignored.

The relationship between crime and the anti-Francoist guerrilla is complex. The existing historiography has avoided the subject, preferring instead to focus on criteria relating to morality or legitimacy. However, this lack of analysis has generated considerable confusion and ambiguity. The resistance, whether it took the form of *neighbours in arms* or the *modern guerrilla*, always sought to eradicate petty crime and banditry, but this did not guarantee to put an end to the phenomenon, nor did it prevent instances of impersonation and emulation, or, indeed, the emergence of grey areas where certain resistance groups themselves operated.

The study of both phenomena should allow for focused case studies while also shedding light on broader issues that have been banished from the scholarly agenda for moral reasons. An enormous proportion of Spanish society in the 1940s suffered extreme material and economic hardship. A large section of the population was also subjected to marginalization as well as social, political and economic segregation. In these circumstances, dozens of individuals resorted to traditional day-to-day resistance practices, found among the peasantry and subaltern groups. Although there were undoubtedly professional criminals, a huge proportion of thefts, robberies and hold-ups in the 1940s and 1950s were carried out by rural and urban workers who were desperately trying to cope with the harsh economic and political conditions imposed on them. Survival was the predominant motive although this would sometimes blend with other motives, turning self-preservation into protest. Survival strategies and multifaceted forms of resistance would sometimes clash but could also converge and even fuse in a shadowy area which may be difficult to delineate but which the present chapter is intended to analyse, understand and explain.

Conclusion

Let's talk now about the guerrillas, which constitute the true national army; about people rising in villages in the countryside; about those spontaneous armies, emerging out of the earth like native grass and whose mysterious seed was not planted by man; I want to talk about that military organisation created behind the State's back by miraculous instinct; about that regulated anarchy which primitive times reproduced.

(*Juan Martín "El Empecinado"*, Benito Pérez Galdos)

On January 10th 1949, the Civil Guard recovered the body of Cecilio Guerrero Moles, a guerrilla fighter in the AGG who had been shot the previous night. Among the material that the sergeant confiscated was a notebook in which Cecilio had struggled to complete a short writing exercise. The attempt had been marked by Francisco Sánchez Girón, who was responsible for guerrilla fighters' cultural training and education. It is still possible to observe Cecilio's hesitant handwriting and Francisco's corrections, joining words wrongly split in two or separating words mistakenly joined together. The exercise involved reproducing an article from the guerrilla newspaper, *Por la República*. In this case the text was "clearly written" but still contained "72 mistakes".[1]

As daily life in the resistance was full of long waits, restlessness and boredom the Agrupaciones dedicated many hours to the education of their fighters. In most cases the students were peasants who were unfamiliar with the basic rules of reading and writing. Nevertheless, the educational efforts made by the Agrupaciones were fundamentally political and ideological. Many peasants "became class-conscious" and learned to "think politically" when they joined the AGG, according to an old guerrilla fighter interviewed by the author.[2] This simple declaration illustrates a crucial conflict within the anti-Francoist guerrilla movement: many of these peasants did, in fact, think politically before joining the guerrilla, it was simply that their political cultures and codes were often alien and incomprehensible to the leaders of the *modern guerrilla*.

The Spanish peasantry had not been immune to political and cultural change in the first decades of the twentieth century. However, rural societies did not passively adopt new political cultures arriving from urban areas but adapted them to fit their own cultural and social frameworks. These adaptational processes can be observed in mobilisation campaigns during the first decades of the twentieth century, during the Spanish Cvil War and in the anti-Francoist guerrilla. Using the category *neighbours in arms*, I have tried to identify in these processes a set of key characteristics, which had previously been hidden or were simply labelled "primitive".

In this book, I have focused on these characteristics and on the conflict which arose between those groups wishing to conserve them and those who wanted to transform them. The task has been arduous as the relevant documentation is fragmented and there are now very few surviving guerrilla fighters who can testify to life in the resistance. Moreover, the struggle between *neighbours in arms* and *the modern guerrilla* was a dynamic process which constantly changed in response to historical contingencies. Even so, throughout the book I have presented a series of characteristics, elements, and conflicts which have, until now, been marginalised by historians. This analysis has been facilitated by the twelve variables listed in the introduction, variables which show that the differences separating the two guerrilla models were more anthropological than ideological.

The quote from the novel by Benito Pérez Galdós, serving as an epigraph to these conclusions, provides a clue as to how the PCE sought to transform the anti-Francoist guerrilla. The *National Episodes* by Galdós, and especially those related to the Peninsular War in the nineteenth century, were the main texts that the Agrupaciones guerrilleras gave to their members.[3] Literature and mythology created figures like "El Empecinado", of peasant origin, who had broken free from local ties in order to fight the French invader at a national level. For the PCE, this story illustrated a key development which would also transform *neighbours in arms* into *modern guerrillas*.

When asked to evaluate his transformative work with the local guerrilla, Ramiro Fuentes Ochoa, the political chief of the initial configuration of the AGG, stressed that "The most effective approach for us is [was] to direct these people and give them a political significance".[4] This type of paternalistic view, oblivious to the cultural references and languages proper to *neighbours in arms*, prompted dozens of armed groups to oppose the Agrupaciones guerrilleras organised by the PCE. Communist leaders who had recently returned from exile tried to convert the *neighbours in arms* into a "real Guerrilla Army", but, to achieve their aims, they resorted to expeditious and coercive methods which produced widespread rejection.

The PCE was the organisation which made the greatest efforts to organise and strengthen the resistance in Spain. It was also the organisation which saw most clearly the need to link the anti-Francoist struggle with the fight against Fascism in Europe. However, the sacrifice of thousands rank-and-file activists ultimately bore little fruit, largely as a result of the high levels of repression applied by the dictatorship, the unfavourable international context, the internal power struggles within the party and the PCE's incomprehension of the political cultures of large sectors of the peasantry. The PCE's dogmatism and slavish obedience to Moscow ended up severely restricting their approach to the struggle against Franco's dictatorship in the 1940s.

At the beginning of 1951, the future of the resistance in Spain was clear. All guerrilla strongholds on the peninsula had been eliminated apart from some areas in the Levante, Aragón and Andalusia, where the Agrupaciones guerrilleras fought hard to survive. The armed strategy against the dictatorship had failed. The international context, now dominated by the Cold War, demanded that the opposition took a new political direction. After more than a decade of fighting in the mountains, the anti-Francoist guerrilla had to disband. This in itself was no easy task, especially as demobilisation had to take place on enemy territory, with no bilateral agreements to mitigate the intense repression. Resources were scarce and communication lines with PCE delegations abroad non-existent. This was the situation in Andalusia. Disorder, personal initiatives and betrayal became the hallmarks of a demobilisation process which continued over the following two years.

In March 1951, "Roberto" ordered the demobilisation of the 7th Battalion. Vicente Martín, lieutenant in a guerrilla unit in Málaga was ordered to go to Granada and communicate the decision. At this point the AGG had only about thirty men in the mountains. Units were to stay in the mountains and maintain a minimum level of activity while the Chief of Staff prepared the logistics of an evacuation of the remaining guerrilla fighters.

Vicente left the camp but did not complete his mission. The Civil Guard had launched a very effective counterinsurgency campaign by this point: guerrilla fighters who turned themselves in and gave vital information about the AGG were promised very lenient sentences. Dozens of members of the Agrupaciones guerrilleras yielded to this promise and Vicente was one of them. In March 1951, he walked in to the Civil Guard barracks in his village and began to actively collaborate with government forces. His information led to dozens of deaths and arrests of former comrades over the following years.

Two months later, in May 1951, "Roberto" abandoned the mountains with "Paquillo", the Agrupación's Press and Propaganda chief and travelled to Madrid to acquire passports and guarantees of safe passage in order to evacuate the last guerrilla fighters in the AGG. On this mission, they were joined by Ana Gutiérrez, a young PCE activist who was born in Tangier (hence her nickname "La Tangerina") and had worked within the Provincial Committee of Málaga.

The three fugitives hid in a small flat at number 26 Hilarión Eslava Street, in the Madrilenian neighbourhood of Moncloa. At this stage, "Roberto" and "La Tangerina" had become lovers, and both had contact with "Clemente", the Head of the Chief of Staff of the AGG. "Roberto" and "Paquillo" informed him of the progress they were making with regards to the documentation and asked that he send money to pay the intermediaries.

O September 26th 1951, four months after their arrival in Madrid, the most senior leaders of the AGG were arrested. The Civil Guard were aware of "Roberto's" presence in Madrid and had followed every step he took. One item of information led to another until they discovered that the guerrilla leadership were meeting an intermediary in a café on Plaza de España that afternoon. The Guardia Civil transferred the ex-guerrilla member Vicente Martín to Madrid for him to identify the leader. At the agreed time, Vicente entered the bar chosen for the meeting, disguised by a hat and a moustache and accompanied by two Civil Guards in civilian clothing. They found "Roberto" with "La Tangerina" and "Paquillo" at one of the tables. According to witnesses, "La Tangerina" opened her handbag for "Roberto" to grab a pistol, but the Civil Guards already had their weapons drawn. The leadership of the AGG had been captured.[5]

After being interrogated in premises belonging to the security services (DGS), Roberto was transferred to the Civil Guard headquarters in Málaga. With the help of his lawyer he reached an agreement with his captors, who promised him a reduced sentence if he collaborated with the Civil Guard. Even so, the best he could hope for was to avoid the death penalty. "Paquillo" and "La Tangerina" also agreed to co-operate. Nobody in the AGG knew about their arrest, so "Roberto" could still stay in contact with "Clemente" as if the evacuation plan was still going ahead. For two months he pretended to be finalising preparations and, in December, set a trap for the remaining members of the AGG. Unarmed, the remaining guerrilla fighters voluntarily jumped on a lorry with Army camouflage, thinking that they would be taken to the coast, where they would find a boat to take them to North Africa. However, their final destination was actually the police headquarters in Málaga. The AGG was practically disbanded.

"Roberto", "Paquillo" and "La Tangerina" continued to work as informers until September 1952, when the authorities considered the problem of the Andalusian guerrilla to be solved. The guerrilla informers were not compensated. The only one to survive was "La Tangerina", who had not participated directly in the armed struggle. In September 1952, the three were transferred to the Provincial Prison of Granada and, a month later, "Paquillo" was executed.

In December the other two were sentenced by court-martial. "La Tangerina" was given two years' imprisonment. "Roberto", military leader of the most active Agrupación guerrillera in the whole of Spain, was not so lucky, despite his agreement with the authorities. On January 22nd 1953, José Muñoz Lozano, better known as "Roberto", was driven by a firing squad to the walls of Granada cemetery. At six o'clock in the morning the voice of an official and the noise of rifles could be heard. A flash of fire lit up the morning. The body of "Roberto", worn out after sixteen years of fighting, fell to the ground, riddled with bullets. His remains were buried in a mass grave in the cemetery together with those of dozens of other guerrilla fighters and go-betweens.

The death of "Roberto" brought the resistance in Andalusia to an end. A few months earlier, the last six survivors of the AGG had managed to elude the encircling police, and, after three months of walking, had crossed the border into France.

I began this book with a short biographical sketch of Ramón Vía, the first guerrilla leader sent to Andalusia from abroad by the PCE . After his death in 1946, Ramon Vía became one of the official heroes of the resistance in Spain. I will now end the book with the last guerrilla leader sent to Andalusia by the PCE, a man who, in contrast to Vía, was branded a traitor and villain.

José Muñoz Lozano, alias "Roberto", was a man of a thousand faces: the immigrant boy in Vallecas, the sharp bellboy at the Hotel Ritz, the charming shop assistant in Perfumería Gal, the opportunist at the start of the war, the young commander of the Fifth Regiment, the wayward leader in the French concentration camps, the hero of the French resistance and the instructor at the Guerrilla School in Toulouse. He was the man who never wanted secretly to return to Spain, who never wanted to lead a guerrilla, the man who resigned from his post as military chief of the AGG four times but whose resignation was never accepted by the PCE, who betrayed his old comrades after his arrest, thus destroying what he himself had created .

Narratives of the history of the antifascist resistance have drawn on a long series of traditional stories of heroes and villains, in much the same way as children's tales. However, the men and women whose actions drive history, and especially those forced to act in difficult circumstances, are full of nuances and contradictions. The task of the historian is to illuminate all these aspects, reconstruct their biographies and to understand and explain their decisions, be they coherent or paradoxical. The history of the resistance movement in Spain is no exception.

Thousands of young antifascists committed themselves to the struggle against Franco's dictatorship, risking their lives and putting their friends and family in danger. In some cases the decision to do so was made voluntarily, in others, participation in the resistance was an almost inevitable response to repression. In any case, this small group of young men rebelled against the subjugation of the defeated at the end of the civil war by joining the anti-Francoist guerrilla. They had learned to defend their antifascist ideals with arms and were not willing to accept defeat. For over a decade they fought Franco's dictatorship and survived under the most precarious of circumstances.

Despite the fact that Spain had experienced the first battle against fascism in Europe, the country's international isolation undermined any attempt to co-ordinate the anti-Francoist and antifascist struggles after 1939. Spanish exiles, together with hundreds of antifascist volunteers from elsewhere, joined the ranks of the French resistance and freed Paris in 1944. Those efforts, based on notions of fraternity and brotherhood, were only compensated by a series of homages and individual badges of honour. When the time came to free Spain, the anti-Francoist guerrilla was abandoned to its fate. In such conditions, the efforts of the Spanish resistance were herculean and bold, but ultimately impotent.

The anti-Francoist guerrilla were both the first and the last groups to belong to the antifascist resistance in Europe. By 1952, all other partisan movements had disappeared from a continent fractured by a new international order. As the historian George Mosse has pointed out, the history of European antifascism has largely been seen through the prism of the Cold War, and, for this reason, has often focused on the extent to which resistance movements operated under Soviet control. This perspective does not permit a real understanding of the magnitude of the struggle nor of the enthusiasm that it generated in a whole generation, forever marked by its fight against fascism. Guided by its belief in the future, this was a generation which lived for its hopes, dreams and ideals, a generation which accepted the consequences of the fight until the bitter end. They fought for survival, freedom and justice, for revolution and social change. They were the catalyst for a blossoming of solidarity and an awakening of passionate political consciousness. They provided a lesson for the future, where anonymous men of humble origins could decide not to be passive subjects but rather to make their own history. No one was going to write the crooked ines of their ephemeral biographies for them. Even if it had to be done in halting handwriting, like that of Cecilio Guerrero Moles, they were determined to shape the content of their lives themselves.

Appendix

Tables

Table 1 Census of guerrilla groups. Eastern Andalusia (1937–1952)

Chronology	Name	Provinces	Members	Model
1937–1940	Casares	Málaga	16	Neighbours
1937–	Tabarrito	Málaga	10	Neighbours
1939	Santana	Málaga	3	Neighbours
1939	Cantarero	Málaga	5	Neighbours
1939–1944	Tejero	Málaga	11	Neighbours
1939–1942	Raya	Málaga, Granada	16	Neighbours
1939–1947	Yatero	Granada	37	Neighbours
1939–1940	Niño de la Inés	Granada	4	Neighbours
1939–1940	El Rey	Granada	3	Neighbours
1939–1944	Capacho	Granada	2	Neighbours
1939–1945	Portugués	Jaén	16	Neighbours
1939–1941	Perdiz	Jaén	3	Neighbours
1939–1943	Rojo Terrinchez	Jaén	4	Neighbours
1939–1944	Sastre	Jaén	3	Neighbours
1940–1946	Manolo el Rubio	Málaga, Cádiz	15	Modern
1940–1946	Diego de la Justa	Málaga	6	Neighbours
1940–1941	Marcelino	Málaga	7	Neighbours
1940–1944	Pellejero	Málaga	9	Neighbours
1940–1949	Rubio de Brecia	Málaga	29	Modern
1940–1948	Baza	Granada	12	Neighbours
1940–1947	Quero	Granada	16	Neighbours
1940	Motril	Granada	2	Neighbours
1940–1946	Galindo	Granada	11	Neighbours
1940	Zarco	Jaén	13	
1940–1944	Salsipuedes	Jaén	21	Neighbours
1940–1941	Carbonero	Almería	6	Neighbours
1941–1945	Perejil	Málaga	12	Neighbours
1941	Chico Pérez	Granada, Almería	4	Neighbours
1941–1943	Belloto	Granada	13	Neighbours
1941–1945	Tuerto de Jorairatar	Granada	3	Neighbours
1941–1944	Obispo de Cárdeña	Jaén	4	Neighbours
1941–1946	Chaparros	Jaén	12	Neighbours
1941–1945	Mota	Almería	5	Neighbours
1942–1947	Moreno	Málaga	10	Neighbours

Table 1 *Continued*

Chronology	Name	Provinces	Members	Model
1942–1948	Culito	Granada	12	Neighbours
1942–1948	Olla Fría	Granada	21	Neighbours
1942–1951	Matías	Granada, Almería	6	Neighbours
1942–1949	Clares	Granada	29	Neighbours
1942–1947	Jubiles	Córdoba, Jaén	29	Neighbours
1942–1946	Catena	Jaén	5	Neighbours
1942–1947	Cuco	Almería, Granada	30	Modern
1943	Tejerina	Málaga, Cádiz	5	Neighbours
1943–1948	Casero	Málaga	17	Modern
1943–1946	Bernabé	Málaga, Cádiz	9	Modern
1943–1944	Velázquez	Granada	5	Neighbours
1943–1948	Peste	Granada	4	Neighbours
1943	Checa	Jaén	4	Neighbours
1944–1947	Cuarterón	Málaga	13	Modern
1944–1945	Madrileño	Málaga	6	Neighbours
1944–1948	Mandamás	Málaga	27	Neighbours
1944–1946	6° Batallón o AGM	Málaga	67	Modern
1944–1950	Cencerro	Jaén, Granada	30	Neighbours
1944–1950	Sixto Marchena	Jaén	5	Neighbours
1945–1947	Collares	Málaga	12	Modern
1945–1950	Patalete	Málaga	9	Neighbours
1945	López Quero	Granada	7	Modern
1945–1951	2° Agrupación	Jaén, Ciudad Real	45	Modern
1945	Bonilla	Almería	5	Neighbours
1945	Meruelo	Almería	11	Modern
1946	Robles	Málaga	9	Modern
1946	Polopero	Granada	12	Modern
1947–1952	AGG	Granada, Málaga	340	Modern
1947–1948	Moya	Almería	6	Modern
1948–1949	Laño	Málaga	11	Neighbours

Sources: Consejos de Guerra (ATTMA), Memorias de Comandancia (SEHGC), Fichas policiales (AGA y AHN). Design by the author.

Table 2 PCE leaders sent to Eastern Andalusia from abroad (1944–1946)

Name	Entry into Spain	Exile	Rank
Alfredo Cabello	Feb. 1944	Argentina	Military Chief of AGM
Ramón Vía	Oct. 1944	Oran/France	Military Chief of AGM
Rafael Armada Rus	Apr. 1945	Mexico	General Sec., C.R., PCE Andalusia
José Merediz Víctores	Apr. 1945	France	Political Chief of AGG
J. Muñoz "Roberto"	May-45	France	Military Chief of AGG
Luis Campos Osaba	May-45	France	Member of C.R., PCE Andalusia
Nicolás García Béjar	Oct. 1945	France	Member of C.R., PCE Andalusia
Ricardo Beneyto	Dec. 1945	Oran/France	Political Chief of Andalusian Guerrilla
Félix Cardador	1946	Oran/France	General Sec., C.R., PCE Andalusia
José Mayo Fernández	1946	Oran/France	Member of C.R., PCE Andalusia
Julián Pérez Morante	1946	Oran/France	Member of C.R., PCE Andalusia
Manuel López Castro	1946	Oran/France	Member of C.R., PCE Andalusia

Sources: Consejos de Guerra (ATTMA), Informes internos (ACCPCE). Design by the author.

Table 3 Main PCE leaders: Date of birth and date
of arrival in Eastern Andalusia (1944–1946)

Leader	Date	D.O.B.
Ramón Vía	Oct. 1944	1910
Alfredo Cabello	May 1944/Sep. 1945	1910
Ramiro Fuentes Ochoa	Oct. 1945	1916
Luis Campos Osaba	Oct. 1945	
J. J. Muñoz "Roberto"	Jan. 1946	1914
Rafael Armada Rus	Jan. 1946	1915
Ricardo Beneyto	Jan. 1946	1910
José Merédiz Víctores	Feb. 1946	1919

Sources: Consejos de Guerra (ATTMA), Informes Internos
(ACCPCE). Design by the author.

Table 4 Local Guerrillas and unifying processes, Eastern Andalusia

Chronology	Name	Province	Unification	Nº
1939–1944	Tejero	Málaga	YES*	11
1939–1947	Yatero	Granada	NO	37
1939–1944	Capacho	Granada	NO	2
1939–1945	Portugués	Jaén	NO	16
1939–1944	Sastre	Jaén	NO	3
1940–1946	Manolo el Rubio	Málaga, Cádiz	YES	15
1940–1946	Diego de la Justa	Málaga	YES*	6
1940–1944	Pellejero	Málaga	YES*	9
1940–1949	Rubio de Brecia	Málaga	YES	29
1940–1948	Baza	Granada	NO	12
1940–1947	Quero	Granada	NO	16
1940–1946	Galindo	Granada	NO	11
1940–1944	Salsipuedes	Jaén	NO	21
1941–1945	Perejil	Málaga	YES*	12
1941–1947	Sevilla	Granada	YES*	5
1941–1943	Belloto	Granada	NO	13
1941–1945	Tuerto de Jorairatar	Granada	NO	3
1941–1944	Obispo de Cárdeña	Jaén	NO	4
1941–1946	Chaparros	Jaén	NO	12

Table 4 *Continued*

Chronology	Name	Province	Unification	N°
1941–1945	Mota	Almería	YES*	5
1942–1947	Costeño	Málaga	YES*	10
1942–1948	Culito	Granada	YES*	12
1942–1948	Olla Fría	Granada	NO	21
1942–1951	Matías	Granada, Almería	YES	6
1942–1949	Clares	Granada	YES*	31
1942–1947	Jubiles	Córdoba, Jaén	NO	29
1942–1946	Catena	Jaén	NO	5
1942–1947	Cuco	Almería, Granada	YES	30
1943–1948	Casero	Málaga	YES	17
1943–1946	Bernabé	Málaga, Cádiz	YES	9
1943–1944	Velázquez	Granada	NO	5
1943–1948	Peste	Granada	NO	4
1944–1947	Cuarterón	Málaga	NO	13
1944–1945	Madrileño	Málaga	YES*	6
1944–1948	Mandamás	Málaga	YES*	27
1944–1950	Cencerro	Jaén, Granada	NO	30
1944–1950	Sixto Marchena	Jaén	NO	5
1945–1947	Collares	Málaga	YES*	12
1945–1950	Patalete	Málaga	YES*	9
1945	López Quero	Granada	YES	7
1945	Bonilla	Almería	YES	5
1946	Polopero	Granada	YES	12
1947–1948	Moya	Almería	NO	6

Sources: Consejos de Guerra (ATTMA), Memorias de Comandancia (SEHGC), Fichas policiales (AGA y AHN). Design by the author.

Note: The * symbol corresponds to 'groups who initially accepted unification with doubts and/or demands . Some of them decided later on to leave the main guerrilla group and operate independently'.

Table 5 Levels of command: Leaders in AGM and AGG

Name	Post	Group	Date	Origin
Ramón Vía	Military Chief	AGM	1944–1945	Outsider
Alfredo Cabello	Military Chief	AGM	1945–1946	Outsider
José Muñoz "Roberto"	Military Chief	EGA/AGM/ AGG	1945–1952	Outsider
Ricardo Beneyto	Political Chief	EGA	1946–1947	Outsider
José Merediz "Tarbes"	Military Chief	AGG	1946	Outsider
Ramiro Fuentes Ochoa	Military Chief	AGG	1946	Outsider
Francisco "Sevilla"	Military Chief	AGG	1947	Local
Enrique Arroyo Lozano	Political Chief	EGA	1947–1952	Local

Sources: Consejos de guerra (ATTMA), Fichas guardia civil (AGA), Informes (ACCPCE). Design by the author.

Table 6 Levels of command: Chief of Staff and Senior Staff, AGM and AGG

Name	Post	Group	Date	Origin
Ildefonso Armenta	Head of Chief of Staff	AGM	1944–1945	Outsider
Manuel Jurado Martín	Head of Chief of Staff	AGM/AGG	1946–1951	Local
Francisco Sánchez Girón	Agit-Prop	AGG	1947–1951	Outsider
Manuel Martín Rico	Party Chief	AGG	1948–1951	Local
José Chicano Camacho	Commandant	6° Bat.	1946–1947	Local
Joaquín Centurión Centurión	Commandant	6° Bat.	1946–1948	Local
Sebastián Martín Vozmedio	Lieutenant	6° Bat.	1947–1951	Local
Antonio Jurado Martín	Commandant	6° Bat.	1947–1952	Local
Antonio García Martín	Commandant	6° Bat.	1949–1951	Local
Manuel Lozano Laguna	Commandant	7° y 8°	1947–1949	Outsider
José Díaz Durán	Commandant	7° Bat.	1948–1050	Local
Juan Ortiz López	Lieutenant	7° Bat.	1949–1951	Local
Francisco López Pérez	Commandant	8° Bat.	1948–1951	Local

Sources: Consejos de guerra (ATTMA), Fichas guardia civil (AGA), Informes (ACCPCE). Design by the author.

Table 7 Levels of command: Unit leaders, AGM and AGG

Name	Post	Battalion	Date	Origin
Antonio Gutiérrez Sáez	Captain	6° Bat.	1946–1948	Local
Antonio Jurado Martín	Captain	6° Bat.	1946–1949	Local
Francisco Centurión Centurión	Captain	6° Bat.	1947–	Local
Antonio Núñez Montosa	Captain	6° Bat.	1948–1950	Local
Vicente Martín Vozmedio	Lieutenant	6° Bat.	1948–1951	Local
José García Muñoz	Lieutenant	6° Bat.	1949–1950	Local
José Centurión Jiménez	Lieutenant	6° Bat.	1949–1950	Local
José Muñoz García	Captain	7° Bat.	1947–1948	Local
Juan Alaminos Palacios	Captain	7° Bat.	1948–1950	Local
Manuel Calderón Jiménez	Captain	7° Bat.	1948–1952	Local
Antonio Recio Martín	Captain	7° Bat.	1949	Local
Antonio García Romero	Lieutenant	7° Bat.	1949–1951	Local
Daniel Villena Ruíz	Lieutenant	7° Bat.	1950–1951	Local
Francisco Ruíz Alimirón	Lieutenant	7° Bat.	1950–1951	Local
Manuel Pérez Rubiño	Captain	7° Bat.	1950–1952	Local
Antonio López Morales	Captain	7° Bat.	1951	Local
Antonio González Vázquez	Captain	8° Bat.	1947	Local
Manuel Martín Vargas	Lieutenant	8° Bat.	1948–1949	Local
José Sánchez Porras	Lieutenant	8° Bat.	1948–1949	Local
Antonio Frías González	Captain	8° Bat.	1949	Local
José Martín García	Lieutenant	Liaison Group	1949–1951	Local

Sources: Consejos de guerra (ATTMA), Fichas guardia civil (AGA), Informes (ACCPCE). Design by the author.

Table 8 Internal executions, Málaga-Granada, 1939–1952

Name	Group	Date	Motive	Method
Fernando Arias García	AGM	1946	Dissidence	
Miguel Martín López	AGG	1947	Deserter	Beaten
José Merediz Víctores	AGG	1947	Treason	Persecution
José Manuel Sáez Jerónimo	AGG	1948	Deserter	
Francisco Centurión Centurión	AGG	1948	Defeatist	Hanged
Francisco Díaz Rodríguez	AGG	1948	Deserter	
Antonio Sánchez Martín	AGG	1948	Dissidence	Shot
*Andrés Mignorance Rodríguez	AGG	1948	Desertion?	
Francisco López Samos	AGG	1948		
Manuel Alaminos Rodríguez	AGG	1949		
Ramón Castilla Sánchez	AGG	1949	Banditry	Shot
Francisco López Centurión	AGG	1949	Dissidence	
*Manuel Lozano Laguna	AGG	1949	Dissidence?	Shot
Francisco García López	AGG	1949	Banditry	
Antonio López Ruíz	AGG	1950		
Francisco López Ruíz	AGG	1950		
Enrique Moreno Pérez	AGG	1950	Treason	Hanged
Francisco Nieto Romero	AGG	1950	Dissidence	
Antonio Corpas Molina	AGG	1950	Defeatist	Hanged
Rafael Romero Ramírez	AGG	1950		Persecution
Alfonso Navarro Caballero	AGG	1950	Banditry	Hanged
José Vega Ramos	AGG	1950		
Antonio Arrabal Fernández	AGG	1950	Desertion	Hanged
Diego Alaminos Alaminos	AGG	1951	Dissidence	Hanged
Antonio Platero Ayllon	AGG	1951	Lover	
Vicente González Jiménez	AGG	1951		Hanged
*Sebastián Martín Navas	AGG	1951	Desertion?	Pushed off a cliff

Sources: Consejos de guerra (ATTMA) J. A. Romero Navas, *Censo de guerrilleros y colaboradores de la Agrupación Guerrillera de Málaga-Granada…*, op. cit. Design by the author.
Note: The cases of Andrés Mignorance Rodríguez, Manuel Lozano Laguna and Sebastián Martín Navas (*) should be treated with caution, as the documentary evidence does not make it absolutely clear whether or not their deaths resulted from a guerrilla *ajusticiamiento*.

Table 9 Armed guerrilla action, Eastern Andalusia, 1943–1952

Province	Civilian Deaths	Non-Civilian Deaths	Kidnappings	Robberies	Combats	Sabotage
Almería	2	5	2	41	10	4
Granada[1]	73	43	188	426	151	34
Jaén	11	4	17	247	98	9
Málaga	82	31	141	352	149	28
Total	168	83	348	1.066	408	75

Sources: AGUADO, Francisco: *El maquis en España*, Madrid, Editorial San Martín, 1975, pp. 253–254.

Note 1: The lieutenant coronel Eulogio Limia presented similar numbers with regards to Granada, though the period studied was longer (1940–1952): Civilian deaths, 73 Kidnappings, 193 Hold-ups, 429 Sabotage, 4. See *Informe general del proceso seguido contra el bandolerismo en la provincia de Granada*. Caja 106. Movimiento guerrillero (ACCPCE).

Table 10 Robberies committed by the Resistance in Eastern Málaga and Granada, June 1946–June 1947

Province	Money	Food and Clothing	Arms	Food and Money	Arms and Money
Granada	17	12	9	12	6
Málaga	9	2	2	0	1
Total	26	14	11	12	7

Sources: Consejo de Guerra 719/18 (ATTMA). Design by the author.

Table 11 Takings, robberies and kidnappings carried out by the Resistance in Eastern Málaga and Granada, June 1946–June 1947

Province	N° of Robberies	Takings	Average	N° of Kidnappings	Takings	Average
Granada	35	204.362	5.838	48	1.623.555	33.824
Málaga	10	351.85	35.185	14	1.244.500	88.892
Total	35	556.212		62	2.868.055	

Sources: Consejo de Guerra 719/18 (ATTMA). Design by the author.

Table 12 Clandestine press in Eastern Andalusia, 1939–1952

Title	Distribution	Character	Organisation
Ataque	National	Guerrilla	PCE
CNT	National	Opposition	CNT
Juventud Libre	National	Opposition	CNT
Mundo Obrero	National	Opposition	PCE
Mundo Obrero	Regional	Opposition	PCE
Por la República	Regional	Guerrilla	PCE
Reconquista de España	National	Guerrilla	PCE
Resistencia	Regional	Guerrilla	PCE
Solidaridad Proletaria	Regional	Opposition	CNT
Unidad	Regional	Opposition	PCE
Voz Obrera	Regional	Opposition	PCE

Sources: Documentación PCE (ACCPCE), CNT (FAL) and Consejos de Guerra. Design by the author.

Table 13 International campaigns, 1939–1950[1]

Campaign	Date	Role	Organisation
José Vitini	1945	Guerilla	PCE
Álvarez Y Zapirain	1945–1946	Central Committee	PCE
Ramón Vía	1945–1946	Guerilla	PCE
Cristino García Granda	1945–1946	Guerilla	PCE
Agustín Zoroa	1946–1947	Central Committee	PCE
Los Nueve Jóvenes	1947	Cell	PCE
Ricardo Beneyto	1947	Political Chief of Guerrilla	PCE

Sources: Foreign Office (The National Archives, Public Record Office). Design by the author.

Note 1: 49.575 (FO 371, TNA-PRO), 49.576 (FO 371, TNA-PRO), 49.577 (FO 371, TNA-PRO), 60.325(FO 371, TNA-PRO), 60.326 (FO 371, TNA-PRO), 60.327 (FO 371, TNA-PRO), 60.328 (FO 371, TNA-PRO), 60.330 (FO 371, TNA-PRO), 67.887 (FO 371, TNA-PRO), 67.888 (FO 371, TNA-PRO), 67.889 (FO 371, TNA-PRO), 67.890 (FO 371, TNA-PRO), 67.891 (FO 371, TNA-PRO).

Appendix

Graphs

Graph 1 Guerrilla fighters according to resistance modality in Eastern Andalusia (1939–1952)

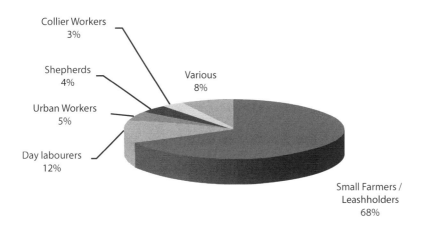

Graph 2 Guerrilla fighters by professions, Eastern Andalusia (1939–1952)

Graph 3 Guerrilla fighters by age when joining, Eastern Andalusia (1939–1952)

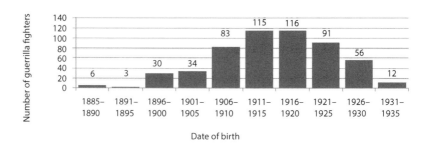

Graph 4 Guerrilla fighters by date of birth, Eastern Andalusia (1939–1952)

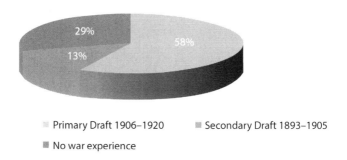

Primary Draft 1906–1920   Secondary Draft 1893–1905

No war experience

Graph 5 Guerrilla fighters by call-ups during the Spanish Civil War, Eastern Andalusia

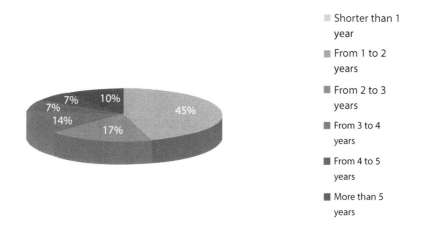

Graph 6 Length of stay in the mountains, Eastern Andalusia (1939–1952)

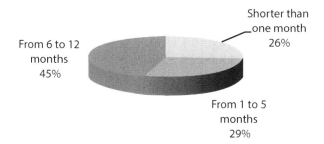

Graph 7 Length of stay that is shorter than one year, Eastern Andalusia (1939–1952)

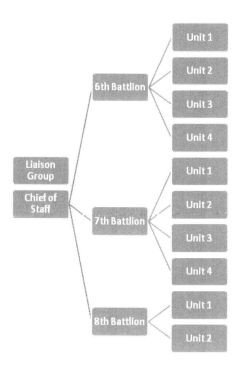

AGG's Internal Structure

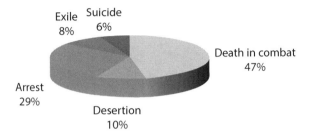

Graph 8 Ways of leaving: Neighbours in arms, Eastern Andalusia (1939–1952)

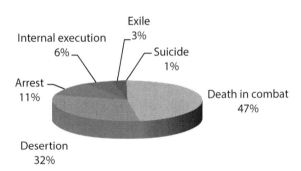

Graph 9 Ways of leaving: Modern guerrilla, Eastern Andalusia (1939–1952)

Notes

Introduction

1 *Informe sobre Ramón Vía*, Jacq 1944–1945 (ACCPCE).
2 *La Libertad*, 17 July 1927.
3 *ABC*, 16 July 1928; *Heraldo de Madrid*, 16 June 1928; *La Libertad*, 16 June 1928.
4 Consejo de Guerra 1431/45 (ATTMA).
5 A canonical definition of resistance in the context of occupation and the Second World War can be found in Henri Michel, "General Report", in *European Resistance Movements, 1939–1945: First International Conference on the History of the Resistance Movements* (Oxford: Pergamon Press, 1960), p. 1.
6 A clear example of this can be found in Tony Judt (ed.), *Resistance and Revolution in Mediterranean Europe, 1939–1948* (New York: Routledge, 1989).
7 George L. Mosse, *Confronting History: A Memoir* (Madison: University of Wisconsin Press, 2000), pp. 101–106.
8 Jorge Marco, "The Long Nocturnal March: The Spanish Guerrilla Movement in the European Narrative of Antifascist Resistance (1936–1952)", in Peter Anderson and Miguel Ángel del Arco (eds.), *Grappling with the Past: Mass Killings and Violence in Spain, 1936–1952* (New York: Routledge, 2015).
9 Helen Graham, *The Spanish Civil War: A Very Short Introduction* (Oxford: Oxford University Press, 2005), pp. 42–53; Helen Graham, *The War and its Shadow: Spain's Civil War in Europe's Long Twentieth Century* (Brighton: Sussex Academic Press, 2012), pp. 75–96.
10 Stathis N. Kalyvas, *The Logic of Violence in Civil War* (New York: Cambridge University Press, 2006), pp. 35–38.
11 Jorge Marco, "Ecos partisanos. La memoria de la Resistencia como memoria conflictiva", *Historia del Presente*, 17-1 (2011).
12 Secundino Serrano, *Maquis: Historia de la guerrilla antifranquista* (Madrid: Temas de Hoy, 2002), p. 376.
13 *Informe de Santiago Carrillo*, 30 de julio de 1945. Jacq 1–2 Dirigentes.
14 In this sense my research builds on the pioneering work of Mercedes Yusta Rodrigo, *Guerrilla y resistencia campesina. La resistencia armada contra el franquismo en Aragón, 1939–1952* (Zaragoza: Prensas Universitarias de Zaragoza, 2003); Mercedes Yusta Rodrígo, *La guerra de los vencidos. El maquis en el Maestrazgo turolense 1940–1950* (Zaragoza: Institución Fernando El Católico, 2005).
15 "Los guerrilleros en el combate por la salvación de España", *Nuestra Bandera*, 30 September 1942.

16 *Informe de Santiago Carrillo.* 30 July 1945. Jacq 1–2 Dirigentes (ACCPCE). On the AGE and the XIV Cuerpo Guerrillero, see: Secundino Serrano, *La última gesta. Los republicanos que vencieron a Hitler, 1939–1945* (Barcelona: Punto de Lectura, 2006), pp. 349–359, 442–446.

17 Paul Preston, *The Last Stalinist: The Life of Santiago Carrillo* (London: HarperCollins, 2014).

18 Interview with Miguel Salado Cecilia, guerrilla fighter in the AGG. 3 October 2008.

19 Francisco Aguado, *El maquis en España* (Madrid: Editorial San Martín, 1975), pp. 165–169; Natacha Lillo, "El PCE en Francia: relaciones con el PCF y evolución (1945–1975)", *Papeles de la FIM*, 22 (2004), p. 132.

20 Andrew J. Birtle, *U.S. Army Counterinsurgency and Contingency Operations Doctrine, 1942–1976* (Washington: Center of Militarily History, 2006), pp. 42–43.

21 Manuel Tagüeña Lacorte, *Testimonios de dos guerras* (Barcelona: Planeta, 1978), p. 331.

22 "Programa de Táctica Guerrillera", in Francisco Aguado Sánchez, *El maquis en sus documentos* (Madrid: Editorial San Martín, 1976), pp. 59–68.

23 Ibid., p. 59.

24 *Informe Político. 1 de septiembre de 1947*, en: Ibid., p. 105.

25 Enrique Lister, "De la experiencia de la lucha guerrillera en España", *España Republicana*, 586, 1966, p. 3.

26 For other examples of these kinds of changes, see Gerard Chaliand, "Introduction", in Gerard Chaliand (ed.), *Guerrilla Strategies: An Historical Anthology from the Long March to Afghanistan* (Berkeley: University of California Press, 1982), p. 10. An extended and revised version: Gérard Chaliand, *Les guerres irégulières. XX–XXI siècle* (Paris: Gallimard, 2008), pp. 30–31; Roger Trinquier, *Modern Warfare: A French View of Counterinsurgency* (Westport: Praeger Security International, 2006).

27 The chain structure and the troikas: Consejo de Guerra 1249/416 (ATTMA); *Informe de Santiago Carrillo, 6 de febrero de 1945.* Jacq 5–8 (ACCPCE). See also: Encarnación Barranquero Texeira, "La reorganización del PCE en Málaga después de la guerra civil", in Lucía Prieto (coord.), *Guerra y franquismo en la provincia de Málaga: nuevas líneas de investigación* (Málaga: Universidad de Málaga, 2005), pp. 87–88. The organisation of cells and ratios, etc.: Consejo de Guerra 510/582 (ATTMA), Consejo de Guerra 951/339 (ATTMA).

28 Vjeran Pavlakovič, "Twilight of the Revolutionaires: 'Naši Španci' and the End of Yugoslavia", *Europe-Asia Studies*, 62-7 (2010), p. 1177.

29 Santiago Carrillo, *Memorias* (Barcelona: Planeta, 2008), pp. 510–513.

30 Robert Gellately, *Stalin's Curse: Battling for Communism in War and Cold War* (Oxford: Oxford University Press, 2013), pp. 317–323.

31 Criticisms of Tito could soon be found in the PCE press, as could new praise of Stalin, which was meant to prove the PCE's loyalty to the Soviet leader. For

examples, see: *Mundo Obrero*, 6 January 1949; *Nuestra Bandera*, December 1949; *Nuestra Bandera*, January 1950, etc.

32 Carrillo, *Memorias*, pp. 412–521; Dolores Ibárruri, *Memorias de Dolores Ibárruri "Pasionaria". La lucha y la vida* (Barcelona: Planeta, 1985), pp. 618–621; Gregorio Morán, *Miseria y grandeza del Partido Comunista de España, 1939–1985* (Barcelona: Planeta, 1986), pp. 137–138; Francisco Moreno Gómez, *La resistencia armada contra Franco. Tragedia del maquis y la guerrilla* (Barcelona: Crítica, 2001), p. 702.

33 "Los guerrilleros, instructores políticos y organizadores de los campesinos", *Mundo obrero*, 3 February 1949. Other articles with similar slogans: "Los Consejos de Resistencia, su composición y funciones", *Revista de información político-militar*, 1 September 1949; "A los camaradas del Partido Comunista de los Pueblos en que se ha organizado el Consejo Local de la Resistencia", 1 November 1949, in Aguado, *El maquis en sus documentos*, pp. 143–149.

34 Hartmut Heine, *La oposición política al franquismo* (Barcelona: Crítica, 1983), p. 467; Josep Sánchez Cervelló (ed.), *Maquis el puño que golpeó el franquismo, La Agrupación Guerrillera de Levante y Aragón* (Barcelona: Flor del Viento, 2003), pp. 295–298; Francisco Moreno Gómez, *Historia y memoria del maquis: El cordobés Veneno, el último guerrillero de la Mancha* (Madrid: Editorial Alpuerto, 2006), pp. 220–221.

35 Sánchez Cervelló, *Maquis*, pp. 380–385.

36 Antonio Tellez Solá, *Sabaté. Guerrilla Urbana en España, 1945–1960* (Barcelona: Virus, 1992); Antonio Tellez Solá, *Facerías. Guerrilla urbana, 1939–1957* (Barcelona: Virus, 2004); Ferran Sánchez Agustí, *El maquis anarquista: De Toulouse a Barcelona por los Pirineos* (Lleida: Editorial Milenio, 2006); Antonio Brevers, *Juanín y Bedoya. Los últimos guerrilleros* (Santander: Cloux Editores, 2008).

37 "Por la Reconciliación nacional, por una solución democrática y pacífica del problema español", *Boletín de Información*, 1 July 1956 (ACCPCE).

1   From Peasants to Soldiers, from Soldiers to Guerrilla Fighters: Youth, masculinity and camaraderie

1 Philippe Ganier Raymond, *L'Affiche rouge* (Paris: Librairie Arthème Fayard, 1975).

2 Olivier Wieviorka: *Une certaine idée de la Résistance. Défense de la France, 1940–1949* (Paris: Éditions du Seuil, 1995), pp. 164–166; Olivier Wieviorka, *Histoire de la Résistance, 1940–1945* (Paris: Perrin, 2015), pp. 427–429; Dominique Veillon and Jacqueline Sainclivier, "Quelles différences sociales entre réseaux, mouvements et maquis?" in: Antoine Prost (dir.), *La Résistance, une histoire sociale* (Paris: Les Éditions de l'Atelier/Les Éditions Ouvriéres, 1997), pp. 47–50.

3 Donald C Hodges and Abraham Guillén, *Revalorización de la guerrilla urbana* (México DF, Ediciones El Caballito, 1977), p. 35.

4 Roberto Sancho Larrañaga, *Guerrilla y terrorismo en Colombia y España*

(Bucaramanga: Colombia, 2003), p. 112; José Luis Cruz Burguete, *Identidades en fronteras, fronteras de identidades: la reconstrucción de la identidad étnica entre los Chujes de Chiapas* (México DF:, Colegio de México/Centro de Estudios Sociológicos, 1998), p. 358; Kalyvas, *The Logic*, p. 136; Boon Kheng Chead, *Red Star over Malaya: Resistance and Social Conflict during and after the Japanese Occupation, 1941–1946* (Singapore: Singapore University Press, 2003), p. 168.

5   Marcel Vigreux: "Sociologie de maquis de Bourgogne", in François Marcot (dir.), *La Résistance et les Français. Lutte armée et maquis* (Paris: Annales litéraires de l'Université de Franché-Comté, 1996), pp. 309–319; François Marcot, "Pour une socioliogie de la Résistance: intentionnalité et fonctionnalité", in Antoine Prost (dir.), *La Résistance, une histoire sociale* (Paris: Les Éditions de l'Atelier/Editions Ouvrières, 1997).

6   H. R. Kedward, *In search of the Maquis: Rural resistance in Southern France, 1942–1944* (Oxford: Oxford University Press, 1994); David H. Close (ed.), *The Greek Civil War: Studies of Polarization* (Nueva York: Routledge, 1993); John Sakkas, "The Civil War in Evvrytania", in Mark Mazower (ed.), *After the War was Over: Reconstructing the Family, Nation, and State in Greece, 1943–1960* (Princeton: Princeton University Press, 2000), pp. 184 et seq.; Kalyvas, *The Logic*, pp. 246–363; Mark Mazower, *Inside Hitler's Greece: The Experience of Occupation, 1941–1944* (New Haven: Yale University Press, 2001), p. 305.

7   Moreno Gómez, *La resistencia armada*, p. 5.

8   The only exception: Fernanda Romeu Alfaro, *Más allá de la utopía: Agrupación Guerrillera de Levante* (Cuenca: Ediciones de la Universidad de Castilla–La Mancha, 2002), pp. 184–186.

9   Manuel González de Molina, *La historia de Andalucía a debate: el campo andaluz* (Barcelona: Anthropos, 2002).

10   Francisco Cobo Romero, *¿Fascismo o democracia?: campesinado y política en la crisis del liberalismo europeo, 1870–1939* (Granada: Universidad de Granada, 2012).

11   For a critique of the theory of middle-class support for fascism, see Michael Mann, *Fascists* (New York: Cambridge University Press, 2004), pp. 17–23.

12   Francisco Cobo Romero, *Revolución campesina y contra-revolución franquista en Andalucía* (Granada: Universidad de Granada, 2004).

13   Ibid., p. 162.

14   Sergio Riesco Roche, *La reforma agraria y los orígenes de la Guerra Civil, 1931–1940* (Madrid: Biblioteca Nueva, 2006).

15   Herbert McClosky and Harold E. Dahlgren, "Primary groups influence on Party Loyalty", *The American Political Science Association*, 53-3 (1959).

16   Cobo Romero, *Por la Reforma Agraria hacia la Revolución. El sindicalismo agrario durante la II República y la Guerra Civil, 1930–1939* (Granada: Universidad de Granada, 2007), pp. 330–340.

17   Federación Socialista de Granada (1937), in: Rafael Gil Bracero, *Revolucionarios sin revolución Marxistas y anarcosindicalistas en guerra: Granada-Baza, 1936–1939* (Granada: Universidad de Granada, 1998), pp. 227–228.

18   Helen Graham, *Socialism and War: The Spanish Socialist Party in Power and*

Crisis, 1936–1939 (Cambridge: Cambride University Press, 1991), pp. 202–210; Fernando Hernández Sánchez, *Guerra o Revolución. El PCE en la guerra civil* (Barcelona: Crítica, 2010), pp. 117–120, 278–280.

19   Romeu Alfaro, *Más allá de la utopía*, p. 183; José Aurelio Romero Navas, *Censo de guerrilleros y colaboradores de la Agrupación Guerrillera de Málaga–Granada* (Málaga: CEDMA, 2004), p. 394.

20   Serrano, *Maquis*, pp. 218–223.

21   Sandra Souto, "Introducción: teoría e historia", *Hispania*, 225 (2007), pp. 12–13, 19.

22   Alberto Melucci, *Challenging Codes: Collective Action in the Information Age* (Cambridge: Cambridge University Press, 2002), p. 119.

23   David S. Reher, *La familia en España, pasado y presente* (Madrid: Alianza, 1996), pp. 291–323.

24   Sandra Souto, "'El mundo ha llegado a ser consciente de su juventud como nunca antes': Juventud y movilización política en la Europa de entreguerras", *Mélanges de la Casa de Velazquez*, 34/1 (2004); Sandra Souto (ed.): "Ser joven en la Europa de entreguerras: política, cultura y movilización", *Hispania*, 225 (2007); Eric Hobsbawm, *Revolutionaries: Contemporary Essays* (London: Phoenix, 1994), pp. 49–50.

25   Eduardo González calleja and Sandra Souto, "De la dictadura a la República: orígenes y auge de los movimientos juveniles en España", *Hispania*, 225 (2007), p. 87.

26   Sandra Souto, "Las organizaciones juveniles: entre el frentepopulismo y el izquierdismo socialista", in Manuel Ballarín and José Luis Ledesma (eds.), *La República del Frente Popular. Reformas, conflictos y conspiraciones* (Zaragoza: Fundación de Investigaciones Marxistas, 2010), p. 61.

27   Sandra Souto, *Paso a la juventud. Movilización democrática, estalinismo y revolución en la República Española* (Valencia: Universitat de València, 2013).

28   Mary Nash, *Rojas: Las mujeres republicanas en la guerra civil* (Madrid: Taurus, 1999), pp. 69–75; María Dolores Ramos, "Identidad de género, feminismo y movimientos sociales en España", *Historia Contemporánea*, 21-II (2000); Marta del Moral, *Acción colectiva femenina en Madrid, 1909–1931* (Santiago: Universidade de Santiago, 2012).

29   Nash, *Rojas*, pp. 155–161; Sofia Rodríguez López, *Mujeres en Guerra: Almería, 1936–1939* (Almería: Arráez Editores, 2003).

30   George Mosse, *The Image of Man: The Creation of Modern Masculinity* (New York: Oxford University Press, 1996), pp. 107–132; Geoff Eley, *Forging Democracy: The History of the Left in Europe, 1850–2000* (New York: Oxford University Press, 2002), p. 9; Enzo Traverso, *A sangre y fuego. De la guerra civil europea, 1914–1945* (Valencia: Universidad de Valencia, 2009), pp. 170–175; Robert Gerwarth, "The Central European Counter-Revolution: Paramilitary Violence in Germany, Austria and Hungary after the Great War", *Past and Present*, 200 (2008).

31   Nerea Aresti, *Masculinidades en tela de juicio* (Madrid: Cátedra, 2010), pp.

121–177; Mary Vincent, "The Martyrs and the Saints: Masculinity and the Construction of the Francoist Crusade", *History Workshop Journal*, 47 (1999).

32 Brian D. Bunk, *Ghosts of Passion. Martyrdom, Gender, and the Origins of the Spanish Civil War* (Durham: Duke University Press, 2007), pp. 88–119; Maria Thomas, *The Faith and the Fury: Popular Anticlerical Violence and Iconoclasm in Spain, 1931–1936* (Brighton: Sussex Academic Press, 2013), pp. 100–120.

33 Graham, Helen, *The Spanish Republic at War, 1936–1939* (Cambridge: Cambridge University Press, 2002), p. 176. Italics in original.

34 *Informe sobre la guerra civil española* (in Russian). Carpeta 19/11. Manuscritos, Tesis, Memorias (ACCPCE) A translation can be found in Ángel Viñas, *El honor de la República* (Barcelona: Crítica, 2009).

35 Julio Aróstegui, "Sociedad y milicias de la guerra civil española, 1936–1939. Una reflexión metodológica", in Santiago Castillo (coord.), *Estudios de Historia de España* (Madrid: Universidad Internacional Menéndez Pelayo, 1981), Vol. 2, pp. 307–326; Vicente Rojo, *¡Alerta los pueblos! Estudio político-militar del periodo final de la guerra española* (Barcelona: Ariel, 1974), pp. 176–184.

36 Juan Andrés Blanco, *El Quinto Regimiento en la política militar del PCE en la guerra civil* (Madrid: UNED, 1993); Michael Alpert, *The Republican Army in the Spanish Civil War, 1936–1939* (New York: Cambridge University Press, 2013).

37 On the campaign for conscription, see La Vanguardia and ABC between 9 and 17 February 1937. On the decree issued by the Generalitat, see La Vanguardia, 12 February 1937. On the decree issued by the Republic, see La Vanguardia and ABC, 17 February 1937.

38 A summary of the figures can be found in Michael Seidman, *Republic of Egos: A Social History of the Spanish Civil War* (Madison: University of Wisconsin Press, 2002), p. 40.

39 *Informe sobre la guerra civil española* (in Russian). Carpeta 19/11. Manuscritos, Tesis, Memorias (ACCPCE). For more on the Fifth Regiment, see Blanco, *El Quinto Regimiento*.

40 John Albert Lynn, *The bayonets of the Republic: Motivation and Tactics in the Army of Revolutionaries France, 1791–94* (Urbana: University of Illinois Press, 1984); J. M. Winter, *The Great War and the British People* (Cambridge, MA: Harvard University Press, 1986), pp. 25–39; Omer Bartov, *Hitler's Army: Soldiers, Nazis, and war in the Third Reich* (Oxford: Oxford University Press, 1992), pp. 29–58, etc.

41 Javier Ugarte, *La nueva Covadonga insurgente Orígenes sociales y culturales de la sublevación de 1936 en Navarra y el País Vasco* (Madrid: Biblioteca Nueva, 1998), pp. 101–139; Carlos Gil Andrés, *Lejos del frente. La guerra civil en la Rioja Alta* (Barcelona: Critica, 2006), pp. 126–129.

42 Seidman, *Republic of Egos*, p. 54; Graham, *The Spanish Republic*, p. 103; Jorge Marco, *Hijos de una guerra. Los hermanos Quero y la resistencia antifranquista* (Granada: Comares, 2010), pp. 73–74.

43 E. A. Shils and M. Janowitz, "Cohesion and Disintegration in the Wehrmacht in World War II", *Public Opinion Quarterly*, 12 (1948).

44 Bartov, *Hitler's Army*, pp. 33–34.

45 Eduardo González Calleja and Sandra Souto, "De la dictadura a la República: orígenes y auge de los movimientos juveniles en España", *Hispania*, 225 (2007), pp. 98–102; Hernández, *Guerra o revolución*, pp. 303–306.

46 Marco, *Hijos*, pp. 80–85.

47 Juan Manuel Fernández, *Educación y cultura en la guerra civil* (Valencia: Nau Llibres, 1984); Christopher H. Cobb, "The Educational and Cultural Policy of the Front Popular Government in Spain, 1936–9", in Martin S. Alexander and Helen Graham (eds.), *The French and Spanish Popular Fronts: Comparative Perspectives* (Cambridge: Cambridge University Press, 1989); Verónica Sierra, *Palabras huérfanas. Los niños y la guerra civil* (Madrid: Taurus, 2009); Ana Martínez Rus, "Editoriales bajo las bombas", *Cultura escrita y Sociedad*, 4 (2007).

48 ABC, 18 February 1937. On the 'popular' character of the new army, see Vicente Rojo, *España heroica. Diez bocetos de la guerra española* (Barcelona: Ariel, 1975), pp. 21–41.

49 Eduardo González Calleja, "La cultura de guerra en la España del siglo XX", *Historia Social*, 61 (2008).

50 George L. Mosse, "Two World Wars and the Myth of the War Experience", *Journal of Contemporary History*, 21–4 (1986), p. 494; George L Mosse, *Fallen Soldier: Reshaping the Memory of the World Wars* (Oxford: Oxford University Press, 1991).

51 Eric J. Leeds, *No man's Land: Combat & Identity in World War I* (Cambridge: Cambridge University Press, 2009); Joanna Bourke, *An Intimate History of Killing: Face to Face Killing in the Twentieth Century Warfare* (New York: Granta Books, 1999), pp. 127–158.

52 Carlos Jiménez Margalejo, *Los que teníamos dieciocho años* (Madrid: Incipit Editores, 2000).

53 Carlos Jiménez Margalejo, *Memorias de un refugiado español en el Norte de África, 1939–1956* (Madrid: Fundación Largo Caballero y Cinca, 2008), p. 71.

54 Santiago Carrillo, *Los viejos camaradas* (Barcelona: Planeta, 2010), p. 15.

55 Julio Aróstegui, *La historia vivida. Sobre la historia del presente* (Madrid: Alianza, 2004), pp. 111–122; Julio Aróstegui, "Traumas colectivos y memorias generacionales: el caso de la guerra civil", in Julio Aróstegui and François Godicheau (eds.), *Guerra civil. Mito y memoria* (Madrid : Marcial Pons, 2009), pp. 57–92.

56 Olivier Galland, *Sociologie de la jeunesse. L'entrée dans la vie* (Paris: Armand Colin, 2007), p. 104.

57 Olivier Wievioka, "La génération de la Résistance", *Vingtième Siècle*, 22 (1989).

58 Vicente Castillo, *Recuerdos y Vivencias* (Barcelona: 1976), unpublished memoir.

59 There are only a few studies on ex-soldiers in Spain, and these deal exclusively with soldiers who fought in the Francoist army. See Ángel Alcalde, *Los excom-*

batientes franquistas, 1936–1965 (Zaragoza: Prensas Universitarias de Zaragoza, 2014).

60   The last call-up was announced on 4 January 1939. Gaceta de la República, 5 January 1939.

61   Marco, *Hijos*, pp. 103–106.

62   Consejo de Guerra 498/46941 (ATTMA), Consejo de Guerra 561/19651 (ATTMA).

63   Consejo de Guerra 1207/649 (ATTMA), Consejo de Guerra 1174/243 (ATTMA).

64   Consejo de Guerra 1349/883 (ATTMA), Consejo de Guerra 1159/245 (ATTMA).

65   Mann, *Fascists*, p. 29.

66   See, for example, the magazine *La Voz del Soldado*. Publicaciones Periódicas. Carpeta 15–18. (ACCPCE).

67   *Por la República*, n° 39. Publicaciones Periódicas. Carpeta 16. (ACCPCE).

68   See, for example, Consejo de Guerra 1047/659 (ATTMA).

69   Interview with Antonia Triviño Martín, in David Baird, *Between Two Fires: Guerrilla War in the Spanish Guerrillas* (Frigiliana: Maroma Press, 2008), p. 186.

70   Ibid., p. 184.

71   Interview with Salomé Pérez Moreno, in Baird, *Between*, p. 212.

72   Consejo de Guerra 450/443 (ATTMA).

73   Paula Schwartz, "Partisanes and Gender Politics in Vichy France", *French Historical Studies*, 16-1 (1989); Margaret Collins Weitz, "Soldiers in the Shadows: Women of the French Resistance", in Gerard J. DeGroot and Corinna Peniston Bird (eds.), *A Soldier and a Woman: Sexual Integration in the Military* (Essex: Pearson Education Limited, 2000), pp. 135–151; L. Capdevila (et al.), *Sexes, genre et guerres: France, 1914–1945* (Paris: Éditions Payot & Rivages, 2010), pp. 81–108.

74   Albert Camus, *Caligula and Three Other Plays* (New York: Vintage Books, 1958.), p. 301.

75   Serrano, *Maquis*, p. 221.

76   Dirigentes. Caja 30. Carpeta 1/2 (ACCPCE).

77   Dolores Ibárruri, "Por un 8 de marzo en libertad", *Mundo Obrero*, 4 (1946).

78   Fernanda Romeu Alfaro, *Silencio Roto: Mujeres contra el franquismo* (Barcelona: El Viejo Topo, 2002), pp. 27–48; Mercedes Yusta, "Rebeldía individual, compromiso familiar, acción colectiva: las mujeres en la resistencia al franquismo durante los años cuarenta", *Historia del Presente*, 4 (2004); Irene Abad Buil, *En las puertas de prisión: de la solidaridad a la concienciación política de las mujeres de los presos* (Barcelona: Icaria, 2012).

2   Carrillo's Men: PCE and the anti-Francoist guerrilla

1   Estruch, *El PCE*, pp. 27–47; Heine, *La oposición*, pp. 95–102.

2   "Llamamiento del PC de España. A la Unión Nacional de todos los españoles

contra Franco, los invasores italo-germanos y los traidores", *Nuestra Bandera*, México (August–September 1941).

3 Manuel Azcárate, *Derrotas y Esperanzas. La República, la Guerra Civil y la Resistencia* (Barcelona: Tusquets, 1994), pp. 202–206; Carlos Fernández Rodríguez, *Madrid clandestino: La reestructuración del PCE, 1939–1945* (Madrid: Fundación Domingo Malagón, 2002), pp. 129–297.

4 David Ginard y Feron, *Heriberto Quiñones y el movimiento comunista en España, 1931–1942* (Palma: Edicions Documenta Balear, 2000), pp. 137–152.

5 Informes del Interior. Sig 10–11 (ACCPCE); Fernández Rodríguez, *Madrid Clandestino*, pp. 189–193.

6 Azcárate, *Derrotas*, pp. 259–265.

7 On the complex unification process in the French Resistance, see Alan Clinton, *Jean Moulin, 1899–1943: The French Resistance and the Republic* (Basingtoke: Palgrave, 2002), pp. 151–176.

8 Heine, *La oposición política*, pp. 142–146.

9 *Unión Nacional Española. Julio de 1944*. Republicanos. 121/1/15 UNE (ACCPCE).

10 Azcárate, *Derrotas*, p. 284.

11 *El Movimiento Guerrillero Vanguardia de la Lucha por la Reconquista de España. 20 de septiembre de 1944*. Dirigentes. Dolores Ibárruri. Escritos. 16/2. (ACCPCE).

12 Enrique Líster, *¡Basta!, Una aportación a la lucha por la recuperación del Partido* (Madrid: G. del Toro, 1978), pp. 180–181.

13 Jacq 1–2 Dirigentes. (ACCPCE).

14 Líster, *¡Basta!*, pp. 184–185.

15 Carrillo, *Memorias*, pp. 450–470; Ibárruri, *Memorias*, pp. 566–567.

16 Fernando Martínez de Baños, *Hasta su total aniquilación. El ejército contra el maquis en el Valle de Arán y en el Alto Aragón, 1944–1944* (Madrid: Almena, 2002); Daniel Arasa, *La invasión de los maquis* (Barcelona: Belacqva, 2004).

17 Informe de Carrillo a Dolores. 6 de febrero de 1945. Jacq 5–8. Dirigentes. (ACCPCE); Carrillo, *Memorias*, pp. 470–472.

18 Azcárate, *Derrotas*; López Tovar, "Operación, pp. 191–223.

19 Daniel Arasa, *Años 40: el maquis y el PCE* (Barcelona: Argos Vergara, 1984); Serrano, *La última gesta*, pp. 597–604; Fernando Martínez de Baños, *El maquis. Una cultura del exilio español, Zaragoza* (Madrid: Delsan, 2007), pp. 218–223; Moreno Gómez, *La resistencia armada*, p. 697.

20 Arthur London, *La confesión: En el engranaje del Proceso de Praga* (Vitoria-Gasteiz: Ikusager Ediciones, 2000); Claudin, *La crisis del movimiento comunista*, pp. 469–499; Josie McLellan, *Antifascism and Memory in East Germany: Remembering the International Brigades, 1945–1989* (Oxford: Oxford University Press, 2004); Duncan Shiels, *Los hermanos Rajk. Un drama familiar europeo* (Barcelona: Acantilado, 2009).

21 Fernando Claudin, *La crisis del movimiento comunista*, pp. 494–495; Azcárate,

Derrotas y esperanzas, pp. 327–340; Hernández Sánchez, *Comunistas sin partido: Jesús Hernández* (Madrid: Raíces, 2007), pp. 179–206.

22 Carpeta 16/2. Dirigentes. Dolores Ibárruri (ACCPCE).

23 Morán, *Miseria*; Fernández Rodríguez, *Madrid clandestino;* Enrique Lister, *Así destruyó Carrillo el PCE* (Barcelona: Planeta, 1983), p. 79. Heine, *La oposición política*, pp. 225–226.

24 Ibárruri, *Memorias*, pp. 571–575.

25 Líster, *¡Basta!*, pp. 181–182; Carrillo, *Memorias*, pp. 479–480.

26 Cristóbal Criado Moreno, *Mi juventud y mi lucha* (Málaga: Edición del autor, 1993), pp. 207–209; Cristóbal Criado Moreno, *El PCE que viví en Málaga, 1920–1977* (Málaga: Edición del autor, 2004), p. 96; Encarnación Barranquero Texeira, "La reorganización del PCE en Málaga después de la guerra civil", in Prieto Borrego, Lucía (coord.), *Guerra y franquismo en la provincia de Málaga* (Málaga: Universidad de Málaga, 2005).

27 Consejo de Guerra 1249/416; José María Azuaga Rico, "El PCE granadino, 1940–1952", in *II Congreso de Historia del PCE* (Madrid: FIM, 2006).

28 Encarnación Lemus, "Permanencia y reconstrucción del PCE en Andalucía durante la posguerra (1939–1949)", *Espacio, Tiempo y Forma. Historia Contemporánea*, 11 (1998).

29 Consejo de Guerra 556/573 (ATTMA).

30 Ibid.

31 Carrillo, *Memorias.*

32 *Informe Alfredo Cabello*. Jacq 762. Informe camaradas (ACCPCE).

33 Consejo de Guerra 556/573 (ATTMA).

34 *Informe Alfredo Cabello*. Jacq 762. Informe camaradas (ACCPCE).

35 *Informe de Andrés Paredes "Gromán"*. Caso Monzón (ACCPCE); Arasa, *La invasión*, p. 381.

36 *Informe Alfredo Cabello*. Jacq 762. Informe camaradas (ACCPCE).

37 Consejo de Guerra 556/573 (ATTMA).

38 Consejo de Guerra 1431/45 (ATTMA).

39 Jiménez Margalejo, *Memorias*, pp. 70–92.

40 Jacq 1944–1945 (ACCPCE).

41 Jiménez Margalejo, *Memorias*, pp. 105–109; Jacq 1944–1945 (ACCPCE).

42 Jacq 1944–1945 (ACCPCE).

43 Consejo de Guerra 1431/45 (ATTMA).

44 Ibid.

45 Informe sobre Ramón Vía. Jacq 1944–1945. (ACCPCE).

46 Consejo de Guerra 1431/45 (ATTMA); Carrillo, *Memorias*, p. 465; Heine, *La oposición*, pp. 220–221; Hartmut Heine and José María Azuaga, *La oposición al franquista en Andalucía Oriental* (Madrid: Fundación Salvador Seguí, 2005), pp. 126–127, 191–193; Baird, *Between*, pp. 20–24.

47 Carrillo, *Memorias*, p. 465.

48 Informe sobre Ramón Vía. Jacq 1944–1945 (ACCPCE).

49 Consejo de Guerra 1431/45 (ATTMA).

50   Jacq 653–654. Informe Camaradas (ACCPCE).

51   Dirigentes. Caja 34. Carpeta 22 (ACCPCE); Jacq 1–2. Dirigentes (ACCPCE); Baldomero Ortiz Requena, *Frente a la Historia que escriben los vencedores* (Sevilla: 1990) Unpublished memoir (FES-AHCCOO), p. 34.

52   Consejo de Guerra 1431/45 (ATTMA).

53   Ibíd.

54   Consejo de Guerra 1431/45 (ATTMA); Ortiz Requena, *Frente a la Historia*, p. 55.

55   Azcárate, *Derrotas*, pp. 285–288.

56   Consejo de Guerra 1431/45; Romero Navas, *Censo*, p. 351.

57   *Informe de Agustín Zoroa (Darío) 22 de noviembre de 1945.* Jac1 14–18. Documentos PCE no incluidos (ACCPCE); *Informe Ramón Vía. Octubre 1945.* Jacq 1044–1045 (ACCPCE).

58   Consejo de Guerra 1249/416 (ATTMA).

59   Ibid.

60   *Informe de Agustín Zoroa (Darío) 22 de noviembre de 1945.* Jac1 14–18. Documentos PCE no incluidos (ACCPCE).

61   *Informe Ramón Vía. Octubre 1945.* Jacq 1044–1045 (ACCPCE).

62   *Informe Ramón Vía*, found in *Informe de Agustín Zoroa (Darío) 22 de noviembre de 1945.* Jac1 14–18. Documentos PCE no incluidos (ACCPCE).

63   Consejo de Guerra 556/573 (ATTMA); *Informe de Agustín Zoroa (Darío) 22 de noviembre de 1945.* Jacq 14–18. Documentos PCE no incluidos (ACCPCE); *Testimonio de Ramiro Fuentes Ochoa.* Caja 18. Carpeta 7. Tesis Manuscritas (ACCPCE).

64   Consejo de Guerra 556/573 (ATTMA).

65   *Informe Ramón Vía. Octubre 1945.* Jacq 1044–1045 (ACCPCE).

66   Consejo de Guerra 556/573 (ATTMA); *Testimonio de Ramiro Fuentes Ochoa.* Caja 18. Carpeta 7. Tesis Manuscritas (ACCPCE).

67   *Informe Ramón Vía. Octubre 1945.* Jacq 1044–1045 (ACCPCE).

68   Consejo de Guerra 556/573 (ATTMA).

69   Interview with the guerrilla fighter Enrique Urbano, in Romero Navas, *Censo*, pp. 278.

70   Consejo de Guerra 939/1951 (ATTMA).

71   Ibid.

72   *Informe José Muñoz Lozano.* Jacq 920. Informe Camaradas (ACCPCE).

73   Consejo de Guerra 939/1951 (ATTMA).

74   Azcárate, *Derrotas*, p. 242.

75   Consejo de Guerra 939/1951 (ATTMA).

76   *Informe José Muñoz Lozano.* Jacq 920. Informe Camaradas (ACCPCE).

77   *Informe José Muñoz Lozano.* Jacq 920. Informe Camaradas (ACCPCE).

78   Consejo de Guerra 939/1951 (ATTMA).

79   Consejo de Guerra 1195/75 (ATTMA); Consejo de Guerra 939/1951 (ATTMA).

80 *Testimonio de Ramiro Fuentes Ochoa*. Tesis manuscritas. Caja 18. Carpeta 7 (ACCPCE).
81 Consejo de Guerra 939/1951 (ATTMA).
82 Consejo de Guerra 1195/75 (ATTMA).
83 Consejo de Guerra 1195/75 (ATTMA); Consejo de Guerra 719/18 (ATTMA); Consejo de Guerra 939/1951 (ATTMA); *Testimonio de Ramiro Fuentes Ochoa*. Tesis manuscritas. Caja 18. Carpeta 7 (ACCPCE).
84 Consejo de Guerra 1195/75 (ATTMA).
85 *Informe sobre Ricardo Beneyto Sapena*. Jacq 749. Informes camaradas (ACCPCE).
86 Interview with Alicia Langa Laorga (Madrid, febrero de 2011).
87 Ibid.
88 Consejo de Guerra 719/18 (ATTMA).
89 Consejo de Guerra 1195/75 (ATTMA).

3 The Long Journey Towards Unification: Resolution and resistance

1 "Los guerrilleros en el combate por la salvación de España", *Nuestra Bandera*, 30 September 1942; Dolores Ibárruri speech in Radio España Independiente, in Dirigentes 16/2 (ACCPCE), etc.; Jorge Marco, "'Encender la guerra de guerrillas': El PCE y la guerrilla antifranquista", in Jorge Marco, Helder Gordim and Jaime Valim (eds.), *Violência e sociedade em ditaduras ibero-americanas no século XX: Argentina, Brasil, Espanha e Portugal* (Porto Alegre: Editora da Pontifícia Universidade Católica do Rio Grande do Sul, 2015).
2 Luis Soto, "Las nacionalidades de España en la lucha común contra Franco y la falange", *Nuestra Bandera*, 6 October 1942.
3 *Carta del Secretario de la Delegación Nacional de Información e Investigación de la FET de la JONS al Ministro Secretario General de la FET de la JONS. Madrid, 9 de junio de 1941*. Caja 51/20.569 (AGA); Consejo de Guerra 6/3071 (ATTMS); Información Especial n° 26. Dirección General de Seguridad (FFF); Consejo de Guerra 820/595 (ATTMA).
4 Consejo de Guerra 1249/416 (ATTMA).
5 Marco, *Hijos*, pp. 310–311.
6 Ibid., pp. 316–321.
7 Consejo de Guerra 890/572 (ATTMA).
8 For an acccount of a similar attempt between disparate forces in the Federación Guerrillera de León-Galicia, see Secundino Serrano, *La guerrilla antifranquista en León, 1936–1951* (Madrid: Siglo XXI, 1988), pp. 231–232, 360.
9 Consejo de Guerra 440/207 (ATTMA).
10 José Aurelio Romero Navas, *La guerrilla en 1945: Proceso a dos jefes guerrilleros: Ramón Vías y Alfredo Cabello Gómez-Acebo* (Málaga: CEDMA, 1999).
11 *Informe de Ramón Vía a Agustín Zoroa*. Jacq 1044–1045 (ACCPCE).
12 Consejo de Guerra 1235/465 (ATTMA). The subsequent information is also taken from this document, until otherwise indicated.
13 Consejo de Guerra 1238/279 (ATTMA).

14 Consejo de Guerra 1235/465 (ATTMA).

15 Consejo de Guerra 908/692 (ATTMA); Consejo de Guerra 1238/278 (ATTMA).

16 *Informe Ramón Vía* found in *Informe de Agustín Zoroa (Darío) 22 de noviembre de 1945*. Jacq 14–18. Documentos PCE no incluidos (ACCPCE).

17 Ibid.

18 Consejo de Guerra 1431/45 (ATTMA). The subsequent information is also taken from this document, until otherwise indicated.

19 Romero Navas, *Censo.*

20 *Informe Ramón Vía* found in *Informe de Agustín Zoroa (Darío) 22 de noviembre de 1945*. Jacq 14–18. Documentos PCE no incluidos (ACCPCE).

21 Carpeta 25. Tesis, manuscritos (ACCPCE).

22 Consejo de Guerra 1431/45 (ATTMA). The subsequent information is also taken from this document, until otherwise indicated.

23 Jacq 1–2. Dirigentes (ACCPCE).

24 *Informe Ramón Vía* found in *Informe de Agustín Zoroa (Darío) 22 de noviembre de 1945*. Jacq 14–18. Documentos PCE no incluidos (ACCPCE).

25 Consejo de Guerra 556/573 (ATTMA).

26 *Informe Ramón Vía* found in *Informe de Agustín Zoroa (Darío) 22 de noviembre de 1945*. Jacq 14–18. Documentos PCE no incluidos (ACCPCE).

27 Consejo de Guerra 556/573 (ATTMA).

28 *Informe Ramón Vía* found in *Informe de Agustín Zoroa (Darío) 22 de noviembre de 1945*. Jacq 14–18. Documentos PCE no incluidos (ACCPCE).

29 Consejo de Guerra 556/573 (ATTMA).

30 *Informe Ramón Vía* found in *Informe de Agustín Zoroa (Darío) 22 de noviembre de 1945*. Jacq 14–18. Documentos PCE no incluidos (ACCPCE).

31 Consejo de Guerra 556/573 (ATTMA); Romero Navas, *Censo*, p. 128.

32 *Informe Ramón Vía* found in *Informe de Agustín Zoroa (Darío) 22 de noviembre de 1945*. Jacq 14–18. Documentos PCE no incluidos (ACCPCE).

33 Consejo de Guerra 556/573 (ATTMA).

34 Consejo de Guerra 910/245 (ATTMA).

35 Consejo de Guerra 1431/45 (ATTMA); *Informe Ramón Vía* found in *Informe de Agustín Zoroa (Darío) 22 de noviembre de 1945*. Jacl 14–18. Documentos PCE no incluidos (ACCPCE).

36 Jacq 653–654. Informe camaradas (ACCPCE); Ortiz Requena, *Frente a la historia*, pp. 44–48.

37 *Informe de Agustín Zoroa (Darío) 22 de noviembre de 1945*. Jacl 14–18. Documentos PCE no incluidos (ACCPCE).

38 Consejo de Guerra 510/582 (ATTMA).

39 Consejo de Guerra 556/573 (ATTMA); Jacq 653/654. Informes Camaradas (ACCPCE).

40 Consejo de Guerra 556/573 (ATTMA).

41 *Carta de Ramón Vía. Mayo de 1946*. Jacq 1944–1945 (ACCPCE). The subsequent information is also taken from this document, until otherwise indicated.

42 Consejo de Guerra 1431/45 (ATTMA).

43 Consejo de Guerra 1431/45 (ATTMA); Consejo de Guerra 556/573 (ATTMA); Romero Navas, *La guerrilla*, pp. 12–13.

44 Consejo de Guerra 556/573 (ATTMA).

45 Consejo de Guerra 719/18 (ATTMA).

46 Consejo de guerra 1195/75 (ATTMA); Azuaga Rico, *La guerrilla antifranquista*, p.131; Alfonso Domingo, *El canto del búho. La vida en el monte de los guerrilleros antifranquistas* (Madrid: Oberón, 2002), p. 243.

47 *Testimonio de Ramiro Fuentes Ochoa*. Caja 18. Carpeta 7. Tesis manuscritas (ACCPCE).

48 Consejo de Guerra 657/24 (ATMTS); Consejo de Guerra 1195/75 (ATTMA); Francisco Rodríguez Sevilla, *Así me metieron en la política* (Granada: 1977) Unpublished memoirs.

49 Consejo de Guerra 719/18 (ATTMA).

50 Consejo de Guerra 1195/75 (ATTMA).

51 Consejo de Guerra 890/572 (ATTMA).

52 Consejo de Guerra 1195/75 (ATTMA). The subsequent information is also taken from this document, until otherwise indicated.

53 Interview with Manuel Prieto López, 27 September 2003.

54 Ibid.; Consejo de Guerra 719/18 (ATTMA).

55 Rodríguez Sevilla, *Así me metieron en política*.

56 Marco, *Hijos*, pp. 106–111, 200–229, 275–284, 375–382, 409–411.

57 Marco, "'Una Corea en pequeño': Contrainsurgencia y represión de la guerrilla en España, 1939–1952", *Contenciosa*, 1 (2013).

58 Consejo de Guerra 657/24 (ATMTS).

59 Consejo de Guerra 657/24 (ATMTS).

60 Consejo de Guerra 1186/595 (ATTMA).

61 *Informe de Agustín Zoroa (Darío) 22 de noviembre de 1945*. Jac1 14–18. Documentos PCE no incluidos (ACCPCE).

62 Consejo de Guerra 1157/526 (ATTMA).

4 "A Strange Guerrilla Group": Identities and local community

1 Jesús Izquierdo, *El rostro de la comunidad. La identidad del campesino en la Castilla del Antiguo Régimen* (Madrid: Consejo Económico y Social, 2001); Jesús Izquierdo, "De palabras y cosas en el cambio agrario: el desafío de la historia conceptual", *I Seminario Anual de la SEHA* (Madrid: SEHA, 2010).

2 La denominación procede de: Juan Díaz del Moral, *Las agitaciones campesinas del periodo bolchevique, 1919–1920* (Sevilla: Editoriales Andaluzas Unidas, 1985).

3 Izquierdo, "De palabras", p. 12.

4 Ibid., pp. 13–14.

5 Ibid., p. 16.

6 Keri E. Yllal Smith, "Hybrid Identities: Theoretical Examinations", in Keri

E. Yllal Smith and Patricia Levay (eds.), *Hybrid Identities: Theoretical and Empirical Examinations* (Leiden: Brill, 2008), pp. 3–4.

7 For examples, see A. M. Rivas, "Los marcos territoriales y sociales de identificación regional en el mundo rural cantábrico", in *Los espacios rurales cantábricos y su evolución* (Santander: Universidad de Cantabria, 1990), pp. 213–230; Luis Díaz, *Aproximación antropológica a Castilla y León* (Barcelona: Anthropos, 1988).

8 A. M. Rivas, *Ritos, símbolos y valores en el análisis de la identidad en la provincia de Zaragoza* (Zaragoza: Caja de Ahorros de la Inmaculada, 1986); Pitt-Rivers, *The People*.

9 Gil Andrés, *Lejos del frente*, p. 73.

10 J. Blum, "The Internal Structure and Polity of the European Village Community from Fifteenth to the Nineteenth Century", *Journal of Modern History*, 43–4 (1971); Adrian Shubert, *A Social History of Modern Spain* (London & New York: Routledge, 1990), pp. 193–197; Ledesma, *Los días*, p. 120.

11 Rafael Cruz, *En el nombre del pueblo. República, rebelión y guerra en la España de 1936* (Madrid: Siglo XXI, 2006).

12 Ugarte Tellería, *La nueva Covadonga*, p. 15; Hamza Alavi, "Peasant Classes and Primordial Loyalties", *The Journal of Peasant Studies*, 1-1 (1973).

13 James C. Scott, *Weapons of the Weak: Every Forms of Peasant Resistance* (New Haven & London: Yale University Press, 1985), pp. 212–240.

14 Mykel Verkuyten, *The Social Psychology of Ethnic Identity* (East Sussex: Psychology Press, 2005), pp. 50–53, 151–155.

15 Ledesma, *Los días de llamas*, pp. 117–127.

16 Gil Andrés, *Lejos del frente*; Carlos Gil Andrés, "La zona gris de la España azul. La violencia de los sublevados en la guerra civil", *AYER*, 76-4 (2009); Peter Anderson, *The Francoist Military Trials*, pp. 63–91; Peter Anderson, "Singling Out Victims: Denunciation and Collusion in the Post-Civil War Francoist Repression in Spain, 1939–1945", *European History Quarterly*, 39 (1), 2009; Peter Anderson, "In the Interest of Justice? Grass-roots, Prosecution and Collaboration in Francoist Military Trials, 1939–1945", *Contemporary European History*, 18–1 (2009).

17 Intreview with Antonia Triviño Martín, in Baird, *Between*, p. 183.

18 Kalyvas, *The Logic*, pp. 77–83.

19 Mark Mazower, *Hitler's Empire: How the Nazis Ruled Europe* (New York: Penguin, 2009), p. 520.

20 There are many studies highlighting the importance of primary groups for mobilization efforts in local and peasant communities: Timoty P. Wickham-Cowley, *Guerrillas and Revolution in Latin America: A Comparative Study of Insurgents and Regimes since 1956* (Princeton: Princeton University Press, 1992), p. 142; Eric Hobsbawn and George Rude, *Captain Swing: A Social History of the Great English Agricultural Uprising of 1830* (New York: W. W. Norton & Company, 1968), p. 205; James C. Scott, *The moral Economy of the Peasant* (New Haven & London: Yale University Press, 1976), pp. 222–227; Craig J. Calhoun, *The Question of Class Struggle: Social Foundations of Popular Radicalism*

during the Industrial Revolution (Chicago: University of Chicago Press, 1982), pp. 7–8; Mark Irving Lichbach, *The Rebel's Dilemma* (Michigan: The University of Michigan Press, 1995), pp. 146–149; Mario Diani, "Networks and Participations", in D. A Snow (et al.), *The Blackwell Companion to Social Movements* (Oxford: Blackwell Publishing, 2004) p. 341; Paul Staniland, *Networks of Rebellion: Explaining Insurgent Cohesion and Collapse* (Ithaca: Cornell University Press, 2014), pp. 5–11, etc.

21   *Memoria Histórica de la Guardia Civil. Provincia de Jaén* (SEHGC); *Informe General sobre el proceso seguido por el problema del bandolerismo en la provincia de Granada* (ACCPCE).

22   Marco, *Hijos.*

23   Consejos de Guerra: 1140/17867; 1224/426; 1229/1246; 1236/310; 1238/1304 (ATTMA); Consejo de Guerra 20/425 (ACGG) Fichas personales de la guardia civil (AGA).

24   Consejos de Guerra: 288/37; 470/168; 496/242; 620/1149; 1157/414; 398/46941; 510/244; 561/19651; 774/172; 846/1063; 862/185; 862/1901; 871/2002; 929/605; 1216/208; 1224/598; 1225/1037; 1251/841; 1170/413; 1194/794; 1157/526; 876/341; 1169/757; 1225/2387; 520/273 (ATTMA); Consejos de Guerra: 555/411; 580/996 (ACGG) Fichas personales de la guardia civil (AGA).

25   Ho Chi Minh, "The Party's Military Work among the Peasants", in A. Neuberg, *Armed Insurrection* (London: NLB, 1970 [1928]), p. 261. Similar arguments in Hobsbawn, *Revolutionaries*, pp. 163–175.

26   Eric Hobsbawm, *Primitive Rebels* (Manchester: Manchester University Press, 1971).

27   Manuel González de Molina, "Los mitos de la modernidad y la protesta campesina: A propósito de Rebeldes Primitivos de Eric Hobsbawm", *Historia Social*, 25 (1996); Jorge Marco, "Guerrilla, bandolerismo social, acción colectiva: Algunas reflexiones metodológicas sobre la resistencia armada antifranquista", *Cuadernos de Historia Contemporánea*, 28 (2006).

28   Consejo de Guerra 1239/970 (ATTMA) The rest of the account is based on this document.

29   On the local character of collective action, see Charles Tilly, *The Contentious French. Four Centuries of Popular Struggle* (Cambridge, MA: Harvard University Press, 1986), pp. 390–398; Charles Tilly, "Contentious Repertoires in Great Britain, 1758–1834", in Mark Traugott (ed.), *Repertoires and Cycles of Collective Action* (Durham: Duke University Press, 1995), pp. 32–34; Carlos Gil Andrés, *Echarse a la calle. Amotinados, huelguistas y revolucionarios: La Rioja, 1890–1936* (Zaragoza: Prensas Universitarias de Zaragoza, 2000).

30   Consejo de Guerra 443/48 (ATTMA). Italics in original.

31   Josepa Cucó Giner, "Familia, amistad y cultura asociativa en el País Valenciano", *Revista de Antropología social*, 1 (1992); Josepa Cucó Giner, *La amistad: perspectiva antropológica* (Barcelona: Icaria, 1995), pp. 117–125.

32   The recontruction of events is based on Consejo de Guerra 1189/830; Consejo

de Guerra 1169/32 (ATTMA); Consejo de Guerra 1348/705 (ATTMA).

33   Consejo de Guerra 1169/32 (ATTMA).

34   See, for example, Consejo de Guerra 1221/20 (ATTMA).

35   Interview with Enrique Urbano Sánchez, in José Aurelio Romero Navas, *Recuperando la memoria*, (Málaga: CEDMA, 1997), pp. 158, 175. The italics are mine.

36   Ricardo Sanmartín, *Identidad y creación. Horizontes culturales e interpretación antropológica* (Barcelona: Editorial Humanidades, 1993), pp. 200–201.

37   Julian A. Pitt-Rivers, *The People of the Sierra* (Chicago: Chicago University Press, 1971), p. 7.

38   Intreview with Ángel Sánchez García, in Baird, *Between*, p. 109.

39   Consejo de Guerra 1431/45 (ATTMA).

40   Consejo de Guerra 1225/429 (ATTMA); Consejo de Guerra 510/582 (ATTMA); Consejo de Guerra 556/573 (ATTMA), etc.

41   Consejo de guerra 1157/526 (ATTMA) The declaration of another of the five guerrilla fighters, describing the same situation, can be found in Consejo de Guerra 1170/423 (ATTMA). The italics are mine.

42   Consejo de Guerra 876/341 (ATTMA); Consejo de Guerra 1157/526 (ATTMA).

43   Bertolt Brecht, *Poetry and Prose* (New York: Continuum, 2006), p. 75.

5   "I Swear on My Honour as a Guerrilla Fighter": Discipline, recruitment and desertions

1   *Juramento guerrillero*, published in *Nueva Historia*, 8 (September 1977).

2   Consejo de Guerra 1232/892 (ATTMA).

3   Consejo de Guerra 1180/34 (ATTMA); Consejo de Guerra 551/136 (ATMTS); Interview with Enrique Urbano, in Romero Navas, *Recuperando la memoria*, p. 103.

4   *Manual de orientación política-militar del Ejército Guerrillero de Andalucía*. Consejo de Guerra 443/48 (ATTMA).

5   *Informe de la AGM*. 13 April 1946; *Informe de la AGM*. 1 May 1946; *Informe de la AGM*. 9 May 1946. All found in Consejo de Guerra 556/573 (ATTMA).

6   Consejo de Guerra 1431/45 (ATTMA); Consejo de Guerra 556/573 (ATTMA).

7   Consejo de Guerra 510/582 (ATTMA); Consejo de Guerra 719/18 (ATTMA); Consejo de Guerra 556/573 (ATTMA); Consejo de Guerra 657/24 (ATMTS).

8   Consejo de Guerra 1348/705 (ATTMA).

9   Eulogio Limia Pérez, *Informe general del proceso seguido por el problema del bandolerismo en la provincia de Granada*. Caja 106. Movimiento guerrillero (ACCPCE).

10   Consejo de Guerra 1349/883 (ATTMA).

11   Consejo de Guerra 1348/705 (ATTMA).

12   Consejo de Guerra 1431/45 (ATTMA); Jacq 653–654. Informes Camaradas (ACCPCE); Jacq 700. Informes Camaradas (ACCPCE).

13 Consejo de Guerra 1154/950 (ATTMA).

14 *Informe AGM*. 1 May 1946. Consejo de Guerra 556/573 (ATTMA).

15 Consejo de Guerra 1221/20 (ATTMA).

16 Consejo de Guerra 1218/839 (ATTMA).

17 Consejo de Guerra 1174/45 (ATTMA); Interview with Enrique Urbano, in Romero Navas, *Recuperando la memoria*, pp. 122–123.

18 Consejo de Guerra 1207/649 (ATTMA); Romero Navas, *Censo de guerrilleros*, p. 152.

19 Consejo de Guerra 1221/20 (ATTMA); Consejo de Guerra 1207/649 (ATTMA); Romero Navas, *Censo de guerrilleros*, p. 352.

20· *Manual de orientación política-militar del Ejército Guerrillero de Andalucía*. Consejo de Guerra 443/48 (ATTMA).

21 Consejo de Guerra 556/573 (ATTMA); Jacq 762. Informes Camaradas (ACCPCE); Jacq 1944–1945. Informes Camaradas (ACCPCE); Consejo de Guerra 719/18 (ATTMA).

22 London, *La confesión*, p. 26.

23 Consejo de Guerra 496/242 (ATTMA); Consejo de Guerra 620/1149 (ATTMA).

24 *Nota Informativa nº 24 de la 205 Comandancia* (SEHGC); Marco, *Hijos de una guerra*, pp. 218–239.

25 Consejo de Guerra 620/1149 (ATTMA); Romero Navas, *Censo de guerrilleros*, p. 87.

26 *Instrucciones para el cumplimiento de las unidades. Ejército Guerrillero de Andalucía. Estado Mayor*, in Aguado Sánchez, *El maquis en sus documentos*, p. 346.

27 Consejo de Guerra 620/1149 (ATTMA); Romero Navas, *Censo de guerrilleros*, p. 87.

28 Consejo de Guerra 1186/595 (ATTMA); Consejo de Guerra 1348/705 (ATTMA).

29 Eulogio Limia Pérez, *Informe general del proceso seguido contra el bandolerismo en la provincia de Granada*. Caja 106. Movimiento guerrillero (ACCPCE).

30 Consejo de Guerra 1348/705 (ATTMA).

31 *Información sobre la Agrupación de Granada*. Miguel Salado Cecilia. Carpeta 4/2. Caja 106. Movimiento Guerrillero (ACCPCE).

32 Consejo de Guerra 1186/595 (ATTMA); Romero Navas, *Censo de guerrilleros*, pp. 212–214.

33 *Manual de orientación política-militar del Ejército Guerrillero de Andalucía*. Consejo de Guerra 443/48 (ATTMA).

34 Fernanda Romeu Alfaro, *Más allá de la utopía*, pp. 445–456.

35 *Acta de la Unidad 28 de la AGG. 6 de junio de 1947*. Consejo de Guerra 552 bis 39 (ATMTS).

36 Consejo de Guerra 939/51 (ATTMA) Rodríguez Padilla, *El Ejército Guerrillero*, p. 425.

37 *Programa de la Escuela guerrillera de Toulouse*.

38 *Informe Ramón Vía* found in *Informe de Agustín Zoroa (Darío) 22 de noviembre de*

1945. Jacq 14–18. Documentos PCE no incluidos (ACCPCE); Consejo de Guerra 1188/708 (ATTMA).

39   Interview with José López Centurión, guerrilla fighter in the AGG and brother of Francisco, in Romero Navas, *Recuperando la memoria*, pp. 27–46; Romero Navas, *Censo de guerrilleros*, pp. 204–206, 295.

40   Consejo de Guerra 1221/20 (ATTMA); Consejo de Guerra 1207/649 (ATTMA); Interview with Rafael Castilla, brother of Ramón, in Romero Navas, *Censo de guerrilleros*, pp. 83–84.

41   Consejo de Guerra 1154/262 (ATTMA).

42   Consejo de Guerra 1346/979 (ATTMA).

43   Consejo de Guerra 908/692 (ATTMA); Consejo de Guerra 1238/278 (ATTMA); Consejo de Guerra 1189/831 (ATTMA); Consejo de Guerra 910/245 (ATTMA); Consejo de Guerra 1238/236 (ATTMA).

44   Consejo de Guerra 1103/111 (ATTMA); Consejo de Guerra 1237/181 (ATTMA).

45   Romero Navas, *Censo de guerrilleros*, p. 104.

46   Rodríguez Sevilla, *Así me metieron en política*; Consejo de Guerra 1154/262 (ATTMA).

47   Consejo de Guerra 1237/181 (ATTMA); Romero Navas, *Censo de guerrilleros*, pp. 318–319.

48   Informe de Santiago Carrillo. Dirigentes. Carpeta 1/2. Caja 30 (ACCPCE).

49   Marco, *Hijos de una guerra.*

50   Sánchez Cervelló, *Maquis*, pp. 380–385.

51   Juan Antonio Sacaluga, *La resistencia socialista en Asturias, 1937–1962* (Madrid: Fundación Pablo Iglesias, 1986), pp. 52–53; Francisco Moreno Gómez, "La represión en la posguerra" in Santos Juliá (ed.), *Víctimas de la guerra civil* (Madrid: Temas de Hoy, 1999), p. 385.

52   José María Azuaga Rico, "Cambio de Táctica del PCE con relación a la lucha guerrillera: el caso de Granada y Málaga", in *I Congreso sobre la historia del PCE, 1920–1977* (Oviedo: FIM, 2005).

53   Castillo, *Recuerdos*, p. 247; Legajo 620, Causa 1149 (ATTMA); Causa 384/51 (ATMTS).

54   José Aurelio Romero Navas, "1952: Huida de los seis últimos guerrilleros a Francia", *Jábega*, 88 (2001).

6   Beyond Sabotage: Combat, robbery, kidnapping and murder

1   James C. Scott, *Weapons of the Weak*, p. 248.

2   "Los guerrilleros en el combate por la salvación de España", *Nuestra Bandera*, 30 September 1942.

3   *Informe de Santiago Carrillo.* Jacq 1–2. Dirigentes (ACCPCE).

4   *Resumen de la lucha guerrillera en España de 1945 a 1950.* Carpeta 2. Caja 105. Movimiento guerrillero (ACCPCE).

5   Consejo de Guerra 516/1052 (ATMTS).

6   *Programa de la Escuela guerrillera de Toulouse*, in: Aguado Sánchez, *El maquis en sus documentos*, pp. 58–68.

7   Carpeta 1. Caja 105. Movimiento Guerrillero (ACCPCE).

8   Consejo de Guerra 890/572 (ATTMA).

9   *Llamamiento de la Agrupación Guerrillera de Granada. Estado Mayor. 1 de marzo de 1947*, in: Aguado Sánchez, *El maquis en sus documentos*, p. 352.

10 Aguado Sánchez, *El maquis en España*, pp. 253–254; Eulogio Limia Pérez, *Informe general del proceso seguido contra el bandolerismo en la provincia de Granada*. Caja 106. Movimiento guerrillero (ACCPCE).

11 Consejo de Guerra 879/1090 (ATTMA); Consejo de Guerra 1157/812 (ATTMA); Consejo de Guerra 1189/830 (ATTMA); Consejo de Guerra 1189/831 (ATTMA).

12 An example of this confusion: Consejo de Guerra 925/2922 (ATTMA).

13 Marco, "'Una Corea en pequeño'.

14 *Informe Vía*. Jacq. 1044–1045 (ACCPCE); *Instrucciones generales por las que ha de regirse la lucha guerrilla. Estado Mayor. AGG. Ejército Guerrillero de Andalucía. 1 de agosto de 1947*, in Aguado Sánchez, *El maquis en sus documentos*, pp. 358–362.

15 Carpeta 25. Tesis, manuscritos (ACCPCE); Interview with guerilla fighter José López Centurión, in: Romero Navas, *Recuperando la memoria*, pp. 31–32; Consejo de Guerra 1157/414 (ATTMA).

16 Enrique Urbano, guerrilla fighter in the AGG, describes in an interview one of the exceptional ambushes orchestrated by the guerrilla: Romero Navas, *Recuperando la memoria*, p. 137.

17 Rodríguez Padilla, *El Ejército Guerrillero en Andalucía*, pp. 490–491.

18 Ibid., pp. 495–496.

19 Consejo de Guerra 672/49 (ATTMA) and Consejo de Guerra 678/49 (ATTMA); Rodríguez Padilla, *El Ejército Guerrillero en Andalucía*, pp. 520–521.

20 Marco, "'Una Corea en pequeño'.

21 Aguado Sánchez, *El maquis en España*, pp. 253–254.

22 Moreno Gómez, *Historia y memoria*, pp. 226–228.

23 *Informe de Dolores Ibárruri. 28 de Junio de 1952*. Carpeta 13/2. Caja 31. Dirigentes (ACCPCE); PCE Budget 1946–1947. Carpeta 22, Caja 34. Dirigentes (ACCPCE).

24 Aguado Sánchez, *El maquis en España*, pp. 253–254.

25 Consejo de Guerra 719/18 (ATTMA).

26 Consejo de Guerra 1218/564 (ATTMA); Consejo de Guerra 1218/349 (ATTMA); *Parte de operaciones de la AGG. Año 1948*. Carpeta 4/3. Caja 106. Movimiento guerrillero (ACCPCE).

27 *Instrucciones de la AGG. Ejército Guerrillero de Andalucía. 1 de abril de 1946*, en: Aguado Sánchez, *El maquis en sus documentos*, p. 344.

28 Marco, *Hijos de una guerra*.

29 Consejo de Guerra 719/18 (ATTMA).

30 Sánchez Pérez, *La protesta del pueblo*, pp. 41–48; Marco, *Hijos de una guerra*, p. 144.

31 *Parte de operaciones de la AGG. Año 1948.* Carpeta 4/3. Caja 106. Movimiento guerrillero (ACCPCE).

32 *Resumen de las acciones guerrilleras durante el periodo 1 de enero al 23 de mayo de 1947.* Carpeta 2. Caja 105. (ACCPCE); *Parte de operaciones de la AGG. Año 1948.* Carpeta 4/3. Caja 106. Movimiento guerrillero (ACCPCE).

33 *Instrucciones de la AGG. Ejército Guerrillero de Andalucía. 1 de abril de 1946*, in: Aguado Sánchez, *El maquis en sus documentos*, p. 344.

34 Colin Lucas, "The Theory and Practice of Denunciation in the French Revolution", *The Journal of Modern History*, 68–4 (1996), pp. 781–783.; Sheila Fitzpatrick, "Signals from Below: Soviets Letters of Denunciation of the 1930s", *The Journal of Modern History*, 68–4 (1996), p. 107; Kalyvas, *The Logic*, pp. 176–195.

35 Consejo de Guerra 1349/883 (ATTMA).

36 Consejo de Guerra 1519/44 (ATTMA); Consejo de Guerra 556/573 (ATTMA); Marco, *Hijos de una guerra*, p. 178.

37 *Instrucciones sobre las bases económicas de la guerrilla. AGG. Ejército Guerrillero de Andalucía. 1 de octubre de 1946*, in: Aguado Sánchez, *El maquis en sus documentos*, pp. 347–349; Consejo de guerra 522/39 (ATTMA); Consejo de Guerra 5/50 (ATTMA); Consejo de Guerra 1349/883 (ATTMA); Consejo de Guerra 1180/34 (ATTMA).

38 *Informe sobre la actividad de las guerrillas en España. 1944–1945.* Carpeta 2, Caja 105. Movimiento guerrillero (ACCPCE).

39 *Parte de operaciones de la AGG. Año 1948.* Carpeta 4/3. Caja 105. Movimiento guerrillero (ACCPCE).

40 Consejo de Guerra 1431/45 (ATTMA); *Informe Vía.* Jacq. 1044–1045 (ACCPCE); *Información sobre la Agrupación de Granada. Miguel Salas Cecilia "Gómez".* Carpeta 4/2. Caja 106. Movimiento guerrillero (ACCPCE).

41 Eulogio Limia Pérez, *Resumen del problema del bandolerismo en la provincia de Granada. 4 de septiembre de 1951.* Movimiento guerrillero. Carpeta 1/3. Caja 106. Movimiento guerrillero (ACCPCE).

42 Interview with Enrique Urbano, in Romero Navas, *Recuperando la memoria*, p. 145.

43 Consejo de Guerra 5/50 (ATTMA).

44 Consejo de Guerra 1154/180 (ATTMA).

45 Consejo de Guerra 1170/861 (ATTMA).

46 Consejo de Guerra 1154/950 (ATTMA).

47 Eulogio Limia Pérez, *Reseña General del bandolerismo en España después de la Guerra de Liberación.* Carpeta 3/2. Caja 106. Movimiento guerrillero (ACCPCE).

48 Marco, *Hijos de una guerra*, pp. 133–138, 331–352; Consejo de Guerra 288/37 (ATTMA).

49 *Circular de la AGM. Estado mayor. 20 de marzo de 1946*, in: Aguado Sánchez, *El maquis en sus documentos*, p. 343.

50   Aguado Sánchez, *El maquis en España*, pp. 253–254.
51   Kalyvas, *The Logic*, pp. 266–290.
52   See, for example, the case of anti-Soviet guerrillas in the Ukraine, Belarus, Latvia, Lithuania, and Estonia during the 1940s, in Alexander Statiev, *The Soviet Counterinsurgency in the Western Borderlands* (Cambridge: Cambridge University Press, 2010), pp. 9, 123–137.
53   Consejo de Guerra 556/573 (ATTMA).
54   See the Greek case, in Stathis N. Kalyvas, "Red Terror: Leftist Violence during the Occupation", in Mark Mazower (ed.), *After the War was Over*, pp. 142–183; Kalyvas, *The Logic*, pp. 246–329.
55   Consejo de guerra 1346/979 (ATTMA).
56   Consejo de Guerra 1094/948 (ATTMA).
57   Consejo de Guerra 960/46 (ATTMA).
58   Consejo de Guerra 443/48 (ATTMA).
59   Consejo de Guerra 1134/51 (ATTMA).
60   Marco, "'Una Corea en pequeño'.
61   Consejo de Guerra 1134/51 (ATTMA).
62   Consejo de Guerra 946/47 (ATTMA); Consejo de Guerra 863/46 (ATTMA); Consejo de Guerra 443/48 (ATTMA); Consejo de Guerra 640/47 (ATTMA); Consejo de Guerra 477/49 (ATTMA); Consejo de Guerra 522/49 (ATTMA); Consejo de Guerra 439/50 (ATTMA); Consejo de Guerra 66/51 (ATTMA); Consejo de Guerra 950/51 (ATTMA); Rodríguez Padilla, *El Ejército Guerrillero en Andalucía*, pp. 421, 426, 431, 442, 444, 445, 452, 456, 460.
63   Marco, *Hijos de una guerra*, pp. 200–216, 282–284, 434–437.
64   Consejo de Guerra 752/49 (ATTMA); Consejo de Guerra 762/49 (ATTMA).
65   Romeu Alfaro, *Más allá de la utopía*, pp. 473–507
66   Consejo de Guerra 179/48 (ATTMA); Consejo de Guerra 820/48 (ATTMA); Consejo de Guerra 264/50 (ATTMA); Consejo de Guerra 220/51 (ATTMA); Rodríguez Padilla, *El Ejército Guerrillero en Andalucía*, pp. 437, 442, 452, 456, 458.
67   Consejo de guerra 1207/649 (ATTMA); Romero Navas, *Censo de guerrilleros*, p. 152.
68   Consejo de Guerra 556/573 (ATTMA).
69   Consejo de Guerra 211/47 (ATTMA).
70   Marco, *Hijos de una guerra*, pp. 407–435.
71   Consejo de Guerra 1207/649 (ATTMA).
72   Consejo de Guerra 1237/181 (ATTMA).
73   Consejo de Guerra 939/52 (ATTMA).
74   Consejo de Guerra 1157/81 (ATTMA).
75   Consejo de guerra 1154/180 (ATTMA); Consejo de Guerra 1157/650 (ATTMA); Consejo de Guerra 522/39 (ATTMA).
76   Consejo de Guerra 1216/208 (ATTMA); Marco, *Hijos de una guerra*, pp. 434–437.

7 Voices of the Resistance: Propaganda and communication

1 Quote from V. Edwards, *Group Leader's Guide to Propaganda Analysis* (New York: Columbia, University Press, 1938), p. 40. Some authors distinguish between propaganda and persuasion, claiming that only certain kinds of propaganda aim to persuade. See G. S. Jowett and V. O'Donell, *Propaganda and persuasion* (California: Sage Publications, 2006), pp. 1–48. However, the analysis presented here draws on authors who insist on the persuasive character of propaganda. See Alejandro Pizarroso Quintero, "La historia de la propaganda: una aproximación metodológica", *Historia y Comunicación social*, 4 (1999).

2 Sidney Tarrow, *Power in Movement: Social Movements and Contentious Politics* (Cambridge: Cambridge University Press, 1998), pp. 95–119; Bert Klandermans and Sjoerd Goslinga, "Media Discourse, Movement Publicity and the Generation of Collective Action Frames: Theoretical and Empirical Exercises in Meaning Construction", in: D. McAdam (et al.), *Comparative Perspective on Social Movements: Political Opportunities, Mobilizing Structures, and Cultural Framings* (Cambridge: Cambridge University Press, 1996).

3 Antonio Castillo Gómez (coord.), *La conquista del alfabeto: Escritura y clases populares* (Gijón: Trea, 2002).

4 The claim comes from the first propaganda scholar: H. D. Laswell, *Propaganda Technique in the World War* (New York: Knopf, 1927), p. 220.

5 Ramón Mendezona, *La Pirenaica: historia de una emisora clandestina* (Madrid: Edición del autor, 1981); Luis Zaragoza Fernández, *Radio Pirenaica. La voz de la esperanza antifranquista* (Madrid: Marcial Pons, 2008); Armand Balsebre and Rosario Fontova, *Las cartas de la Pirenaica: Memorias del antifranquismo* (Madrid: Cátedra, 2014).

6 Dirigentes 14/3 y 16/2 (ACCPCE).

7 Consejo de guerra 1431/45 (ATTMA), Informe Camaradas. Jacq 653–654 (ACCPCE).

8 Dirigentes 16/2 (ACCPCE).

9 Consejo de Guerra 1249/416 (ATTMA); Consejo de Guerra 1195/75 (ATTMA).

10 A. Escolano Benito (dir.), *Leer y escribir. Doscientos años de alfabetización* (Madrid: Fundación Germán Sánchez Ruipérez, 1997); Jesús Martínez Martín, "La lectura en la España contemporánea: lectores, discursos y prácticas de lectura", *AYER*, 58, (2005).

11 Consejo de Guerra 1225/429 (ATTMA).

12 Carlos Gordon, "Prensa clandestina y movimiento obrero en el franquismo", in José Babiano (coord.), *Amordazada y perseguida. Catálogo de prensa clandestina y del exilio* (Madrid: Fundación 1° de Mayo, 2005) pp. 286–296; Ana Martínez Rus, *La persecución del libro: Hogueras, infiernos y buenas lecturas, 1936–1951* (Gijón: Trea, 2014).

13 *Nuestra Bandera*, n° 4 (January–February 1946).

14 Consejo de Guerra 1249/416 (ATTMA); Consejo de Guerra 510/582 (ATTMA); Consejo de Guerra 951/339 (ATTMA).

15 Carmen González Vicente, "Fuentes para el estudio del movimiento guerrillero. El archivo del PCE", in Santiago Álvarez (et al.), *El movimiento guerrillero de los años 40* (Madrid: Fundación de Investigaciones Marxistas, 2003), p. 21.

16 Francisco Madrid, "La prensa clandestina libertaria", in *La oposición libertaria al régimen de Franco, 1936–1975* (Madrid: Fundación Salvador Seguí, 1993), p. 768.

17 Gordón, "Prensa clandestina, p. 269.

18 *Resumen de la lucha guerrillera en España de 1945 a 1950.* Carpeta 2. Caja 105 (ACCPCE).

19 *Reconquista de España*, 19 y 20 (October and November 1942), Publicaciones Periódicas (ACCPCE). Reproduced in Gordón, "Prensa clandestina, p. 277.

20 *Resistencia*, 10 January 1947. Publicaciones periódicas (ACCPCE).

21 *Por la República*, n° 30. Publicaciones Periódicas. Carpeta 16 (ACCPCE).

22 "Alaminos gime y llora / en lo alto de la sierra; /Alaminos implora / arrodillado en la tierra. / Alaminos se esconde; / lo buscan por los rincones; / lo llaman y no responde; / se oculta tras los peñones / Alaminos terminó huyendo / sin esperar a razones; / y el pobre pierde corriendo / hasta los rústicos botones / de su raída guerrera / en la pedestre carrera". *Por la República*, n° 30. Publicaciones Periódicas. Carpeta 16 (ACCPCE).

23 Consejo de Guerra 1249/416 (ATTMA), Consejo de Guerra 510/582 (ATTMA), Fernández Rodríguez, *Madrid clandestino.*

24 *Manual de orientación política-militar del Ejército Guerrillero de Andalucía.* Consejo de Guerra 443/48 (ATTMA).

25 Consejo de Guerra 1431/45 (ATTMA), Jacq 1944–1945 (ACCPCE); J. Herrera Petere, "Ramón Vía", *Cultura y Democracia*, 4 (1950).

26 Consejo de Guerra 556/573 (ATTMA).

27 Informes Camaradas 992 (ACCPCE).

28 Romero Navas, *Censo de guerrilleros*, p. 367.

29 *Manual de orientación político-militar".* Ejército Guerrillero de Andalucía. Estado Mayor. Causa 443/48. (ACGG).

30 Consejo de Guerra 910/245 (ATTMA) and Consejo de Guerra 1238/236 (ATTMA).

31 Consejo de Guerra 265/50 (ATTMA).

32 *Parte de operaciones de la AGG. Año 1948.* Carpeta 4/3. Caja 105. Movimiento guerrillero (ACCPCE).

33 Consejo de Guerra 510/582 (ATTMA).

34 Consejo de Guerra 719/18 (ATTMA).

35 *Parte de operaciones de la AGG. Año 1948.* Carpeta 4/3. Caja 105 (ACCPCE).

36 On the issue of "urban" political language and the peasantry, see Orlando Figes and Boris Kolonitskii, *Interpreting the Russian Revolution: The Language and Symbols of 1917* (New Haven: Yale University Press, 1999), pp. 127–152.

37 Interview with "Pepito", in Romeu Alfaro, *Más allá de la utopía*, p. 141.

38 Studies of international campaigns and collective action have so far focused on new social movements; little attention has been paid to earlier campaigns of international scope. On campaign coalitions between different groups, see J. Gerhards and D. Rucht, "Mesomobilization: Organizing and Framing in Two Protest Campaigns in West Germany", *American Journal of Sociology*, 98 (1992). On international campaigns, see Paul Routledge, "Converge spaces: process geographies of grassroots globalization networks", *Transactions of the Institute of British Geographers*, 28-3 (2003).

39 For an account of the most important campaign in Greece, launched in the first months of 1946, see Luciano Hassiotis, "Grecia ante la cuestión española (1946–1950)", *AYER*, 78 (2010), pp. 261–263.

40 Consejo de Guerra 510/582 (ATTMA).

41 49.575 (FO 371, TNA-PRO), 49.576 (FO 371, TNA-PRO), 49.577 (FO 371, TNA-PRO), 60.325(FO 371, TNA-PRO), 60.326 (FO 371, TNA-PRO), 60.327 (FO 371, TNA-PRO), 60.328 (FO 371, TNA-PRO), 60.330 (FO 371, TNA-PRO), 67.887 (FO 371, TNA-PRO), 67.888 (FO 371, TNA-PRO), 67.889 (FO 371, TNA-PRO), 67.890 (FO 371, TNA-PRO), 67.891 (FO 371, TNA-PRO).

42 Jean-Marié Gillón and Pierre Laboire (dir.), *Mémoire et histoire: La Résistance* (Toulouse: Privat, 1995).

43 Serrano, *La última gesta*, pp. 649–658; Natacha Lillo, "Los maquis antifranquistas en la prensa francesa", in Marie-Claude Chaput (et. al), *Maquis y guerrillas antifranquistas* (Nanterre: Université de Paris X, 2004), pp. 33–37.

44 On the case of Julián Grimau: Pedro Carvajal Urquijo, *Julián Grimaú. La última víctima de la Guerra Civil* (Madrid: Aguilar, 2003). On the case of Delgado y Granados: Octavio Albeloa and Ariane Gransac, *El anarquismo español y la acción revolucionaria, 1961–1974* (París: Ruedo Ibérico, 1975), pp. 95–127.

45 *Manual de orientación política-militar del Ejército Guerrillero de Andalucía*. Consejo de Guerra 443/48 (ATTMA).

46 Ranajit Guha, *Elementary Forms of Peasant Insurgency in Colonial India* (Dheli: Oxford University Press, 1983), pp. 250–257; James C. Scott, *Domination and the Arts of Resistance: Hidden Transcripts* (New Haven: Yale University Press, 1990), pp. 141–149.

47 David Stafford, *From Anarchism to Reformism: A Study of the Political Activities of Paul Brousse within the First International and the French Socialist Movement, 1870–1990* (Toronto: University of Toronto University Press, 1971); Eduardo González Calleja, *El laboratorio del miedo: una historia general del terrorismo* (Barcelona: Crítica, 2012), pp. 127–152. On Spain, see Rafael Nuñez Florencio, *El terrorismo anarquista, 1888–1909* (Madrid: Siglo XXI, 1983); Julián Casanova, *De la calle al frente. El anarcosindicalismo en España, 1931–1939* (Barcelona: Crítica, 1997), pp. 102–131.

48 Flora Davis, *Inside Intuition: What We Know about Non-Verbal Communication* (New York: McGraw-Hill, 1973), p. 22.

49 R. H. Williams, "The Cultural Context of Collective Action: Constraints, Opportunities, and the Symbolic Life of Social Movements", in D.A. Snow (et al.), *The Blackwell Companion to Social Movements*, pp. 91–115; Clifford Geertz, *The Interpretation of Cultures: Selected Essays* (New York: Basic Books, 1973), p. 94.

50 Eric Hobsbawm, *Bandits* (London: Weidenfeld & Nicolson, 1969), pp. 14, 35; Scott, *Domination*, p. 184.

51 For a microhistorical study of these relations in a mountain community in Cádiz, see Pitt-Rivers, *The People*.

52 Interview with Sebastián Navas, Baird, *Between*, p. 114.

53 Hobsbawm, *Bandits*, p. 39.

54 Claude Lévi-Strauss, *Anthropologie structurale* (Paris: Librairie Plon, 1958), p. 231.

55 Manuel García Pelayo, *Los mitos políticos* (Madrid: Alianza, 1981), pp. 11–37.

56 Georges Sorel, *Reflections on Violence* (London: George Allen & Unwin Ltd., 1925), p. 33.

57 Emilio Gentile, *The Struggle for Modernity: Nationalism, Futurism, and Fascism* (Westport: Praeger, 2003), pp. 2–8, 77–88.

58 George L. Mosse, *The Nationalization of the Masses: Political Symbolism and Mass Movements in Germany from the Napoleonic Wars Through the Third Reich* (New York: Howard Fertig, 1975), pp. 11–14; Figes and Kolonitskii, *Interpreting the Russian Revolution*, pp. 9–29.

59 L. Collin Harguindeguy, "Personajes históricos de la revolución mexicana transformados en héroes culturales y gemelos míticos", *Mitológicas*, 14 (1999); F. Navarrete and G. Olivier (coord.), *El héroe. Entre el mito y la historia* (México DF: UNAM, 2000); D. J. Ávalos, *La guerrilla del Ché y Masseti en Salta-1964: ideología y mito en el Ejército Guerrillero del Pueblo* (Córdoba: La Intemperie, 2005). A good example of the political myth surrounding Fidel Castro in the Cuban revolution can be found in the hagiographical work by A. Númez Jiménez, *En marcha con Fidel: 1959* (La Habana: Editorial Letras Cubanas, 1982).

60 On myth as a lived reality, see Bronisław Malinowski, *Magic, Science and Religion and Others Essays* (Massachusetts: Beacon Press, 1948), pp. 74–89.

61 José R. Gómez Fouz, *Bernabé. El mito de un bandolero* (Barcelona: Silverio Cabaña Editor, 1998); Antonio Brevers, *Juanín y Bedoya. Los últimos guerrilleros* (Santander: Cloux Editores, 2008); V. Luis Lamela García, *Foucellas. El riguroso relato de una lucha antifranquista* (A Coruña: Edicios do Castro, 2002); Santiago Macías, *El monte o la muerte. La vida legendaria del guerrillero antifranquista Manuel Girón* (Madrid: Temas de Hoy, 2005).

62 Nicolás Manzanares Artés, *Consecuencias de la tragedia española (1936–1939) y los hermanos Quero* (Murcia: Edición del autor, 1978), p. 89; Interview with Alfonso Guerra, 14 December 2005.

63 Hobsbawm, *Bandits*, pp. 34–40.

64 Marco, *Hijos de una guerra*, pp. 218–239; Consejo de Guerra 288/37 (ATTMA).

65 Manzanares Artés, *Consecuencias*.

66 On dissident discourses transmitted via oral cultures, stories, legends, and myths, see Scott, *Domination*, pp. 187–201; Ana Cabana, *La derrota de lo épico* (Valencia, PUV, 2013), pp. 229–276.

67 Eulogio Limia Pérez, *Informe General del proceso seguido por el problema del bandolerismo en la provincia de Granada*. Caja 106. Movimiento guerrillero (ACCPCE).

68 Jefatura Provincial del Movimiento. Parte mensual correspondiente al mes de agosto 1944. Caja 51/20.640 (AGA); Información especial n° 26, DGS, 28 de noviembre de 1944 (FFF).

8 The Invisible Front: False guerrillas and crime

1 Interview with Ramiro Fuentes Ochoa, in Romero Navas, *Recuperando la memoria*, pp. 259–260.

2 Interview with Miguel Salado Cecilia. Santa Cruz de Moyá (Cuenca), 3 October 2008.

3 Carlos Barciela and María Inmaculada López, "El fracaso de la política agraria del primer franquismo, 1939–1959. Veinte años perdidos para la agricultura española", in Carlos Barciela (ed.), *Autarquía y mercado negro. El fracaso económico del primer franquismo, 1939–1959* (Barcelona: Critica, 2003), pp. 56–93; Francisco Cobo Romero and María Teresa Ortega López, "Franquismo y cuestión Agraria en Andalucía Oriental, 1939–1968. Estancamiento económico, fracaso industrializador y emigración", *Historia del Presente*, 3 (2004), pp. 105–126.

4 J. F. Gómez Westermeyer, *Historia de la delincuencia en la sociedad española: Murcia, 1939–1949* (Murcia: Universidad de Murcia, 2006); Arco Blanco, *Hambre de siglos*, pp. 291–370; Ana Cabana, *Entre a resistencia e a adaptación: a sociedade rural galega no franquismo, 1936–1960* (Santiago de Compostela: Universidade de Santiago de Compostela, 2007); Óscar Rodríguez Barreira, *Migas de miedo. Prácticas de resistencia al primer franquismo. Almería, 1939–1952* (Almería: Universidad de Almería, 2008), pp. 167–281.

5 Julián Casanova, "Resistencias individuales, acciones colectivas: nuevas miradas a la protesta social agraria en la historia contemporánea española", in Manuel González de Molina (ed.), *La historia de Andalucía*, pp. 289–301; M. Baumeister, *Campesinos sin tierra. Supervivencia y resistencia en Extremadura, 1880–1923* (Madrid: Ministerio de Agricultura, 1997); Oscar Bascuñán, *Protesta y supervivencia. Movilización y desorden en una sociedad rural: Castilla La Mancha, 1875–1923* (Valencia: Fundación Instituto de Historia Social, 2008).

6 Ana Cabana, "Minar la paz social: retrato sobre la conflictividad rural en Galicia durante el primer franquismo", *AYER*, 61, 2006; Óscar Rodríguez Barreira, "Lazarillos del Caudillo. El hurto moral como micropolítica subalterna frente a la autarquía franquista", *Historia Social*, 72 (2012).

7 Edward P. Thompson, "The Crime of Anonymity", in *E. P. Thompson: The Essential* (New York: W. W. Norton, 2001); Rita M. Cristina Albino,

"Escribir <cartas aterradoras> en el palacio Do Limoeiro (Portugal, 1822–1825)", *Hispania*, LXV/3, 221 (2005); Hobsbawm and Rudé, *Captain Swing*, pp. 203–206.; Scott, *Domination*, pp. 144–149.

8 Consejo de Guerra 510/582 (ATTMA); Consejo de Guerra 951/330 (ATTMA).

9 Consejo de Guerra 481/829 (ATTMA).

10 For examples, see Consejo de Guerra 626/1214; Consejo de Guerra 931/506; Consejo de guerra 1186/602; Consejo de Guerra 802/361; Consejo de Guerra 1151/1076; Consejo de Guerra 903/1583; Consejo de Guerra 1147/351; Consejo de Guerra 1186/1040; Consejo de Guerra 1189/839 (ATTMA).

11 Rafael Chirbes, *La larga marcha* (Barcelona: Anagrama, 2008), p. 35.

12 Consejo de Guerra 802/361 (ATTMA).

13 Consejo de Guerra 1158/1126 (ATTMA). Translation from a literal transcription.

14 Michael Richards, *A Time of Silence: Civil War and the Culture of Repression in Franco's Spain, 1936–1945* (Cambridge: Cambridge University Press, 1998), p. 24.

15 Gómez Westermeyer, *Historia de la delincuencia*, p. 176.

16 Manuel de la Plaza Navarro, *Memoria elevada al Gobierno Nacional* (Madrid: Editorial Reus, 1948), p. 116.

17 Ramón García del Valle y Salas, *Memoria elevada al Gobierno Nacional* (Madrid: Editorial Reus, 1945), p. 49.

18 Albino Feijóo Gómez, *Quintas y protesta social en el siglo XIX* (Madrid: Ministerio de Defensa, 1996); J. Fidel Molina Luque, *Quintas y servicio militar: aspectos sociológicos y antropológicos de la conscripción* (Lleida: Servei de Publicacions Universitat de Lleida, 1996).

19 Consejo de Guerra 1214/688 (ATTMA).

20 Consejo de Guerra 1178/43 (ATTMA).

21 Luis Miguel Sánchez Tostado, *La guerra no acabó en el 39: lucha guerrillera y resistencia republicana en la provincia de Jaén. 1939–1952* (Jaén: Ayuntamiento de Jaén, 2000) pp. 184–193; Moreno Gómez, *La resistencia armada*, pp. 146–148.

22 Consejo de Guerra 658/167 (ATTMA). The rest of the account is taken from this document, unless further references indicate otherwise.

23 Interview with Francisco Castro Márquez and Rosa López Maestre, both residents of Alhama de Granada. Madrid, 12 March 2005.

24 Robert Gellately, *The Gestapo and German Society: Enforcing Racial Policy, 1933–1945* (Oxford: Clarendon Press, 1990), pp. 144–151; Sheila Fitzpatrick, *Stalin's Peasants: Resistance and Survival in the Russian Village after the Collectivization* (New York: Oxford University Press, 1994), p. 254; Kalyvas, *The Logic*, pp. 336–355.

25 Paul Berman, *Revolutionary Organization: Institution-Building within the People's Liberation Armed Forces* (Lexington Books, 1974); Robert Maranto and Paula S. Tuchman, "Knowing the Rational Peasant: The creation of Rival Incentive

Structures in Vietnam", *Journal of Peace Research*, 29-3 (1992); Kalyvas, *The Logic*, pp. 91–104.

26 Regarding opportunism and egoism as motivations departing from the altruism of classical resistance models, see James C. Scott, "Everyday Forms of Peasant Resistance", *The Journal of Peasant Studies*, 13-2 (1986); Bert Klandermans, *The Social Psychology of Protest* (Oxford: Blackwell, 1997); J. Goodwin (et al.), *Passionate Politics. Emotions and Social Movements* (Chicago: University Press of Chicago, 2001); Helena Flam and Debra King (ed.), *Emotions and Social Movements* (New York: Routledge, 2005).

27 Consejo de Guerra 5/50 (ATTMA).

28 Interview with Esteban Martín, in Romero Navas, *Censo de guerrilleros*, p. 89.

29 Consejo de Guerra 1238/278 (ATTMA); Consejo de Guerra 1188/450 (ATTMA); Romero Navas, *Censo de guerrilleros*, p. 125.

30 *Manual de orientación político-militar del Ejército Guerrillero de Andalucía*, in Consejo de Guerra 443/48 (ATTMA).

31 Consejo de Guerra 1159/245 (ATTMA).

32 Marco, *Hijos de una guerra*, pp. 353–359.

33 Consejo de Guerra 1159/245 (ATTMA) The rest of the account is taken from this document, until further references indicate otherwise. See also Romero Navas, *Censo de guerrilleros*, pp. 209–211.

34 Consejo de Guerra 1349/883 (ATTMA).

35 Consejo de Guerra 2083/154 (ATTMA); *Memoria Histórica de la Comandancia de Granada* (SEHGC).

36 Interview with Miguel Padial Martín. Madrid, 1 April 2006.

37 Consejo de Guerra 1349/883 (ATTMA). The rest of the account is taken from this document, unless further references indicate otherwise.

38 Consejo de Guerra 658/167 (ATTMA).

39 Interview with Miguel Padial Martín. Madrid, 1 April 2006; Consejo de Guerra 1349/833 (ATTMA).

40 Consejo de Guerra 1349/833 (ATTMA).

41 Consejo de Guerra 1346/979 (ATTMA). Translation of a literal transcription.

42 Consejo de Guerra 1349/883 (ATTMA).

43 Consejo de Guerra 1221/20 y Consejo de Guerra 1237/181 (ATTMA); *Nota informativa de la Guardia Civil nº 199*. 11 de Octubre de 1950 (SHGC).

44 Consejo de Guerra 1346/979 (ATTMA); Consejo de Guerra 1349/883 (ATTMA) The rest of the account is taken from both documents.

45 Interview with Victoriano Sánchez Ramos, in Romero Navas, *Recuperando la memoria*, pp. 312–313; Romero Navas, *Censo de guerrilleros*, pp. 21–211.

Conclusion

1 Consejo de Guerra 1180/34 (ATTMA).

2 Interview with Miguel Salado Cecilia, guerrilla fighter in the AGG. 3 October 2008.

3 Interview with José López Centurión, in Romero Navas, *Recuperando la memoria*, p. 33.

4 Interview with Ramiro Fuente Ochoa, in Romero Navas, *Recuperando la memoria*, p. 260.
5 All of the details about this episode and the AGG in: Consejo de Guerra 939/51 (ATTMA).

References

Primary Sources

Archives

Archivo del Comité Central del Partido Comunista de España (ACCPCE).
Archivo General de la Administración (AGA).
Archivo Histórico Nacional (AHN).
Archivo del Ministerio del Interior (AMI).
Archivo del Tribunal Militar Territorial Segundo.
Archivo del Tribunal Togado Militar nº 23, Almería (ATTMA).
Centro de Estudios Históricos de la Guardia Civil (CEHGC).
Fundación Anselmo Lorenzo (FAL).
Fundación Estudios Sindicales. Archivo Histórico CCOO (FES-AHCCOO).
Fundación Francisco Franco (FFF).
Fundación Pablo Iglesias (FPI).
The National Archives: Public Records Office (TNA: PRO)

Newspapers and contemporary journals

ABC.
Ataque.
Boletín de Información.
CNT.
Cultura y Democracia.
Gaceta de la República.
Heraldo de Madrid.
Juventud Libre.
La Libertad.
Mundo Obrero.
Nuestra Bandera.
Nueva Historia.
El País.
Por la República.
Reconquista de España.
Resistencia.
Revista de información político-militar.
Solidaridad Proletaria.
Unidad.
La Vanguardia.

La Voz del Soldado.

Voz Obrera.

Interviews conducted by the author

Manuel Prieto López (27 September 2003).

Francisco Castro Márquez and Rosa López Maestre (12 March 2005).

Encarnación Quero (9 April 2005) and (21 August 2010)

Alfonso Guerra (14 December 2005).

Gregorio Gallego (8 May 2006).

Andrés Sorel (26 October 2006).

Miguel Padial Martín 'Campañito' (1 April 2007).

Amada Martínez García 'Rosita' (1 April 2007).

Dolores Resina Quero (15 August 2006) and (18 March 2007).

Manuel García Fernández (17 March 2007).

Miguel Salado Cecilia (3 October 2008).

Bernardo Quero Robles (21 August 2010).

Alicia Langa Laorga (7 February 2011).

Diaries, memoirs, collections of documents and other contemporary or eyewitness accounts

Aguado Sánchez, Francisco, *El maquis en sus documentos* (Madrid: Editorial San Martín, 1976).

Azcárate, Manuel, *Derrota y Esperanzas. La República, La Guerra Civil y la Resistencia* (Barcelona: Tusquets, 1994).

Azcárate, Pablo de, *En defensa de la República. Con Negrín en el exilio* (Barcelona: Critica, 2010).

Baird, David, *Between Two Fires: Guerrilla War in the Spanish Guerrillas* (Frigiliana: Maroma Press, 2008)

Carrillo, Santiago, "Sobre la experiencia de dos años de lucha", *Nuestra Bandera*, 31 (1948).

Carrillo, Santiago, "Los guerrilleros, instructores políticos y organizadores de los campesinos", *Mundo Obrero*, 155, (1949).

Carrillo, Santiago, *Memorias* (Barcelona: Planeta, 2008).

Carrillo, Santiago, *Los viejos camaradas* (Barcelona: Planeta, 2010).

Castillo, Vicente, *Recuerdos y Vivencias* (unpublished memoirs, author's archives)

Claudín, Fernando, *La crisis del movimiento comunista. De la Komintern al Kominform* (París, Ruedo Ibérico, 1970).

Criado Moreno, Cristobal, *Mi juventud y mi lucha* (Málaga: Edición del autor, 1993).

Criado Moreno, Cristobal, *El PCE que viví en Málaga, 1920–1977* (Málaga: Edición del autor, 2004).

Fernández López, Federico, *Apunte histórico* (unpublished memoirs, FPI).

García del Valle y Salas, Ramón, *Memoria elevada al Gobierno Nacional* (Madrid: Editorial Reus, 1945). 1969).

Herrera Petere, José, "Ramón Vía", *Cultura y Democracia*, 4 (1950)

Ibárruri, Dolores, *Memorias de Dolores Ibárruri "Pasionaria". La lucha y la vida* (Barcelona: Planeta, 1985).

Jiménez Margalejo, Carlos, *Los que teníamos dieciocho años* (Madrid: Incipit Editores, 2000).

Jiménez Margalejo, Carlos, *Memorias de un refugiado español en el Norte de África, 1939–1956* (Madrid: Fundación Largo Caballero y Cinca, 2008)

Lister, Enrique, "De la experiencia de la lucha guerrillera en España (1939–1951)", *Revista Internacional*, 1966.

Lister, Enrique, *¡Basta! Una aportación a la lucha por la recuperación del Partido* (Madrid: G. del Toro, 1978).

López Tovar, Vicente, "Operación del Valle de Aránen octubre de 1944", in Cos Borbolla, Jesús, *Ni bandidos, ni vencidos* (Santander: Edición del autor, 2006).

Martínez López, Francisco, *Guerrillero contra Franco. La guerrilla antifranquista de León, 1936–1951* (León: Diputación Provincial de León, 2002).

Ortiz Requena, Baldomero, *Frente a la Historia que escriben los vencedores* (unpublished memoirs, FES/AHCCOO)

Plaza Navarro, Manuel de la, *Memoria elevada al Gobierno Nacional* (Madrid: Editorial Reus, 1948).

Rodríguez Sevilla, Francisco, *Así me metieron en política* (unpublished memoirs, author's archive)

Rojo, Vicente, *España heroica. Diez bocetos de la guerra española* (Barcelona: Ariel, 1975).

Rojo, Vicente, *¡Alerta los pueblos! Estudio político-militar del periodo final de la guerra española* (Barcelona: Ariel, 1974).

Romero Navas, José Aurelio, *Recuperando la memoria* (Málaga: CEDMA, 1997).

Tagüeña Lacorte, Manuel, *Testimonios de dos guerras* (Barcelona: Planeta, 1978).

Sorel, Andrés, *Búsqueda reconstrucción e historia de la guerrilla española del siglo XX a través de sus documentos, relatos y protagonistas* (Paris: Editions Libraire du Globe, 1970).

Secondary Sources

Articles, chapters and contributions

Alavi, Hamza, "Peasant Classes and Primordial Loyalties", *The Journal of Peasant Studies*, 1-1 (1973).

Ampudia de Haro, Fernando: "Distinción social y franquismo: la dicotomía 'vencedor/vencido'", in Navajas, Carlos and Iturriaga, Diego (coord.), *II Congreso Internacional de Historia de nuestro tiempo* (Logroño: Universidad de La Rioja, 2010).

Anderson, Peter, "Singling Out Victims: Denunciation and Collusion in the Post-Civil War Francoist Repression in Spain, 1939–1945", *European History Quarterly*, 39-1 (2009).

Anderson, Peter, "In the Interest of Justice? Grass-roots, Prosecution and

Collaboration in Francoist Military Trials, 1939–1945", *Contemporary European History*, 18-1 (2009).

Aróstegui, Julio, "Sociedad y milicias de la guerra civil española, 1936–1939. Una reflexión metodológica", in Castillo, Santiago (coord.), *Estudios de Historia de España* (Madrid: Universidad Internacional Menéndez Pelayo, 1981).

Aróstegui, Julio, "Traumas colectivos y memorias generacionales: el caso de la guerra civil", in Aróstegui, Julio and Godicheau, François (eds.), *Guerra Civil. Mito y Memoria* (Madrid: Marcial Pons, 2006).

Aróstegui, Julio, González Calleja, Eduardo and Souto, Sandra, "La violencia política en la España del siglo XX", *Cuadernos de Historia Contemporánea*, 22 (2000).

Avilés, Juan, "Propaganda por el hecho y regicidio en Italia", in Aviles, Juan and Herrerín, Ángel (eds.), *El nacimiento del terrorismo en Occidente* (Madrid: Siglo XXI, 2008).

Azuaga Rico, José, "Cambio de Táctica del PCE con relación a la lucha guerrillera: el caso de Granada y Málaga", in*: I Congreso sobre la historia del PCE, 1920–1977* (Oviedo: FIM, 2004).

Azuaga Rico, José, "El PCE granadino, 1940–1952", in *II Congreso de Historia del PCE* (Madrid: FIM, 2006).

Barciela, Carlos and López, Mª Inmaculada: "El fracaso de la política agraria del primer franquismo, 1939–1959. Veinte años perdidos para la agricultura española", in Barciela, Carlos (ed.), *Autarquía y mercado negro. El fracaso económico del primer franquismo, 1939–1959* (Barcelona: Critica, 2003).

Barranquero Texeira, Encarnación: "La reorganización del PCE en Málaga después de la guerra civil", in Prieto Borrego, Lucía (coord.), *Guerra y franquismo en la provincia de Málaga: nuevas líneas de investigación* (Málaga: Universidad de Málaga, 2005).

Blanco, Juan Andrés, "Las MAOC y la tesis insurreccional del PCE", *Historia Contemporánea*, 11 (1994)

Blum, J., "The Internal Structure and Polity of the European Village Community from Fifteenth to the Nineteenth Century", *Journal of Modern History*, 43–4 (1971)

Cabana, Ana, "Minar la paz social: retrato sobre la conflictividad rural en Galicia durante el primer franquismo", *AYER*, 61, (2006)

Casanova, Julián, "Resistencias individuales, acciones colectivas: nuevas miradas a la protesta social agraria en la historia contemporánea española", in González de Molina, Manuel (ed.), *Historia de Andalucía a debate* (Barcelona: Anthropos, 2000).

Chaput, Marie-Claude, "Representaciones de la guerrillas en la prensa: ABC, Madrid, La Vanguardia Española, 1944–1951", in Chaput, Marie-Claire, Martínez-Mailer, Odette and Rodríguez, Fabiola (eds.), *Maquis y guerrillas anti-franquistas* (Nanterre: Université de Paris X, 2004).

Cobb, Christopher H., "The Educational and Cultural Policy of the Front Popular Government in Spain, 1936–9", in Martin S. Alexander and Helen Graham (eds.), *The French and Spanish Popular Fronts: Comparative Perspectives* (Cambridge: Cambridge University Press, 1989)

Cobo Romero, Francisco, "El franquismo y los imaginarios míticos del fascismo europeo de entreguerras", *AYER*, 71 (2008)

Cobo Romero, Francisco and Ortega López, María Teresa: "Franquismo y cuestión agraria en Andalucía Oriental, 1939–1968. Estancamiento económico, fracaso industrializador y emigración", *Historia del Presente*, 3 (2004)

Collin Harguindeguy, L., "Personajes históricos de la revolución mexicana transformados en héroes culturales y gemelos míticos", *Mitológicas*, 14 (1999).

Collins Weitz, Margaret, "Soldiers in the Shadows: Women of the French Resistance", in DeGroot, Gerard J. and Peniston Bird, Corinna (eds.), *A Soldier and a Woman: Sexual Integration in the Military* (Essex: Pearson Education Limited, 2000).

Cristina Albino, Rita M., "Escribir <cartas aterradoras> en el palacio Do Limoeiro. Portugal, 1822–1825", *Hispania*, LXV/3, 221 (2005).

Cruz, Rafael, "El mitin y el Motín. La acción colectiva y los movimientos sociales en la España del siglo XX", *Historia Social*, 31 (1998).

Cruz, Rafael, "Olor a pólvora y Patria. La limpieza política rebelde en el inicio de la Guerra de 1936", *Hispania Nova. Revista de Historia Contemporánea*, 6 (2006).

Cucó Giner, Josepa, "Familia, amistad y cultura asociativa en el País Valenciano", *Revista de Antropología social*, 1 (1992).

Diani, Mario, "Networks and Participations", in Snow, D. A., Soule, S. A. and Kriesi, H. (eds.): *The Blackwell Companion to Social Movements* (Oxford: Blackwell Publishing, 2004).

Dunlap, Charles J. Jr., "Preliminary Observations: Asymmetrical Warfare and the Western Mindset", in Matthews, Lloyd J. (ed.), *Challenging the United States Symmetrically and Asymmetrically: Can America Be Defeated?* (Strategic Studies Institute, Army War College, 1998).

Esdaile, Ch. J., "Popular Resistance to the Napoleonic Empire", in Dwyer, P. G.: *Napoleon and Europe* (Harlow: Pearson Education Limited, 2001).

Fitzpatrick, Sheila, "Signals from Below: Soviets Letters of Denunciation of the 1930s", *The Journal of Modern History*, 68-4 (1996)

Gerhards, J. and Rucht, D., "Mesomobilization: Organizing and Framing in Two Protest Campaigns in West Germany", *American Journal of Sociology*, 98 (1992).

Gerwarth, Robert, "The Central European Counter-Revolution: Paramilitary Violence in Germany, Austria and Hungary after the Great War", *Past and Present*, 200 (2008).

Gil Andrés, Carlos, "La zona gris en la España azul", *AYER*, 76 (2010).

González Calleja, Eduardo, "El Estado ante la violencia", in Juliá, Santos (dir.), *Violencia política en la España del siglo XX* (Madrid: Taurus, 2000).

González Calleja, Eduardo, "La cultura de guerra en la España del siglo XX", *Historia Social*, 61 (2008).

González Calleja, Eduardo, and Souto Kustrin, Sandra, "De la dictadura a la

República: orígenes y auge de los movimientos juveniles en España", *Hispania*, 225 (2007).

González de Molina, Manuel, and Sevilla Guzmán, Eduardo: "Perspectivas socio-ambientales de la historia del movimiento campesino andaluz", in: González de Molina, Manuel (ed.): *La historia de Andalucía a debate* (Barcelona: Anthropos, 2000).

González de Molina, Manuel "Los mitos de la modernidad y la protesta campesina: A propósito de Rebeldes Primitivos de Eric Hobsbawm", *Historia Social*, 25 (1996).

González Vicente, Carmen, "Fuentes para el estudio del movimiento guerrillero. El archivo del PCE", in Álvarez, S., Hinojosa, J. and Sandoval, J. (coord.), *El movimiento guerrillero de los años 40* (Madrid: Fundación de Investigaciones Marxistas, 2003).

Gordón, Carlos, "Prensa clandestina y movimiento obrero en el franquismo", in Babiano, José (coord.), *Amordazada y perseguida. Catálogo de prensa clandestina y del exilio* (Madrid: Fundación 1° de Mayo, 2005).

Hassiotis, Luciano, "Grecia ante la cuestión española (1946–1950)", *AYER*, 78 (2010)

Heine, Hartmut, "El Partido Comunista de España durante el franquismo", *Papeles de la FIM*, 22 (2004).

Hernan, Paul F., "Asymmetric Warfare: Sizing the Threat", *Low Intensity Conflict and Law Enforcement*, 6-1 (1997).

Ho Chi Minh, "The Party's Military Work among the Peasants", in Neuberg, A., *Armed Insurrection* (London: NLB, 1970 [1928]).

Izquierdo, Jesús, "De palabras y cosas en el cambio agrario: el desafío de la historia conceptual", *I Seminario Anual de la SEHA* (Madrid: SEHA, 2010).

Kalyvas, Stathis N., "Red Terror: Leftist Violence during the Occupation", in Mazower, Mark (ed.), *After the War was Over. Reconstructing the Family, Nation, and State in Greece, 1943–1960* (Princeton: Princeton University Press, 2000).

Klandermans, Bert and Sjoerd Goslinga, Sjoerd, "Media Discourse, Movement Publicity and the Generation of Collective Action Frames: Theoretical and Empirical Exercises in Meaning Construction", in: D. McAdam (et al.), *Comparative Perspective on Social Movements: Political Opportunities, Mobilizing Structures, and Cultural Framings* (Cambridge: Cambridge University Press, 1996).

Lemus, Encarnación, "Permanencia y reconstrucción del PCE en Andalucía durante la posguerra (1939–1949)", *Espacio, Tiempo y Forma. Historia Contemporánea*, 11 (1998).

Lillo, Natacha, "Los maquis antifranquistas en la prensa francesa", in Chaput, Marie-Claude, Martínez-Maler, Odette and Rodríguez, Fabiola (eds.), *Maquis y guerrillas antifranquistas* (Nanterre: Université de Paris X, 2004).

Lillo, Natacha, "El PCE en Francia: relaciones con el PCF y evolución (1945–1975)", *Papeles de la FIM*, 22 (2004).

Lucas, Colin, "The Theory and Practice of Denunciation in the French Revolution", *The Journal of Modern History*, 68-4 (1996).

Madrid, Francisco, "La prensa clandestina libertaria", in VVAA, *La oposición libertaria al régimen de Franco, 1936–1975* (Madrid: Fundación Salvador Seguí, 1993).

Maranto Robert and Tuchman, Paula S., "Knowing the Rational Peasant: The creation of Rival Incentive Structures in Vietnam", *Journal of Peace Research*, 29-3 (1992).

Marco, Jorge, "Guerrilla, bandolerismo social, acción colectiva. Algunas reflexiones metodológicas sobre la resistencia armada antifranquista", *Cuadernos de Historia Contemporánea*, 28 (2006).

Marco, Jorge, "Ecos partisanos. La memoria de la Resistencia como memoria conflictiva", *Historia del Presente,* 17-1 (2011).

Marco, Jorge, "'Una Corea en pequeño': Contrainsurgencia y represión de la guerrilla en España, 1939–1952", *Contenciosa*, 1-1 (2013).

Marco, Jorge, "The Long Nocturnal March: The Spanish Guerrilla Movement in the European Narrative of Antifascist Resistance, 1936–1952", in Peter Anderson and Miguel Ángel del Arco (eds.), *Grappling with the Past: Mass Killings and Violence in Spain, 1936–1952* (New York: Routledge, 2015).

Marco, Jorge, "'Encender la guerra de guerrillas': El PCE y la guerrilla antifranquista", in Jorge Marco, Helder Gordim and Jaime Valim (eds.), *Violência e sociedade em ditaduras ibero-americanas no século XX: Argentina, Brasil, Espanha e Portugal* (Porto Alegre: Editora da Pontifícia Universidade Católica do Rio Grande do Sul, 2015).

Marcot, François, "Pour une socioliogie de la Résistance: intentionnalité et fonctionnalité", in Prost, Antoine (dir.), *La Résistance, une histoire sociale* (Paris: Les Éditions de l'Atelier/Editions Ouvrières, 1997).

Martínez, Odette, "Testimonios orales sobre las guerrillas antifranquistas de León (1947–1951)", in Chaput, Marie-Claude, Martínez-Maler, Odette and Rodríguez, Fabiola (eds.), *Maquis y guerrillas antifranquistas* (Nanterre: Université de Paris X, 2004).

Martínez Martín, Jesús, "La lectura en la España contemporánea: lectores, discursos y prácticas de lectura", *AYER*, 58, (2005).

Martínez Rus, Ana, "Editoriales bajo las bombas", *Cultura escrita y Sociedad*, 4 (2007).

McClosky, Herbert and Dahlgren, Harold E., "Primary groups influence on Party Loyalty", *The American Political Science Association*, 53-3 (1959).

Michel, Henri, "General Report", in VVAA, *European Resistance Movements, 1939–1945: First International Conference on the History of the Resistance Movements* (Oxford: Pergamon Press, 1960).

Moreno Gómez, Francisco, "La represión en la posguerra", in Juliá, Santos (ed.), *Víctimas de la guerra civil* (Madrid: Temas de Hoy, 1999).

Mosse, George L., "Two World Wars and the Myth of the War Experience", *Journal of Contemporary History*, 21-4 (1986).

Pavlaković, Vjeran, "Twilight of the Revolutionaires: 'Naši Španci' and the End of Yugoslavia", *Europe-Asia Studies*, 62-7 (2010).

Pizarroso Quintero, Alejandro, "La historia de la propaganda: una aproximación metodológica", *Historia y Comunicación social*, 4 (1999).

Ramos, María Dolores, "Identidad de género, feminismo y movimientos sociales en España", *Historia Contemporánea*, 21-II (2000).

Rivas Rivas, A. M, "Los marcos territoriales y sociales de identificación regional en el mundo rural cantábrico", in VVAA: *Los espacios rurales cantábricos y su evolución* (Santander: Universidad de Cantabria, 1990).

Rodríguez Barreira, Óscar, "Lazarillos del Caudillo. El hurto moral como micro-política subalterna frente a la autarquía franquista", *Historia Social*, 72 (2012).

Romero Navas, José Aurelio, "1952: Huida de los seis últimos guerrilleros a Francia", *Jábega*, 88 (2001).

Romeu Alfaro, Fernanda, "Panorámica sociopolítico de los primeros movimientos guerrilleros", in García Delgado, José Luis (ed.), *El primer franquismo. España durante la Segunda Guerra Mundial* (Madrid: Siglo XXI, 1989).

Routledge, Paul, "Converge spaces: process geographies of grassroots globalization networks", *Transactions of the Institute of British Geographers*, 28-3 (2003).

Sakkas, John, "The civil war in Evrytania", in Mazower, Mark (ed.), *After the War was Over: Reconstructing the Family, Nation, and State in Greece, 1943–1960* (Princeton: Princeton University Press, 2000).

Schwartz, Paula, "Partisanes and Gender Politics in Vichy France", *French Historical Studies*, 16-1 (1989).

Scott, James C., "Everyday Forms of Peasant Resistance", *The Journal of Peasant Studies*, 13-2 (1986).

Shils, E. A. and Janowitz, M., "Cohesion and Disintegration in the Wehrmacht in World War II", *Public Opinion Quarterly*, 12 (1948).

Souto Kustrín, Sandra, "'El mundo ha llegado a ser consciente de su juventud como nunca antes': Juventud y movilización política en la Europa de entreguerras", *Mélanges de la Casa de Velazquez*, 34/1 (2004).

Souto Kustrín, Sandra, "Ser joven en la Europa de entreguerras: política, cultura y movilización", *Hispania*, 225 (2007).

Souto Kustrín, Sandra, "Introducción: teoría e historia", *Hispania*, 225 (2007).

Souto Kustrín, Sandra, "Las organizaciones juveniles: entre el frentepopulismo y el izquierdismo socialista", in Ballarín, Manuel and Ledesma, José Luis (eds.), *La República del Frente Popular. Reformas, conflictos y conspiraciones* (Zaragoza: Fundación de Investigaciones Marxistas, 2010).

Thompson, Edward P., "The Crime of Anonymity", in E. P. *Thompson: The Essential*, (New York: W. W. Norton, 2001).

Tilly, Charles, "The modernization of Political Conflict in France", in Harvey, Edward B. (ed.): *Perspectives on Modernization: Essays in Memory of Ian Weinberg* (Toronto: University of Toronto Press, 1972).

Tilly, Charles, "Contentious Repertoires in Great Britain, 1758–1834", in Mark

Traugott (ed.), *Repertoires and Cycles of Collective Action* (Durham: Duke University Press, 1995).

Veillon, Dominique and Sainclivier, Jacqueline, "Quelles différences sociales entre réseaux, mouvements et maquis?", in Prost, Antoine (dir.), *La Résistance, une histoire sociale* (Paris: Les Éditions de l'Atelier/Les Éditions Ouvriéres, 1997).

Vigreux, Marcel, "Sociologie de maquis de Bourgogne", in Marcot, François (dir.), *La Résistance et les Français: Lutte armée et maquis* (Paris: Annales litéraires de l'Université de Franché-Comté, 1996).

Vincent, Mary, "The Martyrs and the Saints: Masculinity and the Construction of the Francoist Crusade", *History Workshop Journal*, 47 (1999).

Yllal Smith, Keri E., "Hybrid Identities: Theoretical Examinations", in Yllal Smith, Keri E. and Leavy, Patricia (eds.), *Hybrid Identities: Theoretical and Empirical Examinations* (Leiden: Brill, 2008).

Wickham-Crowley, Timothy P, "Terror and Guerrilla Warfare in Latin America, 1956–1970", *Comparative Studies in Society and History*, 32-2 (1990).

Wieviorka, Olivier, "La génération de la Résistance", *Vingtième Siècle*, 22 (1989).

Williams, R. H., "The Cultural Context of Collective Action: Constraints, Opportunities, and the Simbolic Life of Social Movements", in Snow, D.A., Soule, S.A. and Kriesi, H. (eds.), *The Blackwell Companion to Social Movements* (Oxford: Blackwell Publishing, 2004).

Yusta, Mercedes, "Rebeldía individual, compromiso familiar, acción colectiva: las mujeres en la resistencia al franquismo durante los años cuarenta", *Historia del Presente*, 4 (2004).

Yusta, Mercedes, "Las mujeres en la resistencia antifranquista, un estado de la cuestión", *Arenal*, 12-1 (2005).

Books and monographs

Abad Buil, Irene, *En las puertas de prisión: de la solidaridad a la concienciación política de las mujeres de los presos* (Barcelona: Icaria, 2012).

Aguado Sánchez, Francisco, *El maquis en España* (Madrid: Editorial San Martín, 1975).

Alberola, Octavio and Gransac, Ariane, *El anarquismo español y la acción revolucionaria, 1961–1974* (París: Ruedo Ibérico, 1975).

Alcalde, Ángel, *Los excombatientes franquistas, 1936–1965* (Zaragoza: Prensas Universitarias de Zaragoza, 2014).

Alpert, Michael, *The Republican Army in the Spanish Civil War, 1936–1939* (New York: Cambridge University Press, 2013).

Álvarez, Santiago, Hinojosa, José and Sandoval, José (eds.), *El movimiento guerrillero en los años 40* (Madrid: Fundación de Investigaciones Marxistas, 1990).

Ambler, John Steward, *The French Army in Politics, 1945–1962* (Ohio: Ohio State University Press, 1966).

Anderson, Peter, *The Francoist Military Trials* (New York: Routledge, 2010).

Arasa, Daniel, *Años 40: el maquis y el PCE* (Barcelona: Argos Vergara, 1984).

Arasa, Daniel, *La invasión de los maquis* (Barcelona: Beñacqva, 2004).

Arco Blanco, Miguel Ángel, *Hambre de siglos. Mundo rural y apoyos sociales del franquismo en Andalucía Oriental, 1936–1951* (Granada: Comares, 2007).

Aresti, Nerea, *Masculinidades en tela de juicio* (Madrid: Cátedra, 2010).

Aróstegui, Julio, *La historia vivida. Sobre la historia del presente* (Madrid: Alianza, 2004).

Aróstegui, Julio and Marco, Jorge (eds.), *El último frente. La resistencia armada antifranquista en España, 1939–1952* (Madrid: Los Libros de la Catarata, 2008).

Asprey, Robert B., *War in the Shadows. The Guerrilla in History.* Vol. I (Lincoln: iUniverse, 2002).

Ávalos, D. J., *La guerrilla del Ché y Masseti en Salta-1964: ideología y mito en el Ejército Guerrillero del Pueblo* (Córdoba: La Intemperie, 2005).

Azuaga Rico, José, *La guerrilla antifranquista en Nerja* (Nerja: Izquierda Unida, 1996).

Azuaga Rico, José, *La guerrilla antifranquista de Granada y Málaga, 1948–1952* (Málaga: Universidad de Málaga, 2005).

Balsebre, Armand and Fontova, Rosario, *Las cartas de la Pirenaica: Memorias del antifranquismo* (Madrid: Cátedra, 2014).

Bartov, Omer, *Hitler's Army. Soldiers, Nazis, and War in the Third Reich* (Oxford: Oxford University Press, 1992).

Bascuñán Añover, Óscar, *Protesta y supervivencia. Movilización y desorden en una sociedad rural: Castilla La Mancha, 1875–1923* (Valencia: Fundación Instituto de Historia Social, 2008).

Baumeister, Martín, *Campesinos sin tierra. Supervivencia y resistencia en Extremadura, 1880–1923* (Madrid: Ministerio de Agricultura, 1997).

Berdal, Mats and Ucko, David H. (ed.), *Reintegrating Armed Groups after Conflicts. Politics, Violence, and Transition* (New York: Routledge, 2009).

Berman, Paul, *Revolutionary Organization: Institution-Building within the People's Liberation Armed Forces* (Massachusetts: Lexington Books, 1974).

Birtle, Andrew J., *U.S. Army Counterinsurgency and Contingency Operations Doctrine, 1942–1976* (Washington: Center of Militarily History, 2006).

Blanco Rodríguez, Juan Andrés, *El Quinto Regimiento en la política militar del PCE en la guerra civil* (Madrid: UNED, 1993).

Bourke, Joanna, *An Intimate History of Killing: Face to Face Killing in the Twentieth Century Warfare* (New York: Granta Books, 1999).

Brevers, Antonio, *Juanín y Bedoya. Los últimos guerrilleros* (Santander: Cloux Editores, 2008)

Broers, M. (ed.), *Europe under Napoleon* (New York: Edward Arnold, 1996).

Bunk, Brian D., *Ghosts of Passion. Martyrdom, Gender, and the Origins of the Spanish Civil War* (Durham: Duke University Press, 2007).

Cabana Iglesia, Ana: *Entre a resistencia e a adaptación: a sociedade rural galega no franquismo, 1936–1960* (Santiago de Compostela: Universidade de Santiago de Compostela, 2007).

Cabana, Ana, *La derrota de lo épico* (Valencia: PUV, 2013).

Calhoun, Craig J., *The question of Class Struggle: Social Foundations of Popular*

Radicalism during the Industrial Revolution (Chicago: University of Chicago Press, 1982).

Callwell, Ch. E., *Small Wars. Their Principles & Practices* (Nebraska: Bison Books, 1996).

Carvajal Urquijo, Pedro, *Julián Grimaú. La última víctima de la Guerra Civil* (Madrid: Aguilar, 2003).

Casanova, Julián, *De la calle al frente. El anarcosindicalismo en España, 1931–1939* (Barcelona: Crítica, 1997).

Casanova, Julián, (coord.), *Morir, matar sobrevivir. La violencia en la dictadura de Franco* (Barcelona: Crítica, 2002).

Casanova, Julián, *Anarquismo y violencia política en la España del siglo XX* (Zaragoza: Institución "Fernando el Católico", 2007).

Castillo, Juan José, *Propietarios muy pobres: sobre la subordinación política del pequeño campesino en España* (Madrid: Servicio de Publicaciones Agrarias, 1979).

Castillo Gómez, Antonio (coord.), *La conquista del alfabeto. Escritura y clases populares* (Gijón: Trea, 2002).

Capdevila, L., Rounquet, F., Virgili, F. and Voldman, D., *Sexes, genre et guerres: France, 1914–1945* (Paris: Éditions Payot & Rivages, 2010).

Chaliand, Gerard (ed.), *Guerrilla Strategies: An Historical Anthology from the Long March to Afghanistan* (Berkeley: University of California Press, 1982).

Chaliand, Gerard (ed.), *Les guerres irégulières. XX–XXI siècle* (Paris: Gallimard, 2008).

Clinton, Alan, *Jean Moulin, 1899–1943: The French Resistance and the Republic* (Basingtoke: Palgrave, 2002).

Close, David H (ed.), *The Greek Civil War: Studies of Polarization* (Nueva York: Routledge, 1993).

Clutterbuck, Richard, *The Long Long War: Counterinsurgency in Malaya and Vietnam* (New York: Praeger, 1966)

Cobo Romero, Francisco, *Conflicto rural y violencia política: el largo camino hacia la dictadura: Jaén, 1917–1950* (Jaén: Universidad de Jaén, 1999).

Cobo Romero, Francisco, *De campesinos a electores. Modernización agraria en Andalucía, politización campesina y derechización de los pequeños propietarios y arrendatarios. El caso de Jaén, 1931–1936* (Madrid: Biblioteca Nueva, 2003).

Cobo Romero, Francisco, *Revolución campesina y contra-revolución franquista en Andalucía* (Granada: Universidad de Granada, 2004).

Cobo Romero, Francisco, *Por la Reforma Agraria hacia la Revolución. El sindicalismo agrario durante la II República y la Guerra Civil, 1930–1939* (Granada: Universidad de Granada, 2007).

Cruz, Rafael, *En el nombre del pueblo. República, rebelión y guerra en la España de 1936* (Madrid: Siglo XXI, 2006).

Cruz, Rafael, *Repertorios. La política de enfrentamiento en el siglo XX* (Madrid: CIS, 2008).

Cruz, Rafael and Casquete, Jesús, *Las políticas de la muerte. Usos y abusos del ritual fúnebre en la Europa del siglo XX* (Madrid: Los Libros de la Catarata, 2009).

Cruz Artacho, Salvador, *Caciques y campesinos. Poder político, modernización agraria y conflictividad rural en Granada, 1890–1923* (Madrid: Libertarias, 1994).

Cruz Burguete, José Luis, *Identidades en fronteras, fronteras de identidades: la reconstrucción de la identidad étnica entre los Chujes de Chiapas* (México: Colegio de México/Centro de Estudios Sociológicos, 1998).

Cucó Giner, Josepa, *La amistad: perspectiva antropológica* (Barcelona: Icaria, 1995).

Davis, Flora, *Inside Intuition: What We Know about Non-Verbal Communication* (New York: McGraw-Hill, 1973).

Díaz Del Moral, Juan, *Las agitaciones campesinas del periodo bolchevique, 1919–1920* (Sevilla: Editoriales Andaluzas Unidas, 1985).

Díaz, Luis (coord.), *Aproximación antropológica a Castilla y León* (Barcelona: Anthropos, 1988).

Domingo, Alfonso, *El canto del búho. La vida en el monte de los guerrilleros Antifranquistas* (Madrid: Oberón, 2002).

Edwards, V., *Group Leader's Guide to Propaganda Analysis* (New York: Columbia, University Press, 1938).

Eley, Geoff, *Forging Democracy: the History of the Left in Europe, 1850–2000* (New York: Oxford University Press, 2002).

Escolano Benito, A. (dir.), *Leer y escribir. Doscientos años de alfabetización* (Madrid: Fundación Germán Sánchez Ruipérez, 1997).

Estruch Tobella, Joan, *El PCE en la clandestinidad. 1939–1956* (Madrid: Siglo XXI, 1982).

Feijóo Gómez, Albino, *Quintas y protesta social en el siglo XIX* (Madrid: Ministerio de Defensa, 1996).

Fernádez Rodríguez, Carlos, *Madrid clandestino. La reestructuración del PCE, 1939–1945* (Madrid: Fundación Domingo Malagón, 2002).

Fernández Soria, Juan Manuel, *Educación y cultura en la guerra civil* (Valencia, Nau Llibres, 1984).

Figes, Orlando and Kolonitskii, Boris, *Interpreting the Russian Revolution: The Language and Symbols of 1917* (New Haven: Yale University Press, 1999).

Fitzpatrick, Sheila, *Stalin's Peasants: Resistance and Survival in the Russian Village after the Collectivization* (New York: Oxford University Press, 1994).

Flam, Helena and King, Debra (ed.), *Emotions and Social Movements* (New York: Routledge, 2005).

Fojas, Camilla, *Border Bandits: Hollywood on the Southern Frontier* (Texas: University of Texas Press, 2008).

Forbes, H., *Manual for the Patriotic Volunteer on Active Service in Regular and Irregular War* (New York: W. H. Tinson, 1855).

Foucault, Michael: *Power/Knowledge. Selected Interviews and Other Writings. 1972–1977* (New York: Pantheon Books, 1980).

Galland, Olivier, *Sociologie de la jeunesse. L'entrée dans la vie* (Paris: Armand Colin, 2007).

Ganier Raymond, Philippe, *L'Affiche rouge* (Paris: Librairie Arthème Fayard, 1975).

García-Pelayo, Manuel, *Los mitos políticos* (Madrid: Alianza, 1981).

Geertz, Clifford, *The Interpretation of Cultures: Selected Essays* (New York: Basic Books, 1973).

Gellately, Robert, *The Gestapo and German Society: Enforcing Racial Policy, 1933–1945* (Oxford: Clarendon Press, 1990).

Gellately, Robert, *Stalin's Curse: Battling for Communism in War and Cold War* (Oxford: Oxford University Press, 2013).

Gentile, Emilio, *The Struggle for Modernity: Nationalism, Futurism, and Fascism* (Westport: Praeger, 2003).

Gil Andrés, Carlos, *Echarse a la calle. Amotinados, huelguistas y revolucionarios. La Rioja, 1890–1936* (Zaragoza: Prensas Universitarias de Zaragoza, 2000).

Gil Andrés, Carlos, *Lejos del frente. La guerra civil en la Rioja Alta* (Barcelona: Critica, 2006).

Gil Bracero, Rafael, *Revolucionarios sin revolución. Marxistas y anarcosindicalistas en guerra: Granada-Baza, 1936–1939* (Granada: Universidad de Granada, 1998).

Ginard y Feron, David, *Heriberto Quiñones y el movimiento comunista en España, 1931–1942* (Palma: Edicions Documenta Balear, 2000).

Gómez Bravo, Gutmaro and Marco, Jorge, *La obra del miedo. Violencia y sociedad en la España franquista, 1936–1950* (Barcelona: Península, 2011).

Gómez Fouz, José R., *Bernabé. El mito de un bandolero* (Barcelona: Silverio Cabaña Editor, 1998).

Gómez Westermeyer, Juan Francisco, *Historia de la delincuencia en la sociedad española: Murcia, 1939–1949. Similitudes y diferencias en otros espacios europeos* (Murcia: Universidad de Murcia, 2006).

González Calleja, Eduardo, *El Mauser y el sufragio. Orden público, subversión y violencia política en la crisis de la Restauración, 1917–1931* (Madrid: CSIC, 1999).

González Calleja, Eduardo, *El laboratorio del miedo: una historia general del terrorismo* (Barcelona: Crítica, 2012).

Goodwin, J., Jasper, J. M. and Polletta, F. (ed.), *Passionate Politics. Emotions and Social Movements* (Chicago: University Press of Chicago, 2001).

Graham, Helen, *Socialism and War: The Spanish Socialist Party in Power and Crisis, 1936–1939* (Cambridge: Cambride University Press, 1991).

Graham, Helen, *The Spanish Republic at War, 1936–1939* (Cambridge: Cambridge University Press, 2002).

Graham, Helen, *The Spanish Civil War: A Very Short Introduction* (Oxford: Oxford University Press, 2005).

Graham, Helen, *The War and its Shadows: Spain's Civil War in Europe's Long Twentieth Century* (Brighton: Sussex Academic Press, 2012).

Grimshaw, Allen D. (ed.), *A Social History of Racial Violence* (New Jersey: Transaction Publishers, 2009).

Guevara, Ernesto "Che", *La guerra de guerrillas* (Madrid: Júcar, 1977).

Guha, Ranajit, *Elementary Forms of Peasant Insurgency in Colonial India* (Dheli: Oxford University Press, 1983).

Guillen, Abraham, *Estrategia de la guerrilla urbana* (Montevideo: Ediciones Liberación, 1969).

Gillón, Jean-Marié and Laboire, Pierre (dir.), *Mémoire et histoire: La Résistance* (Toulouse: Privat, 1995).

Gurr, Ted Robert, *Why Men Rebel* (Princeton: Princeton University Press, 1970).

Gurr, Ted Robert (ed.), *Handbook of Political Conflict: Theory and Research* (London & New York: Free Press, 1980).

Gwynn, Charles, *Imperial Policing* (London: Macmillan and Co. Ltd., 1934).

Heine, Hartmut, *A guerrilla antifranquista en Galicia* (Vigo: Xerais, 1980).

Heine, Hartmut, *La oposición política al franquismo* (Barcelona: Crítica, 1983).

Heine, Hartmut, and Azuaga, José María, *La oposición al franquismo en Andalucía Oriental* (Madrid: Fundación Salvador Seguí, 2005).

Hernández Sánchez, Fernando, *Comunistas sin partido: Jesús Hernández* (Madrid: Raíces, 2007)

Hernández Sánchez, Fernando, *Guerra o Revolución. El PCE en la guerra civil* (Barcelona: Critica, 2010).

Hobsbawm, Eric, *Revolutionaries: Contemporary Essays* (London: Phoenix, 1994).

Hobsbawm, Eric, *Primitive Rebels* (Manchester: Manchester University Press, 1971).

Hobsbawm, Eric, *Bandits* (London: Weidenfeld & Nicolson, 1969).

Hobsbawn, Eric and Rude, George, *Captain Swing: A Social History of the Great English agricultural uprising of 1830* (New York: W. W. Norton & Company, 1968).

Izquierdo, Jesús, *El rostro de la comunidad. La identidad del campesino en la Castilla del Antiguo Régimen* (Madrid: Consejo Económico y Social, 2001).

Jowett, G. S. and O'Donell, V., *Propaganda and Persuasion* (California : Sage Publications, 2006).

Judt, Tony (ed.), *Resistance and Revolution in Mediterranean Europe, 1939–1948* (New York: Routledge, 1989).

Jünger, Ernst, *La Guerre comme expérience intérieure* (Paris: Christian Bourgois Editeur, 1997).

Kalyvas, Stathis N., *The Logic of Violence in Civil War* (New York: Cambridge University Press, 2006) .

Kedward, H. R., *In search of the maquis: Rural Resistance in Southern France, 1942–1944* (Oxford: Oxford University Press, 1994).

Kheng Chead, Boon, *Red Star over Malaya: resistance and social conflict during and after the Japanese Occupation, 1941–1946* (Singapore, Singapore University Press, 2003).

Klandermans, Bert, *The Social Psychology of Protest* (Oxford: Blackwell, 1997).

Kriger, Norma, *Guerrilla Veterans in Post-War Zimbabwe. Symbolic and Violent Politics, 1980–1987* (Cambridge: Cambridge University Press, 2003).

Lamela García, V. Luis, *Foucellas. El riguroso relato de una lucha antifranquista* (A Coruña: Edicios do Castro, 2002).

Laswell, H. D., *Propaganda Technique in the World War* (New York: Knopf, 1927).

Lazo, Alfonso: *Retrato del fascismo rural en Sevilla* (Sevilla: Universidad de Sevilla, 1998).

Ledesma, José Luis, *Los días de llamas de la revolución: violencia y política en la retaguardia republicana de Zaragoza durante la guerra civil* (Zaragoza: Instituto Fernando el Católico, 2003).

Leed, Eric J., *No Man's Land: Combat & Identity in World War I* (Cambridge: Cambridge University Press, 2009).

Lévi-Strauss, Claude, *Anthropologie structurale* (Paris: Librairie Plon, 1958).

Lichbach, Mark Irving, *The Rebel's Dilemma* (Michigan: The University of Michigan Press, 1998).

London, Arthur, *La confesión. En el engranaje del Proceso de Praga* (Vitoria-Gasteiz: Ikusager Ediciones, 2000).

López Martínez, Mario, *Orden Público y luchas agrarias en Andalucía* (Madrid: Ediciones Libertarias, 1995).

Lucea Ayala, Víctor, *Rebeldes y amotinados. Protesta popular y resistencia campesina en Zaragoza, 1890–1905* (Zaragoza: Institución Fernando el Católico, 2005).

Lynn, John Albert, *The bayonets of the Republic: motivation and tactics in the army of Revolutionaries France, 1791–94* (Urbana: University of Illinois Press, 1984).

Macías, Santiago, *El monte o la muerte. La vida legendaria del guerrillero antifranquista Manuel Girón* (Madrid: Temas de Hoy, 2005).

Mackey, R. R., *The Uncivil War: Irregular Warfare in the Upper South, 1861–1865* (Oklahoma: University of Oklahoma Press, 2004).

Malaparte, Curzio, *Técnica del golpe de Estado* (Barcelona: Plaza & Janes, 1960).

Malinowski, Bronislaw, *Magic, Science and Religion and Others Essays* (Massachusetts: Beacon Press, 1948).

Mann, Michael, *Fascists* (New York: Cambridge University Press, 2004).

Manzanares Artés, Nicolás, *Consecuencias de la tragedia española, 1936–1939, y los hermanos Quero* (Murcia: Edición del autor, 1978).

Marco, Jorge, *Hijos de una guerra. Los hermanos Quero y la resistencia antifranquista* (Granada: Comares, 2010).

Marco, Jorge, Gordim, Helder and Valim, Jaime (eds.), *Violência e sociedade em ditaduras ibero-americanas no século XX: Argentina, Brasil, Espanha e Portugal* (Porto Alegre: Editora da Pontifícia Universidade Católica do Rio Grande do Sul, 2015).

Marcot, François (dir.), *La Résistance et les Français. Lutte armée et maquis* (Paris: Annales littéraires de l'Université de Franché-Comté, 1996).

Martínez de Baños, Fernando, *Hasta su aniquilación total: el ejército contra el maquis en el Valle Arán y el Alto Aragón, 1944–1946* (Madrid: Almena, 2002).

Martínez de Baños, Fernando, *El maquis. Una cultura del exilio español, Zaragoza* (Madrid: Delsan, 2007)

Martínez Rus, Ana, *La persecución del libro: Hogueras, infiernos y buenas lecturas, 1936–1951* (Gijón: Trea, 2014).

Mazower, Mark, *Inside Hitler's Greece: The Experience of Occupation, 1941–1944* (New Haven and London: Yale University Press, 2001).

Mazower, Mark (ed.), *After the War was Over. Reconstructing the Family, Nation, and State in Greece, 1943–1960* (Princeton: Princeton University Press, 2000).

Mazower, Mark, *Hitler's Empire: How the Nazis Ruled Europe* (New York: Penguin, 2009).

McAdam, D., McCarthy, J. D. and Zald, M. (eds.), *Comparative Perspective on Social Movements: Political Opportunities, Mobilizing Structures, and Cultural Framings* (Cambridge: Cambridge University Press, 1996).

McLellan, Josie, *Antifascism and Memory in East Germany: Remembering the International Brigades, 1945–1989* (Oxford: Oxford University Press, 2004).

Melucci, Alberto, *Challenging Codes: Collective Action in the Information Age*, (Cambridge: Cambridge University Press, 2002).

Mendezona, Ramón, *La Pirenaica: historia de una emisora clandestina* (Madrid, Edición del autor, 1981).

Molina Luque, J. Fidel, *Quintas y servicio militar: aspectos sociológicos y antropológicos de la conscripción. Lleida, 1878–1960* (Lleida: Servei de Publicacions Universitat de Lleida, 1996).

Moral, Marta del, *Acción colectiva femenina en Madrid, 1909–1931* (Santiago de Compostela: Universidade de Santiago de Compostola, 2012).

Moran, Gregorio, *Miseria y grandeza del Partido Comunista de España, 1939–1985*, (Barcelona: Planeta, 1986).

Moreno Gómez, Francisco, *La resistencia armada contra Franco. Tragedia del maquis y la guerrilla* (Barcelona: Crítica, 2001).

Moreno Gómez, Francisco, *Historia y memoria del maquis. El cordobés Veneno, el último guerrillero de la Mancha* (Madrid: Editorial Alpuerto, 2006).

Mosse, George L., *The Nationalization of the Masses: Political Symbolism and Mass Movements in Germany from the Napoleonic Wars Through the Third Reich* (New York: Howard Fertig, 1975).

Mosse, George L., *Fallen Soldier. Reshaping the Memory of the World Wars* (Oxford: Oxford University Press, 1991).

Mosse, George L., *The Image of Man: The Creation of Modern Masculinity* (New York: Oxford University Press, 1996).

Mosse, George L., *Confronting History: A Memoir* (Madison: University of Wisconsin Press, 2000).

Nash, Mary, *Rojas. Las mujeres republicanas en la guerra civil* (Madrid: Taurus, 1999).

Navarrete, F. and Olivier, G. (coord.), *El héroe. Entre el mito y la historia* (México DF: UNAM, 2000).

Neuberg, A., *Armed Insurrection* (London: NLB, 1970 [1928]).

Nuñez Florencio, Rafael, *El terrorismo anarquista, 1888–1909* (Madrid: Siglo XXI, 1983).

Númez Jiménez, A., *En marcha con Fidel: 1959* (La Habana: Editorial Letras Cubanas, 1982).

Ortega López, Teresa María: *Del silencio a la protesta. Explotación, pobreza y conflictividad en una provincia andaluza, Granada 1936–1977* (Granada: Universidad de Granada, 2003).

Parejo Fernández, José Antonio, *La Falange en la Sierra Norte de Sevilla, 1934–1956* (Sevilla: Universidad de Sevilla, 2004).

Parejo Fernández, José Antonio, *Las piezas perdidas de la Falange: el sur de España* (Sevilla: Universidad de Sevilla, 2008).

Pitt-Rivers, Julian A., *The People of the Sierra* (Chicago: Chicago University Press, 1971)

Preston, Paul, *The Last Stalinist: The Life of Santiago Carrillo* (London: Harper Collins, 2014).

Prost, Antoine (dir.), *La Résistance, une histoire sociale* (Paris: Les Éditions de l'Atelier /Les Éditions Ouvriéres, 1997).

Reher, David S., *La familia en España, pasado y presente* (Madrid: Alianza, 1996).

Richards, Michael, *A Time of Silence: Civil War and the Culture of Repression in Franco's Spain, 1936–1945* (Cambridge: Cambridge University Press, 1998).

Riesco Roche, Sergio, *La reforma agraria y los orígenes de la Guerra Civil, 1931–1940* (Madrid: Biblioteca Nueva, 2006).

Rivas Rivas, A. M., *Ritos, símbolos y valores en el análisis de la identidad en la provincia de Zaragoza* (Zaragoza: Caja de Ahorros de la Inmaculada, 1986).

Rodríguez Barreira, Óscar, *Migas de miedo. Prácticas de resistencia al primer franquismo. Almería, 1939–1952* (Almería: Universidad de Almería, 2008).

Rodríguez López, Sofía, *Mujeres en Guerra. Almería, 1936–1939* (Almería: Arráez Editores, 2003).

Rodríguez Padilla, Eusebio, *El Ejército Guerrillero en Andalucía, 1945–1952* (Almería: Arráez Editores, 2010).

Romero Navas, José Aurelio, *La guerrilla en 1945. Proceso a dos jefes guerrilleros: Ramón Vías y Alfredo Cabello Gómez-Acebo* (Málaga: CEDMA, 1999).

Romero Navas, José Aurelio, *Censo de guerrilleros y colaboradores de la Agrupación Guerrillera de Málaga–Granada* (Málaga: CEDMA, 2004).

Romeu Alfaro, Fernanda, *Más allá de la utopía: Agrupación Guerrillera de Levante* (Cuenca: Ediciones de la Universidad de Castilla-La Mancha, 2002).

Romeu Alfaro, Fernanda, *Silencio Roto. Mujeres contra el franquismo* (Barcelona: El Viejo Topo, 2002).

Sacaluga, José Antonio, *La resistencia socialista en Asturias* (Madrid: Fundación Pablo Iglesias, 1986).

Sanmartín, Ricardo, *Identidad y creación. Horizontes culturales e interpretación antropológica* (Barcelona: Editorial Humanidades, 1993).

Sánchez Agustí, Ferrán, *El maquis anarquista. De Toulouse a Barcelona por los Pirineos* (Lleida: Milenio, 2006).

Sánchez Cervelló, Josep (ed.), *Maquis: el puño que golpeó el franquismo, La Agrupación Guerrillera de Levante y Aragón* (Barcelona: Flor del Viento, 2003).

Sánchez Pérez, Francisco, *La protesta de un pueblo. Acción colectiva y organización obrera. Madrid 1901–1923* (Madrid: Ediciones Cinca, 2006).

Sánchez Tostado, Luis Miguel, *La guerra no acabó en el 39: lucha guerrillera y resistencia republicana en la provincia de Jaén. 1939–1952* (Jaén: Ayuntamiento de Jaén, 2000).

Sancho Larrañaga, Roberto, *Guerrilla y terrorismo en Colombia y España* (Bucaramanga: Colombia, 2003).

Scanlon, Geraldine M., *La polémica feminista en la España Contemporánea: 1868–1974* (Madrid: Akal, 1986).

Scott, James C., *The Moral Economy of the Peasant: Rebellion and Subsistence in Southeast Asia* (New Haven & London: Yale University Press, 1976).

Scott, James C., *Weapons of the Weak. Every Forms of Peasant Resistance* (New Haven & London: Yale University Press, 1985).

Scott, James C., *Domination and the Arts of Resistance: Hidden Transcripts* (New Haven: Yale University Press, 1990).

Seidman, Michael, *Republic of Egos: A Social History of the Spanish Civil War* (Madison: University of Wisconsin Press, 2002).

Serrano, Secundino, *La guerrilla antifranquista en León, 1936–1951* (León: Junta de Castilla y León, 1986).

Serrano, Secundino, *Maquis. Historia de la guerrilla antifranquista* (Madrid: Temas de Hoy, 2002).

Serrano, Secundino, *La última gesta. Los republicanos que vencieron a Hitler, 1939–1945* (Barcelona: Punto de Lectura, 2006).

Shiels, Duncan, *Los hermanos Rajk. Un drama familiar europeo* (Barcelona: Acantilado, 2009).

Shubert, Adrian, *A Social History of Modern Spain* (London & New York: Routledge, 1990).

Sierra, Verónica, *Palabras huérfanas. Los niños y la guerra civil* (Madrid: Taurus, 2009).

Sorel, George, *Reflections on Violence* (London: George Allen & Unwin Ltd., 1925).

Soule, S. A. and Kriesi, H. (eds.), *The Blackwell Companion to Social Movements* (Oxford: Blackwell Publishing, 2004).

Souto Kustrin, Sandra, *Y ¿Madrid? ¿Qué hace Madrid? Movimiento revolucionario y acción colectiva, 1933–1936* (Madrid: Siglo XXI, 2004).

Souto Kustrin, Sandra, *Paso a la juventud. Movilización democrática, estalinismo y revolución en la República Española* (Valencia: Universitat de València, 2013)

Stafford, David, *From Anarchism to Reformism: A Study of the Political Activities of Paul Brousse within the First International and the French Socialist Movement, 1870–1990* (Toronto: University of Toronto University Press, 1971).

Staniland, Paul, *Networks of Rebellion: Explaining Insurgent Cohesion and Collapse* (Ithaca: Cornell University Press, 2014).

Statiev, Alexander, *The Soviet Counterinsurgency in the Western Borderlands* (Cambridge: Cambridge University Press, 2010).

Tarrow, Sidney, *Power in Movement: Social Movements and Contentious Politics* (Cambridge: Cambridge University Press, 1998).

Tellez Solá, Antonio, *La guerrilla urbana. Facerías* (Paris: Ruedo Ibérico, 1974).

Tellez Solá, Antonio, *Sabaté. Guerrilla urbana en España, 1945–1960* (Barcelona: Plaza y Janés, 1978).

Thomas, Maria, *The Faith and the Fury: Popular Anticlerical Violence and Iconoclasm in Spain, 1931–1936* (Brighton: Sussex Academic Press, 2013).

Tilly, Charles, *From Mobilization to Revolution* (Massachusetts: Addison-Wesley Publishing Company, 1978).

Tilly, Charles, *The Contentious French. Four Centuries of Popular Struggle* (Cambridge, MA: Harvard University Press, 1986).

Traverso, Enzo, *A sangre y fuego. De la guerra civil europea, 1914–1945* (Valencia: Universidad de Valencia, 2009).

Trinquier, Roger, *Modern Warfare: A French View of Counterinsurgency* (Westport: Praeger Security International, 2006).

Ugarte Tellería, Javier, *La nueva Covadonga insurgente, Orígenes sociales y culturales de la sublevación de 1936 en Navarra y el País Vasco* (Madrid: Biblioteca Nueva, 1998).

Verkuyten. Mykel, *The Social Psychology of Ethnic Identity* (East Sussex: Psychology Press, 2005).

Verstrynge, Jorge, *La guerra periférica y el islam revolucionario. Orígenes, reglas y ética de la guerra asimétrica* (Barcelona: El Viejo Topo, 2005).

Viñas, Ángel, *El Honor de la República. Entre el ocaso fascista, la hostilidad británica y la política de Stalin* (Barcelona: Critica, 2009).

Voglis, Polymeris, *Becoming a Subject: Political Prisoners during the Greek Civil War* (Oxford: Berghahn Books, 2002).

Vinyes, Ricard, *Irredentas. Las presas políticas y sus hijos en las cárceles de Franco* (Madrid: Temas de Hoy, 2002).

VVAA, *European Resistance Movements, 1939–1945: First International Conference on the History of the Resistance Movements* (Oxford: Pergamon Press, 1960).

Wickham-Crowley, Timothy P, *Guerrillas and Revolution in Latin America: A Comparative study of Insurgents and Regimes since 1956* (Princeton: Princeton University Press, 1992).

Wieviorka, Olivier, *Une certaine idée de la Résistance. Défense de la France, 1940–1949* (Paris: Éditions du Seuil, 1995).

Wieviorka, Olivier, *Histoire de la Résistance, 1940–1945* (Paris: Perrin, 2015).

Winter, J. M., *The Great War and the British People* (Cambridge, MA: Harvard University Press, 1986).

Yusta, Mercedes, *La guerra de los vencidos. El maquis en el maestrazgo turolense, 1940–1950* (Zaragoza: Institución Fernando el Católico, 2005).

Yusta, Mercedes, *Guerrilla y resistencia campesina. La resistencia armada contra el franquismo en Aragón, 1939–1952* (Zaragoza: Prensas Universitarias de Zaragoza, 2003).

Zaragoza Fernández, Luis, *Radio Pirenaica. La voz de la esperanza antifranquista* (Madrid: Marcial Pons, 2008).

Novels and Plays

Brecht, Bertolt, *Poetry and Prose* (New York: Continuum, 2006).

Camus, Albert, *Caligula and three other plays* (New York: Vintage Books, 1958).

Chirbes, Rafael, *La larga marcha* (Barcelona: Anagrama, 2008).

Pérez Galdos, Benito, *Juan Martín 'El Empecinado'* (Madrid: Alianza, 2006).

Semprun, Jorge, *El largo viaje* (Madrid: Seix Barral, 1994).

Index

INDEX